Love in the Time of Revolution

Love
in the Time of
Revolution

Transatlantic Literary

Radicalism and Historical Change,

1793–1818

Andrew Cayton

Published for the
Omohundro Institute of Early American History
and Culture, Williamsburg, Virginia, by the University of
North Carolina Press, Chapel Hill

The Omohundro Institute of Early American History and Culture is sponsored jointly by the College of William and Mary and the Colonial Williamsburg Foundation. On November 15, 1996, the Institute adopted the present name in honor of a bequest from Malvern H. Omohundro, Jr.

Designed by Kimberly Bryant and set in Utopia by Tseng Information Systems, Inc.
Manufactured in the United States of America

Library of Congress Cataloging-in-Publication Data
Cayton, Andrew R. L. (Andrew Robert Lee), 1954–
Love in the time of revolution : transatlantic literary radicalism and
historical change, 1793–1818 / Andrew Cayton.
pages cm.
Includes bibliographical references and index.
ISBN 978-1-4696-0750-4 (hardback)
1. English fiction—19th century—History and criticism. 2. Love in literature.
3. American fiction—19th century—History and criticism. 4. Godwin, William, 1756-
1836—Influence. 5. Wollstonecraft, Mary, 1759-1797—Influence. 6. Literature and
society—England—History—19th century. 7. Literature and society—United
States—History—19th century. 8. Politics and literature—England—
History—19th century. 9. Politics and literature—United States—
History—19th century. 10. Radicalism in literature. I. Title.
PR878.L69C39 2013
820.9′3543—dc23
2013002815

The paper in this book meets the guidelines for permanence and durability
of the Committee on Production Guidelines for Book Longevity of the Council on
Library Resources. The University of North Carolina Press has been a member
of the Green Press Initiative since 2003.

17 16 15 14 13   5 4 3 2 1

In memory of my grandmother,
IRENE STEPHENS PELLEY
(1902–1993),
in whose kitchen I learned much more
than how to bake a cake

contents

illustrations

Love in the Time of Revolution

A Revolution in Favor of Love

Gilbert Imlay was a citizen of the United States, and Mary Wollstonecraft a subject of George III of Great Britain. He avoided confrontation, she embraced it. He had been a soldier and speculator, she a teacher and governess. They were both writers. His *Topographical Description of the Interior of North America* had appeared in 1791, and he would soon publish a novel, *The Emigrants,* which would achieve a well-deserved obscurity. Her *Vindication of the Rights of Woman* became enormously influential. To Paris in 1793 these restless adventurers came to join other radicals in the heady business of renegotiating all aspects of human life. In the capital of revolution in the last decade of the eighteenth century, they talked, wrote, flirted, and fell in love and into bed with each other. It was a "PLEASANT exercise of hope and joy!" famously recalled William Wordsworth of life in Paris in the early 1790s.

> For mighty were the auxiliars which then stood
> Upon our side, we who were strong in love!
> Bliss was it in that dawn to be alive,
> But to be young was very heaven![1]

In actuality, neither Wollstonecraft nor Imlay was very young when they met each other. She was thirty-four; he was probably thirty-nine. Nor did they fall in love in a time of unlimited bliss. Members of a generation born

---

1. William Wordsworth, "French Revolution, as It Appeared to Enthusiasts at Its Commencement" (1804, 1809), in *The Poetical Works of William Wordsworth: With Memoirs and Notes* (New York, [1880]), 158.

between the late 1740s and the early 1760s, Wollstonecraft, Imlay, and their friends in Paris and London were old enough to know disappointment well. They would come to know it even more intimately in the summer and fall of 1793 as they found themselves or witnessed their friends inhabiting filthy prisons, mounting the steps of the guillotine, fleeing Paris in search of a safe haven in the midst of a Continental war, and protesting repression from frightened governments in London and Philadelphia. By spring, even the once happy bond between Wollstonecraft and Imlay was fraying. Around the time Wollstonecraft gave birth to a daughter, Fanny, in May 1794, Imlay took up with another woman in London, precipitating a series of bitter exchanges, suicide attempts, and fleeting reconciliations.

None of this was especially remarkable. Unhappy love affairs were commonplace in the floating community of British and American writers to which Wollstonecraft and Imlay belonged. The twenty-three-year-old Wordsworth, for example, had returned to London in late 1792, about the time Wollstonecraft arrived in Paris, leaving behind his lover, Annette Vallon, and their illegitimate daughter, Anne Caroline, neither of whom he saw again for a decade. More generally, a woman seduced and betrayed by a scoundrel was a ubiquitous trope in eighteenth-century Anglo-American literature and, indeed, in transatlantic popular culture. By 1798, however, people throughout the English-speaking world were talking about the Wollstonecraft-Imlay affair as a particularly revealing moment in a decade of dramatic episodes. Why? Why did anyone care about the problems of two people when the world as a whole was turned upside down?[2]

They cared because Mary Wollstonecraft was no ordinary Clarissa, the heroine of the eponymous novel by Samuel Richardson. She, of all women, should have known better. And yet she had embraced her own Lovelace, Clarissa's seducer, if that in fact was what Imlay was. Wollstonecraft was the celebrated author of *A Vindication of the Rights of Woman,* in which

2. See Nicola Trott, "Sexing the Critic: Mary Wollstonecraft at the Turn of the Century," in Richard Cronin, ed., *1798: The Year of the Lyrical Ballads* (New York, 1998), 32–67; Anna Clark, *Scandal: The Sexual Politics of the British Constitution* (Princeton, N.J., 2004); Rodney Hessinger, *Seduced, Abandoned, and Reborn: Visions of Youth in Middle-Class America, 1780–1850* (Philadelphia, 2005); Julie A. Carlson, *England's First Family of Writers: Mary Wollstonecraft, William Godwin, Mary Shelley* (Baltimore, 2007); Marion Rust, *Prodigal Daughters: Susanna Rowson's Early American Women* (Chapel Hill, N.C., 2008); and Tom Mole, *Romanticism and Celebrity Culture, 1750–1850* (Cambridge, 2009). On the political transatlantic political context, see Philipp Ziesche, *Cosmopolitan Patriots: Americans in Paris in the Age of Revolution* (Charlottesville, Va., 2010); and Seth Cotlar, *Tom Paine's America: The Rise and Fall of Transatlantic Radicalism in the Early Republic* (Charlottesville, Va., 2011).

Figure 1. Mary Wollstonecraft. *By John Opie. Oil on canvas, circa 1797.*
© *National Portrait Gallery, London*

she contended that women were subordinated to men by culture rather than nature. The book was one of the most widely debated books of the decade. Originally published in London in 1792 by Joseph Johnson, *Vindication* was almost immediately reprinted in Philadelphia and Boston, and in Paris it was published as *Défense des droits des femmes.* A Dublin edition and a German one, *Rettung der Rechte des Weibes,* appeared the next year. Yet another version was published in Philadelphia in 1794, and a third edition in London in 1796. Wollstonecraft's personal life became notorious in part because she was a woman who had dared to attack the patriarchal culture that denied women the rights and responsibilities to which they were entitled as human beings.[3]

They cared because William Godwin made them care. Godwin, the author of the essay *Political Justice* and the novel *Caleb Williams,* was Wollstonecraft's second lover and only legal husband. The couple married in April 1797, roughly five months before she died after giving birth to their daughter, Mary. Months later, in 1798, he published a deeply personal narrative, *Memoirs of the Author of "A Vindication of the Rights of Woman,"* which engaged Wollstonecraft's character more than her writing and highlighted the affair with Imlay as a turning point in her life. Godwin's account remains the most influential interpretation of the Wollstonecraft-Imlay relationship. He tells a story of a woman so in thrall to her sensibility, so eager to be loved, that she was easily seduced by a charming confidence man. Once he had satiated his desire for her body, he abandoned her and their daughter for another woman. Godwin presents himself as the hero of his wife's life: a lover who disdained marriage until Wollstonecraft became pregnant with their child; a husband who refused to exercise patriarchal authority and treated his wife as his equal; and a father who took full responsibility for both Mary and Fanny after Wollstonecraft's death. Much to Godwin's surprise, journalists, moralists, and novelists transformed the details of his book into one of the first great celebrity scandals, packed with the ingredients with which we today are so familiar: famous people bedding one another, fighting, throwing themselves into rivers, abandoning babies, and declaring eternal love on a deathbed.

They cared because Wollstonecraft, Godwin, and Imlay were prominent literary figures in the cultural capital of the late-eighteenth-century Atlantic world. What people said and did in London attracted the attention of people from Glasgow, to Dublin, to Philadelphia, to Cincinnati because London was the most important center of publishing in the world. The rapid expansion in the numbers of literate middling peoples combined with a proliferation of printers and venues to make it possible for hundreds of individuals to support themselves as professional writers. Books written and published in London circulated throughout Europe and the Americas and set the terms of intellectual discourse throughout the English-speaking world. Most of these volumes were religious tracts, travel narratives, and collections of poetry. But a small group of intellectuals, including Woll-

3. John Windle, *Mary Wollstonecraft Godwin, 1759–1797: A Bibliography of the First and Early Editions* . . . (New Castle, Del., 2000), 15–20.

stonecraft, Imlay, and Godwin, composed books in the early to mid-1790s that amounted to blueprints for an all-encompassing social revolution.[4]

Inspired by ideas about sociability developed in Western Europe in the late seventeenth and eighteenth centuries, radical writers were particularly obsessed with culture, that is, the rules and assumptions under which human beings operate. As concerned with *why* and *how* human beings think and feel as they were with *what* they think and feel, they argued that human nature and human society were dynamic and susceptible to transformation through education and social intercourse. Following Adam Smith in particular, Wollstonecraft and other writers insisted that monarchy, monopoly, guilds, and established churches caused social injustice and fueled prejudice and conflict. Developed over centuries to ensure stability, these institutions had become destructive of that end. They inhibited progress by encouraging people to respond to fear rather than hope, to believe that they were so incapable of managing themselves that they had to defer to the judgments of a handful of men who monopolized wealth, information, and power. The institutions of civil society had become so ossified, artificial, and corrupt, so out of touch with the interests of the rapidly expanding numbers of literate, middling people in growing cities, that they had lost legitimacy.

As an alternative, Wollstonecraft, Godwin, and others advocated a culture of natural commerce. Rather than repress their desires, individuals should act on them. They should be ambitious. They should pursue their self-interest, their happiness, within a society united by the bonds of social affection. They should exercise their imagination to conjure possibilities in conversation with other people. Commerce—the regular exchange of commodities, goods, ideas, and sentiments through trade, conversation, and books—would allow them to locate themselves within networks of friends who would cultivate social affection as the most effective means of managing their desires. Commercial society would cohere in a shared celebration of choice, in the cultivation of sympathy or empathy, and in the conviction that persuasion was the most effective means of promoting social order and human improvement. Empowered to seek fulfillment of their desires, individuals would learn the benefits of social engagement. Mutual sympathy would promote a spirit of benevolence, a respect for the capacity of human beings to imagine possibilities, to improve themselves, to balance desire and obligation, to find individual independence in social

---

4. For the thinking of a historian who has had a decisive impact on my historical sensibility, if not necessarily on this point, see Michael O'Brien, "Response to My Critics," *Mississippi Quarterly,* LVIII, nos. 1–2 (Winter–Spring 2005), 205–213.

interdependence. Benevolence would make people feel better about themselves, bring them approbation and profit.[5]

Learning about these ideas, coming of age during the American Revolution, and witnessing the power of benevolence in rallying individuals for humanitarian movements against the slave trade, corporal punishment, and a host of other forms of brutality, Wollstonecraft, Godwin, Imlay, and many others of their generation became ardent advocates of a revolution in favor of commerce. Their particular interest was in what we would call a cultural revolution, a complete reorganization in the basic assumptions and rules under which a society operates. Making their case within the realm of personal intimacy rather than politics, they began to argue that friendship and love were the firmest foundation of a new social order.

In their eyes, the central institution of the artificial ancien régime was marriage. As readers of novels by authors from Samuel Richardson to Jane Austen know, marriage was all about the exchange of property and genes among patriarchal families. The institution affirmed the absolute legal and economic power of men; it also offered women and children some protection by forcing men to honor obligations created by desire. But, in the late eighteenth century, Wollstonecraft, Imlay, and Godwin were among those denouncing marriage as an impediment to human happiness and improvement achieved through mutuality and exchange. Literate, middling men and women like Wollstonecraft, Imlay, and Godwin argued that the fundamental question for a woman and a man contemplating intimacy was not what their fathers thought or how much property they owned; rather, it was whether they loved each other enough to sustain mutuality, consent, and equality over an extended period of time. Wollstonecraft was the most prominent advocate of the position—shared by many others—that the model of commerce should encompass personal as well as political relationships. In *A Vindication of the Rights of Woman,* a sequel to her previous book, *A Vindication of the Rights of Men* (1790), she applied her variation on the theory of a commercial society to the institution of the family and to the nature of intimacy between men and women. What was the point of eliminating kings and priests, of attacking monopolies of wealth and ideas, if the patriarchal institution of marriage remained intact? Why create what would come to be called a liberal society—to celebrate the possibilities of self-interest, education, competition, and the creation of meaning, or what they would have called morality—and not include the most basic of ties,

---

5. Among many secondary sources, I have particularly relied on Emma Rothschild, *Economic Sentiments: Adam Smith, Condorcet, and the Enlightenment* (Cambridge, Mass., 2001).

those between men and women, parents and children? Why challenge the power of patriarchs in public but not in private?[6]

Like many writings of the 1790s, *A Vindication of the Rights of Woman* was written in part in response to the politician and philosopher Edmund Burke's critique on the implications of the French Revolution. His *Reflections on the Revolution in France,* twenty thousand copies of which appeared between 1790 and 1805, was probably the most read and certainly the most influential text of the decade. The Irish-born Burke, the champion of tradition and hierarchy, advocated a culture of social commerce that rooted authority in reason, in respect for the beauty human beings had constructed in spite of their natural terror in the face of the mysterious workings of their own bodies. "The most important of all revolutions," observed Burke, was not a revolution in politics; it was "a revolution in sentiments, manners, and moral opinions." It dated, not from July 4, 1776, or July 14, 1789, but from October 6, 1789, and it occurred, not in Independence Hall or the Bastille, but in the Royal apartments in the Palace of Versailles. There lived a king, a queen, and their children, a family that was more than a family, the living embodiment of a unified social and political order and divinely sanctioned authority. Suddenly, a "band of cruel ruffians and assassins" burst into the queen's bedroom and forced her to run "almost naked . . . to seek refuge at the feet of a king and husband not secure

---

6. My thinking on these questions reflects the influence of many scholars. Particularly important were G. J. Barker-Benfield, *The Culture of Sensibility: Sex and Society in Eighteenth-Century Britain* (Chicago, 1992); Toby L. Ditz, "The New Men's History and the Peculiar Absence of Gendered Power: Some Remedies from Early American Gender History," *Gender and History,* XVI, no. 1 (April 2004), 1–35; Daniel Walker Howe, *Making the American Self: Jonathan Edwards to Abraham Lincoln* (Cambridge, Mass., 1997); Lynn Hunt, *The Family Romance of the French Revolution* (Berkeley, Calif., 1992); Chris Jones, "Radical Sensibility in the 1790s," in Alison Yarrington and Kelvin Everest, eds., *Reflections of Revolution: Images of Romanticism* (London, 1993), 68–82; Mary Kelley, *Learning to Stand and Speak: Women, Education, and Public Life in America's Republic* (Chapel Hill, N.C., 2006); Sarah Knott and Barbara Taylor, eds., *Women, Gender, and Enlightenment* (New York, 2007); Michael Meranze, "Culture and Governance: Reflections on the Cultural History of Eighteenth-Century British America," *William and Mary Quarterly,* 3d Ser., LXV (2008), 713–744; Catherine O'Donnell Kaplan, *Men of Letters in the Early Republic: Cultivating Forums of Citizenship* (Chapel Hill, N.C., 2008); William M. Reddy, *The Navigation of Feeling: A Framework for the History of Emotions* (Cambridge, 2001); Ivy Schweitzer, *Perfecting Friendship: Politics and Affiliation in Early American Literature* (Chapel Hill, N.C., 2006); Jenny Uglow, *The Lunar Men: Five Friends Whose Curiosity Changed the World* (New York, 2002); Dror Wahrman, *The Making of the Modern Self: Identity and Culture in Eighteenth-Century England* (New Haven, Conn., 2004); Bryan Waterman, *Republic of Intellect: The Friendly Club of New York City and the Making of American Literature* (Baltimore, 2007).

of his own life." Louis XVI could do nothing to prevent his family from being escorted to a palace in Paris "now converted into a Bastile for kings," thus ending the "age of chivalry." The "glory of Europe is extinguished forever," exclaimed Burke. "Never, never more, shall we behold that generous loyalty to rank and sex, that proud submission, that dignified obedience, that subordination of the heart, which kept alive, even in servitude itself, the spirit of an exalted freedom!" Burke's sociability was one practiced within institutions—Parliament, law, an urban society of commerce—developed largely in the eighteenth century in response to the fragmentation of authority into multiple competing groups, including political factions and religious denominations.[7]

Consent, Burke suggested, was won not only through manly conversation and honest commerce but also through the beauty and majesty of institutions. Without the latter, there was neither harmony nor balance in the world. "All the pleasing illusions which made power gentle and obedience liberal" were gone. "All the decent drapery of life is to be rudely torn off." A "king is but a man, a queen is but a woman, a woman is but an animal,— and an animal not of the highest order. . . . laws are to be supported only by their own terrors, and by the concern which each individual may find in them from his own private speculations, or can spare to them from his own private interests. . . . Nothing is left which engages the affections on the part of the commonwealth. . . . our institutions can never be embodied . . . in persons,—so as to create in us love, veneration, admiration, or attachment." October 6 mattered to Burke because he saw it as the triumph of the tendency of human beings to act impulsively rather than to reason together within the confines of mutually constructed institutions such as a constitutional monarchy and patriarchal households. Burke's nightmare was the fear, often associated with Thomas Hobbes, that without time-honored institutions to monitor human behavior individuals would pursue their interests at the expense of the good of the whole. Ultimately, a culture of natural commerce would produce a firestorm of competing interests that would only be extinguished by the application of brute force. Power would survive in some form, Burke believed, most likely one more repressive and dangerous to liberty than the monarchical world denounced by its critics.[8]

7. Edmund Burke, *Reflections on the Revolution in France* . . . (1790), in *The Writings and Speeches of the Right Honourable Edmund Burke,* 12 vols. (Boston, 1901), III, 325, 326, 331, 332, 333, 334, 337. On the publishing history and influence of Burke's work, see William St. Clair, *The Reading Nation in the Romantic Period* (Cambridge, 2004), 13, 253–254, 257, 278–279.

8. Burke, *Reflections,* in *Writings and Speeches,* III, 332, 333, 334. On the connections be-

Wollstonecraft, Imlay, Godwin, and other radical writers did not imagine a world without power. Indeed, they fully intended to exercise power in a new form. At the core of their revolutionary vision was the idea that authority, far from a fixed, mysterious right enforced by kings, aristocrats, priests, and fathers, was a dynamic process that emerges from continual conversation among educated individuals who celebrate mutuality, honesty, and change. If power is the ability to get people to do what others want them to do, then men and women like Wollstonecraft and Godwin exercised power through a cultivated ability to persuade others of the justice of certain propositions about human behavior and human society. In many ways, the 1790s was the climax of more than a century of creative scrambling to respond to the disintegration of the unified authority of Christian monarchs and churches. Thomas Paine succinctly summarized this attitude in introducing *The Age of Reason.* Paine asked his "FELLOW-CITIZENS OF THE UNITED STATES OF AMERICA" "to remember, that [he had] always strenuously supported the right of every man to his own opinion, however different that opinion might be to [his]." "He who denies to another this right, makes a slave of himself to his present opinion, because he precludes himself the right of changing it." Controversy over this epistemological position—the belief that truth is that which people find the most persuasive of many competing propositions—became deeply personal. Without a general acceptance of authority and the right to exercise power, whether in the American Republic, the French republic, the English constitutional monarchy, or domestic households, crisis became a way of life.[9]

Like the men and women who invaded Versailles, Wollstonecraft, Godwin, Imlay, and their peers rejected the authority of patriarchs who monopolized power. What Burke feared, they embraced. Chivalry, they believed, entailed a social order that not only subordinated subjects to monarchs and women to men but also children to parents. Wollstonecraft, Imlay, and Godwin did not propose to substitute a world of total individual freedom or, as some of their critics have suggested, anarchy. They feared enthusiasm, too. They did not seek government by a mob of unruly men, the selfish speculators and adventurers Burke despised. Instead, they imag-

---

tween personal and political revolution, see Hunt, *Family Romance,* xv; Holly Brewer, *By Birth or Consent: Children, Law, and the Anglo-American Revolution in Authority* (Chapel Hill, N.C., 2005); and Jennifer Ngaire Heur, *The Family and the Nation: Gender and Citizenship in Revolutionary France, 1789–1830* (Ithaca, N.Y., 2005).

9. Thomas Paine, *The Age of Reason,* in Philip S. Foner, ed., *The Complete Writings of Thomas Paine,* 2 vols. (New York, 1945), I, 463. I elaborate on this point in "The Authority of the Imagination in an Age of Wonder," *Journal of the Early Republic,* XXXIII (2013), 1–27.

ined a social order that emerged from commerce practiced by men and women who respected one another, who talked and listened and negotiated. They would ultimately become "independent and free" less through "the strength of arms," in the words of Jean-Jacques Rousseau, than through "the moderation of hearts." The foundation of revolution was the possibility of revolution: the ability to *imagine* one's self as a malleable historical actor living among other historical actors who could (in conversation with others) revise themselves and thus reinvent society.[10]

Wollstonecraft, Imlay, and Godwin did not change the world, at least not immediately. But they did participate in changing the ways in which English-speaking peoples *understood* change and the world because they focused on form as well as content. Among their enduring contributions was their role in revising contemporary modes of discourse, especially the still relatively new genre of the novel, not only to make sense of their problems but also to link them to the experiences of thousands of readers and writers around the North Atlantic. In their view, a novel was an imagined personal history, a contingent narrative in which characters (and by extension readers), by learning something critical about themselves and one another, learn something critical about the world as a whole. As often as not, they were written by women about women for women. Many contemporaries worried about this development, not simply because of gender, but also because novels insisted that the quotidian, the personal, the making and unmaking of families as well as friends were just as important as political acts that defined public life. Novels inquired into the nature of power and the construction of meaning by contemplating the nature of relationships. They were more about family than the state, more concerned with love than policy. Above all, they were about the possibilities and perils of commerce.[11]

---

10. Jean-Jacques Rousseau, *Emile; or, On Education* (1762), trans. and ed. Allan Bloom (New York, 1979), 235, 236. See Mike Goode, *Sentimental Masculinity and the Rise of History, 1790–1890* (Cambridge, 2009); and Hannah Spahn, *Thomas Jefferson, Time, and History* (Charlottesville, Va., 2011).

11. In thinking about writing, I learned much from Nancy Armstrong, *Desire and Domestic Fiction: A Political History of the Novel* (New York, 1987); Paula R. Backscheider, ed., *Revising Women: Eighteenth-Century "Women's Fiction" and Social Engagement* (Baltimore, 2000); Eve Tavor Bannet, *The Domestic Revolution: Enlightenment Feminisms and the Novel* (Baltimore, 2000); Liz Bellamy, *Commerce, Morality, and the Eighteenth-Century Novel* (Cambridge, 1998); Pamela Clemit, *The Godwinian Novel: The Rational Fictions of Godwin, Brockden Brown, Mary Shelley* (Oxford, 1993); E. M. Dadlez, *Mirrors to One Another: Emotion and Value in Jane Austen and David Hume* (Malden, Mass., 2009); Cathy N. Davidson, *Revolution and the Word: The Rise of the Novel in America* (New York, 1986); Markman Ellis, *The Politics of Sensibility: Race, Gender, and Commerce in the Sentimental Novel* (Cambridge, 1996); Paul Giles, *Transatlantic In-*

Through the practice of rational affection, Wollstonecraft and her friends believed, human beings could manage problems they could never fully understand, let alone overcome, on their own. Individual happiness was the foundation of social progress. What they did not anticipate—and never fully comprehended—was their own imperialism. Because their ideas about commerce reflected the world of a particular class of English-speaking men and women, its appeal to other peoples was often limited or at cross-purposes. Still, the sheer ambition of attempting to maintain that life was socially constructed was a breathtaking assertion of confidence in the ability of human beings to change. If Wollstonecraft, Imlay, Godwin, and many others learned how complicated it was to persuade even a sympathetic man to do what he did not want to do—to pay taxes, obey laws, or stay with a woman he no longer loved—they were merely confronting in their own lives an intractable cultural dilemma that fascinated their contemporaries. Their efforts—and those of their friends, rivals, critics, and, ultimately, their children—to make sense of that dilemma constitute the subject of *Love in the Time of Revolution*.[12]

---

surrections: *British Culture and the Formation of American Literature, 1730–1860* (Philadelphia, 2001); Harriet Guest, *Small Change: Women, Learning, Patriotism, 1750–1810* (Chicago, 2000); Angela Keane, *Women Writers and the English Nation in the 1790s: Romantic Belongings* (Cambridge, 2000); Beth Lau, ed., *Fellow Romantics: Male and Female British Writers, 1790–1835* (Farnham, Eng., 2009); Sharon Marcus, *Between Women: Friendship, Desire, and Marriage in Victorian England* (Princeton, N.J., 2007); Ruth Perry, *Novel Relations: The Transformation of Kinship in English Literature and Culture, 1748–1818* (Cambridge, 2004); Tilottama Rajan and Julia M. Wright, eds., *Romanticism, History, and the Possibilities of Genre: Re-forming Literature, 1789–1837* (Cambridge, 1998); Rust, *Prodigal Daughters;* Stephen Shapiro, *The Culture and Commerce of the Early American Novel: Reading the Atlantic World-System* (University Park, Pa., 2008); Leonard Tennenhouse, *The Importance of Feeling English: American Literature and the British Diaspora, 1750–1850* (Princeton, N.J., 2007).

In thinking about reading, I learned much from Gary Saul Morson, *"Anna Karenina" in Our Time: Seeing More Wisely* (New Haven, Conn., 2007); Keith Oatley, "Emotions and the Story Worlds of Fiction," 39–70, and James W. Polichak and Richard J. Gerrig, "Get Up and Win! Participatory Responses to Reading," 71–96, both in Melanie C. Green, Jeffery J. Strange, and Timothy C. Brock, eds., *Narrative Impact: Social and Cognitive Foundations* (Mahwah, N.J., 2002); and James L. Machor, *Reading Fiction in Antebellum America: Informed Response and Reception Histories, 1820–1865* (Baltimore, 2011).

12. On the empire, see Maya Jasanoff, *Edge of Empire: Lives, Culture, and Conquest in the East, 1750–1850* (New York, 2005); Kathleen Wilson, *The Island Race: Englishness, Empire, and Gender in the Eighteenth Century* (London, 2003); and Kathleen Wilson, ed., *A New Imperial History: Culture, Identity, and Modernity in Britain and the Empire, 1660–1840* (Cambridge, 2004). On the experiences of women in a colonial city whose lives allowed little time for self-reflection, see Clare A. Lyons, *Sex among the Rabble: An Intimate History of Gender and Power in the Age of Revolution, Philadelphia, 1730–1830* (Chapel Hill, N.C., 2006).

I

"Quite Alone in a crowd"

Armed with a letter of credit for thirty pounds from her publisher, Mary Wollstonecraft traveled from London to Paris in December 1792 determined to experiment with the possibilities of life at the epicenter of revolution. She was thirty-three years old and the acclaimed author of *A Vindication of the Rights of Woman*. In many ways, the journey was an affirmation of her hard-won status as an independent professional woman. Wollstonecraft had at long last found her voice within imperial London's radical literary circles, supporting herself by writing reviews, essays, and books. As important, she had honed an acute sense of what was wrong with her world and how it might be improved through the cultivation of a culture of mixed-gender sociability. Why not try Paris? It was on the cutting edge of revolution, only three and a half years from the fall of the Bastille and a couple of months from the replacement of a monarchy with a republic. The National Assembly had even made divorce a legal option for women on September 20, 1792. Perhaps, she joked, the "Spinster on the wing . . . might take a husband for the time being, and get divorced when [her] truant heart" missed her friends in London.[1]

In fact, Wollstonecraft had just experienced a kind of emotional divorce. Disappointment drove her from London as much as hope brought her to Paris. She was still trying to let go of her "rational desire" for the married painter Henry Fuseli, who had recently refused her proposal that she live

1. Mary Wollstonecraft (MW) to Everina Wollstonecraft, [circa early December 1792], in Janet Todd, ed., *The Collected Letters of Mary Wollstonecraft* (New York, 2003), 212–213, to William Roscoe, Nov. 12, [17]92, 208.

with him and his wife. The pain was intense. She missed him. She missed their intimacy. Above all, she missed *them*. Wollstonecraft had "always [caught] something from the rich torrent of [his] conversation, worth treasuring up in [her] memory, to exercise [her] understanding." As she absorbed Fuseli's decision, she recoiled from her own behavior. To her "horror," she realized she had become "a sacrifice to a passion which may have a mixture of dross in it." Perhaps she was confronting her sexuality, something she had yet to indulge with another person. Perhaps she was just hurt and embarrassed. Whatever it was, she had thought she could "conquer" such a passion or "die in the attempt." Why had she failed—again—to sustain a relationship that had moved from friendship to love? Fuseli was not the first person with whom she had found intimacy that proved fleeting. Why? Was she "a mere animal" in whom "instinctive emotions too often silence the suggestions of reason"?[2]

Paris provided no answer, no refuge, and no satisfaction. Wollstonecraft entered a dark, dirty, chilly city very much alone. Arriving just before Christmas Day, she stayed at a friend's house, barren of all but servants. Unable to shake a cold, she fought a lingering cough and struggled to improve her French. Beyond the house, Paris was consumed with the fate of one man. On the morning of December 26, Wollstonecraft watched from her window as guards escorted the former king of France to his trial. There were no insults, no jeers, no rude gestures, just an eerie silence broken only by the regular beating of a drum. Impressed with the behavior of the crowd, she was equally impressed with Louis's dignified demeanor, a composure he would sustain until his execution in the Place de la Révolution on January 21. Trying to write after the tumult of the procession had faded into the distance, Wollstonecraft was haunted by images of "bloody hands." Unnerved, she missed her cat. "I want to see something alive," she wrote, "death in so many frightful shapes has taken hold of my fancy." That night she went to bed "for the first time in [her] life" with a candle still burning.[3]

In February, intent on adjusting to the rhythms of her new home, making friends, and learning French, she still could not shake a "lowness of Spirits" so persistent that one of her sisters speculated that she must have suffered "some great disappointment." Life in the republican capital, she confessed, was more diverting than satisfying. "Those who wish to live for themselves without close friendship, or wa[rm] affection ought to live in Paris," Woll-

2. MW to Roscoe, Nov. 12, [17]92, ibid., 206, to Henry Fuseli, [late 1792], 205, to Joseph Johnson, [October 1792], 205.

3. MW to Johnson, Dec. 26, 1792, ibid., 216, 217.

stonecraft wrote, "for they have the pleasantest way of *whiling away time—* and their urbanity, like their furniture is *tres commode.*" She complained of the "very bad" weather and "very disagreeable" streets, frustrated that she could not walk at will and enjoy fresh air. Wollstonecraft knew she was "not well," citing as a symptom the "fatigue" resulting from the "vivacity that should amuse [her]." In her distress, she almost accepted the sudden offer of a ride back to England.[4]

Wollstonecraft's disillusionment with Paris reflected her distrust of her imagination. "Before [she] came to France," she had "cherished . . . an opinion, that strong virtues might exist with the polished manners produced by the progress of civilization." She was wrong. Paris had persuaded her that "vice, or, if you will, evil, is the grand mobile of action." The villain was "that wanton, the Imagination, with her artful coquetry, who lures us forward, and makes us run over a rough road, pushing aside every obstacle merely to catch a disappointment." Selfishness, "the narrow principle of commerce," was overcoming "the simple emotions of the heart, which, being natural, are always moral." Despite her "hope, that a fairer day is dawning on Europe," she feared that the Revolution had transformed rather than tamed the "desire of power." Now "every petty municipal officer, [has] become the idol, or rather the tyrant of the day, stalk[ing] like a cock on a dunghil." Wollstonecraft conjured a future dominated by isolated individuals. She feared "the turpitude of a cold calculator who lives for himself alone." Lacking sympathy, he would legally crush "thousands with impunity." It seemed that "names, not principles, are changed." Revolution had replaced kings with clerks.[5]

Nobody who knew Mary Wollstonecraft would have been surprised by this extended bout of melancholy in the winter of 1792–1793. Her low spirits were hardly unusual. Always moody, she struggled with a genetic tendency toward depression that she inherited from her restless, volatile, and angry father. Making a virtue out of necessity, Wollstonecraft embraced brutal honesty—what she and her contemporaries termed *manly* behavior. At the end of a century in which many Europeans and Americans constructed life as a drama and themselves as actors, Wollstonecraft refused to pretend to be anything other than what she was. She defined herself in opposition to "arti-

4. Eliza Bishop to Everina Wollstonecraft, quoted ibid., 221 n. 514, MW to Bishop, Jan. 20, [1793], 218, to Ruth Barlow, Feb. [1–14], [1793], 220–221.

5. MW, "Introductory to a Series of Letters on the Present Character of the French Nation," Feb. 15, 1793, in Janet Todd and Marilyn Butler, eds., *The Works of Mary Wollstonecraft,* 7 vols. (New York, 1989), VI, 445, 446.

ficial" structures and in favor of natural relationships founded on mutual consent rather than patriarchal coercion. She believed that the "birthright of man . . . is such a degree of liberty, civil and religious, as is compatible with the liberty of every other individual with whom he is united in a social compact." Only "an artificial monster" would fail to understand "that true happiness arose from the friendship and intimacy which can only be enjoyed by equals." Imagination conjured possibilities as well as perils.[6]

We would scarcely take note of Mary Wollstonecraft if she had not generalized from her experience to write about the human condition with uncommon passion and intelligence. We care about Wollstonecraft because of her unyielding insistence on persuading men as well as women that romantic love was a means to secure independence rather than to obliterate it and that mutual respect and mutual happiness were possible if women and men regularly engaged with one another. Critics then and now point out that it was an absurdly idealistic enterprise that ignored well-entrenched structures of human behavior and social organization. Wollstonecraft was defying history as well as patriarchy. If it was folly, she would make the most of it. She endured the long winter in Paris without surrendering entirely to her dark mood. After all, as she concluded a litany of complaints, she had "met with affection" as well as disappointment. Everything she had experienced in thirty-three years told her that February would soon end, and March would eventually turn into April. Spring was only a few weeks away.[7]

Education

Born on April 27, 1759, in London, Wollstonecraft spent the first thirty years of her life struggling with the competing claims of independence and interdependence, autonomy and affection. She and her five surviving siblings—Edward (1757-1808), Elizabeth (1763–circa 1829), Everina (1765-1843), James (circa 1768-1806), and Charles (circa 1770-1817)—had grown up in a peripatetic and unpleasant household. Wollstonecraft had no use for her abusive father and no respect for her long-suffering mother. Later she strenuously objected to parents who enforced "a brutal attachment to children" and treated them "like slaves." Individuals ought to be free to follow "the dictates of nature" in all aspects of their lives. As a girl, she sought alternatives to her family with neighbors. When her father moved the family to Hoxton,

6. MW, *A Vindication of the Rights of Men in a Letter to the Right Honourable Edmund Burke . . .* , 2d ed. (London, 1789), in Todd and Butler, eds., *Works of Wollstonecraft,* V, 9, 10–11.

7. MW to Bishop, Jan. 20, [1793], in Todd, ed., *Collected Letters,* 218.

she spent time with a minister and his wife who "took some pains to cultivate [her] understanding," giving her books and encouraging her to read out loud. Much as she craved independence, she desired a mutual attachment. She despised "company without any soci[a]bility" as a "false kind of politeness" in which "neither the heart nor sentiments appear in their true colours." In many ways, her life's ambition was to avoid what she would experience in Paris in the long winter of 1792–1793: to be "quite alone in a crowd."[8]

Wollstonecraft reached that conclusion in the wake of the death of her first great friend. Two years older, the better-educated Fanny Blood seemed a perfect blend of "masculine understanding" and "feminine virtue[s]" when the twenty-year-old Wollstonecraft met her in early 1780. Through unreserved conversation, the women developed an easy intimacy that allowed them to "do . . . good" for each other without the complications of "any matrimonial tie," by which she meant an artificial connection. Together they were something more than they were when alone. Wollstonecraft moved into the Bloods' house in Walham Green, a suburb west of London, and became friends with Fanny's siblings George and Caroline. Increasingly, she doubted that birth families promoted happiness because they involved more coercion than consent. Better to choose friends than obey parents.[9]

Marriage was also suspect because it was so rarely rooted in mutuality. The failure of her sister Eliza Bishop's marriage affirmed the troubled image offered by the example of their parents. In 1783, Wollstonecraft went to stay with Eliza, who was suffering from postpartum depression after the birth of her first child. According to Wollstonecraft, Eliza and her husband were enduring "the fate of most married pairs": they had no serious relation-

---

8. MW, *Vindication of the Rights of Men,* in Todd and Butler, eds., *Works of Wollstonecraft,* V, 22; MW to Jane Arden, [early 1780], 24, in Todd, ed., *Collected Letters,* 80, to Everina Wollstonecraft, Oct. 9, [1786]. Throughout I have relied on the careful and thoughtful work of Janet Todd, author of the most thorough biography, *Mary Wollstonecraft: A Revolutionary Life* (New York, 2000). Gary Kelly captures Wollstonecraft's restless, radical character in *Revolutionary Feminism: The Mind and Career of Mary Wollstonecraft* (New York, 1992). Richard Holmes offers a lively portrait in *Footsteps: Adventures of a Romantic Biographer* (New York, 1996), 90–132. Other biographies include Lyndall Gordon, *Vindication: A Life of Mary Wollstonecraft* (New York, 2005); Diane Jacobs, *Her Own Woman: The Life of Mary Wollstonecraft* (New York, 2001); and Claire Tomalin, *The Life and Death of Mary Wollstonecraft* (New York, 1974). Barbara Taylor, *Mary Wollstonecraft and the Feminist Imagination* (Cambridge, 2003), combines biography and astute criticism. Claudia L. Johnson, ed., *The Cambridge Companion to Mary Wollstonecraft* (Cambridge, 2002), contains more than a dozen informative essays.

9. MW to Arden, [early 1780], in Todd, ed., *Collected Letters,* 24–25, [April 1781?], 30.

ship, no rational friendship, once the initial "joy, and all that"—the "raptures" of sensuality—had dissipated. Mary and Fanny persuaded Eliza to leave her husband and child (who subsequently died), "contrary to all the rules of conduct that are published for the benefit of new married Ladies." Rescuing Eliza from an insensitive tyrant—the "poor girl will never again be in this man's power"—was exhilarating. But what came next? How were three young women to manage in a society that assumed they would spend their lives as wives and mothers? Mary, Fanny, and Eliza opted for teaching (an extension of a domestic role) and opened a school for girls in 1784 in a rented house on Newington Green, north of London.[10]

As the experiment failed, Mary's life fell apart. Fanny's confidence in the possibility of female independence waned. She grew closer to her friend, Hugh Skeys, and accepted his marriage offer in 1785. Because Skeys had business interests in Portugal, the couple moved to Lisbon. Wollstonecraft blamed the husband for the wife's choice. She had initially considered Skeys the kind of man her "fancy has painted [and] my heart longed to meet with," a man whose treatment of his wife was "humane and tender." Now he revealed himself to be impatient with human "infirmities." He did not love Fanny for "the qualities that re[nder] her dear to my heart." On a personal level, Wollstonecraft had seen the transience of even close relationships. Her inability to sustain the possibilities she had imagined led her into crashing disappointment. Her mind was "harassed," and she was so "hunted down by cares" that her "spirits [were] quite deprest." Losing "all relish for life," she hoped that death would cure her "almost broken heart." Not for the last time Wollstonecraft determined that, without someone "to be unreserved to," "without some one to love[,] this world is a desart."[11]

Equally characteristic was her determination to overcome her sense of powerlessness by acting impulsively to reclaim what she refused to accept as lost. Sailing to Lisbon, she arrived in time to witness the delivery of Fanny's son. Unfortunately, neither the child nor his mother survived. Fanny Blood Skeys died on November 29, 1785. A bereft Wollstonecraft returned to England brimming with self-pity. Disgusted that she had survived the "tempestuous" voyage, she welcomed death. Her melancholy was evidence that "Nature will sometimes prevail, 'spite of reason.'" Beyond the loss of Fanny, the failure of the school meant that she had to accept the

10. MW to Arden, [circa late 1782], ibid., 38, to Everina Wollstonecraft, [circa January 1784], 47, [circa January 1784], 48.

11. MW to George Blood, July 3, 1785, ibid., 52, 53, July 20, [1785], 55, 56, July 25, [1785], 58.

position of governess with an aristocratic family in rural Ireland. Without friends or prospects, she lamented that she was *"alone"* in the world.[12]

Wollstonecraft thought through her predicament in language widely available to late-eighteenth-century English women and men through the rapidly expanding medium of books. Reading was "the only way to destroy the worm that will gnaw the core." In large part, that was because it allowed her to locate her personal dilemma within a larger cultural movement. Books affirmed her celebration of friendship as a relationship created by choice rather than birth; they also affirmed that friendship was perpetually unpredictable. No matter how hard people worked to cultivate mutual trust through regular commerce, friendships faded or disintegrated. Samuel Taylor Coleridge lamented that friendship was often no more than delusion or a desire to escape loneliness. Time inevitably frayed the most sincere of connections. Family obligations undermined friendships, if only by "occupying the heart." Sexuality could be problematic because it encouraged people to mistake fleeting physical gratification for enduring affection. The institution of marriage substituted an artificial connection for a natural one, limiting the possibilities of friendship within an exchange of property and genes supervised by ministers and lawyers. In the end, however, the ultimate challenge was negotiating difference between two or more people with dynamic sensibilities and shifting interests. Human beings were mercurial and whimsical. Placid calm suddenly gave way to dark storms; the object of desire as the sun set was an object of derision as the sun rose.[13]

Eighteenth-century Britons and British Americans emphasized the supposed inability of dark-skinned, non-Christian individuals to sustain a culture of sociability and to behave in a civilized fashion (that is, to balance mind and body through commerce). This attitude rationalized their conquest and exploitation of different kinds of people around the Atlantic basin and in South Asia. But historians have neglected the extent to which

12. MW to Blood, Feb. 4, [1786], ibid., 65, Mar. 3, 1788, 148, June 18, 1786, 72.

13. MW to Everina Wollstonecraft, Mar. 22, [1788], ibid., 152; Samuel Taylor Coleridge, December 1812–June 1813, in Kathleen Coburn, ed., *The Notebooks of Samuel Taylor Coleridge*, 4 vols. (Princeton, N.J., 1973), III, 4175. On reading as a form of friendship, see William Hazlitt, "Essay XX: On Reading Old Books," in Hazlitt, *The Plain Speaker: Opinions on Books, Men, and Things*, II (London, 1826), in Duncan Wu, ed., *The Selected Writings of Hazlitt*, VIII, 206–214. See also Clarissa Campbell Orr, "Aristocratic Feminism, the Learned Governess, and the Republic of Letters," in Sarah Knott and Barbara Taylor, eds., *Women, Gender, and Enlightenment* (New York, 2005), 306–325; Gurion Taussig, *Coleridge and the Idea of Friendship, 1789–1804* (Newark, Del., 2002); and Ivy Schweitzer, *Perfecting Friendship: Politics and Affiliation in Early American Literature* (Chapel Hill, N.C., 2006).

English-speaking peoples assessed themselves in the same way. The most important "other" for educated middling people such as Wollstonecraft was *themselves*, especially when it came to dealing with the relationship between the body and the mind in shaping relationships with other people. What was friendship—and in its most heightened form, romantic love—if not a perpetual negotiation between bodies and minds?[14]

Many of Wollstonecraft's contemporaries were imagining the possibilities of reconfiguring relations within families and states through commerce, moving from "an axis of kinship based on consanguineal ties or blood lineage to an axis based on conjugal and affinal ties of the married couple." Although this conception applies mainly to a relatively small number of middling peoples, there was a shift in the late-eighteenth-century Anglo-American world from defining family as a group of people who resided together in a multitude of forms to defining it as a nuclear unit of parents and children. Suddenly, the term "friends" meant strictly people with whom there was no connection of blood. Friendship was a bond of choice rooted ultimately in some form of sympathy and in which commerce (or general exchange) substituted for blood in structuring relationships. This shift prompted considerable anxiety. Individuals such as Wollstonecraft were confused about how to behave and what to think. To whom did they owe their primary loyalty, their birth family or the family they created, a situation complicated by increased migration? How did they negotiate their often conflicting roles as children, siblings, parents, and friends? How did they deal with strangers? What were the dangers as well as the possibilities of relationships that depended on something as vague and unstable as affection? How would households support themselves?[15]

Many Western Europeans contemplated these questions by imagining a better society as a free-floating alliance of male and female friends. One of the most prominent advocates of a new social order was the Frenchman Jean-Jacques Rousseau. His essays and novels shaped the conversation of Wollstonecraft and others like her long after his death in 1778. The young Wollstonecraft admired Rousseau's celebration of honest connection. She

14. Kathleen Wilson, *The Island Race: Englishness, Empire, and Gender in the Eighteenth Century* (London, 2003); Wilson, ed., *A New Imperial History: Culture, Identity, and Modernity in Britain and the Empire, 1660–1840* (Cambridge, 2004).

15. Ruth Perry, *Novel Relations: The Transformation of Kinship in English Literature and Culture, 1748–1818* (Cambridge, 2004), 2–6; Naomi Tadmor, *Family and Friends in Eighteenth-Century England: Household, Kinship, and Patronage* (Cambridge, 2001). See also Christopher Flint, *Family Fictions: Narrative and Domestic Relations in Britain, 1688–1798* (Stanford, Calif., 1998).

was less persuaded of his ideas about gender. In Rousseau's view, sexual "inequality" was not "man-made" because men and women clearly had different aptitudes and talents. But, he contended, that divergence should inform, not obstruct, mixed-gender sociability. Recognizing that together they constituted more than the sum of their parts, men and women had to engage with one another in a spirit of mutual respect. Although Sophie, the consort of Émile, the central figure in the novel that bears his name, learns to defer to men and to confine herself to managing a well-ordered household, Émile learns to treat women courteously, to reason rather than command. In the immensely popular novel *Julie,* Rousseau narrated the efforts of a small group of flawed but well-meaning friends to balance the rational pleasures of love, "the sweet habit which makes a man affectionate toward his companion," with the transient enthusiasm of sex, "that unbridled ardor which intoxicates him with the chimerical attractions of an object which he no longer sees as it really is." Rousseau insisted that social commerce would only flourish in rural areas. Paris corrupted and distorted human behavior. Men were "adventurers and bachelors who spend their lives running from house to house," and lovers "passing acquaintances who get together for amusement, for show, out of habit, or for the needs of the moment." Away from the artifice of the city, friends and lovers could work together to develop a balanced sensibility called love, "the rule and bridle of nature's inclinations." This mixed-gender cooperation was "a noble empire, and one well worth the price of its purchase." Men and women united by natural affection in small communities would find contentment. "Human souls need to be coupled to realize their full value," exclaims the ardent male lover in *Julie.* The "combined force of friends, like that of the blades of an artificial magnet, is incomparably greater than the sum of their individual forces." Together people *composed* themselves. Friendship was "an exchange, a contract like others, but it is the most sacred of all." Combining a "mutual attachment, agreement of tastes, [and] suitableness of characters," social affection would flourish in a natural environment replete with natural distinctions.[16]

Wollstonecraft readily agreed that mutual affection was more useful so-

16. Jean-Jacques Rousseau, *Emile; or, On Education* (1762), trans. Allan Bloom (New York, 1979), 38, 39, 214, 215, 233 n. 348, 361, 363–365, 393, 430; Rousseau, *Julie; or, The New Heloise: Letters of Two Lovers Who Live in a Small Town at the Foot of the Alps* (1761), trans. Philip Stewart and Jean Vaché (Hanover, N.H., 1997), 188, 211, 221, 222, 294, 549. See MW, review of *Second Partie des Confessions de J. J. Rousseau,* in Todd and Butler, eds., *Works of Wollstonecraft,* VII, 228–234. See also James H. Warner, "*Émile* in Eighteenth-Century England," *PMLA,* LIX (1944), 773–791.

cial glue than patriarchal command. But she was ultimately more comfortable with the Scottish variation on these themes than she was with Rousseau's celebration of rural simplicity and romantic enthusiasm. Unlike Rousseau, David Hume and Adam Smith argued that an urban society was most likely to encourage harmony and prosperity because it facilitated the pursuit of self-interest within a community bound together by rational affection. Alone, human beings cannot form realistic judgments about how to gain what they desire. Isolation reinforces prejudice and antisocial behavior. "Were it possible that a human creature could grow up to manhood in some solitary place, without any communication with his own species," warned Smith, "he could no more think of his own character, of the propriety or demerit of his own sentiments and conduct, of the beauty or deformity of his own mind, than of the beauty or deformity of his own face." The human senses are too limited to be trusted. Society facilitates ambition because commerce is the only way in which individuals can understand their ambition, let alone act on it with any hope of success. Regular exchange of ideas and sentiments as well as goods enables people to realize their ambitions and honor mutuality. They find happiness by learning to manage their bodies and their emotions in ways that win the respect of others. When individuals "meet in an easy and sociable manner," wrote Hume, "the tempers of men, as well as their behaviour, refine apace." They "feel an encrease of humanity, from the very habit of conversing together, and contributing to each other's pleasure." Among other positive outcomes, men would know that a distinguishing feature of a civilized society was the polite treatment of women. A man of refined sensibility would condescend to notice the plight of all creatures. To dismiss or abuse another human being, no matter their social status, was to incur the opprobrium of one's fellow beings and therefore to risk failure in all aspects of one's life.[17]

17. Adam Smith, *The Theory of Moral Sentiments* (1790), ed. Ryan Patrick Hanley and Amartya Sen (New York, 2010), 133–134; David Hume, "Of Refinement in the Arts" (1742), in Eugene F. Miller, ed., *Essays, Moral, Political, and Literary* (Indianapolis, Ind., 1987), 271. See David Fate Norton, ed., *The Cambridge Companion to Hume* (Cambridge, 1993); Chris Jones, "Radical Sensibility in the 1790s," in Alison Yarrington and Kelvin Everest, eds., *Reflections of Revolution: Images of Romanticism* (London, 1993), 68–82; Liz Bellamy, *Commerce, Morality, and the Eighteenth-Century Novel* (Cambridge, 1998); and, especially, Emma Rothschild, *Economic Sentiments: Adam Smith, Condorcet, and the Enlightenment* (Cambridge, Mass., 2001), 1–51. On the emergence of humanitarianism, see Thomas L. Haskell, "Capitalism and the Origins of the Humanitarian Sensibility, Part 2," 136–160, David Brion Davis, "Reflections on Abolitionism and Ideological Hegemony," 161–179, and John Ashworth, "The Relationship between Capitalism and Humanitarianism," 180–199, all in Thomas Bender, ed., *The Antislavery Debate: Capitalism and Abolitionism as a Problem in Historical Interpretation* (Berkeley, Calif.,

A commercial society nurtured stability, not by isolating individuals or repressing antisocial behavior through coercion, but by encouraging individuals to mix with others in the hope of improving themselves materially and morally. "We can never survey our own sentiments and motives, we can never form any judgment concerning them," claimed Smith, "unless we remove ourselves, as it were, from our own natural station, and endeavor to view them at a certain distance from us. . . . we can do this in no other way than by endeavouring to view them with the eyes of other people, or as other people are likely to view them." Thus everything depends on "the judgment of others." Individuals must function as both "spectator[s]" and "agent[s]." By observing others, they see themselves better. They grasp the profit in knowing that true independence grows from interdependence. Because of the power of fear, the body's first line of defense, human beings will always struggle to manage their passions and cultivate socially acceptable behavior. But they are more likely to succeed if they locate themselves in a network of friends who function as both actors and audience and accept that meaning (or value) emerges from dynamic interaction. In short, the practice of social affection is necessary to the development of self-awareness.[18]

Accepting Hume's dictums about the irregular behavior of human beings and the elusive quality of human understanding (when "we say . . . that one object is connected with another, we mean only that they have acquired a connection in our thought"), members of Wollstonecraft's generation assumed that progress was less about identifying structures, labeling categories of human behavior, and prescribing specific remedies through legislation than about endlessly engaging with others. Avoiding extremes, a healthy person lived "a mixed kind of life." He or she sought out interlocutors, read books, attended the theater, and evaluated his or her performance in conversation with others in person or in print. "A real Friend," according to one British observer in 1793, "is the agreeable Moderator in all our Actions and inward Sensations. His Genius we carefully consult in all that concerns our Amusement and Interest." "Friendship well cultivated . . . will ensure us at least a moderate Passage through the most terrible of all tempestuous Natures *('Human nature')*."[19]

1992); Karen Halttunen, "Humanitarianism and the Pornography of Pain in Anglo-American Culture," *American Historical Review,* C (1995), 303–334; and Christopher Leslie Brown, *Moral Capital: Foundations of British Abolitionism* (Chapel Hill, N.C., 2006).

18. Smith, *Theory of Moral Sentiments,* ed. Hanley and Sen, 133, 136.

19. David Hume, *An Enquiry concerning Human Understanding* (Stilwell, Kans., 2005), 6, 43; Charles Atkinson, *The Mind's Monitor; or, A Serious Discourse on the Advantages of Self-Preservation, Society, Friendship, Love, Learning, Religion, and on Death* (Leeds, 1793), 25, 26.

In Wollstonecraft's world, books counted as best friends. A 1774 decision in the House of Lords to outlaw perpetual copyright fueled a boom in the publishing industry. Suddenly, a long "suppressed" "demand" was "met by a huge surge in the supply of books," including cheap editions of older works, anthologies, and abridgments. All over Britain, organizations sprang up to facilitate reading. By 1800, there were perhaps one thousand circulating libraries in the country and innumerable reading societies, both of which bought books that their members then rented or borrowed. Reading in the late eighteenth century, while more extensive than it had been only decades earlier, remained a communal activity, one shared with family or friends. People read books out loud and talked about them together. The British "reading nation was not so much a scatter of individuals reading this and that, but a group of reading constituencies, with cohorts joining and leaving, a reading class which was geographically well spread and which was not commensurate with social class, income, gender, or with age, and which only in part coincided with the economic and social elites."[20]

Likely Wollstonecraft was introduced to reading in this fashion in the homes of neighbors and the Bloods. But once in Ireland there was limited opportunity for shared reading. Books alone were not enough to satisfy Wollstonecraft's need for connection. She expected reading to have a social dimension. She craved the kind of personal intimacy she had enjoyed with Fanny. Demanding letters from friends and relatives, she declared herself "a sojourner in a strange land" who wanted to "be reminded that I still live in the remembrance of those, whose very names fills me with tenderness." Wary about the fleeting nature of friendship, she emphasized the importance of "rational conversations, and domestic affections." Melancholy flourished in the chasm between imagination and reality. She knew that she had to be careful about "indulg[ing] a delightful tenderness, forget[ting] the convictions of reason, and giv[ing] way to chimerical hopes." But friendships that emerged "in a cultivated mind" and flourished in an abundance of both "reason and sensibility" were something more than "*warm starts of tenderness*" or "*mere ornaments.*" True friends were "manly," which meant they acted "with firmness instead of rashness." They were not *courtiers*, gallants devoted to sensuality and artificiality. Manliness was natural openness, a willingness to cry at the plight of others or the courage to endure

---

On the danger of social isolation, see Thomas W. Laqueur, *Solitary Sex: A Cultural History of Masturbation* (New York, 2003).

20. William St. Clair, *The Reading Nation in the Romantic Period* (Cambridge, 2004), 111, 115, 237–267.

pain. But it had to be a measured sensibility. Harley, the central character of Henry MacKenzie's popular 1771 novel, *The Man of Feeling*, was so sensitive that the sheer weight of others' misery weighed him down and ultimately killed him.[21]

Most educated Europeans were familiar with this dilemma, dramatized effectively in Johann Wolfgang von Goethe's novel, *The Sorrows of Young Werther*. Goethe offered his "little book [to] be [a] friend" to those who needed one. Published in 1774 and translated into English and French, *Werther* tells the story of a young man obsessed with Lotte, a rational woman engaged to Albert, a man so controlled that he lacks "sympathy" and "sensitive perception." The enthusiastic Werther never knows "what is happening" when he is "with [Lotte]; it's as if [his] nerves are turning [his] soul inside out." Love awakens people to possibilities, to imagine something they do not have, even as it enslaves them to a "raging, endless passion." Without Lotte, Werther "cannot get hold of [him]self!" When Lotte marries Albert, her attempts to reason with him, to encourage manly behavior—"control yourself!"—fail. Lotte feels for Werther. But after he forces a kiss on her, she locks him out. And Werther shoots himself. Wollstonecraft admired Goethe's ability to create sympathy for Werther even as he highlighted the character's "ungoverned sensibility." More important, she understood the novel to be a cautionary tale about the imagination. Even if Lotte had loved him, Werther would have found "some unattainable object to pine after."[22]

Experience and books taught Wollstonecraft that people needed one another to navigate between the extremes of isolation and enthusiasm. They also taught her that a patriarchal society so restricted women that the friendships necessary to cultivate understanding were virtually impossible. Women needed friends as much as men, and they needed occupations that brought them regularly into contact with other people. Locked in domestic prisons and trained only in the arts of housewifery, women could scarcely be expected to balance imagination and reality. Men had the advantage of being "forced to see human nature as it is, and are not left to dwell on the

21. MW to Everina Wollstonecraft, [Jan. 15, 1787], in Todd, ed., *Collected Letters*, 99, Mar. 3, [1787], 107, to Johnson, Apr. 14, [1787], 119, to Joshua Cristall, Mar. 19, [1790?], 168, 169; MW, *An Historical and Moral View of the Origin and Progress of the French Revolution; and the Effect It Has Produced in Europe* (London, 1794), in Todd and Butler, eds., *Works of Wollstonecraft*, VI, 23. See Henry Mackenzie, *The Man of Feeling* (1771) (London, 1928).

22. Johann Wolfgang von Goethe, *The Sorrows of Young Werther* (1774), trans. and ed. Burton Pike (New York, 2005), [3], 43, 56, 57, 61, 89, 105, 124; MW, review of *The Sorrows of Werter, a Poem*, by Amelia Pickering, *Analytical Review*, III (January 1789), in Todd and Butler, eds., *Works of Wollstonecraft*, VII, 71.

pictures of their own imaginations. Nothing, I am sure, calls forth the faculties so much as the being obliged to struggle with the world; and this is not a woman's province in a married state."[23]

In Ireland, Wollstonecraft moved from reading to writing. The result was *Thoughts on the Education of Daughters: With Reflections on Female Conduct, in the More Important Duties of Life,* which a friend showed to the London publisher Joseph Johnson. Johnson printed it in 1787. In her first book, Wollstonecraft wondered about the nature of female education. Her specific variation on relatively conventional thinking about education was the radical idea of featuring a wise, balanced, educated woman as the preceptor of both boys and girls. The book's most revolutionary contribution was its author's relatively quiet celebration of female authority. The few vocations open to women were "very humiliating." A teacher or a governess combined the identity of relative, servant, and stranger, always "dependant on the caprice of a fellow-creature." There was no place for an unmarried woman in English society. "She is alone, shut out from equality and confidence." Books could only create so much conversation. "How earnestly does a mind full of sensibility look for disinterested friendship." But, Wollstonecraft warned, "friendship between persons of different sexes" was dangerous. The "heart is very treacherous, and if we do not guard its first emotions, we shall not afterwards be able to prevent its sighing for impossibilities." Anticipating her more famous work, she suggested that the solution lay in the practice of manly mutuality. Banish the arts of male and female coquettes! Loving "a worthy person" was an incentive to improve "the manners and temper. . . . A woman cannot reasonably be unhappy, if she is attached to a man of sense and goodness, though he may not be all she could wish." Women should give up on the idea, encouraged by novels, that love was a raging passion. If marriage was a rational friendship between a man and woman, both partners could cultivate their understanding and honor their familial duties.[24]

The modest success of *Thoughts on the Education of Daughters* encouraged Wollstonecraft to pursue a career option that afforded a woman some prospect of independence. She would live in London as a professional writer. Abandoning her position as governess, she contemplated her "new plan of life" and the pleasing vision of "a little peace and *independence.*" She was

23. MW, *Thoughts on the Education of Daughters: With Reflections on Female Conduct, in the More Important Duties of Life,* in Todd and Butler, eds., *Works of Wollstonecraft,* IV, 32.

24. Ibid., 21, 25, 26, 29, 30. See Mitzi Myers, "Impeccable Governesses, Rational Dames, and Moral Mothers: Mary Wollstonecraft and the Female Tradition in Georgian Children's Books," *Children's Literature,* XIV (1986), 31–59.

tired of "grovelling." Joseph Johnson had assured her that if "[I] exert[ed] my talents in writing I may support myself in a comfortable way. I am then going to be the first of a new genus." Others would reply with "ridicule" and "advice, to which I cannot listen—I must be independent." The next year, Johnson published Wollstonecraft's short novel, *Mary*, which summarized her education to that point by narrating a life similar to her own.[25]

The genre was a strange choice for a woman who believed that novels were too "romantic," that they indulged the imagination and cultivated "sensuality" instead of "principles." Fiction depicted "the struggles of passion—of those *human passions,* that too frequently cloud the reason, and lead *mortals* into dangerous errors." Still, precisely because they were flights of fancy, novels had the power to transform readers by highlighting challenges most everyone eventually faced. The problem for Wollstonecraft lay less in the form than in the uses authors and readers made of it.[26]

The novel—a fictional tale written to be sold in print form and consumed in private by strangers—was invented largely by English men and women in the long eighteenth century. Although the popularity of the genre did not rival that of sermons and biographies, it did appeal to large numbers of middling people, especially women. Novels tended to focus on private relationships, often narrating the adventures of an isolated, naive hero or heroine, far from parents and surrogate parents, whose body is desired by other characters. Increasingly, they were about complicated paths to marriage, moving women from a birth family to a volitional one. Readers identified with characters melodramatically placed in an exaggerated version of a common dilemma. The advantage of fictional stories, according to the American novelist Charles Brockden Brown, was that "the affections are engaged" as well as reason "won by incessant attacks." Novels demonstrated the democratic principle that "every man occupies a station in society in which he is necessarily active to evil or to good." Not surprisingly, many men and some women, especially those who believed in the existence of revealed truth, denounced novels as dangerous and antisocial, for they shifted attention away from traditional sources of authority to the idea that meaning emerged through conversation. Narrative highlighted turning points and unanticipated consequences, allowed for rumination on the un-

25. MW to Johnson, Sept. 13, [1787], in Todd, ed., *Collected Letters,* 134, to Everina Wollstonecraft, Nov. 7, [1787], 139, 140.

26. MW, review of *Edward and Harriet; or, The Happy Recovery . . . , Analytical Review,* I (June 1788), in Todd and Butler, eds., *Works of Wollstonecraft,* VII, 19; MW, review of *Julia, a Novel,* by Helen Maria Williams, *Analytical Review,* VII (May 1790), ibid., 251.

reliability of reason, and granted human beings an unprecedented degree of both agency and responsibility.[27]

Mary, the heroine of Wollstonecraft's novel, posed the challenge of finding a way between solitude and company, imagination and reality. A young girl neglected by a "very tyrannical and passionate" father and an "indole[nt]" mother, she suffered from a deficient education. Chronic loneliness made her "too much the creature of impulse, and the slave of compassion." When the death of an older brother creates a financial tangle related to inheritance, Mary's heartless father and another male relative force their teenage children into a loveless marriage in order to save the family fortune. Luckily for Mary, the fifteen-year-old groom is as reluctant as his bride. Departing immediately after the wedding, he leaves Mary, still a virgin, free to accompany her ailing friend Ann to Lisbon. In Portugal, Mary's education improves dramatically, even as her friend's health fails, because she develops a friendship with a young Englishman named Henry.[28]

A "man of learning," Henry "expanded" Mary's mind by sharing new ideas and improving her taste. As important, his religious piety keeps "his sensibility" within "proper bounds." Manly Henry is as direct as he is "gentle." He chooses to be Mary's "friend," interested in her in ways that no one else had ever been. Unable to distinguish between "love and friendship," an entranced Mary gives into passion, although exactly how is unclear. Mary's inadequate education in a loveless family has left her ill equipped to manage her sexuality. Nevertheless, an unconventional liaison rooted in mutual respect was better than a transfer of property masquerading as a marriage. The consequences of Mary's and Henry's behavior are predictable. After Ann's death, Henry follows Mary back to England, where he soon dies. Melancholy Mary wants to hear no more of love. She finds "a gleam of joy" in "moments of solitary sadness" given over to contemplating "that world *where there is neither marrying,* nor giving in marriage." To be useful and happy, men and women had to avoid the extremes of calculation and en-

27. MW, review of *Edward and Harriet, Analytical Review,* I (June 1788), ibid., 19; MW, review of *Julia,* by Williams, *Analytical Review,* VII (May 1790), ibid., 251; [Charles Brockden Brown], "Walstein's School of History: From the German Krants of Gotha," *Monthly Magazine, and American Review,* I, no. 6 (September–December 1799), 407. See Nancy Armstrong, *Desire and Domestic Fiction: A Political History of the Novel* (New York, 1987); Cathy N. Davidson, *Revolution and the Word: The Rise of the Novel in America* (New York, 1986); and Perry, *Novel Relations.*

28. MW, *Mary, a Fiction* (1788), ed. Janet Todd (London, 2004), 7, 9, 21. See Daniel O'Quinn, "Trembling: Wollstonecraft, Godwin, and the Resistance to Literature," *ELH,* LXIV (1997), 761–788.

thusiasm, and they had to do it together, as natural friends rather than as husband and wife.[29]

Persuasion

With a population between five hundred thousand and six hundred thousand souls, Paris in 1793 was still little more than half the size of London, the imperial capital in which Mary Wollstonecraft took up residence half a decade earlier. The emergence of middling sorts, a cohort constituting perhaps 15 percent of the total, flowed from the availability of jobs in an intertwined world of constitutional government and global finance—and the legal, insurance, construction, and service industries needed to support them. The English capital had a thriving public culture: a proliferation of newspapers, books, and theaters and a remarkable degree of religious tolerance. It was possible to achieve some degree of fame and fortune in London through friends rather than patrons. The global intersection of multiple forms of commerce, London had long encouraged cultural revolution—and nowhere more obviously than in the flourishing mixed-gender networks of professional writers.

Mary Wollstonecraft achieved a degree of financial independence in the early 1790s because there was a demand for books by women. Not only did women read novels, hundreds of women published books between 1780 and 1830. Unlike the aristocratic Bluestocking writers of a previous generation, most were middle-class women eager to support themselves. London offered unprecedented vocational opportunities for women. There were, for example, more than fifteen thousand female shopkeepers in the city in the mid-1780s. Usually literate, many lived by themselves or with other women. Women writers were hardly exceptional in their quest for independence, although it is important to remember that they had opportunities unavailable to most of their contemporaries. For most women, life in the metropolis was a mixture of drudgery and danger. An estimated fifty thousand women (roughly 9 percent of London's female population) qualified as prostitutes in the eyes of those who kept records.[30]

Even the most successful women writers remained dependent on men. They had no control over the means of production; they were neither the

29. MW, *Mary,* ed. Todd, 24, 28, 30, 53.

30. Margaret R. Hunt, *The Middling Sort: Commerce, Gender, and the Family in England, 1680–1780* (Berkeley, Calif., 1996), 133–158; P[atrick] Colquhoun, *A Treatise on the Police of the Metropolis . . .* , 7th ed. (London, 1806), 340.

publishers nor the sellers of books. Wollstonecraft was "for most of her writing career, an indebted employee of her friend and publisher Joseph Johnson, acting as editor, compiler, reviewer, and translator, as his business needs developed, rather than as an independent author deciding which books she would like to write." Her gender exacerbated a common predicament. Equally true, though, is that publishers were eager to take advantage of "the essential flood of writing by women." There was "a climate of encouragement of, even fascination with, women's writing." Professional women consciously asserted their influence as women. Although "they lacked real authority" in economic and political terms, they "kept on writing, continuing a professional career by which many secured their independence."[31]

This small but consequential group of women was participating in the emergence of a class of professional writers. Until the 1790s, most writers, whether they were ministers, poets, or statesmen, had been aristocrats or gentlemen who had no expectation of profiting from their books or in some cases being publicly identified with them. That changed toward the end of the century. The authors of prose fiction, in particular, were generally "previously anonymous, genderless, low-skilled, low-paid, piece-workers" who now demanded "more explicit acknowledgement of their role in the production process, and a greater financial share in the rewards from the market." Wollstonecraft was proud that she expected to make two hundred pounds in 1788. Even if she was not completely independent, she had found a way to follow "the peculiar bent of my nature." Joseph Johnson and Thomas Christie paid her to contribute to the *Analytical Review,* a journal they founded in May 1788. Within a year, she was regularly reviewing travel accounts, poetry, drama, and, especially, novels.[32]

Women writers deployed an array of genres and perspectives to com-

31. St. Clair, *Reading Nation,* 163; Stuart Curran, "Women Readers, Women Writers," *The Cambridge Companion to British Romanticism,* ed. Stuart Curran (Cambridge, 1993), 178, 179, 184, 185, 189; Betty A. Schellenberg, *The Professionalization of Women Writers in Eighteenth-Century Britain* (Cambridge, 2005), 145. On the tension between politeness and sentiment, see Jon Mee, "'Severe Contentions of Friendship': Barbauld, Conversation, and Dispute," in Heather Glen and Paul Hamilton, eds., *Repossessing the Romantic Past* (Cambridge, 2006), 21–39. More generally, see the essays in Knott and Taylor, eds., *Women, Gender, and Enlightenment;* note, particularly in Jane Rendall, "'Women That Would Plague Me with Rational Conversation': Aspiring Women and Scottish Whigs, c. 1790–1830," 326–347, the existence of similar communities of women in other places.

32. St. Clair, *Reading Nation,* 175; MW to Everina Wollstonecraft, Nov. 7, [1787], in Todd, ed., *Collected Letters,* 140. See Todd, *Wollstonecraft,* 124, 137; and Janet Todd, "Prefatory Note," in MW, *Contributions to the "Analytical Review," 1788–1797,* in Todd and Butler, eds., *Works of Wollstonecraft,* VII, 14–18.

ment on the potential of heterosexual sociability as well as its multiple challenges. Some operated within a republican perspective; others embraced
the assumptions of an emerging liberal ideology. Some applauded the new
order; some tried to subvert it; many did both. Some wrote after a career
in the theater; some wrote as quasi-journalists reporting from abroad; still
others continued to write novels or fictional histories. Because women wrote
mainly about women, we tend to categorize them, positively and negatively,
in strictly gendered terms. To do so is of immense importance in highlighting the emergence of a vocation in which women could express themselves
and attain financial independence. But it also obscures the breadth and
significance of a collective cultural project, one shared by many men as
well, which involved the reconfiguration of all human relationships around
notions of consent and mutuality. Late-eighteenth-century writers' fascination with the behavior of women and men in social situations went well beyond familiar questions of romance, marriage, and domesticity: they imagined a world in which women were taken seriously by men.[33]

Of the previous generation of Bluestocking authors, none was more influential on Wollstonecraft than Catharine Sawbridge Macaulay Graham. In
Letters on Education, published in 1790, Macaulay argued that public education was the sine qua non of a successful republic. The history of Rome
demonstrated the need for a government-supported system of mixed-
gender national education that would prepare all children to exercise the
rights and responsibilities of republican citizens. "The happiness and perfection of the two sexes are so reciprocally dependant on one another that,

33. The key secondary text is Gary Kelly, *The English Jacobin Novel, 1780–1805* (Oxford, 1976),
esp. 21–29. Kelly characterizes these novels as works with a political and ethical agenda. They
address social problems, including the status of women, by narrating the experiences of individuals. See also Bellamy, *Commerce, Morality, and the Eighteenth-Century Novel.* See Harriet
Guest's subtle argument that "a series of small changes takes place in the position of women,
or the way women [were] perceived" in the late eighteenth century, laying the foundation of
a nineteenth-century assumption by "some women of liberal education" that "it was their
right and duty to have opinions about what happened in the world; they did not see their exclusion from participation in the public life of the nation as natural; indeed, in some senses
they did not think of themselves as excluded at all" (Guest, *Small Change: Women, Learning,
Patriotism, 1750–1810* [Chicago, 2000], 14). Guest claims that eighteenth-century novelists par-
ticipated in "debates that cut across genres," destabilizing any public / private dichotomy (15).
See also Angela Keane, *Women Writers and the English Nation in the 1790s: Romantic Belongings*
(Cambridge, 2000); Helene Moglen, *The Trauma of Gender: A Feminist Theory of the English
Novel* (Berkeley, Calif., 2001); Paula R. Backscheider, ed., *Revising Women: Eighteenth-Century
"Women's Fiction" and Social Engagement* (Baltimore, 2000); and Adela Pinch, *Strange Fits of
Passion: Epistemologies of Emotion, Hume to Austen* (Stanford, Calif., 1996).

Figure 2. Catharine Macaulay (née Sawbridge). *By Robert Edge Pine.*
Oil on canvas, circa 1775. © *National Portrait Gallery, London*

till both are reformed, there is no expecting excellence in either." Properly educated men would learn to balance pride with empathy; properly educated women would learn to balance emotion with self-respect. Underlying Macaulay's argument was the radical assumption that gender was socially constructed. She rejected essentialist notions of anatomical determinism. If women were emotional, their behavior reflected their education. They could learn "to act a rational part in the world, and not to fill up a niche in the seraglio of a sultan." Coquetry, the art of pleasing men with wiles and deception, amounted to female complicity in their own subjugation. Romantic love was particularly dangerous for women because it was "the most ungovernal propensity of any which attends us" and left them at the mercy of ungoverned men. Macaulay did not expect revolution. Until "that period arrives in which women will act wisely," she wrote archly, "we will amuse ourselves in talking of their follies." Wollstonecraft thought Macaulay a "masculine and fervid writer," a model of "the rank our sex ought to endeavour to attain in the world." "She contends for laurels whilst most of her sex only seek[s] for flowers." The older woman admired Wollstonecraft's work because it verified her "opinion of the power and talents of" women. Unfortunately, Macaulay's death in June 1791 prevented the two women from enjoying a friendship.[34]

Although subsequent writers accepted Macaulay's major argument, they tended to imagine the consequences of inadequate education in personal rather than civic terms. Reformation of power structures had to begin in the realm of the personal and proceed to the political, not the other way round. The challenge was enormous. How were human beings to manage their bodies—the totality of their desires, impulses, passions—without the structures of patriarchal power that had evolved over centuries to restrain them? Love was a case in point. It was one thing to practice mutuality in the throes of an overwhelming physical attraction that flooded bodies with pleasure and made everything seem possible. It was quite another to sustain mutuality over a long period of time in a world dominated by men, a world in which women had virtually no means to seek redress for a grievance except to plead with husbands, fathers, and brothers, a world in which the physical consummation of romance left women pregnant and at the mercy of

34. Catharine Macaulay, *Letters on Education* . . . (1790; rpt. London, 1996), 13–14, 207, 216, 220, 221; MW to Catharine Macaulay, [December 1790], in Todd, ed., *Collected Letters*, 186, Macaulay to MW, Dec. 30, 1790, 186 n. 416, MW, review of *Letters on Education* . . . , by Catharine Macaulay Graham, *Analytical Review*, VIII (November 1790), in Todd and Butler, eds., *Works of Wollstonecraft*, VII, 309.

their bodies and their male kin. Marriage remained primarily an institution that protected the property of men through the legal exchange of women. Wollstonecraft and her peers rarely talked about challenging this situation through legislation. Enduring reform, they believed, had to proceed from within a human being. Successful revolution was the sum total of a mass of individual conversion experiences.[35]

Elizabeth Inchbald, born in 1753 to a middle-class Catholic couple in Sussex, dramatized the dilemma in her 1791 novel, *A Simple Story.* Inchbald had arrived in London in 1772 to pursue a career on the stage. She married actor Joseph Inchbald and stayed with him until his death in 1779. Overcoming a serious stutter, Inchbald became a successful actress and playwright. *A Simple Story* was her first novel. Told in two parts, the book contrasted a mother's coquettish defiance of her distant husband with her daughter's demure obedience to her distant father, thus illustrating the counterproductive options available to women (and men). None of the characters seems capable of finding, let alone sustaining, an understanding that balanced imagination and reality.[36]

In the first half of *A Simple Story,* beautiful eighteen-year-old orphan Miss Milner becomes the ward of the Jesuit priest Dorriforth (later Lord Elmwood). Hoping to love her guardian "with all the passion of a mistress, and with all the tenderness of a wife," Miss Milner acts the coquette. Dorriforth is charmed by her flirty sparring, charmed in other words by precisely the attributes that ought to put him on his guard. When he is released from his religious vows so that he can accept his inheritance as Lord Elmwood, the couple becomes engaged. But what future is there for an "unthinking woman" and a proud man "blinded by his passion?"[37]

The second part of *A Simple Story* occurs seventeen years later. Lady Elmwood (the once lively Miss Milner) has died in disgrace, a public adul-

35. See Karen O'Brien's comparative analysis of Macaulay and Wollstonecraft in *Women and Enlightenment in Eighteenth-Century Britain* (Cambridge, 2009), 152–200.

36. Jo Alyson Parker, "Complicating *A Simple Story:* Inchbald's Two Versions of Female Power," *Eighteenth-Century Studies,* XXX (1997), 255–270. See also Terry Castle, *Masquerade and Civilization: The Carnivalesque in Eighteenth-Century English Culture and Fiction* (Stanford, Calif., 1986); Emily Hodgson Anderson, "Revising Theatrical Conventions in *A Simple Story:* Elizabeth Inchbald's Ambiguous Performance," *Journal for Early Modern Cultural Studies,* VI, no. 1 (2006), 5–30; George E. Haggerty, "Female Abjection in Inchbald's *A Simple Story,*" *Studies in English Literature,* XXXVI, no. 3 (Summer 1996), 655–671; and Daniel O'Quinn, "Scissors and Needles: Inchbald's *Wives as They Were, Maids as They Are* and the Governance of Sexual Exchange," *Theater Journal,* LI (1999), 105–125.

37. Elizabeth Inchbald, *A Simple Story* (1791), ed. J. M. S. Tompkins (New York, 1998), 72, 139.

Figure 3. Elizabeth Inchbald. *By George Dance. Pencil, 1794.*
© *National Portrait Gallery, London*

terer deserted by her husband. Their daughter, Matilda, who mixes her mother's physical features with the "mind and manners" of her father, has not seen either parent in a decade. Lord Elmwood is "implacab[le]" in his determination not to lay eyes on Matilda because of her mother's betrayal. If "Love, that produces wonders, that seduces and subdues the most determined and rigid spirits, had" once "over[come] [his] inflexibility . . . the magic which once enchanted away this spirit of immutability was no more." Elmwood's heir, unable to resist his cousin's charms, risks his uncle's wrath by proclaiming his love for Matilda. The young couple then enacts a variation on the experience of their elders. Matilda is more disciplined than her mother, and the nephew is more empathetic than Elmwood. He promises her that "she has one sincere friend—that upon every occurrence in life, there is a heart so devoted to all she feels, she can never suffer without the sympathy of another." Elmwood not only refuses to countenance the union, he and a friend try to overcome his nephew's romantic notions.[38]

Elmwood relents when his parental negligence threatens Matilda's virtue and therefore his reputation. Rescuing his daughter before she is raped by an impetuous aristocrat, Elmwood realizes the folly of his stubborn heartlessness. Part of his reconciliation with Matilda is to yield to her "alone, the power" to choose her husband. Matilda's newfound autonomy is illusory, however. If the choice of husband was a concession to a daughter, it was paternalistic. More important, it would be the last free choice she would enjoy. Matilda's marriage to Elmwood's nephew preserves the estate and restores the social order. As important, Matilda remains a remarkably passive creature, as irrationally dutiful as her mother was irrationally defiant. Will the younger couple be any happier than the older one? Inchbald is coy, advising readers to contrast the mother's "improper" education with the daughter's training in the "school of prudence."[39]

Wollstonecraft admired Inchbald's craftsmanship and her intention "to show the advantage of a good education." But she did not like that the mother and daughter were extremes; the former lacked "sensibility," and the latter "dignity of mind." "Why do all female writers, even when they display their abilities," asked Wollstonecraft in her review, "always give a sanction to the libertine reveries of men? Why do they poison the minds of their own sex, by strengthening a male prejudice that makes women systematically weak?" Wollstonecraft wanted to see women functioning as rational

38. Ibid., 221, 250, 251, 296.
39. Ibid., 337–338.

creatures. Maintaining Macaulay's "empire of reason" was a challenge that men and women must accept together.[40]

This widespread attention to mixed-gender sociability was apparent in the title of Mary Hays's *Appeal to the Men of Great Britain in Behalf of Women*, published by Joseph Johnson in 1798 but apparently written much earlier in the decade. Hays had been born into a Dissenting family in 1760 in Southwark, outside London. Her fiancé died when she was twenty. She became a professional writer. Hays thought Wollstonecraft "the true disciple of her own system," a woman who "commands at once fear and reverence, admiration and esteem." Wollstonecraft, for her part, critiqued the "vain humility" of the preface to Hays's proposed book of essays. She objected to an apology for defects attributed to an inadequate education. Even more troubling was that Hays included praise for her work from men. The preface was "so full of vanity, [that] your male friends will still treat you like a woman," advised Wollstonecraft. Hays ought "to try rather to be useful than to please." If the "essays have merit they will stand alone." To apologize was to affirm hierarchy, for "when weakness claims indulgence it seems to justify the despotism of strength." In this sense, Hays was perpetuating the system she sought to critique. She was "a petitioner," "a friend and companion" rather than "an Amazon" committed to her sense of "right or wrong."[41]

Nevertheless, Hays posed a fundamental question: How did women get men to give up power? Why would liberty-loving British men "wish to counteract the benevolent designs of Providence in their favour; by leading in chains, too often galling to their sensible and tender natures, those, whom heaven having in its wisdom formed their equals, could never surely, save in its wrath, doom[ed] to be the slaves of man[?]" The answer was simple: it was in their interest to do so. If only men had the "courage" to "come forth and look Reason boldly in the face," to abandon "the fiend Prejudice." Joining with women, they might accomplish together what neither could accomplish alone: conquer "the most powerful and universal passions interwoven in the human heart." If women indulged "violent extremes" that were neither "natural [n]or voluntary," if their ambition was

---

40. MW, review of *A Simple Story*, by Elizabeth Inchbald, *Analytical Review*, X (May 1791), in Todd and Butler, eds., *Works of Wollstonecraft*, VII, 370.

41. Mary Hays, *Appeal to the Men of Great Britain in Behalf of Women* (1798), ed. Gina Luria (New York, 1974), unnumbered pages 4–5 in "Advertisement"; MW to Mary Hays, Aug. 11, [1792], in Todd, ed., *Collected Letters*, 202, Nov. 25, [17]92, 210; Hays to unknown correspondent, in A. F. Wedd, ed., *The Love-Letters of Mary Hays (1779–1780)* (London, 1925), 5.

channeled into obsession with clothes, frivolity, domesticity, and an "eternal round of giddy intercourse with the world," it was because they were kept "in a state of PERPETUAL BABYISM." Men "sacrifice[d their] truest happiness, and [their] dearest interests, by denying to women . . . the noble privilege of telling [them the] truth, with that honest freedom, which is, and ought to be, equally distant from ill-nature and fury, as from flattery and hypocrisy." Too often, love degenerated into "violent and capricious tempers, [in]to contempt, and even hatred, with very little reason or provocation; sometimes none at all." Men, too, were "subject as all human beings more or less, are,—to error, to passion, and caprice." Why should a woman's dream of "a true and virtuous attachment" with "an amiable man whom she loves" depend on the "chance" that her husband was "a sensible, a reasonable, a humane man"? What was required was "the gradual emancipation of women" as part of "the gradual emancipation of every one bearing the stamp of the human species." In this sense, Hays argued, the rights of woman were one aspect of the rights of man.[42]

In retrospect, the attitude of the male friends of women such as Wollstonecraft, Inchbald, and Hays—men of similar age and background—toward the rights of women seems ambiguous, confused, and sometimes contradictory. Welcoming women in mixed company, their motives often seemed more instrumental than intellectual. Equality did not necessarily create mutuality. Social commerce became an opportunity for sexual commerce; dealing directly with women became license to indulge desire. Still, some men were taking women seriously, none more so than Thomas Holcroft.[43]

Taught to read by his shoemaker father, Holcroft consumed books while accompanying his parents on peddling tours of the English countryside. Failing to make a living as a teacher, Holcroft became a strolling actor until his big break, the 1778 Drury Lane production of his play, *The Crisis; or, Love and Famine.* By the 1780s, Holcroft was a well-established member of the London theater community, and in the 1790s he became a leading figure in radical political circles. His activities with the Society for Constitutional Information led to his arrest for high treason. Acquitted in December 1794, he never recovered professionally and died in 1809. Holcroft had drama

42. Hays, *Appeal*, ii, 29, 47, 49, 57, 97, 123, 168, 263, 264, 275, 276, 277, 282, 288.

43. Helen P. Bruder, *William Blake and the Daughters of Albion* (New York, 1997). See Nicholas M. Williams, *Ideology and Utopia in the Poetry of William Blake* (Cambridge, 1998); Magnus Ankarsjö, *William Blake and Gender* (Jefferson, N.C., 2006); and Bruder, ed., *Women Reading William Blake* (New York, 2007).

aplenty in his personal life. Three of his four wives died, and his eldest son committed suicide in 1789 at the age of sixteen.[44]

In 1792, the forty-seven-year-old Holcroft published *Anna St. Ives,* a popular work often cited as the first Jacobin novel. Wollstonecraft termed it "a vehicle to convey what are called democratical sentiments." The plot is commonplace. Anna St. Ives, an educated and intelligent daughter of minor gentry, loves Frank Henley, the son of her family's steward. She nevertheless promises to marry the aristocratic Coke Clifton out of deference to her family and her class. Marriage to the low-born Frank, while imaginable, is impossible; it makes her relatives and her friends "miserable" and sets "a bad example to [her] sex." Accepting his rejection, a devastated Frank decides to migrate to America. Soon enough, Coke Clifton's true nature becomes apparent. Coke mocks Frank. Women like him because he is not a "naughty cat"; they are safe with him because he has "principles." Consumed by sexual desire, Coke vows to "die a foaming maniac" if he cannot possess Anna. "If not by persuasion, she shall be mine by chicanery, or even by force." In the end, all is well. Frank helps a kidnapped Anna save herself and urges a badly wounded Coke to reform. The novel concludes with the happy couple on the verge of marriage. *Anna St. Ives* is remarkable in several respects, not the least of which is that its resourceful heroine manages to end up with someone whose sole claim on her is that he is a man "worthy of being loved."[45]

Frank and Anna imagine a world in which "the free discussion of every opinion, true or false," thrives. They talk through their various challenges, work together to manage their bodies, and inspire each other to defy convention. Rejecting Coke's assumption that a woman should surrender to her lover, Anna grows into a strong person because she learns to respect her own judgment. In trying to escape her captors, Anna finds herself thwarted by her maid's insistence that they cannot climb a high wall. Could "a man climb it," Anna asks? Yes, replies the maid, "but she could not think how." Well, Anna can, and does. It was "weakness and folly," she asserts, "to suppose that men were better able to climb walls than women."[46]

---

44. Peter Faulkner, "Introduction," in Thomas Holcroft, *Anna St. Ives,* ed. Faulkner (London, 1970), viii–xx. See Elbridge Colby, ed., *The Life of Thomas Holcroft* (London, 1925); and David Karr, "'Thoughts That Flash Like Lightning': Thomas Holcroft, Radical Theater, and the Production of Meaning in 1790s London," *Journal of British Studies,* XL (2001), 324–356.

45. MW, review of *Anna St. Ives, a Novel,* by Thomas Holcroft, *Analytical Review,* XIII (May 1792), in Todd and Butler, eds., *Works of Wollstonecraft,* VII, 439; Holcroft, *Anna St. Ives,* ed. Faulkner, 37, 178, 328.

46. Holcroft, *Anna St. Ives,* ed. Faulkner, 98, 464, 465.

Holcroft does not deny the complexity of mixed-gender relationships. It was "a question of infinite importance" that Frank was "not fully prepared to answer." He did not propose that "the intercourse of the sexes will be altogether promiscuous and unrestrained," but he was certain that marriage involved coercion. "Of all the regulations which were ever suggested to the mistaken tyranny of selfishness, none perhaps to this day have surpassed the despotism of" marriage. Instead of "a civil institution," marriage ought to be "the concern of the individuals who consent to this mutual association, and they ought not to be prevented from beginning, suspending, or terminating it as they please." When Anna expresses satisfaction with Frank's conception of marriage, Coke interjects the standard riposte: this was libertinism, not liberty, and very bad for women. Among the "alarming" "consequences" was the surety that the "man who only studied the gratification of his desires would have a new wife each new day." Frank insists that it is possible to imagine a society other than the one "as perverse and vitiated as the present." True, men treat women badly under the banner of "unjust laws and customs." Some are "demons in the human form, who come tricked out in all the smiles of love, the protestations of loyalty, and the arts of hell." But he is unwilling to surrender a vision of what the world might become.[47]

As Anna remarks during a crisis, Frank's virtue will save him, "or nothing can." Individuals cannot rely on the state, or the church, or family. Recognizing that she is a mortal creature, Anna advocates manliness in the face of death or dishonor. Fear cannot dictate her behavior. Anna and Frank move toward a better world because they learn to respect themselves as well as each other. They reason together. Engaging with each other strengthens them as individuals and makes their association mutual. The novel ends with Frank exhorting a seriously ill Coke to grasp that he is not forever "a most guilty, foul, and hateful monster." "Frantic man, forbear! Recall your wild spirits and command them to order. . . . Be yourself." Coke's behavior was not innate. The product of "ignorance," it was correctable. *Anna St. Ives* indicates that the desire for more egalitarian, mutual relationships was hardly limited to women. Holcroft, for many years one of William Godwin's best friends, is better known today for his political activism. But his critique of marriage was every bit as subversive as his opposition to the repressive measures of the government of William Pitt the Younger.[48]

Holcroft was only one of many men sympathetic to a critique of marriage in particular and patriarchy in general. For Wollstonecraft personally, the

47. Ibid., 279, 280, 281.
48. Ibid., 398, 478, 479.

most important was her publisher, Joseph Johnson. Eminently persuadable, he was the kind of principled man Coke despised. But precisely because Johnson and Wollstonecraft were such intimate friends, their often fraught relationship reveals tensions inherent in even the best-intentioned efforts to practice revolution in private lives.

The son of Baptists from a village near Liverpool, Johnson had been apprenticed as a youth to a bookseller in London. By the early 1760s, when he was in his mid-twenties, he had opened his own shop. A quarter century later, his enterprise was one of the most successful in the densely concentrated community of booksellers along Paternoster Row. He occupied what was probably the largest building in Saint Paul's Churchyard, parallel to Paternoster, where he stocked a variety of books, not all of them his own publications. Johnson's medical and religious texts underwrote less profitable works about Unitarianism and political reform.[49]

Bookselling was a sociable trade. Men like Johnson kept their shops (where they usually lived) open twelve hours a day, seven days a week, inviting customers to drop in, browse, and chat. They nurtured relationships with potential authors. Both their places of business and nearby coffeehouses were sites where readers, sellers, and authors met to talk. Writers, for whom "the creation of a text was seldom a solitary activity," often welcomed the opportunity to share manuscripts and discuss possibilities. Like other publishers, Johnson cultivated a circle of friends that included Joseph Priestley, Henry Fuseli, William Cowper, Thomas Christie, William Blake, William Godwin, Thomas Paine, and Joel Barlow. Godwin, who became a regular member of Johnson's circle in 1795, remembered him as "a man of a generous, candid, and liberal mind" who "delighted in doing good." His shop had been "the perpetual resort of all his connections in seasons of difficulty and embarrassment." Godwin only wished that Johnson had said more in the lively conversations that took place at "his table."[50]

49. James Raven, "Location, Size, and Succession: The Bookshops of Paternoster Row before 1800," in Robin Myers, Michael Harris, and Giles Mandelbrote, eds., *The London Book Trade: Topographies of Print in the Metropolis from the Sixteenth Century* (New Castle, Del., 2003), 89–126. A straightforward account is Gerald P. Tyson, *Joseph Johnson: A Liberal Publisher* (Iowa City, Iowa, 1979). More valuable in locating Johnson in a larger cultural context is Helen Braithwaite, *Romanticism, Publishing, and Dissent: Joseph Johnson and the Cause of Liberty* (New York, 2003). See also John Barrell, *The Spirit of Despotism: Invasions of Privacy in the 1790s* (Oxford, 2006), 72–74; and Andrea A. Engstrom, "Joseph Johnson's Circle and the *Analytical Review*: A Study of English Radicals in the Late Eighteenth Century" (Ph.D. diss., University of Southern California, 1986).

50. *Morning Chronicle and London Advertiser,* Dec. 21, 1809. See William Zachs, *The First*

Women were welcome at Johnson's gatherings. Knowing that she could not "live without loving [her] fellow creatures," Wollstonecraft attended dinners at three in "his hospitable mansion." Most of the guests were "sensible men," often older than she. Wollstonecraft saw them as family members. "Involuntarily lament[ing] that I have not a father or brother," she informed Johnson, she found solace in his kindness and that of "a few others." Johnson claimed that "she spent many of her afternoons and most of her evenings with" him. At his house, she "met the kind of company" she found "most pleasure in."[51]

Complicating the Johnson-Wollstonecraft relationship were the usual suspects, money and sex. A confirmed bachelor, Johnson was a physically unattractive man with a formal demeanor that disguised a tender sensibility. He liked Wollstonecraft and encouraged her ambition. He was struck by her manliness. "She was incapable of disguise," remembered Johnson; "whatever was the state of her mind it appeared when she entered, and the turn of conversation might easily be guessed." Conversation with friends was critical. When she felt "harassed, which was very often [the] case, she was relieved by unbosoming herself and generally returned home [a house on George Street from 1787 to 1791 and then one on Store Street until December 1792] calm, frequently in spirits." Johnson soon became her "only friend—the only person [she was] *intimate* with." Wollstonecraft liked Johnson, too. He was "*a man* before [he was] a bookseller." "Allow me to love you, my dear sir, and call friend a being I respect." She was grateful to Johnson for reminding her that she could not "live without loving my fellow-creatures—nor can I love them, without discovering some virtue."[52]

But Johnson also reminded her that she was not autonomous. Wollstonecraft hated her debts and her "irksome" "state of dependance," a condition she shared with male as well as female authors who had to pay attention not only to the vagaries of the market but to the whims of their publishers. She was enraged that men had a wider range of choices than women. "Your sex

John Murray and the Late Eighteenth-Century London Book Trade (Oxford, 1998); St. Clair, *Reading Nation*, 158.

51. MW to Johnson, [late 1788?–early 1789], in Todd, ed., *Collected Letters*, 159, to Blood, Mar. 3, [1788], 149, to Everina Wollstonecraft, [circa November 1787], 141; [Joseph Johnson to William Godwin], "A Few Facts," n.d., in Godwin, *Memoirs of the Author of "A Vindication of the Rights of Woman"* (1798), ed. Pamela Clemit and Gina Luria Walker (Peterborough, Ont., 2001), 162. See Todd, *Wollstonecraft*, 116–117.

52. [Johnson to Godwin], "A Few Facts," n.d., in Godwin, *Memoirs*, ed. Clemit and Walker, 163; MW to Johnson, [early 1788?], in Todd, ed., *Collected Letters*, 148, [late 1788?–early 1789], 159, [early 1789?], 160, [1790?], 166.

generally laugh at female determinations," she told Johnson in 1787, "but let me tell you, I never yet resolved to do, any thing of consequence, that I did not adhere resolutely to it, till I had accomplished my purpose, improbable as it might have appeared to a more timid mind." In nearly three decades of life, she had "gathered some experience, and felt many *severe* disappointments—and what is the amount? I long for a little peace and *independence!* Every obligation we receive from our fellow-creatures is a new shackle, takes from our native freedom, and debases the mind, makes us mere earthworms—I am not fond of grovelling!" When Johnson proposed marriage in 1790 through an intermediary in order to support her financially, Wollstonecraft lost her temper. He insulted her if he thought that she "could for a moment think of *prostituting* [her] person for a maintenance." It would violate everything she had sought to achieve in her life.[53]

"Enlighten [Men] and You Will Elevate Them"

Mixed-gender social commerce was a sentimental solution to a patriarchal society. That some women persuaded some men to embrace some degree of mutuality did not affect a vast patriarchal structure in which women had no legal existence. Why should men want to surrender power that not only promoted their interests to the exclusion of others but also that centuries of tradition, religion, law, and practice affirmed was ultimately beneficial to all people? If power is on some level the ability to get people to do what they do not want to do, then women such as Wollstonecraft and Inchbald had no obvious power. Nor did they have any discernible short-term impact on the political or legal rights of women, unlike their contemporaries whose sentimental appeals led a majority in Parliament to abolish the slave trade in 1807. From a longer historical perspective, however, the significance of Wollstonecraft and other radical writers in the 1790s was to fashion enduring arguments for the rights of woman from a dynamic eighteenth-century discourse about the rights of man. More specifically, they contended that gender, like all relationships, was a dynamic construction that evolved over time.

Wollstonecraft was in attendance on November 4, 1789, when her friend the Welsh-born Dissenting minister Richard Price preached "A Discourse on

53. MW to Johnson, Dec. 5, [1786], in Todd, ed., *Collected Letters*, 96, Sept. 13, [1787], 134, to ———, [Summer 1790?], 174. See Cora Kaplan's smart if ahistorical analysis of Wollstonecraft's "combination of equal rights and self-abnegating sexuality" in *A Vindication of the Rights of Woman:* "Wild Nights: Pleasure / Sexuality / Feminism," in Kaplan, *Sea Changes: Essays on Culture and Feminism* (New York, 1986), 31–56 (quotation on 50).

the Love of Our Country," a "simple, unaffected" sermon that captured the sense of progress and possibility that inspired her and others. Wollstone-craft had become friends with Price in the early 1780s, when she, Fanny, and Eliza were operating their school for girls on Newington Green, north of London. He and other religious Dissenters living in her neighborhood met together weekly for supper and conversation. Wollstonecraft regularly joined them. She particularly admired Price, a leading spokesman for the "idea of *Self-direction,* or *Self-government.*" Dissenters challenged the status quo by arguing that educated men and women were capable of thinking for themselves. They valued reading, writing, and speaking—anything that awakened enlightened individuals to themselves as historical actors inextri-cably intertwined with other human beings. Although their attitude toward women rarely approached the egalitarian notions of Quakers, Shakers, and other sects, male Dissenters generally welcomed women into their circles.[54]

In his 1789 sermon, Price contended that rational devotion to spirituality and education—to the love of God and truth—would lead men to affirm their own self-worth, which was the prerequisite to recognizing the worth of all people. "Enlighten [men] and you will elevate them," urged Price. "Shew them they are *men,* and they will act like *men.*" Despite the Glorious Revo-lution of 1688—which had introduced "that *era* of light and liberty" that made Britain "an example to other kingdoms" and "the instructors of the world"—toleration was incomplete because Dissenters did not enjoy the full rights of Englishmen. But history was moving in the right direction. Nations now "pant[ed] for liberty." In the wake of the American Revolution, thirty million Frenchmen had stood up like men, denouncing slavery and "demanding liberty."[55]

Price's sermon sparked a famous reply from Edmund Burke, entitled *Re-flections on the Revolution in France.* Burke asserted that the "effect of lib-erty to individuals is, that they may do what they please: we ought to see

54. MW, review of *A Discourse on the Love of Our Country . . . ,* by Richard Price, *Analytical Review,* V (December 1789), in Todd and Butler, eds., *Works of Wollstonecraft,* VII, 185; Richard Price, *Observations on the Nature of Civil Liberty, the Principles of Government, and the Justice and Policy of the War with America; to Which Is Added, an Appendix and Postscript, Contain-ing, a State of the National Debt, an Estimate of the Money Drawn from the Public by the Taxes, and an Account of the National Income and Expenditure Since the Last War,* 9th ed. (London, 1776), 6. See Taylor, *Mary Wollstonecraft,* 103; and Phyllis Mack, "Religion, Feminism, and the Problem of Agency: Reflections on Eighteenth-Century Quakerism," in Knott and Taylor, eds., *Women, Gender, and Enlightenment,* 434–459.

55. Richard Price, *A Discourse on the Love of Our Country, Delivered on Nov. 4, 1789, at the Meeting-House in the Old Jewry, to the Society for Commemorating the Revolution in Britain; with an Appendix,* 2d ed. (London, 1789), 3, 4, 8, 12, 32, 49, 50.

what it will please them to do, before we risk congratulations, which may be soon turned into complaints. Prudence would dictate this in the case of separate, insulated, private men. But liberty, when men act in bodies, is *power*." People ought to think before they act; they ought to consider consequences as well as intentions. Wary of the idea that they are the best judges of their own actions, they must understand that they have to surrender "the whole" of liberty in order to "secure some liberty." Alas, as the French were demonstrating, "by having a right to everything they want everything." Human beings are imperfect creatures who cannot be trusted to exercise "a sufficient restraint upon their passions." Social commerce alone, Burke contended, would not suffice. The subjugation of passions could "only be done *by a power out of themselves*." Restraints, ironically, were also rights. Revolutionaries in England as well as France "are so taken up with their theories about the rights of man, that they have totally forgot his nature." Denying the complexity of human nature, they indulged their fancies and rent the fabric of civilization. Revolutionary Paris was as vulgar and violent as any primitive society, as brutal and compulsory as any monarchy.[56]

Burke's reflections inspired Wollstonecraft to write her first major work, *A Vindication of the Rights of Men,* which Joseph Johnson published in 1790. A grateful Price told the author he was "happy in having such an advocate." Refusing to accept that fear governs human beings, requiring institutions and tradition to keep them under control, she asserted that people have a "capacity of improvement, which gives [them] a natural scepter on earth." Human beings could manage themselves "if the voice of nature was allowed to speak audibly from the bottom of the heart, and the *native* unalienable rights of men were recognized in their full force." The key to a new order, in Wollstonecraft's view, was self-respect. Rather than be governed by the *likelihood* of failure, people should be governed by the *possibility* of success. Because she feared God she reverenced herself. She had "enlightened self-love," which "forces me to see; and, . . . to *feel,* that happiness is reflected, and that, in communicating good, my soul receives its noble aliment." Liberty was social glue, and *natural* a synonym for *mutual*.[57]

56. Edmund Burke, *Reflections on the Revolution in France . . .* (1790), in *The Writings and Speeches of the Right Honourable Edmund Burke,* 12 vols. (Boston, 1901), III, 242, 310, 316. See Luke Gibbons, *Edmund Burke and Ireland: Aesthetics, Politics, and the Colonial Sublime* (Cambridge, 2003); Tom Furniss, *Edmund Burke's Aesthetic Ideology: Language, Gender, and Political Economy in Revolution* (Cambridge, 1993); and Ian Crowe, ed., *An Imaginative Whig: Reassessing the Life and Thought of Edmund Burke* (Columbia, Mo., 2005), 1–58.

57. [Richard] Price to MW, Dec. 17, 1790, Oxford, Bodleian, MS Abinger c. 41, fol. 2; MW, *Vindication of the Rights of Men,* in Todd and Butler, eds., *Works of Wollstonecraft,* V, 8, 33, 34.

In a better world, merit would be rewarded, and content would matter more than form. Mocking Burke, Wollstonecraft denounced British society as corrupt. Surely Burke knew "that a man of merit cannot rise in the church, the army, or navy," that few men achieved eminence "without submitting to a servility of dependence that degrades the man." What was the value of stability if it encouraged "unmanly servility," if men and women could not embrace the potential afforded them by reason? What was the value of property and family if they encouraged men and women to become *parasites* rather than to assert their natural dignity? "Happy would it be for the world . . . if pride, in the shape of parental affection, did not absorb the man, and prevent friendship from having the same weight as relationship." Then ambition among men would be virtuous rather than gallant and domesticity among women a rational choice. As in the nation, "affection in the marriage state can only be founded on respect."[58]

Burke had it backward. Kings and courtiers had interrupted the progress of reason. Priests had retarded "the cultivation of the understanding, and refinement of the affections, [which] naturally make a man religious." Monopoly and tradition had established and protected slavery and turned women into pretty, thoughtless dolls, as eager to please men as men are eager to please their superiors. The system was rotten to the core. Only liberty would produce manliness. Only manliness would defy slaveholders and turn "British senators" into men. Only manliness would allow "the natural feelings of humanity" to silence "the cold cautions of timidity," to allow all men "to enjoy their birth-right—liberty." Burke would have men "enjoy" rather than "think." To fight for *the rights of men* was hard work. But the result was worth the toil. In a just world, where all people were educated, where property was more equitably distributed, where people deferred to one another from self-interest, where "man was contented to be the friend of man" rather than a master, men and women would relish their labor and enjoy "affection . . . built on rational grounds." Revolution was all about a God who had created human beings capable of improvement. Richard Price, sending his "best thanks" for Wollstonecraft's work, was especially happy about "the very kind and handsome manner in which she had mentioned him."[59]

Two years later, Wollstonecraft extended her argument in her most in-

58. MW, *Vindication of the Rights of Men,* in Todd and Butler, eds., *Works of Wollstonecraft,* V, 21, 23, 24.

59. Ibid., 39, 46, 51, 52, 56, 57, 59; Price to MW, Dec. 17, 1790, Oxford, Bodleian, MS Abinger c. 41, fol. 2.

fluential work, *A Vindication of the Rights of Woman.* Published by Joseph
Johnson and addressed to Charles Maurice de Talleyrand-Périgord, author
of a recent report on public education in France, *Vindication* elaborated on
Catharine Macaulay's call for the equal education of both women and men.
Wollstonecraft denied that she was engaged in special pleading for her sex.
She advocated the rights of woman from "an affection for the whole human
race" and a "wish to see woman placed in a station in which she would advance, instead of retarding, the progress of those glorious principles that
give a substance to morality." Her conviction that "women cannot, by force,
be confided to domestic concerns" reflected her more general concern that
there be "no coercion *established* in society" as a whole. Wollstonecraft
imagined a world in which women and men engaged in mutual commerce
on relatively equal terms, exercising power through persuasion rather than
force or tradition. Her book exemplified her larger goal. Rejecting an artificial, affected "flowery diction," she would directly and sincerely "persuade"
men that the world would be a better place if the relationships of men and
women were rooted in esteem rather than prejudice. It was "time to effect
a revolution in female manners" and encourage women to "labour by re-
forming themselves to reform the world."[60]

In the first chapters of *Vindication,* Wollstonecraft detailed the culture of
an ancien régime that prevented men and women from working together
to cultivate their understanding, that is, to make sense of themselves and
their world using emotion and reason. Defective education made women
and men unfit and therefore antisocial companions, spouses, parents, and
citizens. Women were trained to please men rather than benefit themselves; they decorated their bodies, neglected their minds, and indulged
their sensibility by reading novels and dreaming of romance. Men, "considering females rather as women than human creatures," had been too "anxious to make them alluring mistresses" instead of "affectionate wives and
rational mothers." Thus, most women were "only anxious to inspire love,
when they ought to cherish a nobler ambition, and by their abilities and
virtues exact respect." Properly educated, women would choose to fulfill
their social responsibilities. Rather than endure their "slavish dependence,"
women should seek "a character as a human being, regardless of the distinction of sex." Whatever differences separated women from men, women
could reason, and men could respect them for doing so.[61]

60. MW, *A Vindication of the Rights of Woman* (1792), 2d ed., ed. Carol H. Poston (New York,
1988), 3, 5, 6, 10, 11, 45.

61. Ibid., 7, 9–10, 24.

The general improvement of mankind depended on a revolution in education that would in turn inspire a revolution in personal relationships and eventually in political relationships. Wollstonecraft concentrated on a basic social unit—the family—and the ways in which its members ought to function as friends. Together a husband and wife should seek "a humble mutual love." A woman should "become the friend, and not the humble dependent of her husband." To fall in love was to risk the dominion of an unstable enthusiasm in which "chance and sensation" took the "place of choice and reason." The value of marriage lay in "allowing the fever of love to subside" into "the calm tenderness of friendship." The only other option, given the natural course of any passion, was "indifference." Wollstonecraft insisted that understanding allowed women to distinguish "strong, persevering passions" from "romantic wavering feelings." A strong woman with a strong mind marries "from affection, without losing sight of prudence, and . . . secures her husband's respect before it is necessary to exert mean arts to please him and feed a dying flame, which nature doomed to expire when the object became familiar, when friendship and forbearance take place of a more ardent affection.—This is the natural death of love." "Love and friendship cannot" flourish together. Narrow passions, by "guarding the heart and mind, destroy also all their energy.—It is far better to be often deceived than never to trust; to be disappointed in love than never to love; to lose a husband's fondness than forfeit his esteem." Enlightened women will "resign all the prerogatives of love, that are not mutual." Otherwise, they enslaved themselves to enthusiasm. In short, a healthy relationship progressed from love as intense physical desire into settled emotional intimacy.[62]

In order to achieve mutuality and nurture understanding, men and women must deal with the other in an honest fashion. To deny imperfections and weaknesses was counterproductive. Only through engagement with others could women and men manage the ultimate other—themselves. Together they could see that love was "easily distinguished from esteem, the foundation of friendship, because it is often excited by evanescent beauties and graces." Women trained to behave like pretty ornaments, to cajole and connive rather than to reason and speak directly, must be excused "for their attachment to rakes." But women of intelligence would not confuse a husband with a lover, "for a lover the husband, even supposing him to be wise and virtuous, cannot long remain." Good friends (and effective parents) were sincere and honest advocates of social commerce. "The world cannot

62. Ibid., 25, 29, 30, 50, 73, 75, 100, 104.

be seen by an unmoved spectator, we must mix in the throng, and feel as men feel before we can judge of their feelings. If we mean, in short, to live in the world to grow wiser and better, and not merely to enjoy the good things of life, we must attain a knowledge of others at the same time that we become acquainted with ourselves." Honest conversation, however difficult and painful, was necessary. Parents should not expect children to be either "wise" or "virtuous" if they spared them "labour and sorrow."[63]

Marriage and family mattered because "public spirit must be nurtured by private virtue." So, too, did mixed-gender schools that got children in the habit of interacting with one another. The only way to get them "excited to think for themselves" was "by mixing a number of children together, and making them jointly pursue the same objects." If girls and boys were educated together, if girls studied history and boys learned to esteem rather than desire girls, they were far more likely to become useful friends, spouses, and parents. Keeping their hearts pure, their understandings exercised, and their imagination under control, women would no longer be "cunning envious dependents." Men would also change. Those "voluptuous tyrants" would control their desire to dominate others. Wollstonecraft thought it "an indisputable truth" that the "two sexes mutually corrupt and improve each other." Well-educated women would help well-educated men practice chastity. "Public affections, as well as public virtues, must ever grow out of the private character," Wollstonecraft concluded, "or they are merely meteors that shoot athwart a dark sky, and disappear as they are gazed at and admired."[64]

With esteem as the foundation of relationships, friendships would encourage independence. "Natural affection" would grow when women were "in some degree, independent of men." "Rational fellowship" rather than "slavish obedience" would nurture better daughters, sisters, wives, and mothers—"in a word, better citizens." Women would "love . . . with true affection" because they would "respect" themselves. They would become their husbands' "companions rather than their mistresses," and men would learn that love was about "esteem" and "affection" rather than "selfish gratification." Elaborating on ideas shared by many of her contemporaries, Wollstonecraft's achievement in *Vindication* was to emphasize the importance of "the rights of woman" in the larger work of transforming social relations. Revolution was a process of individual awakenings, nurtured in

---

63. Ibid., 112, 118, 119, 124.
64. Ibid., 140, 144, 157, 162.

social exchange, to the strength of independence created through inter-dependence.[65]

A Vindication of the Rights of Woman was widely read and admired when it first appeared. The reaction of English reviewers was almost unanimously favorable. In Philadelphia, publisher Mathew Carey optimistically printed fifteen hundred copies of his edition of the popular book, and American magazines ran long excerpts. Wollstonecraft and the phrase "the Rights of Woman" became synonymous. Men as well as women cited the work and debated its implications. By 1795, three editions had appeared in the United States. "The Rights of Women are no longer strange sounds to an American ear," wrote Congressman Elias Boudinot of New Jersey in 1793; "They are now heard as familiar terms in every part of the United States." *Vindication* became the signature statement of a transatlantic moment. Its readers tended to find its significance in its bold title. "In opposition to your im-mortal Paine," asserted Ann Harker in the December 1794 commencement address of the Young Ladies' Academy of Philadelphia before a crowd that included Martha Washington and other luminaries, "we will exalt our Wol-stencraft," who has "asserted and vindicated our rights."[66]

The cause of the rights of woman was only one aspect of a general imag-ining of a world of freedom for all people, a world without the tyranny of kings, priests, parents, slaveholders, or monopolies, a world of unfettered commerce in all aspects of life, a world in which a sense of independence was achieved through sociability. In the view of Wollstonecraft and her con-temporaries, women required education, not to isolate themselves from men, but to engage them in a conversation between equals. "The inter-course of the sexes which nature and custom have established teaches the propriety of their being mutually beneficial," said Harker. "Conversation is

65. Ibid., 141, 150, 165, 192.

66. Elias Boudinot, *An Oration Delivered in Elizabeth-Town, New-Jersey, Agreeably to a Reso-lution of the State Society of Cincinnati on the Fourth of July M.DCC.XCIII* (Elizabethtown, N.J., 1793), 24; Ann Harker, "The Salutatory Oration," in J. A. Neal, *An Essay on the Education and Genius of the Female Sex; to Which Is Added, an Account, of the Commencement of the Young-Ladies' Academy of Philadelphia* (Philadelphia, 1795), 17-18. See Marcelle Thiébaux, "Mary Wollstonecraft in Federalist America, 1791-1802," in Donald H. Reiman et al., eds., *The Evi-dence of the Imagination: Studies of Interactions between Life and Art in English Romantic Lit-erature* (New York, 1978), 195-235; Susan Branson, *These Fiery Frenchified Dames: Women and Political Culture in Early National Philadelphia* (Philadelphia, 2001), 35-49; Caroline Winterer, *The Mirror of Antiquity: American Women and the Classical Tradition, 1750-1900* (Ithaca, N.Y., 2007), 68-101; and Rosemarie Zagarri, *Revolutionary Backlash: Women and Politics in the Early American Republic* (Philadelphia, 2007), 40-45.

the proper index of the mind." *A Vindication of the Rights of Woman* captured the indignation and aspirations of a generation. An angry critique of artificial patriarchal relationships revealed a remarkable faith that women and men could be friends if they understood how profoundly necessary they were to each other.[67]

"A Tender Friend"

In 1792, the year *Vindication* appeared, Mary Wollstonecraft learned first-hand the divergence between theory and practice, especially the danger of trusting her fancy and letting her sensibility run rampant. As in her book, she envisioned something that did not exist but might yet be, a romantic *friendship* with Henry Fuseli, a painter who was close to Joseph Johnson. Fifty years old, Fuseli was five feet two inches tall with a shock of white hair and commanding blue eyes. He had recently married a much younger woman, Sophia Rawlins of Bath. A third generation painter, Fuseli had been born in 1741 and trained in Zurich. After a brief sojourn in Germany, he migrated to London in the early 1760s and lived there, with occasional stays in Italy, until his death in 1825. Fuseli's friends included Laurence Sterne, Sir Joshua Reynolds, and William Blake. He had known David Hume and Jean-Jacques Rousseau, admired Shakespeare and Milton, and loved the theater.[68]

Fuseli channeled his remarkable personal and creative passion in ways that made him an interesting conversationalist as well as a popular if not always solvent artist. Never one to suffer fools, he was both shy and direct, charming and impatient. A female acquaintance described Fuseli in 1789 as "an extraordinary and very entertaining character." She was particularly taken with his use of the word *"divine"* to describe a drawing by her son. At breakfast Fuseli regaled his hosts with stories of "Spectres . . . told with all the fire of poetic genius" and certain to affect even "the dullest" of imaginations. The only novels he had read were those of Samuel Richardson, although he remarked that he intended to read Frances Burney's *Evelina* and *Cecilia* because Johnson highly recommended them. As a painter, Fuseli boldly represented scenes from Antiquity, Shakespeare, and Milton suf-

---

67. Harker, "The Salutatory Oration," in Neal, *Essay,* 16.

68. John Knowles, *The Life and Writings of Henry Fuseli,* 3 vols. (London, 1831). See Peter Tomory, *The Life and Art of Henry Fuseli* (New York, 1972), 9–46; Franziska Lentzsch, "London's Theatres—Drury Lane and Somerset House: All the City's a Stage," in Lentzsch, *Fuseli: The Wild Swiss* (Zurich, 2005), 189–246.

Figure 4. Henry Fuseli. *By John Opie. Oil on canvas, feigned oval, exhibited 1794.*
© *National Portrait Gallery, London*

fused with dreams, demons, and dread. His most famous work—the one
that made his reputation when it was shown at the annual exhibition of
the Royal Academy in 1782—was *The Nightmare,* subsequently revised on
at least two occasions. An unconscious young woman in a thin white gown
lies on a couch with her arms flung above her head and a gargoyle-like creature perched on her lower abdomen. The painting was inspired by Lorenzo
Ghiberti's representation of a corpse on the Noah panel on the east doors
of the Florentine Baptistery. It likely reflected Fuseli's unrequited and quite

specific desire for the body of a young woman with whom he fell in love but whose family insisted she marry a merchant.[69]

Wollstonecraft liked Fuseli because he took her seriously, paying attention to her in the ingratiating manner that had endeared him to countless others. Johnson later claimed, "They were so intimate and spent so many happy hours in my house that I think I may say he was the first of her friends." With Fuseli, Wollstonecraft imagined she was enjoying a friendship rooted in mutual esteem. As early as 1790, she spoke of someone who was probably Fuseli as "a tender friend who bore with my faults—who was ever anxious to serve" and "comfort" her. He was a person with whom she could converse about anything from politics to male bodies. Fuseli enjoyed Wollstonecraft's company. Fond of flirting, he seemed interested in her mind and talent. Others were not so sure of his sincerity. Godwin thought him "the most frankly ingenuous and conceited man" he had ever known. Closer to the mark was Fuseli's patron William Roscoe's description of the artist as "a wonderful Man and certainly the most agreeable companion that can be when pleased, and even when not so his very anger and resentment may be tolerated for the sake of the wit and liveliness it produces." Wollstonecraft herself was ambivalent. Disgusted with his portrayal of women as pretty, defenseless innocents, she was equally enthralled by his "rich torrent of conversation." She could not resist his "grandeur of soul," his "quickness of comprehension," and his "lively sympathy." Eventually she determined to "unite" herself to his "mind." Wollstonecraft wanted to talk with him daily. But Sophia Fuseli had other ideas and turned Wollstonecraft away after she broached the subject of living—chastely—with the couple. When the painter did not dispute his wife's decision, Wollstonecraft's reaction paralleled her reaction to her loss of Fanny. She became ill, depressed, and left London for Paris, where she complained bitterly about the tyranny of that wanton, her imagination.[70]

The farcical denouement of the relationship with Fuseli should not obscure the importance of Wollstoneraft's experimentation. She disparaged the manners and habits of men as the products of their distorted edu-

69. Mrs. Frederica Lock to Frances Burney, June 17–21, 1789, in David H. Weinglass, ed., *The Collected English Letters of Henry Fuseli* (Millwood, N.Y., 1982), 40–41, 44. See H. W. Janson, "Study 4: Fuseli's *Nightmare*," in Janson, *16 Studies* (New York, 1973), 77–88.

70. Johnson to Godwin, Sept. 12, 1797, Oxford, Bodleian, MS Abinger c. 3, fols. 79–80; MW to Bishop, [circa 1790], in Todd, ed., *Collected Letters*, 183, to Henry Fuseli, [circa late 1792], 205; Godwin to John Knowles, Sept. 28, 1826, in Weinglass, ed., *Letters of Fuseli*, 509, William Roscoe to Jane Roscoe, Feb. 4, 1793, 87.

cation. More than a few men, however, were susceptible to persuasion. If she hadn't believed that, she would never have written *Vindication*, for it was nothing if not an exercise in persuasion predicated on the notion that men and women could together awaken one another to improvement. William Godwin recalled that "she set a great value on a mutual affection between persons of an opposite sex. She regarded it as the principal solace of human life." In the winter of 1792–1793, Wollstonecraft believed that sex should follow from "individual affection," which would surely persist longer than the physical connection. But, although she had experienced emotional intimacy with Fanny, she had never experienced physical intimacy with anyone. Her ideas about sexuality were largely theoretical. Fuseli was a friend who "amused, delighted and instructed her." Alas, he had chosen to remain within the prison of a conventional marriage, or perhaps declined to hurt the woman with whom he had chosen to live by sharing her house with another woman.[71]

Mary Wollstonecraft had other ideas. If her imagination might lead her into enthusiasm, it also might lead her to contentment. She remained remarkably confident of the ability of educated individuals to realize their ambitions. And why not? Wollstonecraft had become a well-known literary figure, a woman of independence who largely supported herself by arguing in print with men such as Edmund Burke. Why not aspire to something equally extraordinary in her personal life? "We have all an individual way of feeling grandeur and sublimity," she had observed earlier in 1792. Women and men could imagine all kinds of possibilities. They did not have to accept the world as it was, certainly not in Paris in 1793. The dreary winter would eventually give way to spring, and Wollstonecraft would "once more breathe on the ashes of hope."[72]

71. Godwin, *Memoirs*, ed. Clemit and Walker, 78, 79.

72. MW to William Roscoe, Jan. 3, 1792, in Weinglass, ed., *Letters of Fuseli*, 79; MW to Bishop, June 13, 1793, in Todd, ed., *Collected Letters*, 226.

2

A "very sensible" American

April came at last. Winter was over, and with it went Mary Wollstonecraft's melancholy mood. Life was better, mainly because she was no longer alone. She had found friends within a community of English-speaking writers, some of whom she had known in London. Through Thomas Paine, she had become acquainted with French men and women such as Jacques-Pierre Brissot de Warville and his wife Felicité and Jean-Marie and Marie-Jeanne Roland de La Platière. Wollstonecraft's friends were generally middling, provincial men and women in their late thirties who had sought fame and fortune through a literary career. The French Revolution, they were certain, had overturned institutions and attitudes that had too long thwarted the ambitions of men and women. It was making visible at last the pleasures and profits of a natural world in which friendship replaced patronage and talent mattered more than flattery.

They were wrong, of course. By the time the weather turned cold and the leaves were falling from the trees in the Luxembourg Garden, many would be making conversation in prison cells and imagining the guillotine rushing toward their necks. We can wonder whether, if they had known what awaited them in October, they would have acted differently in April. But they didn't know. No one knew. In spring, as France went to war with Great Britain and other European nations, as the National Assembly debated a future in the aftermath of the execution of Louis XVI, their confidence seemed entirely reasonable. Anything was possible. Paris was hardly the place to tame one's fancy. What was revolution if not an act of imagination?

In late April, Mary Wollstonecraft's spirits were as high as they had been low in February. She was a woman consumed with hope, bursting with energy. She was a woman in love. It was a feeling she knew; it had happened before, after all. What was novel was the strange sensation created by the knowledge that the feeling was mutual. For the first time in her life, she was experiencing the love of someone she loved. This time, she wanted *and* she was wanted. This time, she found someone necessary to her happiness *and* he found her necessary to his. A liberated Wollstonecraft accepted the existence of something she had begun to doubt she would ever know. Her "love was unbounded," recalled William Godwin, and "for the first time in her life she gave a loose to all the sensibilities of her nature." She had found a companion as well as a lover.[1]

His name was Gilbert Imlay, and he was nothing if not a sensible man, in the eighteenth-century sense of the word. A slave to fancy, Imlay lived a life shaped by his notions of the world as it could be rather than the world as it was. He lurched from possibility to possibility in a seemingly endless series of what his contemporaries called speculations or adventures. Most involved making money; all reflected an extraordinary imagination. Empowered to dream by revolution, Imlay never came to terms with reality. When he met Wollstonecraft, he was an American in his late thirties who had recently published two books in which he blithely argued that the best place to realize a natural society was neither London nor Paris but the Ohio Valley. The first, *A Topographical Description of North America,* detailed a lush, safe, and accessible landscape far from the artificial corruption of Great Britain; the second, *The Emigrants,* imagined educated individuals organizing a society around mixed-gender sociability. Like Wollstonecraft, Imlay, who had written and published his books in London, was in Paris because it was the epicenter of revolutionary power. But, whereas she was there to help promote change in Europe through education and writing, he was there to promote change in North America through trade and war. Just as *A Vindication of the Rights of Men* and *A Vindication of the Rights of Woman* had given her a measure of celebrity and authority, so, too, had his books conferred on him the status of an expert on America, at least with eager French leaders such as Jacques-Pierre Brissot.

Wollstonecraft met Imlay in early April 1793, probably at the home of their mutual friends, Thomas and Rebecca Christie. Their initial encounter was not a success, at least from her perspective. She did not like him, although her disdain soon became "kindness." We do not know how their relationship progressed. We do not know when they first touched, kissed,

1. William Godwin, *Memoirs of the Author of "A Vindication of the Rights of Woman"* (1798), ed. Pamela Clemit and Gina Luria Walker (Peterborough, Ont., 2001), 89.

and embraced, whether they arrived at intercourse quickly, impulsively, or whether they moved slowly, fitfully. What is striking is the speed with which Wollstonecraft wrote to Imlay with the familiar specificity of a lover. Suddenly, she was his "dear girl." Eager to avoid disappointing him, she delighted in seeing his "eyes praise" her. She reveled in the illicit quality of their affair and the rush of hiding her happiness from their friends. "Hush! Here they come—and love flies away in the twinkling of an eye, leaving a little brush of his wing on my pale cheeks." Friends soon figured out that something was happening. "[Mary] has got a sweetheart," Joel Barlow wrote to his wife Ruth on April 19, and "she will finish by going to Am[eric]a a wife. He is of Kentucky and a very sensible man." Two weeks later, the "sweetheart affair goes on well."[2]

From the beginning, Wollstonecraft sought a mutual relationship in which her lover engaged her mind as well as her body, in which conversation was more than flirtation, and in which sexual ardor would evolve into "habitual" "affection." She hoped Imlay would be a permanent partner whose respect would banish the loneliness that had haunted her throughout her life. Finding "peace in [his] bosom," she was able to contemplate "many plans of employment." Confident of Imlay's regard, she resolved to continue her lifelong quest for self-improvement, insisting that he do the same. Wollstonecraft clarified her expectations. "Cherish me with that dignified tenderness, which I have only found in you; and your own dear girl will try to keep under a quickness of feeling, that has sometimes given you pain.—Yes, I will be *good*, that I may deserve to be happy; and whilst you love me, I cannot again fall into the miserable state, which rendered life a burthen almost too heavy to be borne." Love—manly intimacy—encouraged independence, not dependence; to know you were loved was freedom, not slavery. Wollstonecraft yielded to her infatuation with Imlay because she felt stronger. She was happy. With him, she could "once more breathe on the ashes of hope." Stunned by Mary's uncharacteristic optimism, Eliza wondered to their sister Everina about its cause. Was it "the *Continental air.*—Or is it A *Love*? Ambition or Pity? That has wrought the Miracle?"[3]

The romance fueled Wollstonecraft's literary ambition. She alternated

2. Godwin, *Memoirs,* ed. Clemit and Walker, 85; MW to Gilbert Imlay, [circa April–May 1793], in Janet Todd, ed., *The Collected Letters of Mary Wollstonecraft* (New York, 2003), 222, 223, 224; Joel Barlow to Ruth Barlow, Apr. 19, 1793, Joel Barlow Papers [MS AM 1448], 7 vols., III, no. 210, Houghton Library, Harvard University, May 2, 1793, III, no. 211.

3. MW to Imlay, [circa August 1793], in Todd, ed., *Collected Letters,* 228, to Eliza Bishop, June 13, [1793], 226, Bishop to Everina Wollstonecraft, July 14, 1793, 227 n. 531.

between making love and writing, two passions flourishing together, feeding off each other. Abandoning a planned visit to Switzerland, Wollstonecraft moved into "the house of an old Gardener" in the village of Neuilly-sur-Seine, just north of Paris. She spent her time "writing a great book," published in 1794 as *An Historical and Moral View of the French Revolution,* and walking in the garden and neighboring woods. She ate and slept with Imlay, although he continued to live in Saint-Germain-des-Prés. They planned a future together in North America. It included Eliza and Everina; indeed, the prospect of providing her sisters with a comfortable life relieved Wollstonecraft of her anxiety about them. Enjoying the pleasures of sexuality for the first time in her life, she dotted her letters with playful allusions that hint at comfortable intimacy. She liked kissing him, referring to the poet John Milton's suggestion that there are happy moments "when the honey that drops from the lips is not merely words." But even at the height of her happiness, Wollstonecraft remained true to her sense of herself. When they were together, which was not often enough, Imlay "*must* be glad to see [her]—because [he was] glad." Wollstonecraft was confident that she was affecting Imlay as much as he was affecting her, that they were in fact living the life she had called for in *A Vindication of the Rights of Woman.* His main rival, she playfully informed him, was Honoré Gabriel Riqueti, comte de Mirabeau (1749–1791). Mirabeau's love letters confirmed her notion that women could transform men. Had she "not begun to form a new theory respecting men" with Imlay, she "should, in the vanity of [her] heart, have i*magined* that [she] could have made something of [Mirabeau's]—it was composed of such materials." Imlay was persuadable, or so that wanton coquette, her imagination, suggested.[4]

"So-and-So Has Succeeded. Why Shouldn't I?"

At first glance, Gilbert Imlay fits the caricature of the feckless male. But Imlay was actually a variation on a late-eighteenth-century man who assumed the importance of shape-shifting—adjusting his loyalty and accommodating his behavior—as circumstances demanded. Growing up in an era of global warfare, political revolution, and rapid economic change that undermined the authority of traditional institutions from households to monarchy, a cohort of ambitious provincials born in the middle of the

---

4. MW to Bishop, June 13, [1793], ibid., 226, June 24, [1793], 227, to Imlay, Wednesday morning [circa April–May 1793], 223, 224.

century disassociated themselves from families and local communities and gambled on their ability to navigate through a fluid and uncertain world. The key to their lives was mobility, the ability to move freely from possibility to possibility. Liberty to men such as Imlay and Brissot meant autonomy, and revolution the creation of a world in which men of merit became somebody by declaring themselves independent of any and all obligations, connections, and responsibilities that, in their judgment and their judgment alone, inhibited that autonomy. A French journalist captured their ambition when he commented in 1793 that, in a natural society, justice would prevail and Brissot's literary talent would make him enormously wealthy. Brissot himself remarked of Americans in the late 1780s: "They say: 'So-and-so has succeeded. Why shouldn't I? I am nobody here; I will be somebody in Ohio.'" Above all, they demanded the right to construct their careers, their reputations, and their relationships. Identity was created, not by birth, but by the choice of free men and women.[5]

Imlay was an adventurer, a man without particular loyalties who lived by his wits and looked to secure his fortune by taking chances in a wide variety of enterprises. He engaged in speculation, a word that connoted an act of intellectual imagination as well as economic investment. The expo-

5. Gary Kates, *The Cercle Social, the Girondins, and the French Revolution* (Princeton, N.J., 1985), 177; J. P. Brissot de Warville, *New Travels in the United States of America, 1788* (1791), trans. Mara Soceanu Vamos and Durand Echeverria, ed. Echeverria (Cambridge, Mass., 1964), 120. See Christine Holbo, "Imagination, Commerce, and the Politics of Associationism in Crèvecoeur's *Letters from an American Farmer," Early American Literature,* XXXII (1997), 20–65; Christopher Iannini, "'The Itinerant Man': Crèvecoeur's Caribbean, Raynal's Revolution, and the Fate of Atlantic Cosmopolitanism," *William and Mary Quarterly,* 3d Ser., LXI (2004), 201–234. See also Paul Merrill Spurlin, *The French Enlightenment in America: Essays on the Times of the Founding Fathers* (Athens, Ga., 1984); Grantland S. Rice, "Crèvecoeur and the Politics of Authorship in Republican America," *EAL,* XXVIII (1993), 108; Doreen Alvarez Saar, "Crèvecoeur's 'Thoughts on Slavery': *Letters from an American Farmer* and Whig Rhetoric," ibid., XXII (1987), 192–203; Nathaniel Philbrick, "The Nantucket Sequence in Crèvecoeur's *Letters from an American Farmer," New England Quarterly,* LXIV (1991), 414–432; and Thomas A. Foster, ed., *New Men: Manliness in Early America* (New York, 2011). On itinerancy and self-fashioning, see Linda Colley, *The Ordeal of Elizabeth Marsh: A Woman in World History* (New York, 2007); Edward G. Gray, *The Making of John Ledyard: Empire and Ambition in the Life of an Early American Traveler* (New Haven, Conn., 2007); Maya Jasanoff, *Edge of Empire: Lives, Culture, and Conquest in the East, 1750–1850* (New York, 2005); Dror Wahrman, *The Making of the Modern Self: Identity and Culture in Eighteenth-Century England* (New Haven, Conn., 2004); and Kathleen Wilson, "Introduction: Histories, Empires, Modernities," in Wilson, ed., *A New Imperial History: Culture, Identity, and Modernity in Britain and the Empire, 1660–1840* (Cambridge, 2004), 1–26. I also learned a good deal from reading Martha Tomhave Blauvelt, *The Work of the Heart: Young Women and Emotion, 1780–1830* (Charlottesville, Va., 2007), and the work of sociologists Erving Goffman and Arlie Russell Hochschild to which she led me.

nential growth in the circulation of books and periodicals as well as the growth of literacy had stimulated his imagination, allowing him to conjure all kinds of possibilities his parents and grandparents would never have taken seriously. But like his peers, including Wollstonecraft, he came of age in a world that provided little specific guidance on how to become "somebody." Refusing to think locally, to apprentice himself to parents or neighbors in order ultimately to inherit their property, he improvised. Seeking the life of a gentleman freed from labor and devoted to ideas but unwilling to give himself over to hard work and patient development, Imlay gambled. He speculated in land, enslaved Africans, books, and revolution. Seizing any opportunity to advance his own interests, he did not recognize the right of anyone to impede his progress or to hold him responsible. He was oblivious to the impact of his exercise of freedom on other people's ability to exercise theirs.

Gilbert Imlay was born on February 9, 1754, in Imlaystown in the county of Monmouth in the British colony of New Jersey. He was a member of a family that had worked hard for three generations to secure its position economically and socially—and had largely succeeded. Imlays had married well, produced considerable progeny, accumulated property (including a mill), served as militia officers, and become bulwarks of the local Presbyterian congregation. Growing slowly, New Jersey was a landscape of farms and villages in between the burgeoning metropolises of New York and Philadelphia, both of which beckoned to ambitious young men. By the late 1770s, Gilbert's second cousin John was a Philadelphia merchant engaged in the West Indies trade; shortly thereafter, his brother Robert was a partner in the firm of Imlay and Potts.[6]

War shaped Imlay's career. Born shortly before the outbreak of the Seven Years' War, he grew up during a decade of crisis between Great Britain and its North American colonies and was scarcely twenty-one when British troops clashed with Americans on Lexington Green. He heard the Declaration of Independence when he was twenty-two. Toward the end of the summer of 1776, a British army under the command of General Sir William Howe thrashed General George Washington's Continental army in a series of battles around New York City. By late fall, the British and their hired Hessian allies were pursuing the defeated Americans into central New Jersey. Many people greeted the victors with open arms and loud declarations of loyalty to George III, hardly a surprising phenomenon especially after Howe granted pardons and protection to anyone who took an oath of allegiance

---

6. Wil Verhoeven, *Gilbert Imlay: Citizen of the World* (London, 2008), 32.

to the king within thirty days. Some New Jerseyans went further, organizing militia units to fight for the crown. In response, Washington in late November dispatched local resident Colonel David Forman with a regiment to arrest persons in Monmouth County who appeared "to be concerned in any Plot or Design against the Liberty or Safety of the united States." Despite Washington's recommendation that he "be cautious in proceeding against any but such as you have the fullest Grounds of Suspicion," "Black David" Forman ruthlessly pursued loyalists, even after the American victories at Trenton and Princeton in December. In early 1777, Washington authorized Forman to raise a regiment in the Continental Line. Forman and his men called themselves the Association of Retaliation. Functioning as vigilantes, they exploited the situation to harass their enemies and to seize the property of suspected loyalists. As the British pulled back from central New Jersey, they abandoned men who only a few weeks earlier had declared for the crown to the mercy of angry neighbors. Forman's men took their revenge, fueled by political and personal resentment.[7]

Gilbert Imlay did not declare himself until February 10, 1777, when he became a first lieutenant in Forman's regiment. Years later, his rage at the British remained palpable. Much as he admired "the true English," he knew that "men, feeling the spirit of liberty, are always superior to slaves." The Americans had rebelled at "the inflated grandeur of visionary plans for dominion, which the remains of gothic tyranny [had] produced" in Great Britain. Imlay conveniently joined Forman at a time when supporters of Congress had the whip hand in Monmouth County. His most conspicuous act was to arrange pardons for a group of loyalists on the condition that they join with Congress. Imlay understood that men could choose who they were. After some service as a regimental paymaster, he resigned his commission on July 24, 1778, probably for the same reason that Forman's regiment was disbanded on July 1. With the British confined to New York City, opportunities for glory and profit had passed. In addition, Imlay despised standing armies, preferring local militia acting in defense of their communities.[8]

7. [George Washington], "Orders to Colonel David Forman," [Nov. 24, 1776], in W. W. Abbot et al., eds., *The Papers of George Washington,* Revolutionary War Series, 20 vols. (Charlottesville, Va., 1985–2010), VII, 203. See David Hackett Fischer, *Washington's Crossing* (New York, 2004), 171, 172; and Michael S. Adelberg, "The Transformation of Local Governance in Monmouth County, New Jersey, during the War of the American Revolution," *Journal of the Early Republic,* XXXI (2011), 467–498.

8. Gilbert Imlay, *A Topographical Description of the Western Territory of North America . . .* (1797), 3d ed. (New York, 1969), 2, 16. See Verhoeven, *Imlay,* 30–33, 39.

Imlay might have followed in the footsteps of his paternal ancestors. He could have married a suitable local woman, whose major qualifications would have been her connections, dowry, and domestic competence. He could have inherited or purchased land from his father and set up his own household. He might have been a good Presbyterian and held assorted local offices. When he got into trouble with his neighbors (he was arrested more than once for trespass and failure to pay his debts), Imlay could expect his family, especially his male relatives, to restrain as well as support him. Instead, he borrowed several thousand British pounds—perhaps facilitated by his family's local standing or his cousin's and brother's connections in Philadelphia—to embark on a career common among men of his generation: speculating in land in the Virginia district of Kentucky, "the key-stone of the settlements upon the waters of the Mississippi." Almost thirty years old and unmarried, he went west to make his way in a place even more in flux than New Jersey.[9]

The challenges of life in a borderland were hardly novel. War, violence, betrayals, deception, unreliable legal structures, distant and fluctuating markets were familiar problems. Likely Imlay went to Kentucky as an agent for Philadelphian merchants John May and Samuel Beall. The Ohio Valley was attractive because of its relative proximity to Philadelphia, its fertile soil, and its prime location along hundreds of miles of navigable water. As important, Kentucky was the one area west of the Appalachians over which an American government—that of Virginia—exercised legitimate authority. Philadelphia merchants were buying land warrants in Richmond under the Virginia Land Act of 1779, which they intended to resell at a profit. They were also interested in developing "an inland version of the triangular trade routes that merchants often used in the Atlantic basin." Merchants would send dry goods to the Ohio Valley, where agents would exchange them for tobacco, furs, and flour and arrange for them to be traded in New Orleans for specie to be shipped to Philadelphia.[10]

In Kentucky, Imlay purchased ten thousand acres on credit from Daniel Boone, promising eventual payments of ten pounds for every one hundred acres. Close to Limestone (Maysville), "the usual landing-place for people coming down in boats, who mean to settle in the upper part" of Kentucky, the tract was several miles from the Ohio River but on the road to Lexington. No doubt Imlay believed that the inevitable growth of the region would

---

9. Imlay, *Topographical Description*, 16.

10. Thomas M. Doerflinger, *A Vigorous Spirit of Enterprise: Merchants and Economic Development in Revolutionary Philadelphia* (Chapel Hill, N.C., 1986), 295–296.

allow him to resell parcels of land soon at much higher prices. "Far from being disgusted with man for his turpitude or depravity," he rhapsodized later, Kentuckians "feel that dignity nature bestowed upon us at the creation; but which has been contaminated by the base alloy of meanness, the concomitant of [E]uropean education; and . . . laws and governments." Unfortunately, the resistance of American Indians north of the Ohio River confined settlers in stations. Just as troublesome were fluctuating water levels, a lack of specie, and limited demand for lots of three hundred to five hundred acres. Americans dealing with a lack of capital and a spate of foreclosures from Massachusetts through the Carolinas were in no position to buy land in the Ohio Valley.[11]

Despite these challenges, Imlay persisted in the manner of his male ancestors in New Jersey. He sought local offices in order to secure a modest income, make important connections, and acquire land. Others were doing the same thing. Daniel Boone had become a deputy surveyor in Fayette County in 1782, which made it possible to identify and reserve good tracts as well as charge high fees to locate land for others. In April 1785, Imlay was appointed a deputy surveyor of Jefferson County, mainly to take advantage of the multitude of overlapping land claims. A place like Kentucky that "had grown up under the devastation of a most barbarous [I]ndian and civil war, and under the miseries of famine and distress, settled by . . . men of different interests and different politics" needed a simple system of jurisprudence. Problems occurred when there was insistence on form at the expense of justice. In practice, the combination of acquisitiveness and weak institutions made Kentucky a paradise for lawyers and absentee speculators. Few people in the Ohio Valley in the 1780s thought the legal system worked to their benefit. To the contrary, many saw courts and governments as obstacles to the attainment of their individual or household's aspirations. Imlay's strategy for becoming somebody was to attach himself to prominent patrons, well-connected men who acted as surrogate fathers vocationally, ensuring access to information, other men, and economic opportunities. Kentucky was awash with ambitious men eager to embrace the likes of Imlay. He had no trouble connecting himself with powerful patrons. Well-connected Virginians seeking reliable partners and talented agents had to

11. Imlay, *Topographical Description*, 27, 28. See John Mack Faragher, *Daniel Boone: The Life and Legend of an American Pioneer* (New York, 1992), 246; Craig Thompson Friend, *Along the Maysville Road: The Early American Republic in the Trans-Appalachian West* (Knoxville, Tenn., 2005), 9; Terry Bouton, *Taming Democracy: "The People," the Founders, and the Troubled Ending of the American Revolution* (New York, 2007).

choose from a pool of strangers. It was a business as risky as land speculation itself. Men entered into agreements with little knowledge of one another. Neither the local ties that would have been decisive in Virginia and
New Jersey nor the professional credentials that would matter in the nineteenth century existed.[12]

Imlay was soon ensnared in the general mess of Kentucky land sales.
He went into a partnership to develop an ironworks and acquired between 100,000 and 500,000 acres of random lots of land, knowing full
well that he had to move them quickly because he could not afford to pay
for them. Unfortunately, the Kentucky land boom was a bust. As fear of
Indians prompted out-migration and inhibited in-migration, a dearth of
cash and credit resulted in numerous defaults and lawsuits. "The speculators are starving and can sell no Land. Everyman is a seller and no pur-
chasers," complained Colonel William Christian, a neighbor of "Captain
Imlay," in late 1785. Although his family and slaves were well, he feared a
"general Indian war" and complained bitterly of a lack of money and im-
migrants. "Of all America," Kentucky was "the vilest and most unpromis-
ing in its present state." A few months later, Christian was killed tracking
Indians who had taken his horses. By the time a court in Jefferson County
had issued a warrant for Imlay's arrest for failing to make payments, he
had already decamped to the Atlantic Seaboard, where he tried to unload
land in Baltimore, New Jersey, and New York City. He also bought more
land, like a gambler certain his luck has to change on the next role of the
dice. To some extent it did. After he obtained title in late 1785 to more than
15,043 acres in Jefferson County, he sold nine tracts for 12,771 silver Spanish milled dollars and 750 pounds in Pennsylvania paper. Overall, however,
the situation was dire. By October, Philadelphia merchants John May and
Samuel Beall were ready to sever connections with Imlay. "I am at present
in a very disagreeable State of Suspence of not knowing where the Bargain
[with Imlay] stands or not," wrote May, "not having any Person to give me
the least Assistance on Behalf of Imlay, nor one Farthing of Money to pay
his Proportion of Expences." "He has totally given up the Business and left
no one to act for him."[13]

12. Imlay, *Topographical Description*, 11. See Stephen Aron, *How the West Was Lost: The
Transformation of Kentucky from Daniel Boone to Henry Clay* (Baltimore, 1996), 84.

13. William Christian to his mother (and brother-in-law Mr. Fleming and his sister), Nov. 4,
Dec. 12, 1785, Hugh Blair Grigsby Papers, MSS 1 G8782 b 5751–5752, Virginia Historical Society,
Richmond; John May to Samuel Beall, Oct. 27, 1786, Beall-Booth Family Papers, MSS A B365 6,
The Filson Historical Society, Louisville, Ky.

In the depressed economic circumstances of the 1780s, investing in human beings was a more promising enterprise than investing in land across the Appalachians. While in Philadelphia, Imlay met Silas Talbot, a Rhode Island–born privateer now engaged in trading New England produce for Southern tobacco and rice. Talbot had recently bought a half-interest in the ninety-ton slave ship *Industry*. In March 1786, Talbot sold his share to Imlay in return for land in Kentucky, a promissory note, and 4 enslaved Africans. Disaster struck the *Industry* on its voyage from the west coast of Africa to Charleston, South Carolina. Disease killed well over half of the 180 Africans on board, leaving only 34 men, 21 women, and 12 children to be sold in September 1786. Imlay and his partners had lost almost five thousand pounds. By the end of the year, courts and creditors from Kentucky to South Carolina were in pursuit of a man who had promised much and delivered nothing. In December, he told Daniel Boone that he was "sincerely sorry it [was] not in [his] power to pay, for Such is the embarrassing State of affairs in this Country that I have not been able to recover a pound from all the engagements that have been made me." Instead of dealing with his obligations, Imlay traveled to Saint Augustine in Spanish Florida, where he boarded a ship for Europe, apparently carrying letters of credit to purchase goods for sale to American Indians.[14]

Whatever Gilbert Imlay's character, he was never an independent actor. Far from a precursor of unscrupulous nineteenth-century capitalists, Imlay was an ambitious young man trying to make his way in a radically unstable revolutionary environment. Economic contraction as well as economic potential defined his world. In his early thirties, Imlay was an adventurer without an obvious home or occupation, stable points of reference, or the security of patriarchal authority. Young men and women moved around and reinvented themselves free from the artificial shackles of households and villages. Where they went and how they behaved was their choice. As debtors and sheriffs closed in, Imlay decided to seek his fortune in a place where being a cheeky American had considerable cachet.

"Chevaliers d'Industrie"

We do not know what Imlay did from 1786 until 1792. We do know that by the latter date he was a member of London's literary community. His mod-

---

14. Imlay to Daniel Boone, December 1786, Draper 26C152, Wisconsin Historical Society Archives, Madison, Wis. See Wil Verhoeven, "Gilbert Imlay and the Triangular Trade," *WMQ*, 3d Ser., LXIII (2006), 827–842.

est success as a writer suggests he had a decent education in literary genres and commonplace intellectual attitudes. But a literary career involved more than literary knowledge. Imlay knew how to charm, how to adjust, and how to shift his shape as circumstances required. Making a book was a speculative enterprise on its own terms, yet another way to secure an income, meet people, and gain entrée into powerful circles. And it was a way through a classic colonial double bind: striving to carve out an independent existence and find acceptance in the imperial metropole. Americans embraced the title of citizen of the world because it blurred national distinctions and allowed them to pursue multiple opportunities. A visitor from Philadelphia observed in 1791 that Paris abounded "in spongers—fellows who are well dressed, but live by their wits; chevaliers d'industrie, who never could dine if some flat did not pay for their dinner." They included several Americans "anxiously watching the times in order to cut in and carry off a slice, either by preying upon or administering to the wants of the disordered state."[15]

For some men, a literary career complemented a business career. In the streets beyond the publishers in Paternoster Row were a stock exchange, banks, government offices, and merchant houses, like that of Turnbull, Forbes, and Company, which employed Imlay as well as his friends Thomas Christie (through whom he likely met Wollstonecraft) and Joel Barlow. With interests all over the world in an era of global warfare, London merchants understood that success depended on access to information about political decisions and government contracts. That access often came through connections cultivated over lifetimes, in schools, clubs, and social circles, as well as from a reputation for steadiness, reliability, and taste. Powerful men also needed agents in faraway places to handle their affairs, make decisions, gather information, keep them informed, and increase the credit of their firms.[16]

Partners in houses such as Turnbull, Forbes, and Company managed their interests from the comfort of their London townhouses, employing men such as Barlow, Christie, and Imlay to operate as their agents in what amounted to branch offices. These factors hired ships, organized cargoes, and dealt with shipmasters and local officials. Advance (and accurate)

15. H. E. Scudder, ed., *Recollections of Samuel Breck, with Passages from His Note-Books (1771–1862)* (Philadelphia, 1877), 170, 171, 172. See Philipp Ziesche, *Cosmopolitan Patriots: Americans in Paris in the Age of Revolution* (Charlottesville, Va., 2010), 64–87.

16. David Hancock, *Citizens of the World: London Merchants and the Integration of the British Atlantic Community, 1735–1785* (Cambridge, 1995); P. J. Cain and A. G. Hopkins, *British Imperialism, 1688–2000*, 2d ed. (1993; rpt. Harlow, Eng., 2002).

Figure 5. Joel Barlow. *By William Dunlap. Watercolor on ivory, 1806. National Portrait Gallery, Smithsonian Institution; gift of Mr. and Mrs. Joel Barlow*

knowledge of a military campaign or the assistance of a well-connected friend could make all the difference in the fortunes of Turnbull, Forbes, and Company. Traditionally, British factors had behaved as free agents, managing their own goods and rarely revealing their association with specific merchants. Generally, they were paid on commission with the understanding that they could freelance as possibilities presented themselves. Imlay and dozens of others like him were thus rewarded for their ability to take advantage of fluid situations. Today, they seem like confidence men, an image enhanced by their frequent invocation of liberty as the ultimate justification for their behavior. But a combination of opportunism and naïveté, of speculation and social mobility, thrived in an era of instability, as the career of Joel Barlow illustrates.[17]

17. Hancock, *Citizens of the World,* 124; Sheryllynne Haggerty, *The British-Atlantic Trading Community, 1760–1810: Men, Women, and the Distribution of Goods* (Leiden, 2006), 41–46. On

A graduate of Yale College who had participated briefly in the American War of Independence, Barlow seemed addicted to the melodrama of a revolutionary life. He thrived on crisis, on the disjunction between imagination and reality. Wollstonecraft shrewdly observed that he was "devoured by ambition" and reveled in the "present commotions" in France, acting as if "life loses its zest when we find there is nothing worth wishing for, nothing to detain the thoughts in the present scene, but what quickly grows stale, rendering the soul torpid or uneasy." He left Connecticut in 1788 to go to Paris as an agent of the Scioto Company to sell land north of the Ohio River to French men and women. The company was a fraud; it did not own the land it was selling. Emigrants, arriving at a village called Gallipolis, confronted isolation and angry Indians. Much as the disappointed Barlow, who was probably as much of a dupe as the French buyers, missed Connecticut, "the present disposition of Europe . . . toward a general revolution" was too enticing, the "the duty of every individual to assist" it too compelling, to return home. So he hung on in the wake of the Scioto debacle, composing poetry and prose and promoting commercial schemes, usually with London merchants. In 1791, he and his wife Ruth lived in an apartment in the Palais Royale above a "great gambling establishment." They eventually escaped this "attic prison" and returned to London.[18]

In all aspects of his life, Barlow was a devotee of universal revolution and natural sociability. "Men are gregarious in their nature," he wrote in *Advice to the Privileged Orders,* which was published by Joseph Johnson; "they form together in society, not merely from necessity, to avoid the evils of solitude, but from inclination and mutual attachment." In November 1792, Barlow addressed the French National Convention as the agent of the British Society for Constitutional Information. Two months later, he became a citizen of France, a rare designation for a person born elsewhere. But Barlow's faith that other people would rally to revolution when they were forcibly liberated by French troops proved illusory. On a visit to Savoy in early 1793, Barlow decided to seek a seat in the National Convention. The election

the origins of factors with specific reference to the West Indies, see Hancock, *Citizens of the World,* 123–131.

18. MW to Everina Wollstonecraft, Sept. 14, [17]92, in Todd, ed., *Collected Letters,* 203; Joel Barlow to Ruth Barlow, Jan. 1, 1790, Joel Barlow Papers, III, no. 178, Houghton Library, Harvard University; Lewis Leary, "Joel Barlow and William Hayley: A Correspondence," *American Literature,* XXI (1949), 333; Scudder, ed., *Recollections of Samuel Breck,* 170, 171, 172. See Ziesche, *Cosmopolitan Patriots,* 64–87, esp. 75–76. Richard Buel, Jr., *Joel Barlow: American Citizen in a Revolutionary World* (Baltimore, 2011), is a definitive biography. See also James Woodress, *A Yankee's Odyssey: The Life of Joel Barlow* (Philadelphia, 1958).

tested Barlow's faith in universal brotherhood. He told his potential constituents that he loved them as his "fellow-creatures" and "cherish[ed] the
ties which ought to be mutual between us." Together they could "burst the
bands of slavery." But voters refused to support a candidate they thought
likely to associate the interests of mankind with France instead of Savoy.[19]

The glorification of freedom extended to relationships between the
sexes. Many late-eighteenth-century males wanted to celebrate sexuality
as a right, a natural pursuit of pleasure to which all human beings were entitled. The North Atlantic had more than its share of men who moved from
partner to partner at will and demanded, coerced, or purchased the use
of women's bodies. Scorning mutuality, they constructed women as passive facilitators of male pleasure whose social importance was entirely post-
coital, an attitude reinforced by new ideas about reproduction that denied
female agency in conception. No less important, the seduction of multiple
women could secure their reputation as men of formidable talents. Assertive heterosexuality protected men making their way in a literary culture
from charges of effeminacy or weakness. But promiscuous behavior was
also dangerous. It threatened an endless series of venereal diseases that
could scar or kill; it could also as easily ruin as make a man's reputation. Few
characters were more prominent in contemporary novels than the rake,
a man who destroyed himself along with virtuous women because he enslaved himself to desire. The signature figure, Richard Lovelace in Samuel
Richardson's *Clarissa* (1748), had hundreds of literary heirs by the 1790s,
including Coke Clifton in *Anna St. Ives*. A lover who mistreated a woman
might be safe from legal punishment, but he would likely face ostracism or
scorn in polite company. One of the first charges male rivals hurled at each
other was that of libertinism.[20]

19. Joel Barlow, *Advice to the Privileged Orders . . . Part II* (Paris, 1793), 12, 13; Barlow, "A Letter Addressed to the People of Piedmont, on the Advantages of the French Revolution, and the
Necessity of Adopting Its Principles in Italy (1792)," in *The Works of Joel Barlow,* 2 vols. (Gaines-
ville, Fla., 1970), I, 316, 318. See Ziesche, *Cosmopolitan Patriots,* 78–79.

20. Roy Porter, "Mixed Feelings: The Enlightenment and Sexuality in Eighteenth-Century
Britain," in Paul-Gabriel Boucé, ed., *Sexuality in Eighteenth-Century Britain* (Totowa, N.J.,
1982), 4, 7, 13, 18, 20; Clare A. Lyons, *Sex among the Rabble: An Intimate History of Gender
and Power in the Age of Revolution, Philadelphia, 1730–1830* (Chapel Hill, N.C., 2006), 188, 256;
Thomas Laqueur, *Making Sex: Body and Gender from the Greeks to Freud* (Cambridge, Mass.,
1990); Laqueur, "Orgasm, Generation, and the Politics of Reproductive Biology," in Catherine
Gallagher and Laqueur, eds., *The Making of the Modern Body: Sexuality and Society in the
Nineteenth Century* (Berkeley, Calif., 1987), 1–41; Joan Cadden, *Meanings of Sex Difference in
the Middle Ages: Medicine, Science, and Culture* (Cambridge, 1993); Kathleen M. Brown, *Good
Wives, Nasty Wenches, and Anxious Patriarchs: Gender, Race, and Power in Colonial Virginia*

For many men, the new culture of mutuality was about the right to end as well as begin relationships. Just as they could move around politically, so, too, they believed, they could move around sexually. Consent given to a relationship could be rescinded when in the eyes of at least one partner the relationship no longer served its original purpose. After he moved to Paris in 1789, Thomas Christie, cofounder with Joseph Johnson of the *Analytical Review,* formed a liaison with a married Frenchwoman who gave birth to their child. Back in London while the couple awaited her divorce, Christie fell in love with Rebecca Thomson, the granddaughter of a wealthy carpet magnate, and married her, abandoning his previous lover and their child. The Christies immediately set off for an extended honeymoon in Paris. It was in their house that Wollstonecraft and Imlay met. Thomas Paine, an ardent advocate of divorce who had left two wives before he reached Philadelphia in the 1770s, detested marriages contracted out of either the rashness of "ill-grounded passion" or a prosaic utility in which men sought "a wife as they go to *Smithfield* for a horse." But he also believed that virtually all unions, no matter how mutual and ecstatic their origins, tended to "indifference" and "neglect." Eventually, they promoted "separate pleasures" and "utter aversion" and eventually led to "mutual infidelity" and "mutual complaisance." Better to follow the natural practices of American Indians. Native couples stayed together only as long as they shared "'mutual pleasures.'" If "'hate'" existed "'where the only commerce ought to be love,'" a marriage was dissolved. Force might "chain couples together like criminals," but it could not "yoke them like lovers."[21]

The Barlows were continually negotiating the terms of the marriage they had contracted in 1781. More specifically, they were trying to balance the need to cultivate intimacy as lovers with the need to develop relationships with other friends and associates. Husbands deserting wives for long periods of time to devote themselves to trade, war, or politics was hardly a novel phenomenon. What was new was the cultural context. More and

(Chapel Hill, N.C., 1996), 328, 329; Cornelia Hughes Dayton, "Taking the Trade: Abortion and Gender Relations in an Eighteenth-Century New England Village," *WMQ,* 3d Ser., XLVIII (1991), 19–49; Sharon Block, *Rape and Sexual Power in Early America* (Chapel Hill, N.C., 2006), 16–52; and Robert Darnton, *Bohemians before Bohemianism* (Wassenaar, 2006), 36.

21. *An Essay on Marriage; or, The Lawfulness of Divorce, in Certain Cases, Considered; Addressed to the Feelings of Mankind* (Philadelphia, 1788), 3; Thomas Paine, "Reflections on Unhappy Marriages" (1775), in Philip S. Foner, ed., *The Complete Writings of Thomas Paine,* 2 vols. (New York, 1945), II, 1118, 1119, 1120; Paine, "Cupid and Hymen" (1775), ibid., 1116. See Matthew McCormack, *The Independent Man: Citizenship and Gender Politics in Georgian England* (Manchester, 2005), 110, 120, 130.

Figure 6. Thomas Paine. *By William Sharp, after George Romney.*
Engraving, 1793. © *National Portrait Gallery, London*

more spouses saw their relationships as fundamentally romantic, at least in
their origins. Ruth was hardly alone in often interpreting Joel's attention to
politics and business, not as a necessary devotion to the interests of a patriarchal household, but as willful neglect of his best friend and lover. When
Joel sailed alone for Europe in May 1788, he patronizingly reassured his
angry wife. "Don't say I am social and unfeeling when I tell you to cultivate
your fortitude—think that your situation is eligible, write it on the wall every

morning that you are happy and in one week you will find yourself so." Eighteen months later, Barlow was in the midst of a campaign to persuade Ruth, from whom he had not heard a word in months, to join him in Europe. Ruth had good reason to be annoyed. Despite his abiding commitment to his marriage, Joel consistently sacrificed the relationship to his business interests and rarely trusted Ruth to manage her own affairs. Delighted when she decided to join him in Europe, he spelled out how she could arrange for passage and where she should go when she got to London to meet his friends and "agent." All she needed to do was to "be a good girl, by which I mean, have confidence in your self that you are so." But when Ruth wrote from her ship in the English Channel that she was almost in London, her "cruel Husband" apologized for not meeting her in person because he was too busy in Paris. Instead, he sent a friend, Mrs. Blackden, to greet Ruth in London. In the meantime, Joel insisted, he was a faithful lover. He had "not slept with any body but God" since they had parted. Sexual fidelity was not really the issue for Ruth, however; weeks passed before Joel joined his wife in London. His lamentations about enduring "a thousand deaths" could not obscure his choosing "vexatious" business over a reunion with a wife he had not seen in more than two years.[22]

Joel was back in Paris in the winter and spring of 1793, working for Turnbull, Forbes, and Company, seeking election, and claiming that he could not appreciate everything he saw "for want of [his] lovely friend to participate in the pleasure of viewing it." Ruth had had enough. Wishing him a happy new year, she complained of her unhappiness. "Would to Heaven you had not left me, that is, unless it has given you satisfaction." In any case, she had decided to return to Connecticut in the spring. Her "love" had done "wrong" in going to Paris with a disreputable business partner in yet another enterprise. With his affairs "a wreck" and war imminent, she must head home. Joel protested that she would "never think of sailing without [him]. [He] certainly will *never* consent to it." She should come to Paris instead. Ruth should consult with a business partner in London about his prospects in Europe and to let him know what she thought. Paris was safer than she believed. Still, Joel had no choice but to "take no decision" until he heard from Ruth and his partner. If she decided to stay in London, he would respect that decision. But if she was going home he asked her to meet him in Le Havre so they could sail together. In the end, the Barlows reconciled

22. Joel Barlow to Ruth Barlow, May 24, 1788, Barlow Papers, III, no. 177, Jan. 1, 1790, no. 178, Mar. 9, 1790, no. 181, June 20, 1790, no. 182, July 8, 1790, no. 184, July 11, 1790, no. 185, July 19, 1790, no. 187.

again; they remained in Europe for years, but they never stopped arguing with each other.[23]

The negotiation of romantic intimacy between geographically mobile individuals in a fluid revolutionary world was a perpetual challenge. Men and women like the Barlows no longer constituted a local household within a familiar social web of family and neighbors; they thought less in terms of domestic partnership than in terms of emotional connection. They were lovers whose practice of mutuality was always in need of tending. Intimacy was the perpetual exchange, the continual intermingling of sentiments, ideas, and bodies. But men such as Joel Barlow and Gilbert Imlay and women such as Wollstonecraft, Mary Hays, and Ruth Barlow also required multiple friendships as well as ties with political leaders, publishers, and merchants. As much as they craved the concentrated focus of intense passion enjoyed in blissful ignorance of the world around them, they also wanted to speak, write, and encourage revolution, not to mention support themselves financially. As women and men resented competition for the attention of their lovers from friends and associates, so, too, they resented the constraints that the demands of personal intimacy put on their connections with friends and associates. Balancing the role of lover and the role of citizen was a challenge.

Difficult as navigating this new world was for men, it was harder for women, which was part of the reason why they had to contemplate it imaginatively. Women, Wollstonecraft had explained, were handicapped by a culture that denied them not only the legal rights but also the self-confidence enjoyed by men. In a revolutionary order, men and women would cultivate mutuality and choose persuasion over coercion. Wollstonecraft knew men willing to join women in realizing this vision. They did so because they assumed they would benefit both socially and economically; people would respect them because they practiced benevolence. Wollstonecraft also knew that men enjoyed opportunities to turn imagination into reality that were unavailable to women. If and when the time came to choose between private and public lives, between intimacy and society, between love and business, men simply had more freedom than women did. But falling in love in the midst of revolution was all about beginnings, not endings, all about mutuality, not inequality. More than anything else, it was about finding

23. Joel Barlow to Ruth Barlow, Jan. 7, 1793, ibid., no. 199, Ruth Barlow to Joel Barlow, Jan. 1, 1793, IV, no. 538, Jan. 9, 1793, no. 539, Jan. 28, 1793, no. 540, Joel Barlow to Ruth Barlow, Jan. 26, 1793, III, no. 200, Apr. 15, 1793, no. 209, Apr. 19, 1793, no. 210, May 2, 1793, no. 211, June 10, 1793, no. 213.

the confidence in shared intimacy with another person to believe that the future abounded in possibilities.[24]

Planting "the Tree of Liberty in a Foreign Soil"

Imlay arrived in Paris from London around the same time as did Wollstone-craft, armed with a letter of introduction from Thomas Cooper. He was a minor celebrity. *A Topographical Description of North America* had been published on May 21, 1792, by the well-respected John Debrett and had already gone through several editions. Less than a year later, on March 12, 1793, Alexander Hamilton published Imlay's novel, *The Emigrants,* although another edition might have appeared in late 1792. Imlay's behavior was to some extent a product of the particular historical circumstances of the late eighteenth century. An ambitious provincial who had abandoned his family and ventured out into the world to speculate in land, people, language, and politics, Imlay shared with many of his peers conflicting or underdeveloped ideas about the nature of liberty, love, and ambition. Imlay was as much at the mercy of his imagination as Wollstonecraft. But, whereas their imaginations converged in envisioning a natural society of sociable men and women, they diverged in the details of that brave new world. Wollstonecraft focused on women and education, but Imlay came to Paris to harness the resources of the French republic to develop North America in ways that would benefit men like him. He sought state power to encourage war and rebellion, and he found a willing partner in Jacques-Pierre Brissot, a Frenchman interested in extending to the Americas his dream of a liberal order that melded individual ambition, commercial freedom, and political republicanism.[25]

Born in 1754, Jacques-Pierre Brissot de Warville, the thirteenth child of a comfortable proprietor of an inn in Chartres, reveled in alienation from his family. Had he a choice in the matter, he later recalled, he would have preferred to have grown up "under the simple and rustic roof of an American husbandmen." Moving to Paris in the 1770s, Brissot was eager "to com-

24. Julie Ellison, *Cato's Tears and the Making of Anglo-American Emotion* (Chicago, 1999), 9–15; E. J. Clery, *The Feminization Debate in Eighteenth-Century England: Literature, Commerce, and Luxury* (New York, 2004); Barbara Taylor, "Feminists versus Gallants: Sexual Manners and Morals in Enlightenment Britain," 30–52, and Silvia Sebastiani, "Race, Women, and Progress in the Late Scottish Enlightenment," 75–96, both in Sarah Knott and Barbara Taylor, eds., *Women, Gender, and Enlightenment* (2005; rpt. New York, 2007).

25. See W. M. Verhoeven and Amanda Gilroy, "Introduction," in Gilbert Imlay, *The Emigrants* (1793), ed. Verhoeven and Gilroy (New York, 1998), ix–xlix; and Verhoeven, *Imlay,* 96, 124, 138.

mence with an important work." Despite publishing extensively, going to the right places, and meeting the right people, he did not come close to achieving his goal. Like many of his peers, he became obsessive about liberty as the absence of coercion; he opposed capital punishment, torture, and the jailing of debtors. The absolute power of monarchs and aristocrats as well as the absurd influence of established cultural organizations interfered with the natural workings of the world, inhibiting liberty and thwarting ambition. Brissot's life fell apart in 1784 when he was arrested for mocking Queen Marie Antoinette and government officials in print. Likely, Brissot won his release by telling authorities what he knew about the literary underground in Paris. In any case, he left the Bastille an angry man, determined to wreak revenge on his enemies. He wrote articles and pamphlets to benefit his friend Etienne Clavière's investments in the Paris stock market, particularly speculations in the vast debt the Americans had acquired while winning their independence. After a short visit to the United States, Brissot published a glowing account of the Republic intended to revive interest in American land.[26]

In the early 1790s, the irrepressible Brissot rode his journalistic talents and his commitment to *"the universal emancipation of Men"* into the Convention and a position of political influence as an advocate of the abolition of slavery and an aggressive foreign policy. Brissot was a prominent figure in the network of Girondins, men and women who advocated natural commerce as the organizing principle of society and freedom from all restraint on individual choice. Brissot longed to see "a Republican Government established" in France and *"philosophy triumphant every where."* The Girondins merged the defense of the republic against its growing number of enemies with a missionary zeal to transform Europe as a whole. The future of all mankind depended on the revolution, which meant that France could not be conquered nor Paris starved. The Swiss reformer Étienne Dumont

---

26. J. P. Brissot, *The Life of J. P. Brissot . . .* , 2d ed. (London, 1794), 5, 7–8, 17. See Durand Echeverria, "Introduction," in Brissot, *New Travels,* trans. Vamos and Echeverria, x, xix; Robert C. Darnton, "The Grub Street Style of Revolution: J.-P. Brissot, Police Spy," *Journal of Modern History,* XL (1968), 301–327; Darnton, "A Spy in Grub Street," in Darnton, *The Literary Underground of the Old Regime* (Cambridge, Mass., 1982), 41–70; Darnton, "The Brissot Dossier," *French Historical Studies,* XVII, no. 1 (Spring 1991), 191–205; Frederick A. de Luna, "The Dean Street Style of Revolution: J.-P. Brissot, *Jeune Philosophe,*" ibid., 159–190; Simon Burrows, "The Innocence of Jacques-Pierre Brissot," *Historical Journal,* XLVI (2003), 843–871; and Leonore Loft, *Passion, Politics, and Philosophie: Rediscovering J.-P. Brissot* (Westport, Conn., 2002). Eloise Ellery, *Brissot de Warville: A Study in the History of the French Revolution* (1915; rpt. New York, 1970), is dated but useful.

remembered Brissot as a vain enthusiast who "fancied himself a pure and virtuous citizen" because he claimed to be devoid of avarice and ambition. Others ridiculed Brissot as a man who invoked the public good in order to insure his personal profit. Both admirers and detractors miss the point. Brissot, like Imlay and others, refused to distinguish between social change and personal opportunity. His ambition was to thrive in a world transformed.[27]

In the winter of 1792–1793, Brissot set his sights on North America. France had remained a significant presence in the Mississippi Valley long after its defeat in the Seven Years' War in part because sovereignty over the interior of the continent continued to be disputed. The citizens of the United States were volatile; thousands of Spaniards awaited deliverance; and French brethren were hungry for liberty. Brissot and his friends dreamed of liberating Louisiana from Spain and establishing New Orleans as a capital of revolution. A new republic would threaten British interests, contain the unpredictable United States, and destabilize Spanish authority around the Gulf of Mexico and the Caribbean. The practice of free trade would woo alienated Americans in the Ohio Valley eager to open the Mississippi River. Citizens who had shaken off Great Britain would not allow a few Spaniards to close rivers and seas. Kentuckians needed little provocation to move against New Orleans. In this spirit, Brissot and company decided to send thirty-year-old Edmond Genêt to the United States to encourage American expeditions against the British and the Spanish, negotiate a new treaty between France and the United States, and collect money the Americans owed the French. Genêt, who arrived in Charleston, South Carolina, in April 1793, offered Americans an agreement to promote commercial relationships between France and the United States in the shared cause of a liberal revolution.[28]

While Genêt was preparing to sail to North America, Imlay was ingratiat-

27. Brissot, *Life,* 35; J. P. Brissot, *Deputy of Eure and Loire, to His Constituents, on the Situation of the National Convention; on the Influence of the Anarchists, and the Evils It Has Caused; and on the Necessity of Annihilating That Influence in Order to Save the Republic* (London, 1794), 2; Étienne Dumont, *Recollections of Mirabeau and of the First Two Legislative Assemblies of France* (London, 1832), 313.

28. Brissot, *To His Constituents,* 65. See Frederick J. Turner, "The Origin of Genet's Projected Attack on Louisiana and the Floridas," *American Historical Review,* III (1898), 654–655; Stanley Elkins and Eric McKitrick, *The Age of Federalism: The Early American Republic, 1788–1800* (New York, 1993), 330–336, 343; Anna Cornelia Clauder, *American Commerce as Affected by the Wars of the French Revolution and Napoleon, 1793–1812* (Philadelphia, 1932), 28. See Stephen Shapiro's discussion of the impact of these events in *The Culture and Commerce of the Early American Novel: Reading the Atlantic World-System* (University Park, Pa., 2008), 101–107. An excellent overview is François Furstenberg, "The Significance of the Trans-Appalachian Frontier in Atlantic History," *American Historical Review,* CXIII (2008), 647–677.

ing himself with important French men eager to listen to a recent resident of Kentucky. With Brissot's endorsement, Imlay gave a deposition to the Committee of Public Safety in which he attempted to persuade the French republic to sponsor an expedition of Americans against Spanish Louisiana. Seizing New Orleans, which linked the vast expanses of North America with the islands of the Caribbean, would serve the interests of France, the United States, and the cause of freedom everywhere. It would weaken the Spanish by forcing them to defend their colonies throughout the hemisphere; it put pressure on the selfish residents of the Atlantic regions of the United States to join their fellow citizens west of the Appalachians in developing the interior of the continent. Freeing the "millions of miserable inhabitants" of the despotic Spanish empire and promoting the general cause of free trade, the liberation of New Orleans would become another episode in France's "'generous struggle'" to replace "'universal despotism'" with "'universal liberty.'" With French financial and moral support, forty thousand European Americans, many of them military veterans "burning with the Fire of liberty," would act quickly and decisively. Like their European brethren, they were "embittered against Spain, which continues to violate their rights, by erecting barriers against their natural rise to prosperity and by paralyzing key industrial activity and competition." As always, Imlay imagined that the establishment of natural commerce would cure all ills, social and political as well as economic.[29]

Imlay was not exaggerating when he assured his colleagues in Paris that Americans west of the Appalachian Mountains were discontented. Like other Kentuckians, the prominent figure George Rogers Clark felt scorned by his "country." Virginia and the United States had failed to consolidate his "successful and almost unexampled enterprizes" in securing the Ohio Valley. Now, hundreds of former comrades and Indian allies would march together "under [his] banners" against Louisiana. They would join the French war "against almost all the Despots of Europe," an event of even greater consequence than the American War of Independence. Everywhere everyone was "deeply interested" in the struggle against monarchy, aristocracy, and "clerical bigotry." If the French gave him supplies and a legal

29. Brissot to Otto, Mar. 26, 1793, Correspondance Politique, Espagne, vol. 635, doc. 295, Archives des Affaires Éttangères (AAE), Paris, "Observations du Cap. Imlay, Traduites de L'Anglais," Correspondance Politique, État-Unis, Louisiane et Florides, supplement 7, doc. 1. I have generally followed Verhoeven's translations. See Verhoeven, *Imlay,* 249 n. 45, 250 n. 60. I am grateful to Manuel Covo for sending me digital copies of the original documents and to my colleague P. Renée Baernstein for helping me read them in their entirety.

commission, Clark would free Louisiana and perhaps New Spain. More, he and his men would "instantly . . . become citizens of the French Republic." From Paris, Brissot's friend Thomas Paine encouraged Clark's associate and future brother-in-law Dr. James O'Fallon. By extending revolution into the Mississippi Valley, the Kentuckians would secure their land claims and their reputation. "The first characters in Europe are in arms; some with the bayonet, some with the pen, and some with the two-edged sword of Declamation, in favor of Liberty." Despite the best efforts of the "tyrants of the earth," the French persisted "unshaken, unsubdued, unsubdueable, and undaunted." Unlike "slaves chained to the oar of compulsory power," they were free men fighting "for conscience sake." In the nineteenth century, when borders seemed fixed and loyalties more permanent, this behavior would be called treason. But in the unstable borderlands of North America of the 1790s, nothing seemed fixed, including the permanence of the United States or its dominion over the Ohio Valley.[30]

Alas, the same was true in Europe. Military defeats in Belgium encouraged Brissot's enemies, who soon threatened the power he and his friends had enjoyed for months. On April 20, Paine lamented major setbacks to the cause of "extending liberty through the greatest part of Europe," let alone North America. And what did Imlay think? Like his friends, he was gambling on Brissot and his allies staying in power in Paris. Brissot, for his part, was an inveterate gambler who was counting on a multitude of adventurers such as Imlay to galvanize global revolution. Like Mary Wollstonecraft, Brissot trusted Imlay in no small part because he was an American, that is, someone for whom a revolution in favor of natural commerce was supposedly a way of life.[31]

"Another Race of Beings"

Although some Europeans disdained the republican experiment as anarchy, radicals imagined Americans blessed with advantages. Growing up in

---

30. George Rogers Clark to [the French Minister], Feb. 5, 1793, in "Selections from the Draper Collection in the Possession of the State Historical Society of Wisconsin, to Elucidate the Proposed French Expedition Under George Rogers Clark against Louisiana, in the Years 1793–1794," *Annual Report of the American Historical Association for the Year 1896*, 2 vols. (Washington, D.C., 1897), I, 967, 968, 969, 970; Paine to James O'Fallon, Feb. 17, 1793, in Foner, ed., *Writings of Paine*, II, 1328, 1330.

31. Paine to Thomas Jefferson, Apr. 20, 1793, in Foner, ed., *Writings of Paine*, II, 1330. See Richard Munthe Brace, "General Dumouriez and the Girondins, 1792–1793," *American Historical Review*, LVI (1951), 493–509.

a natural environment far from the artificial bulwarks of a corrupt European order—monarchy, aristocracy, and established churches—they practiced social commerce naturally. Thus, when they manfully seceded from degenerate Britain and created a republic, they did so without the enthusiasm convulsing Paris. Thomas Paine argued that America "has something in it which generates and encourages great ideas." "Man becomes what he ought. He sees his species, not with the inhuman idea of a natural enemy, but as kindred; and the example shows to the artificial world, that man must go back to nature for information." The laws "of trade and commerce, whether with respect to the intercourse of individuals, or of nations, are laws of mutual and reciprocal interest." "They are followed and obeyed because it is in the interest of the parties so to do, and not on account of any formal laws their governments may impose or interpose." Wollstonecraft concluded that Americans were more likely to maintain moderation and reciprocity than Europeans. They "appeared to be another race of beings, men formed to enjoy the advantages of society, and not merely to benefit those who governed."[32]

Any number of writers insisted that the manners of Americans sharply diverged from those of Europeans. When Frank Henley, the hero of Thomas Holcroft's *Anna St. Ives,* contemplates where a man like him should live, he thinks "of sailing to America." There he "may aid the struggles of liberty, may freely publish all which the efforts of reason can teach me, and . . . form a society of savages, who seem in consequence of their very ignorance to have a less quantity of error, and therefore to be less liable to repel truth than those whose information is more multifarious." These ideas were shared by a wide range of radical essayists and poets, most famously Samuel Taylor Coleridge and Robert Southey, who, in 1794, imagined what they called a pantisocracy ("government by all") in the Susquehanna Valley of Pennsylvania. Neither Coleridge nor Southey migrated to America. Others did, including Thomas Cooper and Joseph Priestley in 1794. So did French men and women and, later in the decade, tens of thousands of Irish men and women. The United States was a refuge and an opportunity.[33]

Europeans knew about America mainly from books by other Europeans

32. Thomas Paine, *Rights of Man, Part Second,* in Foner, ed., *Writings of Paine,* I, 354, 359; MW, *An Historical and Moral View of the Origin and Progress of the French Revolution* (London, 1794), in Todd and Butler, eds., *Works of Wollstonecraft,* VI, 20.

33. Thomas Holcroft, *Anna St. Ives* (1792), ed. Peter Faulkner (London, 1970), 292. See Suzanne Desan, "Transatlantic Spaces of Revolution: The French Revolution, *Sciotomanie,* and American Lands," *Journal of Early Modern History,* XII (2008), 467–505.

that often constituted a proxy conversation about the past, present, and future of Europe. Some writers imagined the disintegrative tendencies of life on the marchlands of civilization, pointing to American Indians as evidence of the detrimental effect of a wet environment. The inhabitants of North America might someday achieve the standards of living available in Edinburgh, London, or Paris, but they had a long way to go. More radical writers fancied North America as a foil to Europe, an open, natural world that produced and rewarded ambitious men of talent. Somewhere in the middle of this spectrum was J. Hector St. John de Crèvecoeur, the author of the influential *Letters from an American Farmer.* Born into an aristocratic family in Normandy in 1735, Crèvecoeur migrated to Canada two decades later, fought against the British, and then settled on a farm in New York with an American wife. During the War of Independence, he went to France to secure his children's inheritance. Originally published in England and Ireland in 1782, *Letters from an American Farmer* was revised, expanded, translated, and published in France in 1784. The book helped shape European images of the United States, although it made little impact in the American Republic when it appeared in 1793. Despite its reputation as an affirmation of natural commerce, *Letters from an American Farmer* was in fact psychologically complex and often dark.[34]

Crèvecoeur argued that North America generally nurtured "a new mode of living, a new social system." "Here [Europeans] are become men," pursuing their "*self-interest*" in a harmonious balance of nature and civilization. But this sociability flourished almost exclusively in areas between the Atlantic Ocean and "the great woods." North America was a place of extremes. In the relatively undeveloped South, isolated men enslaved Africans and inhibited social commerce; on the highly commercial island of Nantucket, greedy men and women allowed irrational desire to undermine social ties; and, in the backcountry, ignorant hunters perverted liberty into the right to do as one pleased without regard to other human beings. The residents of areas such as the Ohio Valley were "ferocious, gloomy, and unsocial" people who indulged "a strange sort of lawless[ness]" and raised "a

---

34. Susan Manning, "Introduction," in J. Hector St. John de Crèvecoeur, *Letters from an American Farmer,* ed. Manning (Oxford, 1997), vii–xl. See also Durand Echeverria, *Mirage in the West: A History of the French Image of American Society to 1815* (Princeton, N.J., 1957); Colin Bonwick, *English Radicals and the American Revolution* (Chapel Hill, N.C., 1977), 216–266; and Anca Munteanu, "Visionary and Artistic Transformations in Blake's *Visions of the Daughters of Albion,*" *Journal of European Studies,* XXXVI (2006), 61–83. For an astute perspective from an American historian, see Joyce Appleby, "Recovering America's Historic Diversity: Beyond Exceptionalism," *Journal of American History,* LXXIX (1992), 419–431.

mongrel breed, half civilized, half savage." "Unlimited freedom" in a "lonely situation" was as dangerous as tyranny.[35]

The War of Independence had encouraged "a convulsed and a half-dissolved" society whose members were subject to whims and coercion. In the late 1770s, Crèvecoeur and his neighbors in New York had become prisoners in their own homes. Exhausted "with feeling for the miseries of others, every one feels now for himself alone." Fear "transported [them] beyond that degree of calmness which is necessary to delineate our thoughts." Like his sense of empathy, Crèvecoeur's reason seemed to have deserted him. How was he to choose between king and Congress when men "easily . . . pass from loving to hating and cursing one another!" War made men into animals. Saying farewell to "education, principles, [and] love of [his] country," Crèvecoeur devoted himself to "self-preservation." He opted to move his family to an Indian village where—in a vision common among European intellectuals—he imagined a world of natural simplicity and contentment. He also brought a young man who loved his daughter, thus precluding the possibility of an abhorrent connection with an Indian male. Unfortunately for Crèvecoeur, reality was unkind. While he was in France, his property was ruined, his wife killed, and his children lost during vicious fighting between Americans and Indians. Reunited with his children when he returned in 1783, he served as the French consul in New York and speculated in land until he returned to France for good in 1790. *Letters from an American Farmer* was an often horrific depiction of America as an unstable world. Nevertheless, many Europeans persisted in projecting their aspirations onto the new Republic. Among them was Brissot, who went to America in the late 1780s and published his own take on the continent.[36]

Although Wollstonecraft concluded that the author of *New Travels in the United States of America* was naive, Brissot's observations about conjugal felicity intrigued her. According to Brissot, the citizens of Boston were "tender husbands, loving—almost adoring—fathers, and kind masters." Women enjoyed their liberty, too, because they did not have to worry about seduction and deception. Once married, women were "just as natural, kind, and sociable." In Boston, "all marriages" were "happy, and being happy, [were] pure." Wollstonecraft suspected Brissot was overly impressed with the "friendly intercourse" between the sexes because he was used to artificial rather than natural behavior. Still, she agreed that mixed-gender social com-

---

35. Crèvecoeur, *Letters from an American Farmer,* ed. Manning, 42, 43, 44, 46, 51, 52.
36. Ibid., 187, 188, 191, 193.

merce thrived in America. "Men and women mix together like social beings; and, respecting the marriage vow, mutually improve their understandings by discussing subjects that interest the whole race." They did not indulge in the idle and vain conversations of European *gentlemen* and *ladies.*" In general, Brissot averred, Bostonians were becoming sociable and refined, if not intellectual or artistic. Not everything was perfect in the United States, especially slavery. In defiance of the many Americans who defended the institution, some, mostly Quakers, were rising in righteous indignation against the institution. They were learning "to act as though one loved humanity, to consent to sacrificing one's own interests, to being mocked and ridiculed, to dividing one's goods among the poor, to free one's Negroes—to do all these things." Without kings or slaves, with canals enabling commerce, Brissot envisioned a future "festival in which Peruvians, Mexicans, Free Americans, and Frenchmen embrace one another as brothers, anathematizing tyranny and blessing the reign of liberty that brings all men into universal harmony."[37]

Marie-Jean-Antoine-Nicholas de Caritat, marquis de Condorcet, had a more sophisticated vision. Born in Picardy in 1743, Condorcet had become a well-respected mathematician and philosopher in Paris, especially after his admission to the French Academy in 1782. Like many of his contemporaries, he held that there were two major means to human happiness: the "first comprises everything which assures and extends the free enjoyment of man's natural rights," and the second included provisions for human comfort and encouragement. Condorcet believed that human happiness would increase in proportion to the elimination of monopolies and the expansion of commerce in both goods and ideas. Nothing was more valuable than "the communication of knowledge." In this regard, Americans had much to offer Europeans. Thanks to the wide availability of land, they offered the "spectacle of a great people among whom the rights of man are respected." A man secure in his property and person acquired "a more elevated and compassionate soul," finding "probity easy" and courage plentiful. How could Europeans ignore this example? How could they persist in maintaining their "overcomplicated machines in which the multitude of springs make the working violent, irregular, and troublesome; in which so many counterweights, supposed in theory to balance one another, com-

37. MW, review of *Nouveau voyage dans les Etas-Unies de l'Amerique Septentrionale . . .* , by J. P. Brissot, *Analytical Review,* XI (September 1791), in Todd and Butler, eds., *Works of Wollstonecraft,* VII, 390, 391, 392; Brissot, *New Travels,* trans. Vamos and Echeverria, 85, 86, 89–99, 166, 423.

bine in reality to weigh upon the people." The Americans would surely goad Europe into milder laws. Otherwise, Europeans would emigrate in droves.[38]

Thus, when Imlay, trading on being an American and a Kentuckian to boot, wrote a novel called *The Emigrants,* he was entering into a well-established discourse about the possibilities of a community in North America organized around the practice of natural sociability rather than artificial institutions. Whether Imlay believed what he wrote, he gave people what they wanted to read. The novel elaborated on *A Topographical Description of North America*'s commonplace comparison of "the simple manners and rational life of the Americans" in the Ohio Valley "with the distorted and unnatural habits of the Europeans": "We have more of simplicity, and you more of art.—We have more of nature, and you more of the world. . . . You have more hypocrisy—we are sincere." But the novel in which Imlay recapitulates many of the attitudes and arguments of European intellectuals is also a defiant postcolonial denunciation of Great Britain by an angry American fixated on sexuality as the foundation of masculinity.[39]

Written in epistolary form, *The Emigrants* narrates the migration of an English family from Pennsylvania to the Illinois Country in the immediate aftermath of the American War of Independence. As the two central characters—daughter Caroline and the American Captain James Arlington—fall in love, they imagine a society in which people choose each other because of sympathy and self-interest and learn that autonomy and mutuality are complementary. The contrast with imperial Britain is stark. British husbands are brutes whose authority rests on coercion, savages who must force their wives to obey them. The degeneracy of British husbands reinforces the degeneracy of British governors. British law makes romance (including adultery) illegal while it legitimizes domestic tyranny (marriage). The *"barbarous codes of a savage world, have continued to oppress and restrain the acts of volition on the part of women, when the most licentious bounds on the part of men, have found impunity from the prejudices of the world."* Imlay makes his case by narrating the history of marriages in Great Britain in such detail that we can suppose he spoke from experience. But, whereas British radical intellectuals promoted a universal culture of mixed-gender sociability in the place of a universal regime of tyranny, the American identifies these regimes with specific nations. His criticism of Britain is criticism of

38. Marie-Jean-Antoine-Nicholas de Caritat, marquis de Condorcet, *On the Influence of the American Revolution on Europe* (1786), in Keith Michael Baker, ed., *Condorcet: Selected Writings* (Indianapolis, Ind., 1976), 72, 75, 77, 78, 80.

39. Imlay, *Topographical Description*, 1, 179.

British men. They have selfishly exploited their power to pass laws for their "own immediate convenience" rather than the greater good. Because marriage was the means through which men maintained control of women's property and their bodies, any discussion of divorce or alternative relationships ipso facto was subversive of their power.[40]

Imlay illustrates his argument with a tale of a British marriage destroyed by a degenerate husband. In London, when Caroline's older sister Eliza's husband Mr. F—— ruins himself with unrestrained debauchery and reckless spending, he asks Eliza to prostitute herself. It is a "cruel circumstance" that a woman must sacrifice her body because of the imposition of a husband so obviously "impotent." A good husband would respect his wife by restraining his desires and helping her to realize hers; he would never contemplate treating her like a slave or an animal in such a patent defiance of her wishes. If divorce were easily accessible, Eliza could have rescued herself. Alas, she can only find "a refuge against brutality" in dependence on another man. What else could "a *woman*" do? Imlay again presents adultery as a socially acceptable alternative to rape masquerading as marriage. Why should not "a woman of feeling," when she "has been imposed upon and insulted," find solace "in the tender solicitude of some friend or lover?" Adulterous women should be treated like human beings, not property. Conveniently, the suddenly ashamed (and still ruined) husband dies the death of a coward "by putting a loaded pistol to his head." Imlay's point, however, is that neither Eliza nor her husband should have had to endure such misery in the first place. The problem is, not love, but marriage, and making divorce easier for women is only a partial solution. The problems of Imlay's couples parallel imperial problems. The answer is revolution: to emigrate is to secede.[41]

Civilized people could not move to the Ohio Valley and find happiness immediately, however. They had to develop a wilderness into a commercial society, something in between a complete state of nature (associated with Indians) and the artificiality of Europe. Mixed-gender sociability would thrive in the Ohio Valley. Divorce will be legal, and people will "obtain those gratifications" they need for their happiness without "recourse to . . . cunning and stratagem." What was wrong with women as well as men looking "abroad for those amusements which alone can compensate for domestic

---

40. Imlay, *Emigrants,* ed. Verhoeven and Gilroy, 105, 114. See Toby L. Ditz, "The New Men's History and the Peculiar Absence of Gendered Power: Some Remedies from Early American Gender History," *Gender and History,* XVI (2004), 1–21.

41. Imlay, *Emigrants,* ed. Verhoeven and Gilroy, 239, 241, 250, 252.

feuds"? Imlay lamented the "most inhuman" situation of "a woman of honour and delicacy . . . driven to seek for some mitigation of the sufferings of an afflicted bosom, in the friendship of an ingenuous heart." No one should suffer poverty and contempt when friendship naturally prompts "more tender ties—ties which spring from the finest feelings, and which characterize the most humane and exalted souls." Sympathy for afflicted women aside, Imlay spends far more time contemplating how to end relationships than he does considering how to sustain them. As important, he justifies the sexual liberation of British wives as a political act. His logic is clear: British women are married to corrupt brutes; American men are empathetic; therefore, British women should leave British men for American men.[42]

Like Wollstonecraft, Imlay believed "we are by nature sociable beings" who treasure friendship. People should share their "joys," "pains," and "comforts" in "cordial sympathy." But Imlay rarely speaks of heterosocial friendship without highlighting sexuality. Early in the novel, while escorting seventeen-year-old Caroline into dinner at a party in Pittsburgh, Pennsylvania, Arlington—or is he Imlay?—notes her "plain white muslin gown,—her light hair hung in loose ringlets down her back," and the failure of her "thin handkerchief" to cover the "ten thousand beauties" of her "bosom." Later, watching her recover from a chance encounter with three Indians, Arlington "felt in the returning pulsations of her hand, the high beating tones of Nature vibrate through every part of [his] frame; and in this ecstatic moment, when language was mute, and when Caroline's eyes spoke the most ineffable things, [he] was lost in the elysium of intoxicated desire." No wonder Caroline wants him as much he wants her.[43]

American men, unlike their British counterparts, exercise legitimate dominion. They earn respect, even deference, because they pay attention to women and encourage them to embrace sexual as well as domestic liberation. They are decisive as well as sympathetic. Arlington, "one of the most heroic soldiers in the American army," demonstrates "the greatest diffidence, and distant politeness; except it is those with whom he is very intimate, when he is occasionally highly facetious and entertaining." When he holds her hand, Caroline confides to her sister, "my whole soul appeared to be rebelling against the despotism of restraint, and it was not possible any longer for me to controul its emotions." She "felt that supreme bliss which flows from the banquet of pure love, in the genial hours of sentimental rap-

42. Ibid., 32, 43, 47.
43. Ibid., 43, 49, 67.

ture." Caroline, in short, does what Imlay thinks women should do: she accepts natural desire. Sociability works: Caroline helps Arlington restrain his passions while he helps her to indulge hers.[44]

Later in the novel, Arlington flees from Louisville, Kentucky, across the Ohio River looking for peace of mind. Rejecting urban society, he "will live in this uncultivated, and uncivilized waste, until my person shall become as wild as my senses." The region north of the Ohio, however, is no middle ground, no paradise of natural freedom. Caroline pursues Arlington across the river and is captured by Indians whose lack of respect for persons and property testifies to their exclusion from a balanced society. Arlington quickly rescues her. Deprived of her freedom—and much of her clothing—Caroline incites intense sexual interest from her savior. Catching sight of her, Arlington feels his "swelling heart beat with joy." He relishes "a glance from the brilliant eyes of the most divine woman upon earth, torn into shatters by the bushes and briars, with scarcely covering left to hide the transcendence of her beauty." "Embracing her," he is transported by "the divinity of feminine charms" until his servant Andrew covers her with a "*surtoute*" and puts her in the raft that will carry them back to civilization. "Her bosom disclosed the temple of bliss, while her lips distilled nectareous sweets." Arlington stares at her breasts, "more transparent than the effulgence of Aurora . . . and which [were] now half naked." He had "to extinguish the light, to preserve [his] reason." Arlington does not act on his desire in the manner of a British brute; nor does he, like the primitive, childlike Indians who cannot act on desires they do not have, ignore her. Sexuality is a good thing when both partners desire it, not because marriage sanctions it.[45]

In the end, Caroline and Arlington find "mutual happiness" on a plantation north of the Ohio River. They will promote "the dignity of man" with a democratic government that will nurture "love, and harmony." In divisions of labor gendered by nature and choice, Caroline will be busy working with the wives of Arlington's "fellow soldiers." Together they will structure an environment that encourages education and exchange and thus autonomy and mutuality. In "small societies," people are more likely to become friends, to know "the human heart," to converse and think of themselves in terms of their relationships with their neighbors, to nurture usefulness and discourage vulgar and vicious habits. The Arlingtons and their families and

44. Ibid., 41, 180.
45. Ibid., 186, 192–193, 198, 199, 200, 203.

friends were lucky to live in the Ohio Valley, a place where "love seems to have gained absolute and unbounded empire." Interestingly, Imlay says virtually nothing about the consequences of romantic love—children.[46]

Beyond valorizing American masculinity at the expense of British, Imlay qualifies assumptions about American liberty by emphasizing the importance of male agency in its development. Deliberate revolution as much as natural evolution had created the American Republic and promoted the empire of love. Shaped and tempered by war, not only against the degenerate British but also against the altogether too natural American Indians, Imlay puts a premium on decisive action. Caroline needs Arlington to do things she cannot do: engage in trade, transform forests into fields, preside over their small society, and rescue her from Indians. Like many American males, Arlington treasures his personal independence, or rather his freedom from dependence on dissolute English tyrants and European fops; his freedom has been naturalized by the informed consent of an educated woman fully capable of telling a good man from a bad one. Mixed-gender social commerce is in part a means to an end: the love of a beautiful, intelligent woman reflects well on her lover. American men do not have to force women to have sex with them because women desire sex with them, just as generally people will defer to their superiors' judgment naturally, not because they are ordered to obey, but because they will benefit from doing so. By its very nature, all commerce is fluid. Things change. In that spirit, Imlay celebrates an individual's right to withdraw from as well as enter into relationships. Just as American colonists had seceded from an abusive British Empire, so, too, wives ought to be able to leave abusive husbands. Such thinking is a fine indulgence of fancy for young men roaming the Atlantic reinventing themselves as they wished, but far more of a risk for women, who could find themselves pregnant, alone, and unsupported.[47]

---

46. Ibid., 231, 234, 235, 247. See Amanda Gilroy, "'Espousing the Cause of Oppressed Women': Cultural Captivities in Gilbert Imlay's *The Emigrants*," in W. M. Verhoeven and Beth Dolan Kautz, eds., *Revolutions and Watersheds: Transatlantic Dialogues, 1775–1815* (Amsterdam, 1999), 191–205. Gilroy points out that the United States "did not necessarily offer women a country of their own. . . . The novel's espousal of the rights of women is predicated on the stereotype of feminine weakness" (201). See also Catherine Kaplan, "Elihu Hubbard Smith's 'The Institutions of the Republic of Utopia,'" *EAL*, XXXV (2000), 294–308; and Juliet Shields, "Genuine Sentiments and Gendered Liberties: Migration and Marriage in Gilbert Imlay's *The Emigrants*," in Toni Bowers and Tita Chico, eds., *Atlantic Worlds in the Long Eighteenth Century: Seduction and Sentiment* (New York, 2012), 333–348.

47. See Barbara Taylor, "Feminists versus Gallants. Manners and Morals in Enlightenment Britain," 30–52, and Silvia Sebastiani, "'Race,' Women, and Progress in the Scottish Enlighten-

"Habitual Affection"

Wollstonecraft enjoyed a degree of contentment with Imlay in the spring and summer of 1793 previously unknown to her. For many weeks, they met at "the barrier," one of the tollgates in the Paris city wall, and at their lodgings, living in the moment and taking pleasure in each other's company. By August, Wollstonecraft was certain that they had made a long-term commitment. Imlay could "scarcely imagine with what pleasure I anticipate the day, when we are to begin almost to live together." He would "smile to hear how many plans of employment I have in my head, now that I am confident my heart has found peace in your bosom." Wishing him good night, she wanted to kiss him, "glowing with gratitude to Heaven, and affection to you." She liked "the word affection, because it signifies something habitual; and we are soon to meet, to try whether we have mind enough to keep our hearts warm." Thirty-four-year-old Mary Wollstonecraft had found the fulfillment of a rational desire in the arms of a natural man who imagined the future in terms she recognized.[48]

Neither Wollstonecraft nor Imlay allowed their affair to isolate them from their friends. They spent some of the early summer of 1793 with a floating collection of friends later termed the British Club. Dining out together or at Thomas Paine's house in the Rue Fauxbourg in Saint-Denis, a village about seven miles north of central Paris, the friends, who included Paine, the Christies, the Barlows, and the Rolands, spent their evenings in conversation. The Saint-Denis house and its grounds constituted an oasis of sociability. A wall surrounded the house and its yard full of ducks, turkeys, geese, rabbits, and two pigs. An adjacent garden of roughly one acre produced delicious oranges, apricots, and plums that were "the best [Paine] ever tasted."

ment," 75–96, in Knott and Taylor, eds., *Women, Gender, and Enlightenment.* Leonard Tennenhouse, "Libertine America," *Differences: A Journal of Feminist Cultural Studies,* XI (Fall 1999–2000), 1–28, notes the different roles of the libertine in American and British seduction stories. In "American stories," libertines tend "to break up the traditional patriarchal family in a way that ushered in a new family based on mutual consent" (6). As important, American seduction stories tend to be about male competition for women, not, as so often was the case in Britain, about a young woman's finding happiness with a wealthier and cultivated aristocrat (9). In America, libertines disrupt a British system of relationships to create an American one. On British literary types and the role of rascals in securing their reputation and influence through behavior rather than by birth or wealth, see Erin Mackie, *Rakes, Highwaymen, and Pirates: The Making of the Modern Gentlemen in the Eighteenth Century* (Baltimore, 2009).

48. MW to Imlay, "Monday night, past twelve o'clock," [circa August 1793], in Todd, ed., *Collected Letters,* 228.

The friends spent much of their time in the garden. They read newspapers, wrote letters, and entertained themselves with games of marbles, chess, whist, and cribbage. In the evening, if they did not visit the Brissots or other French friends, they talked, sometimes about their previous lives, sometimes about the news of the day. With the rise of their enemies, the Jacobins, recalled one member of the circle, they "used to pass [their] Evenings together very frequently either in conversation or any amusement [which] might tend to dissipate those gloomy impressions." Imlay, he noted, paid Wollstonecraft "more than common attention."[49]

Jean-Jacques Rousseau had celebrated the advantages of mixed company in a setting not unlike the house of Saint-Denis. Away from "the fashions of the city," a society of "select . . . friends who love pleasure and know something about it" could live simple and therefore happy lives. Women and men would work, exercise, play, and dine as they pleased—in the garden, on the grass, or under a tree. Their meals would be "neither orderly nor elegant." Independent people would enjoy one another's company because they chose to do so, because it pleased them. "From this cordial and moderate familiarity there would arise . . . a playful conflict a hundred times more charming than politeness and more likely to bind together [their] hearts." But these friends wanted more than personal harmony. They were practicing their call for a society governed entirely through mutual choice. Social commerce was not an escape from the world; it was the means of transforming it.[50]

The friends met in Paris as well. Helen Maria Williams welcomed visitors to her salon in the winter of 1792–1793. Sophie de Grouchy, the young wife of the marquis de Condorcet and later the definitive translator of Adam Smith's *Theory of Moral Sentiments,* had long entertained the likes of Brissot, Thomas Jefferson, Adam Smith, Madame de Staël, and Olympe de Gouges, author of the 1791 *Declaration of the Rights of Woman and Female Citizen.* Most important to the friends of Wollstonecraft and Imlay was Marie-Jeanne Roland de La Platière, the wife of prominent Girondin Jean-Marie Roland de La Platière. Madame Roland took pride in avoiding "high society," preferring "a studious life" away from "gossip" and "fools." In the first years of the revolution, she held dinners twice a week for her husband's

49. Thomas Paine, "Forgetfulness" (1794), in Foner, ed., *Writings of Paine,* II, 1123; Moncure Daniel Conway, *The Life of Thomas Paine . . .* , 2 vols. (New York, 1909), II, 64–69; I. B. Johnson to William Godwin, Nov. 13, 1797, Oxford, Bodleian, MS Abinger c. 3, fols. 102–103.

50. Jean-Jacques Rousseau, *Émile; or, On Education* (1762), trans. Allan Bloom (New York, 1979), 351, 352.

political friends, and afterward they discussed what had transpired. Roland asserted that her education in history and philosophy and her "devouring passion for human relationships" were the sources of her abiding interest in politics, by which she meant "the art of ruling men and organising their happiness in society." She had no patience for "the petty intrigues of a court or the sterile controversies of gossips and fools." Despite Roland's claim that women should listen to men rather than speak about politics, she talked to close friends about this "worthwhile" subject and mocked old men who thought she was incapable of understanding it. Meanwhile, frustrated by her "lack of equality" with her older husband, she cultivated a relationship with "the man who might be my lover." While she was unable to hide her feelings for her new friend, Roland dutifully "sacrificed" her desire in deference to her husband. Monsieur Roland, in turn, was deeply torn between his resentment of the relationship and his anguish over her refusal to act on her feelings. The Rolands were enacting revolution personally as well as politically. So, too, were Imlay and Wollstonecraft.[51]

Why Imlay chose her, we will never know. He left no explanation. Did he imagine himself as Arlington and Wollstonecraft as Caroline, that they would find happiness together by nurturing sociability in a community in an Ohio Valley shaped by the French as well as the American Revolution? Did he see his political schemes as the sine qua non of his social schemes, that the world he imagined in *The Emigrants* required the conquest of Louisiana? Or did he think about any of this at all? Imlay's relationships before Wollstonecraft are a mystery, although any reader of his novel is likely to conclude that at least one of them involved a married English woman. Did he abandon someone for Wollstonecraft? Was he attracted by her body, as Arlington was by Caroline's? Did he lust more than he loved? What did he see in this smart, prickly woman whose often brittle persona scarcely disguised her deep yearning for intimacy?

Whatever it was, it was enough to sustain an intense relationship that constituted one of the most extended periods of happiness in Mary Wollstonecraft's life. We who know what happened over the course of the next two years must fight the temptation to reach back through time and warn her to be careful. You do not really know him, we would say. He will disappoint you. He will leave you. He will consign you to darkness deeper and blacker than you have ever known—a fate as awful in its own way as that

51. Evelyn Shuckburgh, ed., *The Memoirs of Madame Roland: A Heroine of the French Revolution* (Mount Kisco, N.Y., 1990), 61, 80, 81, 246.

which awaits your friends Brissot and Roland. But even if we explained what was coming, who is to say that she still would not choose as she did, recognizing that her time *with* Imlay was ultimately as much a part of her as her time *without* him? Love might cause pain, but a life without intimacy, however fleeting, was no life at all.

3

"I wish to be necessary to you"

Jacques-Pierre Brissot de Warville and his allies were in serious trouble by the end of May 1793. Neither eloquence nor equivocation could save them from the growing wrath of the Montagnards in the National Convention. Skeptical colleagues and distrustful Parisians transformed Brissot's ambivalence about the execution of Louis XVI, his disastrous handling of the general war with Europe, his farcical efforts to incite unrest in French colonies, and his vague support for federalism into evidence of treason. Increasingly marginalized, Brissot fled the capital before a warrant was issued for his arrest on June 2. Several days later, he was captured in Moulins, returned to Paris, and imprisoned in the Concièrge, where he spent the next few months writing furiously in his own defense.

The assassination of Jean-Paul Marat on July 13 and the desperate situation of the republic consolidated the power of the twelve-man Committee of Public Safety dominated by Maximilien Robespierre. The Committee supported an agenda that amounted to a rejection of local and familial obligations, seeking a civil society in which men and women were primarily, if not exclusively, *citizens* of the French republic. Under the September 17 Law of Suspects, the Revolutionary Tribunal controlled by Robespierre sent thousands of enemies of the state to the guillotine. In the meantime, the government revised the calendar, attacked religion, and made virtually all men between eighteen and twenty-five subject to the *levée en masse,* the conscription of a national army. Leaders, insisting that liberty and France were one and the same, prescribed and proscribed behavior. Revolution was producing loyalty to the state and interfering with the development of natural connections among individuals. Coercion—or Terror—was the order of the day.[1]

Brissot's American and British friends reacted to these events in different ways. An anxious Thomas Paine went for solitary evening strolls that summer to find "some relief" and "[to curse] with hearty good will" what Robespierre and his allies were doing to "the character of the Revolution [he] had been proud to defend." The sweet oranges in the garden of the house offered only temporary respite from the turmoil in Paris and the danger to his friends' bodies as well as their shared vision of revolution. Mary Wollstonecraft's personal happiness shaped her response to political events. Aware of the danger, she could still imagine living in France "should peace and order ever be established in this distracted Land." To be sure, the "rapid changes, the violent, the base and nefarious assassinations . . . cannot fail to chill the sympathizing bosom, and palsy intellectual vigour." But people must respond to the apparent failure of sociability with sociability. Wollstonecraft still believed that no man "chooses evil, because it is evil; he only mistakes it for happiness, the good he seeks." Problems arose, not from an essential character with which men and women were born, but from the culture in which they lived. And that could be changed. The answer was neither to restrain nor eliminate people but to cultivate their understanding through regular commerce. In Wollstonecraft's world, no one—not Robespierre nor Imlay—ever lost the capacity to transform themselves, to *become* who they chose to be. The only question, really, was whether they would have the opportunity to exercise that power.[2]

No One Is "Naturally Inclined to Evil"

In the summer of 1793, while making love with Gilbert Imlay, Wollstonecraft developed her perspective by narrating *An Historical and Moral View of the Origin and Progress of the French Revolution.* Focusing mainly on the events of 1789, Wollstonecraft argued that the revolution was "the natural conse-

1. See Stuart Woolf, "The Construction of a European World-View in the Revolutionary-Napoleonic Years," *Past and Present,* no. 137 (November 1992), 72–101.

2. Thomas Paine, "Forgetfulness" (1794), in Philip S. Foner, ed., *The Complete Writings of Thomas Paine,* 2 vols. (New York, 1945), II, 1124; Mary Wollstonecraft (MW) to Eliza Bishop, June 24, [1793], in Janet Todd, ed., *The Collected Letters of Mary Wollstonecraft* (New York, 2003), 227; MW, *An Historical and Moral View of the Origin and Progress of the French Revolution . . .* (London, 1794), in Janet Todd and Marilyn Butler, eds., *The Works of Mary Wollstonecraft,* 7 vols. (New York, 1989), VI, 6; MW, *A Vindication of the Rights of Men, in a Letter to the Right Honourable Edmund Burke . . . ,* 2d ed. (London, 1790), ibid., V, 53.

quence of intellectual improvement" rather than something "produced by the abilities or intrigues of a few individuals" or "the effect of sudden and short-lived enthusiasm." This interpretation reflected the influence of the stadial theory of human history advocated mainly by Scots such as William Robertson, David Hume, and Adam Smith. Moving through stages of economic and social development, human beings over centuries had arrived at the commercial cities, which were all variations on Edinburgh. A key to historical progress was the expansion of social commerce. The refinement of letters and science, of conversation and trade, had allowed people to overcome man's "miserable weakness as a solitary being, and the crudeness of his first notions respecting the nature of civil society."[3]

Unfortunately, the French had lagged behind their English-speaking neighbors in promoting commerce. "England seems to have led the way" in the general progress of mankind "by a gradual change of opinion." The British were better educated than any other people in the world. After the Glorious Revolution of 1688–1689, the "thinking" British had enjoyed enough liberty "to pursue without interruption their own business" and to join together to combat corruption. In France, however, superstition and oppression had repressed the natural dignity of man. Most problematic was the example of the "idle caprices of an effeminate court." Indolent Louis XV had set a tone by becoming "the slave of his mistresses." Educated in such an environment, Louis XVI was predictably passive, and his queen, Marie Antoinette, predictably frivolous. To be sure, amid the "polished slavery" were Rousseau-like French families whose members behaved like friends. In general, however, France epitomized a monarchical culture in which "every man, in his own eyes, [was] the centre of the world." The American Revolution had accelerated the awakening of the French to their degradation. But the United States, Wollstonecraft noted, was exceptional. It was "in a situation very different from all the rest of the world" because Americans had profited from the experience of the British. In contrast, the French, "worn out by injuries and insults," acted in haste. Rather than seek "gradual improvement," they took advantage of the first opportunity "to strike at the root of all their misery at once." Europe might be "for some years to come, in a state of anarchy."[4]

In the midst of turmoil and terror, Wollstonecraft persisted in believing that progress everywhere depended on individuals awakening to their own power through conversation. It was a tricky process. Ambition was a

3. MW, *Historical and Moral View*, 6, 7, 15, 16.
4. Ibid., 18, 19, 20, 28, 29, 45, 46, 62, 147, 148.

good thing, for it encouraged the French to action; but when imagination took hold and ran away into enthusiasm, complications inevitably ensued. The best way to cultivate true understanding was to recognize "how intimately their own comfort was connected with that of others." If there were "monsters to cope with" in the world, Wollstonecraft insisted, they were created rather than "naturally inclined to evil." Without "the cultivation of the understanding," people indulge "reveries, instead of pursuing a train of thinking; and thus grow romantic, like the croisaders; or like women, who are commonly idle and restless." The erratic French moved overnight from "implicitly obeying their sovereigns" to thinking of themselves as "all sovereigns." But all was not lost. If the "crimes and follies" that revealed "the human character in the most revolting point of view" sickened the heart and appalled the understanding, wrote a woman in love, "things must have time to find their level." It was still possible "that out of this chaotic mass a fairer government is rising than has ever shed the sweets of social life on the world."[5]

Wollstonecraft's protestations were hardly unique. Marie-Jean-Antoine-Nicholas de Caritat, marquis de Condorcet, who spent the late summer and fall of 1793 in hiding, wrote *Sketch for a Historical Picture of the Progress of the Human Mind,* an affirmation of sociability that amounted to a final testament. Quickly reviewing the basic philosophical assumptions of the eighteenth century, Condorcet asserted again that, "as a consequence of [the] capacity [of men to receive and organize sensations] and of his ability to form and combine ideas, there arise between him and his fellow-creatures ties of interest and duty, to which nature herself has wished to attach the most precious portion of our happiness and the most painful of our ills." The perfectibility of man might "vary in speed," but it would "never be reversed." Society, like individuals, was the product of history. "What happens at any particular moment is the result of what has happened at all previous moments, and itself has an influence on what will happen in the future."[6]

Condorcet divided history into ten stages. In the ninth, the era before the creation of the French republic, enlightened people at last recognized "the true rights of man and how they can all be deduced from the single truth, that *man is a sentient being, capable of reasoning and of acquiring moral ideas.*" It was to maintain these rights that men came "together in political

5. Ibid., 21, 22, 23, 47.
6. Marie-Jean-Antoine-Nicholas de Caritat, marquis de Condorcet, *Sketch for a Historical Picture of the Progress of the Human Mind,* in Keith Michael Baker, ed., *Condorcet: Selected Writings* (Indianapolis, Ind., 1976), 210, 211.

societies, and that the social art [became] the art of guaranteeing the preservation of these rights and their distribution in the most equal fashion over the largest area." Notwithstanding "all the astonishing multifariousness of labor and production, supply and demand, with all the frightening complexity of conflicting interests that link the survival and well-being of one individual to the general organization of societies," notwithstanding "this seeming chaos," Condorcet insisted on "a universal moral law" in which "the efforts made by each individual on his own behalf minister to the welfare of all, and that the interests of society demand that everyone should understand where his own interests lie, and should be able to follow them without hindrance." In the tenth stage of human history, the challenge was to complete the perfectibility of mankind.[7]

Condorcet remained optimistic until his arrest in March 1794 when he most likely committed suicide by drinking poison. The adoption of free trade in ideas as well as goods would awaken Europeans to the injustice of the slave trade and the oppression of colonial peoples throughout the world. The latter would benefit enormously from the experience of Europeans. They would progress more quickly because they would avoid obvious mistakes. They could learn from books and conversation. Education would lead people to practice moderation. "Is not the habit of reflection upon conduct, of listening to the deliverances of reason and conscience upon it, of exercising those gentle feelings which identify our happiness with that of others, the necessary consequence of a well-planned study of morality and of a greater equality in the conditions of the social pact?" Someday human beings would have a common language that would allow them to exchange information and insights clearly and regularly.[8]

In the meantime, advocates of social commerce endured as best they could. Arrested in June 1793 along with other friends of Brissot and locked away in Sainte-Pélange prison, Madame Roland found refuge from her initial "extreme agitation" in reading, writing, and drawing. Bereft of her friends, she endured her confinement "with a suitable regime and way of life." Reading Anthony Ashley Cooper, third earl of Shaftesbury, who had argued in *Characteristics of Men, Manners, Opinions, Times* that sociability encouraged the mutual reinforcement of self-regard and social affection, steadied her. But nothing protected her from barking dogs, interrogations, and indecent "orgies." Her jail personified a new order run by "atrocious imbeciles who live by denouncing honest men and filling the prisons with

7. Ibid., 221, 223, 259.
8. Ibid., 273.

innocent people." What would Plato have made of a democracy in which "men of this type dispose of the liberty of their fellow citizens?" He would have seen a world turned up upside down, an antisocial hell. Thieves, prostitutes, and murderers bought their freedom while respectable citizens suffered. "Everything becomes venal and corrupt in this stinking hole, under a vicious administration whose sole passion is to keep people in, with no thought of correction." Meeting a female acquaintance on the August anniversary of the fall of the monarchy, Madame Roland reflected on the irony that that happy occasion had set in motion a string of events that had undone her and that would end for her with the fall of the guillotine on the afternoon of November 8, 1793.[9]

Wollstonecraft and her friends held fast to their belief that revolution was the collective force of individual men and women choosing to transform their sense of themselves and their relationships with other people, and to do all that in collaboration with one another. Their embrace of a new order "based on the reciprocal exchange of conversation among equals" did not blind them to the challenges of realizing a better world. Indeed, it was precisely because they knew human nature, precisely because they knew that personal ambition, jealousy, cruelty, and violence had defined the history of the world as much or more than ideas of honor, compassion, and community, that they insisted that public revolution had to rest on a foundation of multiple personal revolutions. Constitutions and proclamations were worthless unless men and women cultivated their understanding enough to recognize that the securest foundation of individual happiness was the collective happiness of mankind. As long as radical writers imagined people capable of improving themselves, they could hold on to the possibility of change. Nothing was fixed or permanent; nobody was essentially evil.[10]

"Commercial Speculations"

Americans were by and large left alone by French authorities in the late summer of 1793. But British subjects were vulnerable because the republic

9. Evelyn Shuckburgh, ed., *The Memoirs of Madame Roland: A Heroine of the French Revolution* (Mount Kisco, N.Y., 1990), 113, 114, 118, 119, 121. See Anthony Ashley Cooper, third earl of Shaftesbury, *Characteristics of Men, Manners, Opinions, Times* (1711), ed. Lawrence E. Klein (Cambridge, 2000).

10. Dena Goodman, *The Republic of Letters: A Cultural History of the French Enlightenment* (Ithaca, N.Y., 1994), 5.

was at war with their country. To protect his lover, Imlay went to the American ambassador in September and officially affirmed that Mary Wollstonecraft was his wife. The decision was clearly mutual, an expression of their firm belief in a social order defined by consent and natural commerce rather than coercion and artificial institutions. Wollstonecraft started calling herself Mary Imlay and moved into Imlay's apartment in Saint-Germain. The new arrangement occasioned little comment because it was not unusual. After all, the couple was living in a republic whose citizens were rethinking marriage, family, and the social utility of divorce and egalitarian inheritance.[11]

A man and a woman living together without benefit of marriage was not news in the English-speaking world in the 1790s, and not just because of revolution. Indeed, until the middle of the eighteenth century, men and women had created what neighbors and family members recognized as de facto marriages by demonstrating a commitment to each other, usually by sharing a bed or admitting to sexual intercourse. Courts asserted that "the private exchange of promises between a man and a woman to live together as man and wife . . . actually brought marriage into being." In villages throughout Britain and North America, male relatives often assisted a young man in making that commitment, especially when their daughter or sister was pregnant with his child. Then in 1753, Parliament passed the Act for the Better Preventing of Clandestine Marriages, known familiarly as the Marriage Act. In addition to prohibiting the union of people younger than twenty-one without the formal consent of parents or guardians, the legislation required marriages to occur in a church or a chapel in which the banns had been published (that is, the impending nuptials publicly announced) for at least three successive Sundays. Parishes also had to keep formal records of all marriages. Any attempt to marry someone in violation of these requirements constituted a felony. If convicted of the crime, the parties could be transported to North America for a minimum of fourteen years. The Marriage Act offered increased protection, at least in theory, to married women, but it wiped away support for unmarried women. The issue was only vaguely a question of morality or the rights of women. Marriage had developed in part as an institutionalized exchange of property among patriarchal families and generations. The female body and the children conceived within it were age-old forms of economic commerce.

11. Susanne Desan, *The Family on Trial in Revolutionary France* (Berkeley, Calif., 2004); Jennifer Ngaire Heuer, *The Family and the Nation: Gender and Citizenship in Revolutionary France, 1789–1830* (Ithaca, N.Y., 2005).

Wollstonecraft spurned marriage because she rejected an institution that served the interests of men at the expense of women. Her revolution was not about empowering the state to force men to acknowledge obligations or to give the pregnant victims of male lust protection. Wollstonecraft wanted her lover to choose her because they needed each other. She did not want someone to take care of her or shield her from danger. She chose to have sex with a man who would be bound to her by love. To see indulging sexual desire with a sensible man as compromising marital prospects, ruining her virtue, or disgracing her family was to honor the old patriarchal order. Novels of the kind Wollstonecraft despised recounted tale after tale of a young woman ruined by the folly of believing a man would want to be her friend after he had had sex with her. Other writers reminded women that pregnancy as often as not would lead their lovers to desert them. They would be left bereft of more than love. There were questions of authority, financial support, inheritance, and household stability. Wollstonecraft and Imlay confronted these problems too. They simply rejected the contention that females had to defer to the judgment (and the interests) of males. To marry legally—to seek the sanction of the state and the church—was to betray everything they advocated. When she gave herself the name Mary Imlay, she was asserting her right to live as she thought best.[12]

In September 1793, marriage was hardly the greatest challenge the couple faced. Like all people in love—like Ruth and Joel Barlow—they had to balance the time they devoted to their intimacy with the time they devoted to developing relationships with friends and associates. They had to support themselves financially. And, within months, they would have to make room for pregnancy and for the daughter Wollstonecraft would bear in May 1794. All of these things they had to do in a world turned upside down, a relentlessly volatile world defined less by the promise of revolution than by the dangers of war. In the fall of 1793, the lovers started to quarrel, playfully, flirtatiously, at first, and then angrily and resentfully. Despite bouts of frustration with Imlay over his prolonged absences, Wollstonecraft never gave up on the possibility that her American lover was what she thought he was. Imlay, alas, cannot speak for himself because his papers have vanished. All

12. Rebecca Probert, "The Impact of the Marriage Act of 1753: Was It Really 'A Most Cruel Law for the Fair Sex'?" *Eighteenth-Century Studies*, XXXVIII (2005), 247–262; Susan E. Klepp, *Revolutionary Conceptions: Women, Fertility, and Family Limitation in America, 1760–1820* (Chapel Hill, N.C., 2009); Cornelia Hughes Dayton, "Taking the Trade: Abortion and Gender Relations in an Eighteenth-Century New England Village," *William and Mary Quarterly*, 3d Ser., XLVIII (1991), 19–49; Eve Tavor Bannet, *The Domestic Revolution: Enlightenment Feminisms and the Novel* (Baltimore, 2000), 94, 95, 96.

we can do is to consider why he might have found so pressing the demands that friends, associates, and events put on him in the commercial world beyond Wollstonecraft and their daughter.

After the fall of Brissot and the collapse of French ambitions in North America, Imlay had lost his luster in Paris. Undaunted, he joined other men, including Barlow, in pursuing financial opportunities created more by war in Europe than revolution in the Americas. Probably working as a factor for the London merchant house of Turnbull, Forbes, and Company and certainly freelancing on his own as opportunities arose, his focus turned away from Paris to Le Havre, a once-languishing town on the north bank of the Seine estuary that had become France's fourth-largest port. Le Havre's population was twenty thousand when Imlay arrived in September 1793 to engage in what William Godwin later dismissed as "commercial speculations." In response to the British blockade, the French government was about to open all ports to trade with neutral countries, of which the most important were the United States, Norway, Sweden, and Denmark. The French intended to exchange manufactured items at the lowest possible prices for food and arms. The Committee of Safety knew its authority ultimately depended directly on its ability to ensure the basic needs of its citizens. Failure to feed Paris would engender a groundswell of resentment that would threaten the legitimacy of the regime.[13]

Busy Le Havre teemed with sailors, privateers, and tough-minded businessmen with little patience for the social aspects of commerce. Its merchants had struggled for decades to increase their share of Atlantic trade. They had little to offer in return for the grain and food coveted by Parisians. Despite high demand for sugar, French colonies were more of a drain than a boon on the metropolis. French merchants, moreover, were at a competitive disadvantage with their British counterparts. France lacked what Great Britain had: superior financial networks, government bureaucracies, domestic markets, and infrastructure, not to mention colonies that produced more than they consumed. Merchants in Le Havre were rarely in a good mood. On his way to the United States in 1788, Brissot found the town's merchants so eager to increase their profitable share of the Atlantic slave trade that they behaved like swindlers. What choice did they have when the English consistently undersold them? They disparaged benevolence as a threat to their security. Fearful of losing their fine houses and comfortable

13. MW to Gilbert Imlay, [circa September 1793], in Todd, ed., *Collected Letters,* 230 n. 541, 231; William Godwin, *Memoirs of the Author of "A Vindication of the Rights of Woman,"* ed. Pamela Clemit and Gina Luria Walker (Peterborough, Ont., 2001), 89.

lives, these men complained of the antislavery movement in the English-speaking world as "a blind and extremely dangerous form of fanaticism." Characteristically, Brissot blamed their attitude on "prejudice" nurtured in ignorance rather than an essential "inhumanity." The key to eliminating the slave trade was to establish a lucrative alternative. Then "it would not be difficult to persuade them to abandon the traffic in these unhappy Africans." "We must therefore continue to write and to publish," Brissot wrote in a sentiment that Wollstonecraft would have shared, "we must never weary of spreading our message." Five years later, however, the situation was no better.[14]

Almost three centuries old in the 1790s, Le Havre had long been defined by its location on the English Channel. The central artery linking the Atlantic and the seas and rivers of northern Europe, the Channel was a hotly contested space in between perpetual enemies France and Great Britain. For decades the British High Court of Admiralty had issued thousands of letters of marque, authorizing private vessels to attack and confiscate enemy ships. Of the 4,748 letters of marque issued by the British between 1793 and 1801, 454 were to captains from the Channel Islands. They were responsible for 181 of the 266 prizes—almost all of them French or Spanish, and all but 15 merchantmen—taken privately in this period. Privateers seized Americans ships, starting in 1793, because Great Britain did not accept the idea that the vessels of noncombatant nations could carry goods to their enemies. Meanwhile, the residents of the Channel Islands, Guernsey and Jersey, carried on a venerable tradition of smuggling goods in and out of both France and Britain. Vessels thus ventured into the waters from Brest to the north and east at their own considerable risk. American ships bound for Le Havre laden with flour, coffee, potash, and tobacco were frequent victims. In 1793, the American representative in the port struggled to prevent "foreign ships from flying the American flag." He was afraid that Britain's aggressive seizures of U.S. vessels "bringing colonial provisions to France"

---

14. J. P. Brissot de Warville, *New Travels in the United States of America, 1788* (1791), trans. Mara Soceanu Vamos and Durand Echeverria, ed. Echeverria (Cambridge, Mass., 1964), 64, 65. See John Brewer, *The Sinews of Power: War, Money, and the English State, 1688-1783* (Cambridge, Mass., 1990); David Hancock, *Citizens of the World: London Merchants and the Integration of the British Atlantic Community, 1735-1785* (Cambridge, 1995); John G. Clark, *La Rochelle and the Atlantic Economy during the Eighteenth Century* (Baltimore, 1981), 3-4; Pierre Dardel, *Navires et marchandises dans les ports de Rouen et du Havre au XVIIIe siècle* (Paris, 1963); and Michael Duffy, "World-Wide War and British Expansion, 1793-1815," in P. J. Marshall, ed., *The Eighteenth Century*, vol. II of *The Oxford History of the British Empire*, ed. Wm. Roger Louis (Oxford, 1998), 187.

would lead to war. So stressful was his job that he welcomed the appointment of a U.S. consul in Le Havre with obvious relief.[15]

Complicating matters, merchants and factors in ports such as Le Havre were at the mercy of distant military encounters. In early 1793, Prime Minister William Pitt the Younger and his home secretary (and secretary of state for war from 1794) Henry Dundas designed a strategy to protect the Dutch and destroy French naval and commercial power by attacking the French republic through its colonies in the West Indies and the Indian Ocean. From the summer of 1793 through the summer of 1794, British forces everywhere overran strategic French posts, including the Mediterranean port of Toulon. Pitt and Dundas dispatched Sir Charles Grey and nine thousand men to take the French islands of Martinique and Saint Domingue. In Europe, the British were repulsed, most notably by the young Corsican officer Napoleon Bonaparte's recapture of Toulon in December. Things went much better in the West Indies. Grey took Martinique in March 1794, Saint Lucia in April, Guadeloupe in May, and Port-au-Prince on Saint Domingue in June, although he suffered serious setbacks later in the year. Turnbull and Forbes, among many other London firms, staunchly advocated these actions, conjoining their commerce with that of Great Britain. Merchants and shipowners demanded that the British exercise their power over the West Indies, which meant suppressing rebellion, securing the payment of debts and the stability of customs duties, and restoring slavery (abolished by the French). Many had loaned considerable money to absentee planters living in London who mortgaged land and property, including enslaved Africans, in the islands as collateral. War and upheaval, particularly on the French island of Saint Domingue, frightened the likes of Turnbull and Forbes. No regime seemed likely to respect the property rights of absentees, if indeed their property even survived the war.[16]

15. Delamotte to Thomas Jefferson, Aug. 29, 1793, in Julian P. Boyd et al., eds., *The Papers of Thomas Jefferson,* 36 vols. to date (Princeton, N.J., 1950–), XXVI, 783. See Cutting's appointment in "Memorandum on Consuls Recommended for Appointment," Feb. 18, 1793, and general instructions to U.S. consuls in "Circular to Consuls and Vice-Consuls," Mar. 21, 1783, ibid., XXV, 227, 415. See W. R. Meyer, "The Channel Island Privateers, 1793–1815," 180, 181, 182, and A. G. Jamieson, "The Channel Islands and Smuggling, 1680–1850," 195–196, both in Jamieson, ed., *A People of the Sea: The Maritime History of the Channel Islands* (London, 1986). On American commerce in the region, see James Maury to Jefferson, July 4, 1793, Robert W. Fox to Jefferson, Aug. 10, 1793, Jefferson to Thomas Pinckney, Sept. 1, 1793, Fox to Jefferson, Sept. 7, 1793, all in Boyd et al., eds., *Papers of Jefferson,* XXVI, 433, 646, XXVII, 8–9, 52.

16. Duffy, "World-Wide War and British Expansion," in Marshall, ed., *The Eighteenth Century,* vol. II of *The Oxford History of the British Empire,* ed. Louis, 187–188; Carl Ludwig Lokke, "London Merchant Interest in the St. Domingue Plantations of the Émigrés, 1793–1798," *Ameri-*

In the United States, the Washington administration struggled to maintain the neutrality of the new Republic. Many Americans, however, saw in a general European war an opportunity to escape the British stranglehold on international commerce. Reversing the colonial balance of power, Britain and France suddenly needed the Americans, or at least their crops and ships, more than the Americans needed them. The United States was in the midst of a sustained economic and territorial expansion, fueled by poor harvests and war in Europe. The proportion of United States trade carried in American ships rose from 58.6 percent in 1790 to 86.2 percent in 1794. With money and credit abundant, Americans invested in gargantuan land schemes, buying and selling parcels in the interior of North America in a frenzy that would have astonished even Gilbert Imlay. Great Britain attempted to slow the American expansion by encouraging privateers to seize American ships carrying goods in and out of Continental ports and assisting American Indian resistance to the settlement of U.S. citizens in the Ohio Valley.[17]

Neither the Americans nor the British wanted a full-scale war, and in 1794 they would negotiate a treaty designed to resolve their differences. Until then, British merchants worried that the tensions between their nation and the United States constituted another major threat to Atlantic commerce as a whole. Many decided to concentrate their interests in the Channel and the North Sea. Such trade had the advantages of being undertaken on water close to home and regularly patrolled by the Royal Navy. But it had its own problems, not the least of which was the siren song of the Paris market, despite its being off-limits to British subjects. Suddenly, the exigencies of war and the attractions of trade created a demand for the services of citizens of the United States. Imlay went to Le Havre, not as a writer and an expert on

---

can Historical Review, XLIII (1938), 795–802. Many of the commercial details are in Carl Ludwig Lokke, "Documents: New Light on London Merchant Investments in St. Domingue," *Hispanic American Historical Review,* XXII (1942), 670–676. So broad and deep were the London firm's global operations that they loaned Francisco de Miranda £2,000 in the same period. In 1798, when the British left Saint Domingue for good, John Turnbull claimed that thirty-two people owed his firm a total of £8,256, the largest London investment in the island. Combined with the loss of their branch house in Port-au-Prince and plantations they managed or owned, the total loss of Turnbull and Forbes was near £100,000, if we can believe Turnbull's petition for compensation from His Majesty's government.

17. Stanley Elkins and Eric McKitrick, *The Age of Federalism: The Early American Republic, 1788–1800* (New York, 1993), 382–383; Thomas M. Doerflinger, *A Vigorous Spirit of Enterprise: Merchants and Economic Development in Revolutionary Philadelphia* (Chapel Hill, N.C., 1986), 283, 285–286. See also Jacob E. Cooke, *Tench Coxe and the Early Republic* (Chapel Hill, N.C., 1978).

North America, but as a de jure neutral and de facto smuggler who could obtain ships and use them to import grain into Paris, netting a tidy profit for himself and his patrons in London. Early in 1793, Barlow and three other Americans had leased an English ship, the *Cumberland,* for £150 per month. Its cargo of flour and rice, officially headed for Bilbao, Spain, landed at Bordeaux. Later in 1793, Barlow and Imlay sold the French government four thousand quintals of potash, a product derived from wood ashes and used to make glass and soap or as a fertilizer, for approximately $88,000. The cargo came to Le Havre from Scandinavia.[18]

Such windfalls were rare. Events, or rumors of events, could change everything overnight. In September 1793, Thomas Paine asked the Committee of Public Safety to provide protection from British "reprisals" on forty-five American ships anchored in the harbor at Bordeaux; once in the United States, the merchantmen would return laden with flour. The captains were desperate. The American envoy Gouverneur Morris had abandoned them, saying they had thrown themselves "'into the lion's mouth, and it was for them to get out of it as best they could.'" Hearing of attacks on five American ships by Algerians off the Iberian coast, Barlow fired off a letter to Secretary of State Thomas Jefferson in December 1793 calling "the whole of this business . . . a manoeuvre of the English, to prevent our provisions coming to France, and at the same to injure America." Barlow urged Congress to put an impost of 50 percent on English and Irish manufactures until the British backed off. He also noted that "some of the American merchants and captains" in France wanted to accept the republic's offer to lend the United States several frigates to protect American commerce from "these Pirates." The Washington administration declined to act as Barlow suggested.[19]

In the North Atlantic, the power of all nations ebbed and flowed, depending on time and place. French officials often had as much trouble telling American ships from British ships as British privateers had distinguishing American ships from their cargoes. The French might have respected "infinitely more, the Rights of Men, and Nations" than "English Cruizers, who" often "added insult to Injustice," but no government could enforce its will, reliably protect its citizens, or ensure fair treatment for the citizens

18. Sheryllynne Haggerty, *The British-Atlantic Trading Community, 1760–1810: Men, Women, and the Distribution of Goods* (Leiden, 2006), 8; James Woodress, *A Yankee's Odyssey: The Life of Joel Barlow* (Philadelphia, 1958), 143–145, 146.

19. Thomas Paine to Citizen Barrère, Sept. 5, 1793, in Foner, ed., *Writings of Paine,* II, 1332, 1333; Joel Barlow to Jefferson, Dec. 2, 1793, in Boyd et al., eds., *Papers of Jefferson,* XXVII, 469, 470.

of neutral countries. In March 1793, French privateers held three captured American ships at Le Havre until the National Convention allowed them to treat neutral vessels and their cargoes as prizes. The French briefly arrested American consuls and vice-consuls, including the one at Le Havre. Gouverneur Morris correctly recognized the reality of the situation, despite two brief periods of exemption for American ships, when he wrote that "in future the speculations of neutral commerce will, in fact, depend on the naval superiority of the belligerent powers." Later, when American captains complained of the behavior of officials at Bordeaux, Morris asserted that "those who come to a Country torn by the Paroxisms of great Revolution must calculate on the Inconveniences attending such a State of Society. . . . If they come in the Character of Merchants they must set the probable Gain against the probable Loss and if they have made a bad Calculation, they must be content, and try new Plans." Alas, "in a popular Government the Rulers are frequently obligated to act in obedience to the popular voice contrary to their own Judgment." A republican regime could no more guarantee stability than a monarchy. Morris understood the nature of speculation in its broadest sense. "I know that the Language of flattering Hope would be more agreeable," he told an angry petitioner. "But I know also that Truth is a more wholesome and solid Food than Fancy."[20]

No wonder Gilbert Imlay was so preoccupied. Governments around the Atlantic were leaving individuals to make their own way through a darkening maelstrom of war in which a desire for security outweighed commitment to the possibilities of rational affection. Love and friendship might work as a model of society as long as people eschewed violence and coercion. War, however, was the antithesis of sociability.

"Let Us Now Be Friends!"

Wollstonecraft and Imlay nevertheless staunchly persisted in their belief in the power of natural commerce in all its dimensions. Why, having devoted much of their adult lives to social experimentation, would they suddenly abandon everything, admit that Edmund Burke was right, and surrender

---

20. Joseph Fenwick to Jefferson, June 28, 1793, in Boyd et al., eds., *Papers of Jefferson*, XXVI, 387; Gouverneur Morris to M. Lebrun, minister of foreign affairs, May 14, 1793, in Jared Sparks, *The Life and Correspondence of Gouverneur Morris, with Selections from His Correspondence and Miscellaneous Papers*, 3 vols. (Boston, 1832), II, 319; Morris to Fenwick, Nov. 26, 1793, Consular Letterbook, Papers of Gouverneur Morris, Library of Congress; Morris to Jonathan Jones, Oct. 16, 1793, Official Letterbook, ibid.

to despair? There were possibilities still for human beings who refused to accept that revolution had failed. Their conversations from the fall of 1793 through the summer of 1794 reflected an effort to negotiate the complexities of sustaining commerce on multiple levels.

"How are you?" asked the ever direct Wollstonecraft when Imlay was in Le Havre in late September 1793 and she was still in Paris. It was their first lengthy separation, and Wollstonecraft worried it was a harbinger of future trouble. "Of late, we are always separating.—Crack!—crack!—and away you go." She missed Imlay intensely, as if his "presence" or "caresses" had "never gratified [her] senses." If she was talking about the pleasures of physical sensuality, she was also talking about the importance of their so-cial intercourse. The dangers of loneliness were real. Without "those I love, my imagination is as lively" as it was when they were not part of her life. Longing for Imlay, she worried that her devotion to him would last longer than his to her. She needed no "violent effort of reason" to "find food for love in the same object, much longer than" he. If his "spirits" were more "manageable" than hers, she wrote, it was because "the way to my senses is through my heart." There was "sometimes a shorter cut to yours." Char-acteristically, Wollstonecraft generalized from her experience to contem-plate the consequences of superficial sociability. Most men seduced women with a "dash of folly" and did not bother to foster "a passion in their hearts." Foolish females who devoted themselves to pleasing men made it difficult for wiser women to cultivate "the few roses that afford them some solace in the thorny road of life." Wollstonecraft believed that Imlay was one of those roses. Like Caroline in *The Emigrants,* she had encountered a man who blended sociability and independence, self-love and benevolence.[21]

Wollstonecraft thought of love as the joy of a connection with someone who knew his independence was intertwined with hers. In November, when she discovered that she was pregnant, she talked happily of their "mutual interest" in the child. All she desired of Imlay was the knowledge that his "happiness" was "closely connected" with hers. More specifically, Imlay should forget his business and concentrate less on money. What mattered in the end was manliness: his "honest countenance . . . relaxed by tender-ness." To mitigate the pain of separation, Wollstonecraft fantasized about the sensuality she shared with her lover. She thought of Imlay "a little—little wounded by [her] whims"; she saw his "eyes glistening with sympa-

21. MW to Imlay, [circa September 1793], in Todd, ed., *Collected Letters,* 231, [Dec. 31, 1793], 237, [Jan. 9, 1794], 242, [circa Jan. 15, 1794], 246.

thy," his lips feeling "softer than soft"; she fancied them putting their heads together and "forgetting all the world." In her imagination, she pictured the first meeting of Imlay and her brother Charles; her lover would give her sibling "one of your tender looks, when your heart not only gives a lustre to your eye, but a dance of playfulness." What was the "word to express the[ir] relationship"? "Shall I ask the little twitcher?" Part of it was Imlay loving "those [she] love[d]." Part of it was regular communication. Each letter full of "considerate tenderness" made him even "dearer"; they calmed her, erased her "cares." Imlay, she was sure, understood what was happening. His "struggles to be manly" were evidence that they ultimately shared the "same sensibility." He, too, sought to balance "cultivating" his "understanding" with allowing "these springs of pleasure" to flow. He was, in short, a "most worthy man, who joins to uncommon tenderness of heart and quickness of feeling, a soundness of understanding, and reasonableness of temper, rarely to be met with—Having also been brought up in the interior parts of America, he is a most natural, unaffected creature."[22]

The promise of Imlay, as always, was the promise of happiness founded on friendship, on the belief that personal fulfillment was achieved through intimacy. Wollstonecraft wanted a life with Imlay, not because he *made* her happy, but because she *wanted* to be happy with him. And she expected the same in return. She fretted, therefore, when Imlay allowed the demands of his business to take precedence. The answer was to talk about it directly. Her knowledge of his "cheerful temper" made his "absence easy." Yet she warned that, if he did "not return soon" or at least "talk of it," she would "throw [his] slippers out at window, and be off—nobody knows where." Although Imlay did not come back quickly, he did write, often with great affection. His letters reassured her because she feared their separations were making them both more susceptible to the phantoms of their imagination. She worried that she ought to "grow more reasonable" for "a few more of these caprices of sensibility would destroy" her. Her "sorrow" over his absences was making "a child" of her. She expected reciprocity; he ought to feel the same way. And when he said he did, when he imagined them together beside a "fire-side" with six children, she was happy. "Let us now be friends!" she exulted.[23]

Imlay, concluded Wollstonecraft, had, by his "tenderness and worth,

22. MW to Imlay, [circa November 1793], ibid., 233, [circa December 1793], 234, [Dec. 29, 1793], 235, [Dec. 30, 1793], 236, [Dec. 31, 1793], 237, to Everina Wollstonecraft, Mar. 10, [17]94, 249.

23. MW to Imlay, [Jan. 1, 1794], ibid., 238, [Jan. 6, 1794], 240, [Jan. 8, 1794], 241, [Jan. 11, 1794], 243.

twisted [him]self more artfully round my heart, than I supposed possible." She had "thrown out some tendrils to cling to the elm by which I wish to be supported." But she remained certain that this "new language" did not constitute dependency. She was "not a parasite-plant." What she wanted was to live with Imlay and exchange "proofs of affection." The practice of manly commerce allowed them to negotiate the endless struggle to balance her desires and his desires. Reason could direct passion through regular engagement in an atmosphere of mutual respect. "I do not want to be loved like a goddess," she wrote in one of her more memorable sentences, "but I wish to be necessary to you." Imlay would understand because he "has more tenderness and real delicacy of feeling with respect to women, than are commonly to be met with."[24]

In January 1794, the pregnant Wollstonecraft joined Imlay in Le Havre, where they lived until September. Imlay, however, was often away. When he was absent, she missed his kind "looks" and reached across the bed to hug a much contested pillow. She was "acquiring the matrimonial phraseology without having clogged [her] soul by promising obedience etc." She worried about Imlay, not because he was a patriarchal tyrant who enslaved her, but because he was not always as good a friend as he could be. He did not pay enough attention to her; he did not consult her interests as much as he followed his. Love and business, she warned, "will not chime together." Wollstonecraft followed a description of the birth of her daughter Fanny on May 14 with a description of Imlay's impatience over delays in his business. Men were so busy "in the world" that they lost "all sensations, excepting those necessary to continue or produce life!" The problem was not so much Imlay's financial speculations as their tendency to dominate his life to the exclusion of the cultivation of his sensibility through love.[25]

Le Havre did not offer Wollstonecraft many opportunities to develop connections other than her relationship with Imlay. She was far from her networks of friends and from the publishing world that had provided her financial independence. As important, unlike Ruth Barlow, she had to deal with her pregnancy and then with a child. Wollstonecraft loved Fanny. But becoming a mother forced her to engage with new limits and new obligations. She could choose her friends and her lovers, people she could engage in conversation. A child was a different matter. That Wollstonecraft

24. Ibid., [Jan. 1, 1794], 239, [Jan. 14, 1794], 245, Sept. 23, [1794], 265.
25. Godwin, *Memoirs,* ed. Clemit and Walker, 90; MW to Imlay, [Jan. 1, 1794], in Todd, ed., *Collected Letters,* 239, [circa March 1794], 250, Mar. [13], [1794], 250, to Ruth Barlow, Apr. 27, [17]94, 251, May 20, [17]94, 252–253.

employed a nurse to assist her with Fanny's birth did not exempt her from the child's demands for food, stimulation, and relief from discomfort.[26]

Pregnancy and children made visible a profound difference in the experience of women and men. The physical transformation in a woman's body constrained her in ways unimaginable even to the most sympathetic man; her body subverted her autonomy and limited her choices, making her more vulnerable physically, emotionally, economically, and socially. The body of a man, on the other hand, was unaffected by pregnancy, indeed unaware of the fact of conception. Because he was physically free to carry on as before, he had to choose, or be encouraged to accept, changes in his lover's body, behavior, and expectations. Implicit in that acceptance was the recognition of more than an altered connection with a lover; acknowledging paternity also involved taking responsibility for an infant. In theory, lovers could contemplate whatever they wished because they had no attachments to which they had not consented. That equanimity evaporated when they became parents. More so than friends or business associates, a baby was a powerful rival for affection, time, and resources.[27]

In the early summer of 1794, shortly after the birth of Fanny Imlay, the Royal Navy further complicated the already complex lives of Imlay and Wollstonecraft. A fleet of thirty-four ships under the command of sixty-eight-year-old Admiral Richard Howe, Earl Howe, defeated a French fleet of twenty-six ships three hundred miles off the coast of Brittany in the Battle of the Glorious First of June. Crippling French naval power, the British in one day made the world safer for English privateers and more dangerous for smugglers and American ships. At the time, Imlay was busy organizing shipments of food into Paris and looking for cargoes that would pay for them. He was exploiting Le Havre's long-standing commercial ties with Scandinavians in order to transship grains and other goods (perhaps from the United States) through neutral ports on neutral ships. His principal agent in this business lived in Gothenburg, Sweden. Thirty-four-year-old Elias Backman, a Barlow associate who had met Imlay in France, was a Finnish-born supporter of revolution. He was also the American consul general in Gothenburg.[28]

On June 18, 1794, when Fanny Imlay was barely a month old, a Norwegian

26. Claire A. Lyons, *Sex among the Rabble: An Intimate History of Gender and Power in the Age of Revolution, Philadelphia, 1730–1830* (Chapel Hill, N.C., 2006).

27. Marion Rust, *Prodigal Daughters: Susanna Rowson's Early American Women* (Chapel Hill, N.C., 2008), 52. See Holly Brewer, *By Birth or Consent: Children, Law, and the Anglo-American Revolution in Authority* (Chapel Hill, N.C., 2005).

28. Per Nyström, *Mary Wollstonecraft's Scandinavian Journey* (Gothenburg, 1980), 19–24.

shipmaster named Peder Ellefsen bought a vessel called the *Liberty* from two Le Havre merchants and dubbed it *Maria and Margaretha*. The Danish consul affirmed that the boat was a Norwegian vessel bound without cargo for Copenhagen under a Danish flag. The ship did indeed sail from Le Havre in early August. But its destination was Arendal, Norway, Ellefsen's hometown. Later that fall, the *Maria and Margaretha,* without Ellefsen, supposedly disappeared during storms on a journey to Gothenburg. A Swedish merchant filed a complaint about the loss of the ship, which he considered suspicious. Subsequent investigations showed that the real owner of the *Maria and Margaretha* was Gilbert Imlay and that he, not Ellefsen, had arranged things with the Danish consul. As important, the *Maria and Margaretha* had a cargo—thirty-one or thirty-two bars of silver and thirty-six silver dishes and plates totaling around £3,500—fetched from Paris for Imlay by Ellefsen.[29]

Overwhelmed by the uncertainty created by Howe's victory on June 1, Robespierre's increasingly fragile hold on power, and the risky silver shipment, Imlay began to show signs of stress. Wollstonecraft, preoccupied with Fanny, did what she could to help her lover. On May 20, she reported to Ruth Barlow that "Mr. Imlay has been rendered almost impatient by the continual hinderances, which circumstances and the mismanagement of some [of] the people intrusted with the concerns of the party—not to talk of the constant embarrassments occasioned by those whipping embargos, that slip off and on, before you know where you are." Soon Imlay fell ill. On July 8, a concerned Wollstonecraft informed Ruth that he had "not been well for some weeks past, and during the last few days he has [been] seriously feverish." "His mind has been harass[ed] by continual disappointments—Sh[ips] do not return, and the government is perpetually throwing impediments in the way of business." Notwithstanding that "the fulfilling of [social] engagements" meant more to her "than the making [of] a fortune," Wollstonecraft shared her lover's "disquietude." She assumed that, when the crisis passed, Imlay would devote himself to the cultivation of their intimacy, a process interrupted by the demands of war and trade. In the meantime, they were in this thing together. Hardly a helpless victim of a philandering lover, Wollstonecraft, still recovering from her pregnancy, was his nurse, confidante, and partner.[30]

In early August, Imlay, apparently healthy again, rushed back to Paris to

29. MW to Ruth Barlow, Apr. 27, [17]94, in Todd., ed., *Collected Letters*, 251 n. 591, to Imlay, Aug. 17, [1794], 256 n. 602. See Lyndall Gordon, *Vindication: A Life of Mary Wollstonecraft* (New York, 2005), 232–237.

30. MW to Ruth Barlow, May 20, [17]94, in Todd, ed., *Collected Letters*, 253, July 8, [17]94, 255.

protect his interests in the aftermath of the fall of Robespierre on July 28, leaving Wollstonecraft to supervise the departure of the *Maria and Margaretha.* American citizens and British subjects were abandoning the capital. Thomas Paine was not among them; he had been in prison since December 1793. Meanwhile, Thomas Christie had fled to Switzerland to escape severe financial judgments against him. Imlay himself would soon move his base of operations across the Channel to London. And Joel Barlow and his wife Ruth had already left Paris for Hamburg, a bustling port that became a major entrepôt as French control of the coast through Holland and British domination of the seas drove merchants away from northern France. In Hamburg, Barlow did what Imlay had done in Le Havre. He handled the affairs of some of the hundreds of vessels, many of them American, that arrived and then departed for "Lisbon," meaning almost anywhere in the North Atlantic. Much had changed since the spring of 1793. Imlay and his friends were now on the move, living literally on the margins, trying to survive in a world suddenly more concerned with national survival than global revolution.[31]

Taking risks occasionally had fatal consequences. Thomas Christie died in Surinam in October 1796. Somehow the adventurous spirit that had taken him all over Britain a decade earlier in search of friends and knowledge, that had led him to join Joseph Johnson in creating the *Analytical Review* and encouraging women writers, had become an enthusiasm, or so his critics said. Christie lost his way because he could not control himself. "Sceptical company, vanity, and too eager a desire of getting rich all at once were his bane," wrote an acquaintance some months after his death. A creditor reported that, had Christie and his partner been willing to accept "a profit of one thousand pounds per annum each, and a good probability of a gradual increase to each," he could have stayed in England and "restored" the affairs of the partnership. The ever ambitious Christie, however, went to Surinam "to redress the affairs of the house and recover debts." He did not return. At least he escaped the accumulation of small setbacks that usually defined failure.[32]

"A Solitary Madness"

In the eyes of most observers, Wollstonecraft and Imlay were mismatched from the start. Why did an advocate of the rights of woman take up with an adventurer with a penchant for ignoring obligations? Wollstonecraft made a

---

31. Janet Todd, *Mary Wollstonecraft: A Revolutionary Life* (New York, 2000), 243–244.

32. Theophilus Lindsey to Robert Millar, Mar. 3, 1797, in Lindsey Correspondence, MS. 12:46 (15), Dr Williams's Library, London.

life of public defiance; Imlay spent most of his life running away from creditors, sheriffs, and lovers. Her admirers struggle to reconcile her insistence
on rational affection with her obsession with a cad; he has no admirers.
For contemporary critics, their romance was an exercise in antisocial exuberance that proved the folly of pursuing mixed-gender commerce outside
venerable institutions and established custom. In both Paris and Le Havre,
the indulgence of imagination was taking a toll. Jean-Jacques Rousseau had
warned of the danger in his novel *Julie*. Because "we posit the future based
on what suits us today, without knowing whether it will suit us tomorrow,"
we too often find "our misery in what we have contrived for our happiness."
Paris in 1794, its streets filled with the sights and sounds of methodical executions, war, and shortages of food, was as vulgar and violent as any primitive society, as brutish and compulsory as any monarchy. And the couple in
Le Havre, trying to support themselves and their daughter while straining
to sustain their intimacy, were becoming as testy and resentful as any caricature of marital unhappiness.[33]

In retrospect, the idea that the likes of Gilbert Imlay, however sensible
and susceptible to persuasion, were going to become champions of the
rights of woman seems ludicrous. We will look in vain for a movement to
grant women political and legal rights that rivals the successful campaign
to end Britain's role in the international slave trade. On the latter issue,
the rewards of capitalism and benevolence combined to convince members of Parliament to support radical change. But it was hard to persuade
even men sympathetic to women to surrender male prerogatives. Power, as
Edmund Burke had predicted, simply found new forms. In the early nineteenth century, new republics denied rights to people who were neither
male nor white, usually on the grounds that they lacked the independence
and therefore the ability to manage themselves. Dependent creatures were
either children or like children and should be treated as such, with affection
rather than coercion perhaps, but still as children.[34]

The foundation of Wollstonecraft's dissent from this position lay in more
than respect for the rights of woman. Like her radical contemporaries, she
believed that no one, male or female, could manage on his or her own. Fear
and imagination would run rampant without friendship or, better yet, inti-

33. Jean-Jacques Rousseau, *Julie; or, The New Heloise: Letters of Two Lovers Who Live in a
Small Town at the Foot of the Alps* (1761), trans. Philip Stewart and Jean Vaché (Hanover, N.H.,
1997), 553.

34. Brewer, *By Birth or Consent*, 288–368, esp. 364. See Pamela Haag's smart polemic, *Consent: Sexual Rights and the Transformation of American Liberalism* (Ithaca, N.Y., 1999).

macy. Proper education would reveal that the most effective way to promote equality was to recognize the role of dependency in nurturing independence. In short, men and women had to understand that they were necessary to one another. Far from abandoning her principles with Imlay, the author of *A Vindication of the Rights of Woman* was implementing them. Mary Wollstonecraft was never ashamed of her desires, never regretted her choices, never saw her behavior as antisocial, and never gave up on the possibilities of Gilbert Imlay. In her view, the history of Europe was testimony to the failure of efforts to repress desire and coerce acquiescence. Stability would emerge through an acceptance of the need to temper ambition through love. Together they could manage desire through intimacy, through conversation, just as they could manage their desires for money and fame.[35]

Love was not wild romantic passion, an intense surrender to the tyranny of the body; it was a dynamic effort to cultivate mutual happiness on the assumption that human beings can neither recognize nor sustain happiness on their own. The novelist Virginia Woolf was right when she remarked in the early twentieth century that not even Wollstonecraft's admirers really understood her. Fortunately, Wollstonecraft's "revenge" was that her "arguments" and "experiments" gave her "one form of immortality." In her writing, "she is alive and active, she argues and experiments, we hear her voice and trace her influence even now among the living." In her life, she insisted "that nothing mattered save independence," and she desired "something different" from conventional norms. If her friends "were disturbed by her discrepancies," including her affair with the "treacherous" Imlay, they were missing the full range of her personality and her ideas.[36]

Smart women in the late eighteenth century like Wollstonecraft were frustrated by unrequited love or broken affairs, not because they were weak creatures, but because they believed that intimacy was critical to human progress. In 1796, Mary Hays was devastated when William Frend, a Dissenter and Cambridge professor (dismissed from Jesus College in 1788 for blasphemy and the author of a controversial pamphlet for which he was tried for sedition in 1793), declined to become her lover. Ironically, Frend had written to Hays in 1792 to cultivate a friendship in the manner of radical advocates of mixed-gender commerce. Because he and Hays shared an

35. Cornelia Hughes Dayton, "Taking the Trade: Abortion and Gender Relations in an Eighteenth-Century New England Village," *WMQ*, 3d Ser., XLVIII (1991), 19–49; Bannet, *The Domestic Revolution*, 94, 95, 96.

36. Virginia Woolf, "Mary Wollstonecraft," in Woolf, *The Second Common Reader*, ed. Andrew McNeillie (1932; rpt. San Diego, Calif., 1986), 157, 158, 159, 160, 163.

interest in benevolence, they had a "duty to bring the sensibility of our nature under the control of reason." Frend approved of Hays's "sensibility," although his conception of intimacy was formal and paternalistic. Anticipating bourgeois prescriptions about marriage, Frend contended that a good
wife would "love her husband," assist him in his profession, "consider home
as the place of her happiness," and possess "a tolerable share of good sense
that could endure the little mortifications of life without peevishness." Hays
said no to this proposal of marriage. Years later, however, she expressed to
Frend a desire for intimacy without marriage. Could they not enjoy companionship without creating a legal, domestic partnership? Lovers connoted mutuality and equality in ways that husband and wife did not.[37]

Frend, a radical in so many ways, was appalled by Hays's suggestion. His
rejection sent her into an emotional tailspin. She struggled to control "the
importunate suggestions of a too exquisite sensibility—foster'd by the delicacy of female education." Solitude let loose imagination. How could she
handle the rush of emotion? Her choices were few, mainly because she was a
woman. "Happiness," she declared, was "the only valuable end of existence,
or existence must be in vain!" Alas, women had to resort to "eccentricities of
conduct" to achieve that end. Frend's decision, about which she had fretted for months, was "a shock" from which she thought she would "never
wholly recover." She wondered how to proceed. Repression of desire was not
a viable option. She could not be happy "with any thing that did not call forth
strong emotion." For better or worse, she was "an enthusiast in friendship, an
enthusiast in love, an enthusiast in my desire of knowledge!" Traveling and
writing were no substitute for love. Alone she saw "how impotent is *mere* reasoning against reiterated feeling!" Alone, the future looked like prison. Hays
would never be "a mere fine lady, a domestic drudge, or a doll of fashion."
And, though she could "think, write, reason, converse with men and scholars," she did not want to be a "legislator or a reformer of the world." What
did she want? More than anything else, she wrote, "I want to be beloved."[38]

37. Mary Hays to Godwin, Jan. 11, 1796, in "Appendix A—Selections from the Mary Hays and
William Godwin Correspondence," in Hays, *Memoirs of Emma Courtney* (1796), ed. Marilyn L.
Brooks (Peterborough, Ont., 2000), 236–237, William Frend to Hays, Apr. 16, 1792, in "Appen-
dix B—Selected Letters of William Frend," 258, to Mary Frend, [circa Nov. 22, 1785], 259, 260.
See Gina Luria, "Introduction," in Hays, *Appeal to the Men of Great Britain in Behalf of Women*
(1798), ed. Luria (New York, 1974), 8–11; and Brooks, "Introduction," in Hays, *Memoirs of Emma
Courtney*, ed. Brooks, 8–11.

38. Hays to Godwin, Dec. 7, 1794, in "Selections from Hays and Godwin Correspondence,"
in Hays, *Memoirs of Emma Courtney*, ed. Brooks, 226, 227, July 28, 1795, 229, 230, Oct. 13, 1795,
232, Feb. 6, 1796, 238, Feb. 20, 1796, 248, 249.

We know Hays's wish because she shared it with William Godwin. Hays's despair, her fear of more pain, did not keep her from turning for solace to a man. She needed a friend. "Mine, I believe, is almost a solitary madness in the 18th century," Hays exclaimed. Solitude and madness were two sides of the same psychological coin. To be alone was to indulge one's sensibility, to lose perspective, to care too much about one's self and what the imagination conjured. Like Imlay without Wollstonecraft, Frend suffered without her because he had become "a votary at the shrine of Plutus," the Greek god of money. He had worked "to ice his heart and stifle his humanity" against her. But if men "are the infamous, wretched, victims of brutal instinct," then women "if they sink not in mere frivolity and insipidity—are sublimated into a sort of—what shall I call them?—refined, romantic, unfortunate, factitious, beings who cannot [dare] to act, for the sake of the present moment, in a manner, that shou'd expose them to complicated, inevitable, evils—evils, that will, almost, infallibly overwhelm them with misery and regret!" The only answer to this barbaric situation was to engage, to try again and again and again. Let people think she was eccentric. If she was mad to fall in love, it was "the pleasurable madness which none but madmen know!" And so Hays did try again, this time with Godwin. When he, too, rejected her, she was overcome with "frenzy." On her own, she was "forever the victim of contending emotions." Feeling powerless, she was struck that "our passions are never very strong without a mixture of the *sublime* in them—I mean in Mr. Burkes sense—some emotion allied to an apprehension of power—to terror and astonishment." [39]

The instability of romantic relationships was an intractable problem. And yet they were necessary for social as well as personal reasons. Hays would risk failure rather than abandon possibility. So, too, would Mary Wollstonecraft. She had supported herself as a writer in London and Paris, negotiated with her publisher Joseph Johnson, defied the likes of Edmund Burke, traveled on her own to Paris, and chosen a lover with whom she had found happiness. She and Imlay would surely survive their problems. The key was to ensure that the cultivation of their personal intimacy was not sacrificed to the incessant demands of the world in which they lived.

39. Hays to Godwin, Feb. 6, 1796, ibid., 240, 241, 245, [May 1796], 250, 251.

4

"we Are . . . Differently organized"

In September 1794, Mary Wollstonecraft responded to Gilbert Imlay's obsession with "alum or soap" by insisting on the revolutionary quality of their relationship. Imlay ought to stay with her not so much from "love, which is always rather a selfish passion, as reason—that is, I want you to promote my felicity, by seeking your own." She warned that she could not love him unless their "attachment appears to me clearly mutual." Why not "ramble back to the barrier," where they had met on the outskirts of Paris in the summer of 1793? Why not indulge "those fine sympathies that lead to rapture, rendering men social by expanding their hearts, instead of leaving them leisure to calculate how many comforts society affords"? Imlay should ignore "trade and vulgar enjoyments" and "bring me then back your barrier-face," that is, the expression he had when he greeted her at the entrances to Paris. Surely he missed their physical intimacy, those sensations "almost too sacred to be alluded to"? The absence of a legal contract did not mean they did not have familiar ties. Surely he missed their daughter, Fanny? "Come to me, my dearest friend, husband, father of my child!" Nothing Imlay did over the course of the next year—moving to London, obsessing about business, taking up with at least one other woman—shook Wollstonecraft's commitment. Somehow she would persuade Imlay to recognize once again that she was as necessary to his happiness as he was to hers.[1]

1. Mary Wollstonecraft (MW) to Gilbert Imlay, Aug. 19, 1794, in Janet Todd, ed., *The Collected Letters of Mary Wollstonecraft* (New York, 2003), 258, Sept. 22, 1794, 264, Sept. 28, 1794, 267, Dec. 26, 1794, 271.

Wollstonecraft persisted in the midst of a rising tide of skepticism about the utility of sociability, a growing concern that indulging self-interest was putting everyone at risk. More was at stake than her personal future. The dissolution of restraints led republican as well as monarchical governments to more rigorously enforce territorial and cultural borders. Visions of universal brotherhood and global revolution that had widespread support in 1789 became pipe dreams almost overnight. In France, following the fall of Maximilien Robespierre in July 1794, a cadre of army officers rode a series of astounding battlefield victories into positions of influence under a new constitution that concentrated power in a handful of men. In Britain, the once moderate reformer Prime Minister William Pitt the Younger, alarmed, like many of his constituents, by the possibility of a French invasion and domestic insurrection, suspended the writ of habeas corpus in May 1794, put radicals on trial for treason, and led Parliament in the adoption of the Treasonable and Seditious Practices Act and the Seditious Meetings Act in 1795. Across the Atlantic, President George Washington, concerned about the influence of radical societies, dispatched twelve thousand members of the militia in the summer of 1794 to quash a rebellion in western Pennsylvania against the federal tax on whiskey. His administration also sought to secure the loyalty of disaffected residents of the Ohio Valley by protecting their bodies and their economic interests. The Legion of the United States smashed an Indian coalition at the Battle of Fallen Timbers in August 1794. A year later, negotiations produced the Treaty of Grenville. Native peoples acknowledged American dominion over an area north of the Ohio River. Military victory in the west allowed the United States to negotiate treaties in 1795 with Spain and Great Britain that opened the Mississippi River to American citizens and removed the British from posts south of the Great Lakes. From Paris to Philadelphia, proponents of national security had proponents of global revolution on the run.[2]

"Ah! France," exclaimed Thomas Paine from his prison cell in Paris in 1794. "Thou hast ruined the character of a Revolution virtuously begun" and "destroyed those who produced it." The pleasures of conversations and the taste of the fruit in the garden in the summer of 1793 had given way to accusations, executions, and exile. More specifically, Paine noted, the visits in the garden in the summer of 1794 had "finished with the arrestation of my-

2. Jennifer Mori, *William Pitt and the French Revolution, 1785–1795* (New York, 1997). See Edward Royle, *Revolutionary Britannia? Reflections on the Threat of Revolution in Britain, 1789–1848* (Manchester, 2000), 13–25; Stanley Elkins and Eric McKitrick, *The Age of Federalism: The Early American Republic, 1788–1800* (New York, 1995).

self." Life was more contingent than he had imagined. A "misfortune" might become "the means of turning aside [a person's] steps into some new path that leads to happiness yet unknown." Paine's consternation was hardly unique. Indeed, his disillusionment was an attitude commonly ascribed to radicals by the mid-1790s. There was no consolation "in reason, for the mind is at war with reason, and to reason against feelings is as vain as to reason against fire." Perhaps the practice of social commerce, of individuals exchanging perceptions and sentiments, was, after all, no match for human nature. Offering no more than an occasional glimpse of hope, weeping reason was reduced "to wait upon us in the humble station of a handmaid."[3]

Although Paine's friend Wollstonecraft suffered from similar bouts of despair, she rejected a narrative of decline. All was not lost—and never would be. She would not give up on Imlay because she would not give up on the idea that they were necessary to each other's happiness. In 1793, they had spent time together, aware of each other's moods and concerns; each knew what the other was thinking or feeling. But, once Imlay went off to Le Havre, they could not sustain separately what they had created together. There was no surprise in this conclusion. Without him, she had indulged her sensibility. Without her, Imlay had pursued his enthusiasm for adventure and rushed about in "a whirl of projects and schemes." Their relationship affirmed the value of sociability regularly practiced. Two individuals in love could persuade each other of the bounds of self and moderate self-regard by regarding others.[4]

If they spent more time with each other, they could revive their dreams. They could still raise the one thousand pounds needed to buy "a farm in America, which would have an independence" and support her sisters. Wollstonecraft invoked the Imlay with whom she had fallen in love, the man who understood love as a mutual cultivation of the understanding. Willing to adjust her interests to his and experiment with living arrangements, she would not, could not, compromise her belief that they would each find independence in commerce with each other. Love was a process, not an end. Wollstonecraft insisted that Imlay respect her wishes. She did so in her best manly fashion, and she expected him to reply in kind. "*I do not consent* to your taking any other journey," she warned him on one occasion. More generally, she chided him for wasting his "life in preparing to live." Why did "one project, successful or abortive, only give place to two others? . . .

3. Thomas Paine, "Forgetfulness" (1794), in Philip S. Foner, ed., *The Complete Writings of Thomas Paine,* 2 vols. (New York, 1945), II, 1125, 1126.

4. MW to Imlay, Feb. 9, [1795], in Todd, ed., *Collected Letters,* 277.

[Was] it not sufficient to avoid poverty?" He should let go of "these eternal projects" and return to her and Fanny. In no case would she be "a secondary object." She refused to be "dependent on a man, whose avidity to acquire a fortune has rendered him callous to every sentiment connected with social or affectionate emotions," a man who longed for "what we may never enjoy" and proclaimed that he lived "'in the present moment.'" Imlay's attitude was self-destructive because it was profoundly antisocial. True happiness lay in the fulfillment of rational desire through mutual respect.[5]

Imlay did not disagree with this argument. In fact, he supported Wollstonecraft's refusal to abandon their experiment in sociability more than we might expect from a man so inclined to run away—indeed, more than she understood. Wollstonecraft was blind to the possibility that Imlay was endeavoring, albeit erratically, to stay the course, that his problem was, not a callous disregard for her wishes, but a considered *refusal* to exercise dominion over her. Rather than end things, he struggled to maintain their relationship as he became involved with a woman in London. In February 1795, he assured Wollstonecraft that their "'being together is paramount to every other consideration.'" She was certain that he was starting to regret time spent in "pleasure; eating, drinking, and women." Within weeks, Imlay claimed that only "Business" had separated them and invited her to join him in London. "Come to any port [in England], and I will fly down to my two dear girls with a heart all their own." In April, she was "on the wing towards [him]." A cautiously optimistic Wollstonecraft craved the evidence of his eyes: they would tell her whether "the very affectionate tenderness which glows in my bosom" was "mutual." She believed that, when they saw each other, he would respond to her. Without her, he was not, could not be, fully himself. Nor was she. "Though [Imlay] could conduct himself, when absent from her, in a way which she censured as unfeeling," William Godwin later observed, "this species of sternness constantly expired when he came into her presence." Even as their relationship frayed, Wollstonecraft and Imlay repeatedly testified to the power of social commerce.[6]

5. MW to Eliza Bishop, [circa Apr. 23, 1795], ibid., 290–291, to Everina Wollstonecraft, Apr. 27, 1795, 291–292, to Imlay, Dec. 28, [1794], 272, 273, Dec. 29, 1794, 274, 275, Jan. 9, 1795, 278, Feb. 19, 285.

6. MW to Imlay, Feb. 9, 1795, ibid., 281, Feb. 10, 1795, 283, Apr. 7, 1795, 285, [circa December 1795], 335; William Godwin, *Memoirs of the Author of "A Vindication of the Rights of Woman"* (1798), ed. Pamela Clemit and Gina Luria Walker (Peterborough, Ont., 2001), 100.

"What a Long Time It Requires to Know Ourselves"

In London, Wollstonecraft and Fanny lived in a house provided by Imlay from mid-April through mid-May 1795. He was "the most generous creature in the world," although he had no more money than he had two years earlier. Wollstonecraft would not let her sister Eliza Bishop move into her new home, arguing that "the presence of a third person interrupts or destroys domestic happiness." But a third person was already present. Imlay was sleeping with "a young actress from a strolling company of players." The news devastated Wollstonecraft. Losing "hope," she declared herself "nothing." She left Imlay's house and contemplated suicide. Imlay sent her "an affectionate letter," blaming his behavior on his single-minded focus on his "pecuniary difficulties." Wollstonecraft replied by describing her anguish. Asking him to decide whether he desired "to live with [her], or part for ever," she invited him to dine with her several nights later, promising not to "harrass [his] feelings." Imlay stopped an attempt at suicide sometime in this period, and it might well have been an effort to avoid another one that led him to reengage with Wollstonecraft.[7]

Conversation led to a fragile reconciliation. In early June, Wollstonecraft agreed to undertake a business venture for Imlay. She, Fanny, and her maid, Marguerite, traveled to Hull to board a ship that would carry them to Gothenburg, Sweden. Her mission was to meet with Elias Backman and find some way to collect damages awarded to Imlay and Backman from legal proceedings against Peder Ellefsen, whom they suspected of having stolen the *Maria and Margaretha* and its cargo of silver worth thirty-five thousand pounds. Imlay called Wollstonecraft "Mary Imlay my best friend and wife" and instructed her to get a monetary settlement from Ellefsen. In giving her legal power to manage his affairs in Scandinavia, Imlay had found a convenient way to get rid of a distraught Wollstonecraft. But he also publicly acknowledged their relationship. She was his legal agent as well as his "dear beloved friend and companion." For her part, Wollstonecraft accepted the assignment to relieve Imlay of the financial difficulties that he claimed kept them apart. Just as important, she was asserting herself. In Scandinavia, she would be a woman alone, charged with dealing with some

---

7. MW to Eliza Bishop, [circa Apr. 23, 1795], in Todd, ed., *Collected Letters*, 290, to Imlay, May 22, [1795], 292, 293, to Everina Wollstonecraft, Apr. 27, [1795], 291–292; Godwin, *Memoirs*, ed. Clemit and Walker, 93, 94.

very tough characters. How better to demonstrate that she was as necessary to Imlay as he was to her?[8]

Fighting despair, Wollstonecraft imagined that she could find an opening into the "tender avenue of sentiment and affection that leads to [his] sympathetic heart." Rather than see Imlay as an amoral rake, she saw him as a sensible man still susceptible to persuasion. Imlay could transform himself. In collaboration with her, he would recognize that he was an adventurer who loved "to fly about continually—dropping down, as it were, in a new world—cold and strange!—every other day," a lover "hurried away by the impetuosity of inferior feelings," seeking "in vulgar excesses, for that gratification which only the heart can bestow." Imlay's ungoverned sensibility was blinding him to "the ineffable delight" of a settled friendship, to "a unison of affection and desire, when the whole soul and senses are abandoned to a lively imagination, that renders every emotion delicate and rapturous." Imlay's behavior astonished her, given his sympathetic accounts of the "desertion of women" in *The Emigrants.* But, as the title suggested, Imlay's novel was about leaving established relationships and creating new ones. *The Emigrants* was the work of a man who found "the pleasure of being free" more powerful than the "pain" of losing a friend.[9]

Wollstonecraft nevertheless fancied Imlay was not one of "the common run of men" with "gross appetites" and a need for "variety to banish *ennui.*" Enslaved to a mad passion, he retained the "great strength of mind, to return to nature, and regain a sanity of constitution, and purity of feeling— which would open your heart to me." Wollstonecraft did not underestimate the challenge. Imlay's "entanglements in business" and with women reflected his "extreme restlessness of mind." What she had to offer he had to be willing to receive. They could talk. But in the end he had to decide for himself. He had to choose "to restrain [his] caprices, in order to give vigour to affection." He had to choose to sacrifice his "zest for life" for happiness with her and Fanny. He had to "examine [himself] well" to "discover what he wish[ed] to do" and then be "explicit—whether you desire to live with me, or part for ever." She required manliness from him, and offered it in return. Beyond that she was flexible. If his new romance did not work out, she was willing to try again. If there is the pathos of a rejected lover in Wollstone-

---

8. Imlay to MW, May 19, 1795, Oxford, Bodleian, MS Abinger c. 41, fols. 16–17. See Per Nyström, *Mary Wollstonecraft's Scandinavian Journey* (Gothenburg, 1980), 24–25.

9. MW to Imlay, Feb. 10, 1795, in Todd, ed., *Collected Letters,* 283, [June 10, 1795], 295, June 12, [1795], 296–297, June 14, [1795], 300.

craft's letters, there is also the dignity of a woman seeking to hold fast to her vision of the world as it ought to be, as it might yet be.[10]

Safely in Gothenburg, Wollstonecraft stayed at Backman's house until she left a teething Fanny and Marguerite, to journey through Sweden to Norway and on to Copenhagen. Her plan was to meet Imlay in Basel, Switzerland, at the end of the summer. Before her departure, she engaged in an extended bout of self-analysis. Her connections with other human beings empowered defiance of melancholy. Fanny, that "interesting creature" with "her playful smiles," kept her from leaping into the sea. Wollstonecraft chose to live—in no small part because of the enduring possibilities of love. Some thought love "an affair of sentiment," a matter of taste and feeling that could not be "described." But if love was "a want of my heart" that testified to her passion for life, it had to be a mixture of respect for the wishes of both partners. Imlay, she wrote, had to stop allowing the "warmth of your feelings, or rather quickness of your senses, [to harden] your heart" toward her and Fanny. He had to prevent "the grossness of your senses" from overlooking her "graces." Love must combine the "dignity of mind, and the sensibility of an expanded heart."[11]

As Wollstonecraft journeyed away from the company of Fanny and Marguerite, she grew angry with Imlay over his "cruel" failure to write regularly. She increasingly demanded that he take his paternal responsibilities seriously so that Fanny, the "poor lamb," would enjoy, and profit from, his affection. Away from Fanny for the first time, she missed her daughter. There was no way she could part "with her for ever" and leave her "helpless." Could Imlay say the same? Fanny had already endured so much. Must she suffer "the pangs of disappointed affection, and the horror arising from a discovery of a breach of confidence, that snaps every social tie!" Imlay must "acquire an habitual tenderness" for his daughter. Wollstonecraft's happy reunion with Fanny in late August only intensified her fury with Imlay.[12]

Mary Wollstonecraft could take care of herself, she informed her inconstant lover. She would not be "merely an object of compassion." If he must be "free," so be it. He need "not continually tell me that my fortune is inseparable, *that you will try to cherish tenderness* for me." She had no use for "protection without affection." She demanded that he decide whether they

10. Ibid., May 22, 1795, 293, June 12, [1795], 297, 298, June 14, [1795], 300, June 15, [1795], 301, July 1, 1795, 308.

11. Ibid., July 3, [1795], 309, 310, July 4, [1795], 311.

12. Ibid., July 14, [1795], 312, 313, July 30, [1795], 315, Aug. 26, [1795], 318.

"live together, or eternally part!" She suspected he wanted "to heave a load off [his] shoulders" and be done with her. The thought depressed her. Perhaps the world really was a place "in which self-interest, in various shapes, is the principal mobile." Her folly was to seek "a degree of permanent happiness," when he "only sought for a momentary gratification." She was convinced that he had used her, lied to her, was concealing a "new attachment." She had "leaned on a spear, that has pierced me to the heart.—You have thrown off a faithful friend, to pursue the caprices of the moment.—We certainly are differently organized." At the very least, they were at cross-purposes.[13]

By dispatching her to Scandinavia, Imlay had invited Wollstonecraft into his world. No longer sitting at home with a young child, impatiently awaiting the return of her lover, she had become an agent in the masculine arena of wartime trade. Conversation was limited to strangers whose languages she barely understood. Like many travelers, she was disoriented, occasionally entranced by sublime sights, frequently overwhelmed by exotic experiences, and uncertain whom to trust. Compounding the challenge, her sex left her vulnerable to a wide range of threats and deceptions, especially from the kind of men with whom Imlay was dealing. If Wollstonecraft's journey to Scandinavia was an effort to sustain their relationship, it was also an act of physical courage and a defiance of social convention. Imlay might have been exploiting her willingness to serve *his* interests; Wollstonecraft believed she was serving *their* interests.

The outcome of her incursion into the world of trade did not improve her mood. Ellefsen, who had apparently confiscated the silver at Arendal, pleaded poverty, bribed judges, and lied as necessary. His plan, Wollstonecraft concluded, was to exhaust her with delays. We do not know whether she succeeded in getting Ellefsen to reimburse Imlay. Indeed, the fate of the *Maria and Margaretha* remains a mystery. We do know that Imlay failed to meet his lover and their daughter in either Hamburg or Basel, notwithstanding his recognition of the "ties" that bound him to them. When Wollstonecraft returned to London with Fanny and Marguerite, Imlay announced that, although he would "make any sacrifice to promote [her] happiness," he would not live with her. She was wrong in thinking he could not "run about for ever." After moving into an apartment provided by Imlay, Wollstonecraft heard from a servant that he had yet another lover. This time an angry confrontation led her to covet escape from her "hated existence." Kill-

13. Ibid., Aug. 26, [1795], 318, 319, Sept. 6, 1795, 321, Sept. 27, 1795, 322–323, Oct. 4, 1795, 324.

ing herself would persuade Imlay to recalibrate his "sensibility." He would "awake." "In the midst of business and sensual pleasure," "remorse" would fill his heart.[14]

In October 1795, after begging Imlay to send Fanny and Marguerite to a friend in Paris, Wollstonecraft made a serious attempt at suicide. Concluding that Battersea Bridge was too public, she hired a man to take her to Putney Bridge in Fulham. In the dark, she paced back and forth for half an hour "till her clothes were thoroughly drenched and heavy with the wet." When she finally jumped into the Thames, she would not sink. In physical as well as emotional pain, she lost consciousness. Passing fishermen retrieved her from the water and took her to a tavern. Eventually, her old friends, Rebecca and Thomas Christie, gave her shelter.[15]

No one would deny Wollstonecraft's decision reflected serious emotional distress. But, in the late eighteenth century, suicide was not necessarily an antisocial act. Just as melancholy was sometimes understood as a "feminine counter-culture" in which women could acknowledge pain they could not control, suicide was also considered a rational response to an impossible situation. For centuries, Europeans had been of two minds about suicide. Whereas some writers exalted it "as a noble and heroic act" performed by aristocrats in imitation of classical heroes, devout Christians had long denigrated it. By the 1790s, scientists and doctors were tending to categorize suicidal feelings and insanity generally as a temporary alienation that could be diagnosed and treated. Many young people, however, interpreted suicide "as the result of the coherent act of refusing life." There was "a fashion for the suicide of despairing lovers, a taste for solitude, le vague à l'âme (virtual spiritual malaise), and complaints that time was fleeting." Suicides and attempts at suicide became common among the middling and upper classes in eighteenth-century Europe, honored as a rational refusal to live at the mercy of others.[16]

Rousseau, in his novel *Julie,* had captured the debate in an exchange be-

14. Ibid., Oct. 4, [1795], 324, Oct. 10, [1795], 326, 327; Godwin, *Memoirs,* ed. Clemit and Walker, 249. See Lyndall Gordon, *Vindication: A Life of Mary Wollstonecraft* (New York, 2005), 270–280; Janet Todd, *Mary Wollstonecraft: A Revolutionary Life* (New York, 2000), 264; Nyström, *Mary Wollstonecraft's Scandinavian Journey,* 26–27.

15. Godwin, *Memoirs,* ed. Clemit and Walker, 96; MW to Imlay, [circa October 1795], in Todd, ed., *Collected Letters,* 327 n. 693.

16. Mary Jacobus, "'The Science of Herself': Scenes of Female Enlightenment," in Tilottama Rajan and Julia M. Wright, eds., *Romanticism, History, and the Possibilities of Genre: Re-forming Literature, 1789-1837* (Cambridge, 1998), 254–259; Georges Minois, *History of Suicide: Voluntary Death in Western Culture,* trans. Lydia G. Cochrane (Baltimore, 1999), 241, 244, 248.

tween Julie's lover St. Preux and his English mentor. St. Preux made a case for the social utility of killing oneself. "When our life is an ill for us and a good for no one it is therefore permissible to deliver oneself of it." Distraught human beings who did evil were "dishonest." Reason's purpose was to help us deal with our "woes" by leading us "to meditate within ourselves" and to "raise ourselves to sublime contemplation." If that strategy failed, "our passions and errors cause our misfortunes." Recognizing the impossibility of moderation, a person ought to do what is good for everyone. God, after all, had made man the "sole judge of his own acts." To live when we feel it is "right . . . to die" was to defy God's plan. St. Preux's mentor repudiates this argument as an enthusiasm born in a "blind transport." Contemplating suicide was a fleeting desire to escape pain. Wounds to a body that could not be healed might justify suicide. But wounds to a soul ought to be treated with patience. "Did Brutus die a desperate lover, and did Cato rip out his entrails for a mistress?" St. Preux was a "petty, feeble man," a "mad youth" who needed to learn "to love life." And that meant restoring sociability and empathy, for it is "only in the business of an active life that you can hope to recover peace of mind." Rousseau's model of behavior under emotional duress was Julie's valiant struggle to manage her desire.[17]

As always, David Hume made a similar point more subtly. In "On Suicide," written in the 1750s and published in 1783, Hume supported the decision of "a man, who, tired of life, and hunted by pain and misery," sought to overcome "all the natural terrors of death" by killing himself. Such a decision was the ultimate deployment of human reason. Suicide, although never an easy choice, was sometimes a wise one, and almost always one that should be respected. "Has not every one . . . the free disposal of his own life? And may he not lawfully employ that power with which nature has endowed him?" Hume thought so, especially when a person concluded that he could no longer serve the interests of mankind. To be sure, people have social obligations. Still, given that "the life of man is of no greater importance to the universe than that of an oyster," no one ought to have to live "to do a small good to society, at the expence of a great harm to" himself.[18]

Wollstonecraft saw her attempt at suicide as a final effort to bring Gilbert Imlay to his senses. Furious about her rescue—as "the bitterness of death

---

17. Jean-Jacques Rousseau, *Julie; or, The New Heloise: Letters of Two Lovers Who Live in a Small Town at the Foot of the Alps* (1761), trans. Philip Stewart and Jean Vaché (Hanover, N.H., 1997), 311, 312, 313, 315, 317, 322, 323, 324.

18. David Hume, "Of Suicide," in *Essays: Moral, Political, and Literary,* ed. Eugene F. Miller (Indianapolis, Ind., 1987), 582, 583, 586.

was past, [she] was inhumanly brought back to life and misery"—she considered her choice to end her life "one of the calmest acts of reason." Imlay expressed bewilderment at Wollstonecraft's behavior in the passive voice and with an inappropriate metaphor. He told her he knew "'not how to extricate ourselves out of the wretchedness into which we have been plunged.'" Wollstonecraft defiantly rejected his offer of financial support, as she had rejected Joseph Johnson's years earlier. She would not accept "vulgar comfort." But she would accept an unconventional domestic life, as she would have with Henry Fuseli and his wife. If Imlay could not "break off the connection" with his new lover, she would live with them both. In part, she was thinking of the advantages for Fanny. It was important that Imlay "learn habitually to feel for [his] child the affection of a father." Wollstonecraft demanded a clear-cut answer to this proposal. If Imlay said no, she wrote, "here we end. You are now free. . . . [and] I will be to you as a person that is dead." Imlay accepted, and showed her a house he was considering renting. He insisted his new relationship was "merely a casual, sensual connection." Then he changed his mind—again! In November 1795, he and his new friend left London for Paris.[19]

A grief-stricken Wollstonecraft concluded that life was "an exercise in fortitude." Perhaps Imlay was right that some day she would "'judge more coolly of your mode of acting.'" More likely, they were both letting *passion* cloud their "reason." What he called "'exalted'" principles—did he mean liberty?—were really about his "own gratification." In "following your inclination," she wrote, he was "trampling on the affection you have fostered, and the expectations you have excited." Still, through it all, Wollstonecraft asserted that Imlay was "not what you now seem" nor would he "always act, or feel, as you now do." Her "image" would "haunt" him in Paris. Or so she hoped. Meanwhile, she had to face wretchedness created by her "social feelings, and delicacy of sentiment." She had "loved with my whole soul, only to discover that I had no chance of a return—and that existence is a burthen without it." In a larger sense, Imlay's "'most refined'" principles, or, rather, "capricious feelings," undermined "not only the most sacred principles, but the affections which unite mankind." His failure was their failure to collaborate on managing their sensibilities and cultivating their understanding.[20]

19. MW to Imlay, [circa October 1795], in Todd, ed., *Collected Letters*, 327, 328, to Imlay [speculative reconstruction], [circa October 1795], 329; Godwin, *Memoirs*, ed. Clemit and Walker, 98.

20. MW to Imlay, Nov. 27, [1795], in Todd, ed., *Collected Letters*, 332, 333.

Over and over again, Wollstonecraft characterized Imlay's current behavior as aberrant. The man she had known, the man for whom she still felt
affection, was better than this. To conclude that he had surrendered to "old
propensities," that she "and virtue" could not prevail, that he was unable "to
conquer" himself, devastated her. Bad as it was to lose a lover, worse was
to lose him when revolution was everywhere in retreat. That was altogether
too much. So she waited for him to return "to himself." How strange it was
that, despite his continued insistence that "mere animal desire" was "the
source of principle," she remained convinced that he "was not what he now
appeared to be." Perhaps their misunderstanding was merely the failure to
sustain commerce.[21]

"A Greedy Enjoyment of Pleasure without Sentiment"

Always present in Mary Wollstonecraft was a faith in the ability of human
beings to persuade one another of their own power to behave well. This attitude permeated the book she wrote in response to the general crisis precipitated by the confluence of the disintegration of her love affair and the collapse of the French Revolution. In January 1796, Joseph Johnson published
Mary Wollstonecraft's *Letters Written during a Short Residence in Sweden,
Norway, and Denmark*. William Godwin was the first of many readers to
note that this book was more readable than her previous work. The prose
is vivid because the details are concrete and the tone personal, the whole a
merging of the plot of a travel account with the sensibility of a novel. *A Short
Residence* is a narrative meditation on a wide range of subjects, including
Imlay, nature, love, motherhood, business, and the French Revolution, all of
which circle back to the question of commerce. Events unfold in real time;
everything is contingent. The novelty of this published version of her letters to Imlay lay in Wollstonecraft's retrospective creation of a coherent interior monologue from the multitude of sensations that had overwhelmed
her during her actual journey. *A Short Residence* feels modern because of
its psychological depth, because it takes place almost entirely within the
mind of an extraordinarily sensitive and self-aware person engaged in an
unstable conversation with her *self* about who she was.[22]

21. Ibid., Dec. 8, [1795], 334–335, [circa December 1795], 335, to Archibald Hamilton Rowan,
Jan. 26, [1796], 338, to Imlay, [circa March 1796], 339.

22. Godwin, *Memoirs*, ed. Clemit and Walker, 95. In thinking about Wollstonecraft's *Letters
Written during a Short Residence in Sweden, Norway, and Denmark* (1796), I have especially
learned from Syndy McMillen Conger, *Mary Wollstonecraft and the Language of Sensibility*

At the beginning of the trip, Wollstonecraft presented herself as a highly competent person quite capable of overcoming both the turmoil of her mind and the turmoil of the world. When unfavorable winds dissuaded the "good-natured" captain from landing her as promised at Gothenburg, she demanded that he send her, Fanny, and Marguerite to shore in a longboat. Wollstonecraft wore him down until he reluctantly granted permission. The sailors quickly obeyed her order to row her to a lighthouse surrounded by rocks. Wollstonecraft went ahead despite the concern of Marguerite— "whose timidity always acts as a feeler before her adventuring spirit"— about the desolation of the spot miles from Gothenburg. On shore, two old men told her of a pilot's house some eight to ten miles away. She gave the anxious sailors two guineas to convey her party to the new destination. What they found was a rude cottage whose "sluggish inhabitants" rarely saw "strangers, especially women." Dispatching the sailors to arrange for transportation to Gothenburg, Wollstonecraft pondered the impact of such isolation. People cut off from others were lazy in mind and body, so unlike the curious citizens of Paris who had made so much progress in "the art of living—in the art of escaping from the cares which embarrass the first steps towards the attainment of the pleasures of social life." Meanwhile, Marguerite fretted about "robberies, murders or the other evil which instantly, as the sailors would have said, runs foul of a woman's imagination." Eventually, Wollstonecraft encountered a boat with an officer who not only owned the cottage but who spoke English. Inside the house she found her initial unfavorable impression undone by the officer's wife, whose "hands" revealed her gentility and who kept her person and her home clean.[23]

After dining, Wollstonecraft climbed the rocks and surveyed the scene with the officer's telescope. Fanny, meanwhile, delighted in the discovery of "a few wild strawberries." It was a rapturous scene, inspired in no small part by their safe delivery from the sea. Wollstonecraft was happier than she had been "for a long, long time." She was finally able to forget "the "horrors"

(Rutherford, N.J., 1994), 145–159; Mary A. Favret, *"Letters Written during a Short Residence in Sweden, Norway, and Denmark:* Traveling with Mary Wollstonecraft," in Claudia L. Johnson, ed., *The Cambridge Companion to Mary Wollstonecraft* (Cambridge, 2002), 209–227; Jon Klancher, "Godwin and the Genre Reformers: On Necessity and Contingency in Romantic Narrative Theory," in Rajan and Wright, eds., *Romanticism,* 26, 27; and Eleanor Ty, "'The History of My Own Heart': Inscribing Self, Inscribing Desire in Wollstonecraft's *Letters from Norway,*" in Helen M. Buss, D. L. Macdonald, and Anne McWhir, eds., *Mary Wollstonecraft and Mary Shelley: Writing Lives* (Waterloo, Ont., 2001), 69–84.

23. MW, *A Short Residence in Sweden, Norway, and Denmark,* ed. Richard Holmes (New York, 1987), 64, 65, 66.

she had "witnessed in France, which had cast a gloom over all nature." The "enthusiasm" of her "character, too often, gracious God!, damped by the tears of disappointed affection" revived and "care took wing while simply fellow feeling expanded [her] heart." A visit to another family prolonged the pleasure. As the daughters fussed over Fanny, Wollstonecraft talked with the head of the household. He pronounced her "a woman of observation, for [she had] asked him *men's questions*." A day remarkable for courage and competence ended in deep sleep.[24]

Wollstonecraft rose early the next morning to find Fanny sleeping amid stillness. Why, Wollstonecraft wondered, did "melancholy and even misanthropy" so easily possess her? Why when the world "disgusted [her], and friends have proved unkind" did she feel as isolated as people on a rocky coast, "a particle broken off from the grand mass of mankind," in a word, "alone"? What always saved her was "some involuntary sympathetic emotion," which, "like the attraction of adhesion," made her feel that she was "still a part of a mighty whole" from which she could not separate herself. Social commerce was the only way to keep the "cruel experience of life" at bay.[25]

The citizens of Gothenburg, profiting from the burgeoning trade with France, lacked "civilization." Too many of them indulged in gross pleasures, drinking, gambling, and wasting time rather than together exercising their minds or their hearts. Their society was artificial, form without substance, "over-acted" rituals that impeded natural intimacy. Their hospitality amounted to "a fondness for social pleasures," in which drinking predominated over thinking. Vanity encouraged indulgence, as it had in the ancien régime of Europe as a whole. And yet Wollstonecraft found an antidote for despair in her unreliable old friend, her imagination. At "the witching time of night," when the world was peaceful save for the murmuring of water, she enjoyed an "Eternity" in which "worldly cares melt into the airy stuff that dreams are made of; and reveries, mild and enchanting as the first hopes of love, or the recollection of lost enjoyment, carry the hapless wight into futurity, who, in bustling life, has vainly strove to throw off the grief which lies heavy at the heart." If an ungoverned imagination was a coquette, a modulated imagination was a valuable friend.[26]

Scandinavia worried her. Swedish aristocrats maintained their sway, notwithstanding the "manly" resistance of peasants who, inspired by the

24. Ibid., 67, 68.
25. Ibid., 69–70.
26. Ibid., 72–73, 75.

French Revolution, were rejecting the idea that they were "a different order of beings." The prevalence of the French language among the aristocracy was a mixed blessing. A sign of refinement, it also inhibited the development of an indigenous literature, the social cost of which was huge. Wollstonecraft knew that as Swedes read and wrote, they would cultivate "an enlarged plan of usefulness, and with the basis of all moral principles—respect for the virtues which are not merely the virtues of convention." The surest path to progress was a self-awareness that grew from social commerce. "Mixing with mankind, we are obliged to examine our prejudices, and often imperceptibly lose, as we analyze them." That process, experience was teaching her, could occur in the countryside as well as in a city. People who inhabit "an abode absolutely solitary" become "intimate with nature" and thereby cultivate "sentiments dear to the imagination, and inquiries which expand the soul." Wollstonecraft's appreciation for the social utility of nature was limited, however, especially when it came to the impact of commerce on gender.[27]

In a moment of cultural imperialism, Wollstonecraft concluded that Swedes lacked the ambition nurtured in developed Britain. Swedish children were unrefined; in particular, their "country girls" lacked chastity because of the "ignorance of the mothers." Education of a British kind would help them rest their "passions . . . on something more stable than the casual sympathies of the moment." Wollstonecraft admired the natural qualities of Swedish peasants. Their "sincerity of innocence" contrasted sharply with the "artificial manners" of urban dwellers. "There is such a charm in tenderness!—It is so delightful to love our fellow-creatures, and meet the honest affections as they break forth." And yet, she could not live in rural Sweden. Although her "heart would frequently be interested," her "mind would languish for more companionable society." The charming Swedes would never improve themselves until they combined "the advantages of cultivation with the interesting sincerity of innocence."[28]

Wollstonecraft's story grew even more deeply retrospective when she left Marguerite and Fanny at Elias Boardman's house in Gothenburg and set out on her own for Norway. In retrospect, her unnerving journey became an exercise in the dangers of antisocial environments. Away from the town, "nature resumed an aspect ruder and ruder, or rather seemed the bones of the world waiting to be clothed with every thing necessary to give life and beauty." Even the "wild beauties" could not disguise that farms were be-

27. Ibid., 78, 79–80.
28. Ibid., 82, 83, 84.

coming smaller and houses poorer and that gardens were disappearing. The days were gloomy. Man must have originated in the north, she mused, to encourage his ambition, to get him to chase the sun. In the town of Strömstad on the coast, awaiting a ship to Norway, Wollstonecraft saw "the same unvaried immensity of water, surrounded by barrenness." The Norwegians, she decided, were wealthier and more industrious than their Swedish neighbors. They were fascinated by a "woman, coming alone." She found much to admire in them, especially farmers, "a manly race" who acted "with an independent spirit" and refused to countenance "oppression, excepting such as has arisen from natural causes." Yet, despite freedom of the press, education, and religious tolerance, Norwegians were "bastilled by nature—shut out from all that opens the understanding, or enlarges the heart." Someday, that situation would improve. Education and commerce would teach Scandinavians to "promote inquiry and discussion" rather than "gird the human mind round with imaginary circles." Knowledge diffused would "in a great measure destroy the factitious national characters[,] which have been supposed permanent, though only rendered so by the permanency of ignorance." To learn of the French Revolution was to overcome provincialism and enlarge "the heart by opening the understanding."[29]

On her own in an unfamiliar landscape among unfamiliar people, Wollstonecraft herself suffered from a want of company. Alone, she struggled to suppress growing melancholy. The Norwegians' sympathy for one who had dropped down "from the clouds in a strange land" could not overcome the pain of "parting with my daughter for the first time." She was more anxious than the average mother because she knew "the dependent and oppressed state of her sex." Wollstonecraft worried that the failure of her generation to navigate a radical sensibility meant that Fanny "should be forced to sacrifice her heart to her principles, or principles to her heart." All a mother could do was "cultivate sensibility" and "cherish delicacy of sentiment" with a "trembling hand" because of the many "thorns that will wound her breast. . . . I dread to unfold her mind, lest it should render her unfit for the world she is to inhabit. Hapless woman! what a fate is thine!" Increasingly agitated, Wollstonecraft was irritable with her hosts and eager for privacy. Why did "foolish vanity" lead women to lavish so much attention to their clothes? Why could she not have a room in an inn to herself? Why could she not arrange her "own time"? Why had she left Fanny in Gothenburg?[30]

Sublime landscapes produced "misery" as well as "rapture." The "chang-

29. Ibid., 88, 91, 93, 96, 102, 103, 105–106, 131.
30. Ibid., 97, 99.

ing wind" inspired "melancholy" and "extasy." Thinking of Fanny Blood, hearing her "soft voice warbling as [she strayed] over the heath," Wollstonecraft experienced happiness and sadness in equal measure. Recollections of her daughter started "the tear, so near akin to pleasure and pain." Missing her lover, she impatiently awaited his letters. Assuring Imlay that she was his, hoping "that the temporary death of absence may not endure longer than is absolutely necessary," Wollstonecraft sought fleeting solace in nature. She enjoyed spectacular views, bathed in the sea, and viewed embalmed bodies—always to return to the same challenge of controlling the "temperature of [her] soul." To make her "feelings take an orderly course" was to swim "against the stream." Equilibrium was never easily attained or sustained. She must "love and admire with warmth, or . . . sink into sadness." But the chill of "sorrow and unkindness" could not overcome the "tokens of love" that had "rapt [her] in elysium." Walking was reviving her, as did learning to row a boat. What kept her going above all else was "the fear of annihilation," the thought of "being no more—of losing myself— though existence is often but a painful consciousness of misery." Unable to imagine herself as dead, she had to believe that something "resides in this heart that is not perishable—and life is more than a dream." Occasionally, she envied women in domestic situations because they had what she did not: a complete family. What of her "babe" who might "never experience a father's care or tenderness"? The plight of a young mother abandoned by the child's father prompted reflections upon "the instability of the most flattering plans of happiness." Wollstonecraft "hastened" to take her "solitary evening's walk" to think of anything other than "the pangs arising from the discovery of estranged affection, and the lonely sadness of a deserted heart." She had found herself through love, developed independence through interdependence, and cultivated understanding through a blend of passion and reason. Alone, she was disintegrating.[31]

In the midst of an existential crisis brought on by her life in France— both the terror of the guillotine and the terror of desertion—Wollstonecraft searched for hope. The power of the sublime in both nature and social revolution overwhelmed her. She imagined a group of "august pines, towering above the snow" in winter relieving "the eye beyond measure, and [giving] life to the white waste." In the end, only "patient labour" would rescue mankind. "What a long time it requires to know ourselves." "And, considering the question of human happiness, where, oh!, where does it reside? Has it taken up its abode with unconscious ignorance, or with the high-wrought

31. Ibid., 99, 100, 109, 111, 112, 115, 145, 158.

man? Is it the offspring of thoughtless animal spirits, or the elf of fancy continually flitting round the expected pleasure?" All she could do was "catch
pleasure on the wing" and "be happy whilst I can." A mind alone was not
enough to conquer the "sorrow" of a "feeling heart." Wollstonecraft strained
to conjure improvements arising from the "wild coast" of Norway. As her
imagination took her to a future a millions years hence in which all the
world was "perfectly cultivated, and . . . completely peopled," she was filled
with dread. Would there be "universal famine?" Suddenly, "the world appeared a vast prison." Suddenly, she doubted that she had the power to
shape the future. Revolution was a dream. Admiring a "roaring cascade,"
she saw her thoughts as a similar "torrent." Perhaps she would find freedom
only in death. Another falls surrounded by pines and rocks excited "the idea
of chaos" and dwarfed the construction of a canal. The "awful roaring of the
impetuous torrents" made the human works and their tools appear to be
"the insignificant sport of children." Face to face with the terrifying power
of the sublime in all aspects of her life and cut off from regular human contact, an anxious Wollstonecraft had lost what she had found in London and
affirmed with Imlay: confidence in herself and the possibilities of rational
imagination.[32]

Unable to calm her "injured heart" or find refuge from "disappointed affection," she experienced the tyranny of "gloom." Enthusiasm dominated
her life. She "reasoned and reasoned," but her "heart was too full." What
to do but exercise herself into exhaustion and "forgetfulness"? "Friendship and domestic happiness" were rare because they were too hard to sustain. Keeping affection alive required "more cultivation of mind" than most
people supposed. Afraid "to be seen as they really are," people resisted the
"degree of simplicity" and "undisguised confidence" that were "the charm,
nay the essence of love or friendship." Wollstonecraft concluded that, however "sincere" friendship was in the beginning, it became a passing fancy
whose "usual prop" was "a mixture of novelty and vanity." Imlay, she implied, impetuously sought new sensations and relationships rather than
cultivated abiding ties. No wonder her friendship with him had proved to
be "such a wild-goose chase." Consumed by "a sensibility wounded almost
to madness," Wollstonecraft gave into "black melancholy," chastising herself for quarreling with "human nature" over "cruel . . . injuries." Isolation in
nature was no "retreat" from her "disappointments." "Reason drag[ged her]
back, whispering that the world is still the world, and man the same com-

32. Ibid., 118, 122, 128, 130, 152, 153, 160.

pound of weakness and folly, who must occasionally excite love and disgust, admiration and contempt." The struggle was to accept imperfection
without being overwhelmed by it. A stunning cascade of "impetuous[ly]
dashing" water excited both self-pity—why was she "chained to life and
its misery?"—and hope, leading her to stretch out her hand "to eternity,
bounding over the dark speck of life to come."[33]

Wollstonecraft still sought a middle ground in which people could nurture a tender sensibility that would tame psychological demons into manageable feelings. It would be best if she could "divide [her] time between
the town and country." In the latter, "solitary musing" would strengthen her
mind, whereas, in the former, she could "polish the taste which the contemplation of nature had rendered just." If her generation had truly failed to cultivate understanding together, if they admitted defeat, their legacy would
consist of new bastilles erected on the ruins of the old. "Thus do we wish as
we float down the stream of life," Wollstonecraft wrote with the resignation
that often accompanied her bouts of melancholy, "whilst chance does more
to gratify a desire of knowledge than our best-laid plans."[34]

As Wollstonecraft continued her journey into Denmark, she became
increasingly agitated. She saw Imlay's behavior now as an indictment of
the new impersonal world she had condemned in France. Suddenly, like
others in the late 1790s, she was concluding that economic and social commerce were not two sides of the same coin. Indeed, they were often at cross-
purposes. Trade was deceptive, speculative, and inherently self-interested.
It distracted individuals from more important work, as when in Risør, the
"business" of meeting with the English vice-consul "interrupted" her musing about mankind. No doubt Imlay thought her "too severe on commerce."
But the behavior of Scandinavians reinforced her belief that it wore out "the
most sacred principles of humanity and rectitude." "What is speculation,
but a species of gambling, I might have said fraud, in which address [or
manner of presentation, style] generally gains the prize?" Imlay was superficial as well as impulsive. Revolution and war encouraged both a worship of property and efforts to seize the property of others. Wollstonecraft's
sense of commerce was gaining an ironic historical dimension. "England
and America owe[d] their liberty to commerce." Creating "a new species
of power to undermine the feudal system" had the unanticipated "consequence" of creating "a tyranny of wealth . . . more galling and debasing

33. Ibid., 136, 137, 141, 149, 152, 153.
34. Ibid., 132–133.

than that of rank." Now as "commercial frauds" exploded during warfare and men adored property, the people of Copenhagen were more interested in sensuality than friendship. They had "banish[ed] confidence and truth," which were "the charm as well as the cement of domestic life." Love and friendship they did not know.[35]

If Imlay thought she was "harping on the same subject"—"the oppressed state of [her] sex"—he was right. How could it be otherwise? In Denmark, she noted a pattern: women tended to be seduced by their "superiors," whereas men were "jilted by their inferiors." Women were motivated by ambition, and men by tyranny. In any case, sensuality was the product of an "indolence of mind" rather than "an exuberance of life." In Copenhagen as elsewhere, women only had "freedom and pleasure" in the "interregnum between the reign of the father and husband." Courtship was intimate and prolonged. Lest Imlay question her motives, she assured him that her "principal object has been to take such a dispassionate view of men as will lead me to form a just idea of the nature of man." Still, she had to confess that she saw everything through "the jaundiced eye of melancholy—for I am sad—and have cause."[36]

In Copenhagen, she witnessed the ill effects of "Mushroom fortunes" in the "insolent vulgarity" and "groveling views of the sordid accumulators of *cent per cent.*" Men of business were "domestic tyrants, coldly immersed in their own affairs" and "ignorant" of the rest of the world; their wives were "weak" and "indulgent" women. Neither possessed principles. In the "farce" that was "life," wrote a despairing Wollstonecraft, quoting the blind Duke of Gloucester in *King Lear,* "As flies to wanton boys, are we to the gods; / They kill us for their sport." Consumed with trade, Imlay was "strangely altered" in ways of which he was unaware. Reflection had given way to "a continual state of agitation." Imlay epitomized the consequences of abandoning sociability for trade. "Men are strange machines. . . . A man ceases to love humanity, and then individuals, as he advances in the chase after wealth; as one clashes with his interest, the other with his pleasures: to business, as it is termed, every thing must give way; nay, is sacrificed; and all the enduring charities of citizen, husband, father, brother, become empty names." In Hamburg, a bitter Wollstonecraft denounced commerce for making merchants into gamblers, risking the fates of nations, practicing corruption, and perfecting fraud. "Contractors" and "the swarm of locusts who have

35. Ibid., 133, 143, 150, 170, 171.
36. Ibid., 171, 172, 178.

battened on the pestilence they spread abroad" were worse than soldiers. They behaved ignobly without any sense of the human costs of their profit. Like "the owners of negro ships," they "never smell on their money the blood by which it has been gained, but sleep quietly in their beds, terming such occupations *lawful callings.*" In short, they debased the noble promise of commerce into new forms of self-love and self-degradation. They made a virtue of not behaving like sensible men.[37]

At the end of the long journey was nothing but disappointment. Imlay was not in Hamburg to meet Wollstonecraft, as he had promised. He was gone and with him the possibilities of a world she had kept alive in her imagination. She arrived to "find nothing as it should be." Her "agitated spirits" sank. Still, she, who had endured "the cruelest of disappointments" months earlier when she learned of Imlay's betrayal, must "play the child, and weep at the recollection—for the grief is still fresh that stunned as well as wounded me." If men shaped themselves, then Imlay had chosen dreams of economic commerce over those of social commerce. Still, Wollstonecraft would not, could not, give up. Imlay's decision was not final. If he would but listen, she could persuade him of the folly of the choices he had made in her absence and help him rediscover the sensibility that once endeared him to her. Trade encouraged selfish hubris and discouraged empathetic sociability. "An ostentatious display of wealth without elegance, and a greedy enjoyment of pleasure without sentiment, embrutes [men of trade] till they term all virtue, of an heroic cast, romantic attempts at something above our nature; and anxiety about the welfare of others, a search for misery, in which we have no concern." If she was generalizing from personal experience, so be it. For, she whispered to Imlay, "you—yourself, are strangely altered, since you have entered deeply into commerce—more than you are aware of—never allowing yourself to reflect, and keeping your mind, or rather passions in a continual state of agitation." Imlay was not only betraying her, he was betraying himself, or at least the Imlay she imagined he might be. "Nature has given you talents, which lie dormant, or are wasted in ignoble pursuits—You will rouse yourself, and shake off the vile dust that obscures you, or my understanding, as well as my heart, deceives, me, egregiously—only tell me when?" Whatever had made Imlay, he could reform himself if he allied himself with her again. Ironically, he, like the French Revolution, demonstrated the destructive tendencies of allowing self-interest to run rampant without the counterbalance of social com-

37. Ibid., 165, 167, 191, 193, 195.

merce. People who did not grasp how necessary they were to one another would exchange nothing but commodities, care about nothing but themselves, and contribute nothing to mankind but vanity.[38]

"The World [Is] a Vast Prison"

Wollstonecraft's anger at Imlay ultimately fueled her most direct assault on the structures of patriarchy. In *Maria; or, The Wrongs of Woman,* an unfinished novel, she attempted a history of a "woman," not "an individual." Her "main object" was to reveal "the misery and oppression, peculiar to women, that arise out of the partial laws and customs of society." *Maria* was an experiment in realism. Despite her frequent disgust with novels, Wollstonecraft's choice of genre is not so surprising when we consider the tone of *A Short Residence* or the growing imperative to circumvent a repressive regime in Britain that was regularly imprisoning radical writers by the late 1790s, including her publisher Joseph Johnson. As important, fiction allowed her to imagine her audience as women thinking about the plight of women; it made patriarchy personal and consequential in a quotidian sense, not some distant abstraction. Wollstonecraft, like her friends William Godwin and Mary Hays, believed that novels need not be sentimental. Hoping "to pourtray passions [rather] than manners," she intended to illustrate "the wrongs of different classes of women equally oppressive" in a realistic fashion. Readers would not get conventional characters in conventional situations. Her argument that "matrimonial despotism of heart and conduct" were "the peculiar Wrongs of Woman; because they degrade the mind" had tempered her fancy. As Wollstonecraft explained in a letter to a friend, excerpted by Godwin in the novel's preface, no "woman of sensibility, with an improving mind" ought to have to endure patriarchal tyranny of the kind she sketched in *Maria.* No matter how sensible men were, whether they achieved dominance through coercion or consent, they wanted to use women's bodies and control their property. As always, Wollstonecraft insisted this behavior was learned rather than essential. Patriarchal structures, not genes, nurtured brutes and dolls. Men as well as women were bastilled, and any change in that situation had to begin with mixed-gender conversation. The only reasonable path to reform had to start in individual awakenings achieved through social commerce and persuasion. To challenge the authority of patriarchy required a new conception of the

38. Ibid., 189, 191.

origins and nature of authority itself, that is, that authority was historically constructed rather than fixed.[39]

Maria's husband confines his twenty-six-year-old wife, heir to a considerable fortune, in a house for the insane somewhere outside London. Anxious about the fate of her infant daughter, she sustains herself through books and the friendship of her keeper, Jemima. The most fully developed working-class woman in Wollstonecraft's writings, Jemima is the bastard daughter of two servants. Her mother died shortly after her birth, neglected by her seducer and mistreated by her mistress. "Left in dirt, to cry with cold and hunger," Jemima survives cruel treatment by her father and stepmother only to be raped at sixteen by her Methodist master. He deals with her subsequent pregnancy by giving her an "infernal potion" to cause an abortion. Thrown out by the master's angry wife, Jemima prostitutes herself to "the desires of the brutes" she meets. When she finds a position as a servant, she ends up with a man enfeebled by a "thoughtless career of libertinism and social enjoyment." His death renews the cycle of Jemima's life. She depends on a series of men until she allies herself with the master of the madhouse in which Maria and Henry are confined. It is hard to imagine how social commerce might have affected the course of Jemima's life, given the vulgar brutality that surrounds her at every step. Prostitution is the ultimate metaphor for the position of women in a grim society defined by selfish alienation.[40]

Maria has a story, which, despite the differences in class, is remarkably similar to Jemima's—and, ultimately, Wollstonecraft's. She relates her personal history as a cautionary tale for her daughter. Born into a respectable family in the English countryside, Maria had grown up with a tyrannical father and a mother who doted on her son; only her uncle had shown her any kindness. She married George Venables, the son of a merchant who had settled in her village. Fancying herself in love, Maria did not recognize the "selfish soul" of this "heartless, unprincipled wretch" until it was too late. Six years of marriage in London revealed George's true character, which was remarkably similar to that of the brutish British husbands in *The Emi-*

39. MW, *Maria; or, The Wrongs of Woman . . .* (1799), ed. Janet Todd (London, 2004), 59, 60; MW to George Dyson, [circa May 16, 1797], in Todd, ed., *Collected Letters*, 412. See Conger, *Mary Wollstonecraft*, 160–182; and Barbara Taylor, *Mary Wollstonecraft and the Feminist Imagination* (Cambridge, 2003), 231–245. Tilottama Rajan offers a fascinating analysis of William Godwin's interventions in Wollstonecraft's unfinished text. See Rajan, "Whose Text? Godwin's Editing of Mary Wollstonecraft's *The Wrongs of Woman,*" in Rajan, *Romantic Narrative: Shelley, Hays, Godwin, Wollstonecraft* (Baltimore, 2010), 174–214.

40. MW, *Maria,* ed. Todd, 80, 83, 84, 85.

grants. Obsessed with "commerce and gross relaxations," often drunk and brutish in bed, the misogynist George slept with "profligate women" and generally abused Maria. Impregnated after five years, she regretted allowing him to be "familiar" with her "person." George was a man of "tainted breath, pimpled face, and blood-shot eyes," not to mention "gross manners, and loveless familiarity." When he offers her body to one of his friends in return for a loan of five hundred pounds, Maria has had enough. Successfully resisting her prostitution, she removes her wedding ring and rejects his efforts to woo her back.[41]

But what was Maria to do beyond personal defiance? What were her options? The pregnant wife might leave her husband's household. But she had nowhere to go. Landlords refused her when they learned of her husband's threat of legal action against anyone who harbored her. Meanwhile, their disapproving wives reminded Maria of her duty to her husband. So she had discovered that men mistreated women. So what else was new? Maria simply has to endure the common misery. Moving from place to place, Maria concluded that there was no escape from her husband. Then suddenly her kind uncle dies. To keep his estate intact, he has willed it to Maria's infant and appointed Maria as guardian. When she seizes the opportunity to emigrate from England, her husband has her kidnapped from her chaise and locked up in the asylum, where she eventually learns that her child has died.

A chastened Wollstonecraft was brutally direct in drawing lessons from these tales of battered females. The "world [is] a vast prison" into which women are "born slaves." Marriage had "bastilled [Maria] for life." She had no legal existence. A wife was "as much a man's property as his horse, or his ass, she has nothing she can call her own." Men could support themselves and take lovers at will. Convention and law combined to ensure that women had no real choice and certainly no liberty. Men can be sexual; women cannot. Men who leave their wives scarcely suffer; a woman who leaves her husband "is despised and shunned, for asserting the independence of mind distinctive of a rational being, and spurning at slavery." Competitors for the attention of powerful men, women turned against one another, becoming mothers who preferred sons to daughters and wives who demanded from their peers the general obedience they themselves gave to brutish husbands. *Maria* unfolds in a world in which all women are prisoners. "Who ever risked any thing for me? Who every acknowledged me to be a fellow-creature?" asks Jemima. Contrary to the hopes of Wollstonecraft and Hays,

41. Ibid., 104, 107, 109, 114.

men will not voluntarily storm the bastille of marriage or allow women equal access to economic power. Revolution might have swept away kings and priests, it might have redrawn borders and created citizens, but it had not undone the unnatural slavery of women.[42]

Even in the midst of this bleak portrait, Wollstonecraft cannot give up on the possibility of social commerce. For, without it, the world is at an end. On one level, she is talking about female solidarity. In their shared degradation at the hands of men, Jemima and Maria forge a friendship across class lines. Deprived of love and respect, ignored and misused, they converse; they share their love of books. They make do even as Jemima knows that any man half as able and hardworking as she could have found a job. And they are convinced that their problems—and those of thousands like them—are the products of institutions, not their own failings. They reject the judgment that "misery [is] the consequence of indolence" and the advice that it is "the lot of man to submit to certain privations."[43]

Beyond female friendships, Wollstonecraft continues to advocate mixed-gender relationships in the face of oppression and injustice. When another prisoner, Henry Darnford, befriends Maria, Wollstonecraft again flirts with the possibility of a persuadable man. Darnford resembles Imlay, and the arc of his relationship with Maria resembles that of Imlay and Wollstonecraft. The two become friends because they are both unjustly confined, desperate for company, and eager for freedom. He sends her books via Jemima. He corresponds, asking to see her. He needs Maria. As they talk, Maria warms to Henry and empathizes with his situation. His childhood as the son of gamblers who married for convenience was as barren of "domestic affection" as hers. Without a proper education, Darnford raced through his income until he was forced to buy a commission in a regiment raised "to subjugate America." During the War of Independence, he was wounded and captured. Liking Americans so much that he decided to live among them, he "travelled into the interior parts of the country, to lay out my money to advantage." Unfortunately, he discovered that, although American minds were "enthusiastically enterprising," American hearts were full of "cold selfishness." Like Wollstonecraft in Norway, Darnford enjoyed the independence of his remote estate in the interior but missed "more elegant society." To do more than vegetate like an animal, he "determined to travel. Motion was a substitute for variety of objects." America offered little refinement: vice and trade dominated its towns. So he left the "land of liberty and vul-

42. Ibid., 64, 82, 86, 91, 114, 117, 118.
43. Ibid., 88.

gar aristocracy, seated on her bags of dollars," and returned to Britain, only to be kidnapped and confined in the asylum.[44]

The romance of Henry and Maria counters the desperate histories of the two women. A satisfying friendship is one that allows individuals to understand why they are necessary to each other. Like Maria's uncle, Wollstonecraft believed that "a marriage of mutual inclination" was "the only chance for happiness in this disastrous world." Maria and Henry's physical relationship grows from conversation. So attuned are they to each other that their eyes signal mutual consent to a kiss; sexual desire follows from intimacy. Darnford's commitment "to protect [Maria] from insult and sorrow—to make her happy, seemed not only the first wish of his heart, but the most noble duty of his life." He tenderly comforts her when she learns of her daughther's death and assures her "that it should henceforth be the business of his life to make her happy." Eager "to restore her to liberty and love," he repeatedly demonstrates respect for her person. Maria "loved him, for loving her too well to give way to the transports of passion." When they have sexual intercourse, she received him as "her husband," and "he solemnly pledged himself as her protector—and eternal friend." Henry's sensibility compensates for his "volatility." Friends before they are lovers might still be friends after they are lovers.[45]

Or at least they can in the asylum. Ironically and tellingly, Maria and Henry are better off in the relatively egalitarian structure of their prison than they are in the artificial and unjust world beyond it. The couple does well together until they escape into the venal society that destroys their love. The commerce of the prison encouraged love; the trade of the free world stifles it. George Venables sues Henry for adultery and seduction because he wants his dead daughter's inheritance. Although Wollstonecraft stopped writing before the resolution of the case, her notes indicate that George will win damages, that Maria will become pregnant by Henry, that Henry will desert her, and that Maria will kill herself. Sound familiar? Not a happy ending by any means; nor does Wollstonecraft offer hope for reform of entrenched patriarchal power. It was no longer the summer of 1793.

The only independence Maria has is her sense of herself. Acutely self-aware, she refuses to behave as she is expected. Resisting her husband's command to prostitute herself, she has given herself "voluntarily" to Henry. And she defies the authority of laws and men who would unnaturally restrain her. She will "appeal to [her] own sense of justice," to her conscience,

44. Ibid., 74, 75, 76.
45. Ibid., 78, 94, 104, 137, 138, 141.

to her own sense of right and wrong. Maria claims "a divorce [from George Venables], and the liberty of enjoying, free from molestation, the fortune left to me." She will have none of the judge's talk of duty, the dangers of divorce, and "French principles in public or private life." Once her husband violated her person by imprisoning her, she "believed myself, in the sight of heaven, free—and no power on earth shall force me to renounce my resolution." If Maria's was a fleeting autonomy imagined in defiance of the very real power that others exercised over her, her assertion testifies to the stubborn persistence of Wollstonecraft's vision and her abiding, if sorely tested, faith that rational intercourse could inspire some men and some women to rise above, at least briefly, both themselves and institutions developed to manage them.[46]

In the spring of 1796, several months after he had fled London, Gilbert Imlay and his newest lover returned to the British capital. When she heard the news, Wollstonecraft took two-year-old Fanny and confronted Imlay in a crowded parlor in the home of the Christies, the same couple in whose Paris house the estranged lovers had first met. Hearing Wollstonecraft's voice in the hall, Imlay went out immediately to keep her from entering the room and making a scene in front of their friends. She continued, however, in a spirit of "conscious rectitude." Holding Fanny up to Imlay, Wollstonecraft shamed him for his paternal dereliction. An abashed Imlay agreed to meet her the next day. In that conversation, he assured her that he was her friend, and she responded warmly. "At his particular request, she retained the name of Imlay, which, a short time before, he had seemed to dispute with her." Wollstonecraft left the next day to spend the month of March with friends in the country. There she received a letter from Imlay announcing that he had again changed his mind: he would not live with her. This time Wollstonecraft accepted his decision as final. A few weeks later the former lovers happened upon each other by accident on the New Road outside London. They walked together and talked until Imlay mounted his horse and rode off. They never saw each other again.[47]

Imlay and Wollstonecraft constructed what had happened between them differently. Imlay imagined liberty as independence: to be *somebody,* he had to be free to make his own choices. Wollstonecraft fancied mutuality the key to personal happiness and social stability: people must understand that they are "necessary" to one another. Whereas Wollstonecraft

46. Ibid., 144, 145.
47. Godwin, *Memoirs,* ed. Clemit and Walker, 99, 100.

argued that a romantic relationship should evolve into an enduring friendship, Imlay insisted on the right of a lover to withdraw his or her consent from a union created by their consent. In talking about his decision to leave her (and their daughter) for another woman, Imlay and Wollstonecraft emphasized different aspects of their generation's cultural crisis. He insisted he had a right to *divorce* her as informally as he had *married* her. She denounced this assertion as a product of the "impetuosity of [his] senses" and his failure to understand that his notion of independence amounted to social death.[48]

Imlay ultimately paid a huge price for his choice, and not just with scholars. His career deteriorated after he abandoned Wollstonecraft, particularly after her husband published his account of their affair in 1798. He never recovered the considerable social and cultural capital he had enjoyed in 1793 and died in obscurity on the island of Jersey in 1828. Imlay's treatment of Wollstonecraft underscored—indeed became the public signature—of his reputation as an unreliable man. It was an outcome he had clearly hoped to avoid. Unable—or afraid—to make a clean break, he had gone back and forth for months with Wollstonecraft, giving in to her requests to try again, struggling to find a way to keep everyone happy, to end a relationship without anyone thinking the worst of him. Imlay, like many of his peers, never figured out what it meant to be *somebody,* in large part because he never invested in anything to replace the structure of family and village he had abandoned in his youth.

Wollstonecraft was, in her words, "differently organized." Although she gave up on their relationship, she never gave up on him. Imlay, she believed, could still correct himself because his enslavement to his "inclination" reflected, not an essential weakness, but an imbalance between reason and passion. He could start over, become *somebody,* not by rejecting all authority and running off, but by more manfully negotiating the border between his right to choose for himself and his responsibility to "the affections which unite mankind." Until the end of her life, Wollstonecraft "never spoke of Mr. Imlay with acrimony, and was displeased when any person, in her hearing, expressed contempt of him." Never would she be his "enemy," for she was certain that "your mind, your heart, and your principles of action, are all superior to your present conduct." "It is strange," she told him, "in spite of all you do, something like conviction forces me to believe, that you are not what you appear to be." In short, Wollstonecraft held fast to the social value of mutual imagination and ambition. "We see what we wish,

48. MW to Imlay, [circa March 1796], in Todd, ed., *Collected Letters,* 339.

and make a world of our own," a character in *Maria* remarks, "and, though reality may sometimes open a door to misery, yet the moments of happiness procured by the imagination, may, without a paradox, be reckoned among the solid comforts of life." The outcome of the affair with Imlay, like the outcome of the French Revolution, did not invalidate the entire experience. If neither had ended well, it did not follow that they should never have begun.[49]

49. MW to Imlay, Sept. 27, 1795, ibid., 323, Nov. 27, 1795, 332, 333, Dec. 8, [1795], 334, [circa March 1796], 339; Godwin, *Memoirs,* ed. Clemit and Walker, 101; MW, *Maria,* ed. Todd, 138.

5

An "Exchange of sympathy"

Mary Wollstonecraft first met William Godwin at a small party in London in November 1791. "The interview was not fortunate," Godwin later recalled. He had sought an invitation to dinner at a friend's to meet Thomas Paine, who had recently published *The Rights of Man.* Godwin had no interest in Wollstonecraft, whose style he found distasteful. Unfortunately, Paine was "no great talker," and Wollstonecraft was; he therefore "heard her, very frequently," when he "wished to hear Paine." The conversation centered on the characters of famous men and religion. Godwin thought Wollstonecraft eager to criticize, no matter how equivocal the evidence. She saw "every thing on the gloomy side," whereas he was inclined "to the supposition of generous and manly virtue." Godwin and Wollstonecraft encountered each other on two or three occasions before she left for France. But they made little "progress towards a cordial acquaintance."[1]

Circumstances were very different when the two met at a dinner in London on January 8, 1796, a few months after Wollstonecraft had returned from Hamburg. As before, the conversation did not go well. But, by the end of the month, Godwin had read *Letters Written during a Short Residence in Sweden, Norway, and Denmark.* Unlike Wollstonecraft's previous work, it was "a book calculated to make a man fall in love with its author." In the following weeks, Godwin and Wollstonecraft saw each other frequently. Because they lived close to each other, they increased their "intimacy . . . by regular, but almost imperceptible degrees." Godwin retrospectively took

---

1. William Godwin, *Memoirs of the Author of "A Vindication of The Rights of Woman"* (1798), ed. Paula Clemit and Gina Luria Walker (Peterborough, Ont., 2001), 80, 81.

pride in their treatment of each other. Neither was aggressive; neither was "the agent or the patient, the toil-spreader or the prey, in the affair." Like Maria and Henry, they became acquaintances, then friends, and lovers in the natural course of things. When they declared themselves in August, it was an example of "friendship melting into love." This romance could not have been more different from that of Wollstonecraft and Imlay.[2]

A deeply wounded Wollstonecraft warned Godwin that she was not optimistic about a new relationship. When she tried to "catch" the roses he said grew "profusely in every path of life," she "only encounter[ed] the thorns." Perhaps she must be a *"Solitary Walker."* Rather than seek bliss, they should "extract as much happiness, as we can, out of the various ills of life." It was imperative that they act in a manly fashion. If he wanted to engage her, he should not "choose the easiest task," her "perfections"; rather, he should "dwell on [his] own feelings," give her "a bird's-eye view of [his] heart." What Wollstonecraft required was a friend who would always tell her the truth, who would love her, not the idea of love itself. There was no point in even contemplating a close friendship if she could not believe what he told her, if together they could not cultivate understanding.[3]

Godwin was eager to share his opinions on political and philosophical subjects. Profoundly inexperienced in the realm of intimacy, Godwin had never had a lover. Taking up Wollstonecraft's challenge, he revealed himself in unprecedented fashion. This couple grasped early on that they were necessary to each other. Opposites in many ways, they soon discovered a degree of happiness together that they had never known separately. He respected her autonomy, gave her unqualified support, and helped her to maintain her emotional balance; she opened him up, encouraging him to indulge desire, to respect passion as well as reason. Two independent people choosing each other's company, they fulfilled Wollstonecraft's vision of rational desire that was something more than the sum of its parts.

"A Trembling Sensibility"

William Godwin was a delicate man of medium build with a solemn demeanor dominated by large blue eyes and an oversized nose. He had been born in Wisbech, Cambridge, on March 3, 1756, the seventh of thirteen chil-

---

2. Ibid., 95, 103, 104.

3. Mary Wollstonecraft (MW) to William Godwin, [Aug. 17, 1796], in Janet Todd, ed., *The Collected Letters of Mary Wollstonecraft* (New York, 2003), 349, to Mary Hays, [1796], 344, to Godwin, July 1, 1796, 342.

Figure 7. William Godwin. *By James Northcote. Oil on canvas, 1802.*
© *National Portrait Gallery, London*

dren. Godwin felt neglected by his parents and mistreated by teachers. His
father devoted himself to his work as a Dissenting minister, and his mother
was busy burying children when she was not bearing them. He had few
friends. Mostly, he lived through reading and inventing stories. Godwin's
imagination fueled an ambition that overrode his diffidence. Seeking "admiration" and "distinction," he determined to become a minister, although
different in style and substance from his father. After John Godwin's death,
he attended Hoxton Academy in London from 1772 until 1778. His immer-

sion in Dissenting culture had a powerful impact on him. In late 1779, Godwin became the minister to a congregation at Stowmarket in Suffolk. Ignoring his lack of ordination and the disapproval of his peers, he called himself "reverend" and administered the sacraments. His attention to the writings of French philosophes and discussion of alternatives to Calvinism alienated the congregation at Stowmarket and another one at Beaconsfield in Buckinghamshire.[4]

Godwin soon accepted that he had no aptitude for the ministry. In 1783, he moved to London and became a professional writer, or, more precisely, a Grub Street hack. Writing histories, novels, and essays for newspapers and magazines, he managed to earn around one hundred pounds a year. He understood the importance of friendship in fashioning a literary career and worked his way into the city's intellectual circles. By the early 1790s, Godwin was a well-established radical intellectual who underscored his self-constructed outsider status by cutting his hair, wearing bright clothes, and celebrating his agnosticism. Uncomfortable in company, he was a curious mixture of diffidence and confidence. Godwin claimed he had "a trembling sensibility and an insatiable ambition; a sentiment that panted with indescribable anxiety for the stimulus of approbation." Overcompensating for his social unease, he tended to be "rash in assertion . . . and weak in opposition." By his own admission, "bold and adventurous in opinions, not in life," with "a softness, approaching to effeminacy," he was "ill calculated for a practical politician." His "abilities" were "better adapted for contemplation than action." Ashamed of his "timidity," he spoke his mind without regard for his impact on others. He kept the world at a distance even as he critiqued it.[5]

---

4. William Godwin, "Autobiography," in Mark Philp et al., eds., *Collected Novels and Memoirs of William Godwin,* 8 vols. (London, 1992), I, 9, 10, 15, 16, 19, 25, 29, and Godwin, "Autobiographical Fragments," 42, 43. For a physical description of Godwin, see William St. Clair, *The Godwins and the Shelleys: The Biography of a Family* (New York, 1989), 11. Marilyn Butler and Mark Philp, "Introduction," in Philp et al., eds., *Collected Novels and Memoirs,* I, 7–46, is an excellent overview of Godwin's life. See also Peter H. Marshall, *William Godwin* (New Haven, Conn., 1984), 1–92.

5. Godwin, "Autobiography," in Philp et al., eds., *Collected Novels and Memoirs,* I, 24–25, 26, 31, 35, 37, and Godwin, "Analysis of Own Character Begun Sep 26, 1798," 55, 57, 59. See Mark Philp, *Godwin's Political Justice* (Ithaca, N.Y., 1986), 321–354, for an elaborate reconstruction from Godwin's diary of his social contacts. For critiques of Godwin and his circle, see E. P. Thompson, *The Making of the English Working Class* (1963; rpt. New York, 1966); and Gregory Claeys, "The Origins of the Rights of Labor: Republicanism, Commerce, and the Construction of Modern Social Theory in Britain, 1796–1805," *Journal of Modern History,* LXVI (1994), 249–290. Mark Philp has done much to correct the image of Godwin and his friends as dilettantes.

Godwin built a comfortable and predictable life. After mornings devoted to reading the works of Horace, Molière, Shakespeare, David Hume, Jonathan Swift, Thomas Holcroft, and Elizabeth Inchbald, among others, he went out to dine with writers and artists such as Holcroft, Inchbald, George Dyson, John Thelwall, William Nicholson, Joseph Ritson, Charles Sinclair, Alexander Jardine, and Maria and William Reveley. The topics under discussion were often abstract; they included happiness, optimism, sensuality, conversation, education, marriage, obligations, and passions. Rarely did Godwin mention events. Among the exceptions in late 1793 were the execution of the queen of France and the British evacuation of Toulon.[6]

Even as friends complained about his brutal candor and emotional reserve, both to his face and behind his back, they sought out his company. He was smart, curious, and well read. As important, he paid attention to other people, sometimes more than they would have liked. By the mid-1790s, as Godwin became a literary celebrity, he attracted the interest of writers, editors, artists, and professionals in London, Bristol, Edinburgh, Dublin, Philadelphia, and New York. Efforts to formalize endless discussion into organized clubs abounded. Perhaps the most famous in Britain was the Lunar Society in Birmingham. New York had the Friendly Club. Godwin belonged to the Philomathian Society in London and regularly attended its meetings until 1796. He also encouraged Jardine to establish a Select Club, although he ultimately failed. In the end, however, Godwin was not a joiner. He preferred informal discussions over meals with a fluctuating circle of people.[7]

Although Godwin was never entirely comfortable with political radicalism, he supported his friends who were. When William Pitt's government arrested Holcroft, Thelwall, and several other London radicals in the fall of 1795 under an ancient definition of treason, Godwin sprang to their defense. He wrote a powerful essay, published in the *Morning Chronicle* on October 21, claiming the government had overstepped its constitutional bounds. In the face of a widespread outcry, the charges were dropped in November. The Pitt government was not finished, however. It proposed two bills, both of which passed in early 1796, designed to extend officials' power to break

---

See also David Karr, "'Thoughts That Flash Like Lightning': Thomas Holcroft, Radical Theater, and the Production of Meaning in 1790s London," *Journal of British Studies*, XL (2001), 324–356; and Pamela Clemit, "Holding Proteus: William Godwin in His Letters," in Heather Glen and Paul Hamilton, eds., *Repossessing the Romantic Past* (Cambridge, 2006), 100.

6. Godwin, Diary, 1793, Oxford, Bodleian, MS Abinger e. 6, fols. 1–48, esp. 5–15.

7. See Catherine O'Donnell Kaplan, *Men of Letters in the Early Republic: Cultivating Forums of Citizenship* (Chapel Hill, N.C., 2008); and Jenny Uglow, *The Lunar Men: Five Friends Whose Curiosity Changed the World* (New York, 2002).

up public meetings and prosecute sedition. Again, Godwin took up his pen in defense of individual liberty, free speech, and reform of Parliament. *Considerations on Lord Grenville's and Mr Pitt's Bills* was by common consent one of the most effective publications of his career. But Godwin was characteristically as critical of the tactics of the government's opponents as he was of the government. Never a fan of violence or ad hominem attacks, Godwin celebrated rational, open discussion. He sought revolution through persuasion rather than force. When he fell out with friends, as he often did, he attempted reconciliation through even more conversation.[8]

Women writers, including Amelia Alderson, Elizabeth Inchbald, and Mary Hays, were as fascinated by Godwin's straightforward manner and egalitarian ideas as they were appalled by his emotional distance and paternalism. The inquisitive writer liked strong, smart women. He and Inchbald regularly exchanged candid letters about each other's work. Twenty-four-year-old Sarah Parr, the daughter of Dr. Samuel Parr, told her father's friend, Godwin, exactly what she thought of his blunt style. "I have increased antipathy to truth and precision because I daily find fresh reason to believe them more cloaks for rudeness and affectation."[9]

Amelia Alderson was equally forthright. Alderson met Godwin at her Dissenting father's house in Norwich in 1794 and later called on him at his London home. She complained that the few people who constituted society in Norwich displayed an *"eagerness* to deliver their opinion tho' they violate propriety, and good manners by breaking forcibly in on the argument of one else." She valued "silence" in herself and in Godwin. They had "the power of *listening, patiently* and *attentively* even to *bad arguments badly delivered."* Soon the friends were corresponding about their writing and their lives. Neither pulled their punches. Alderson was a serious flirt who liked to tease and taunt. Godwin replied in kind. In one exchange, she exclaimed that she hated him "for always throwing coquette in my teeth—it is a bad habit and you have lately acquired a worse—you called me a bitch the last time I saw you—but no matter." She bristled when he queried whether her affection for her family was rational. After a spirited exchange, Alderson concluded that she "was more of the *woman* than when he saw me last." Godwin's patronizing reference to female emotion had to coexist with his willingness to engage in serious conversation and his fear that his honesty was alien-

8. St. Clair, *Godwins and Shelleys,* 92, 128–135; Godwin to [Thomas Wedgwood], May 30, 1797, Oxford, Bodleian, MS Abinger c. 22, fols. 33–34.

9. [Sarah] Anne [Parr] to Godwin, Mar. 23, 1796, Oxford, Bodleian, MS Abinger c. 3, fols. 25–26. See Marshall, *William Godwin,* 172–175; and St. Clair, *Godwins and Shelleys,* 147–156.

ating her: "Rarely did we agree, and little did he gain on me by his mode of attack, but he seemed alarmed lest he should have offended me, and apologised several times, with much feeling, for the harshness of his expressions. In short, he convinced me that his theory has not yet gotten entire ascendancy over his practice." Godwin subsequently declared "a melancholy regret" if Alderson really was "governed by [her] affections," in the popular meaning of the expression. "To be governed by our affections, in the company we keep, or the conduct we pursue, most usually means, to discard our understanding." His brutal honesty reflected his desire to encourage her to "exercise a penetrating scrutiny" with regard to people and ideas.[10]

Alderson and Godwin remained friends despite, or perhaps because of, this tension. She married his friend, the painter John Opie, in 1798 and wrote several novels that reflected her strong opinions about the status of women. After Godwin and Wollstonecraft became lovers, Alderson explained to her new friend Wollstonecraft that she, like Rousseau's *Julie,* was a person "so capable of feeling affection that you cannot fail to excite it." After reading *A Short Residence,* Alderson overcame her apprehension about meeting the author of *A Vindication of the Rights of Woman.* Like Godwin, she saw "the cold awe which the philosopher had excited . . . lost in the tender sympathy call'd forth by the woman. I saw nothing but the interesting creature of feeling, and imagination" who "had alternately awakened my sensibility and gratified my Judgment." Alas, she told Wollstonecraft, Godwin had proved a disappointment, a man of mind more than heart.[11]

Mary Hays, herself no shrinking violet, was less shocked by Godwin. She sought his friendship in 1794 because she wanted an "opportunity of investigating further the important and interesting subjects of moral truth and political justice" he had discussed in recent books. Godwin was happy to comply. His honesty endeared him to Hays. She "always" greeted him "with pleasure" and was "sorry" when he left. His "conversation excite[d] the curiosity and the activity of [her] mind" and helped her with her tendency toward "confusion." Godwin was a source of comfort. With his "conversation and society," she would not "desert" herself. Hays was unusual. Most people found Godwin intellectually stimulating and emotionally enervat-

---

10. Amelia Alderson to Godwin, Aug. 28, 1795, Oxford, Bodleian, MS Abinger c. 2, fols. 108–109, Alderson to Godwin, Nov. 1, 1796, c. 3, fols. 40–41; Alderson to "My dear Mrs. T[aylor]," 1794, in Cecilia Lucy Brightwell, ed., *Memorials of the Life of Amelia Opie* . . . (Norwich, 1854), 43; Godwin to Alderson, Sept. 8, 1794, in Pamela Clemit, ed., *The Letters of William Godwin,* I, *1778-1797* (Oxford, 2011), 100.

11. Alderson to MW, Aug. 28, [probably 1797], Oxford, Bodleian, MS Abinger c. 41, fols. 9–10.

ing. Cordial with many, he had never experienced true intimacy with anyone. Honoring his independence above all else, Godwin declined to be
"weak." He would not "make my peace depend upon the precarious thread
of another's life or another's pleasure."[12]

Although Godwin and Wollstonecraft did not know each other well in
January 1796, they were aware of each other's reputation. In a burst of concentrated creativity earlier in the decade, Godwin had written two books—a
novel entitled *Things as They Are; or, The Adventures of Caleb Williams* and
*An Enquiry Concerning Political Justice and Its Influence on General Virtues
and Happiness*—that were as celebrated and as controversial as anything
Wollstonecraft had written. *Political Justice* was a sensation that took the
English-speaking world by storm. What Godwin offered was the fullest
available explication of a new social order organized around natural commerce. He was far more specific than Wollstonecraft in showing how rational friendship and manly exchange would function. Here was the strongest
statement for the power of love as the model of revolution.[13]

Written between September 1791 and January 1793, *Political Justice* was
not "a sudden effervescence of fancy." It reflected more than a decade of
thinking catalyzed by "ideas suggested by the French revolution." The central argument was that "government by its very nature counteracts the improvement of individual mind." Godwin started with the commonplace
eighteenth-century assumption that human beings are not innately good
or evil. As important, there is not necessarily any correlation between mo-
tive and outcome. Education involved learning that virtue is "that species
of operations of an intelligent being, which conduces to the benefit of intelligent beings in general, and is produced by a desire of that benefit." The
meaning of virtue emerged through "the collision of mind with mind" in
unfettered social commerce. Human beings needed to engage with one another not only to collect information and see other perspectives but also to
develop a full perspective on themselves. Government interferes with the
cultivation of virtue because it tends toward the preservation of the status
quo. Justice is not the operation of law; it is "a rule of conduct originating

12. Mary Hays to Godwin, Oct. 14, 1794, in "Appendix A—Selections from the Mary Hays and
William Godwin Correspondence," in Hays, *Memoirs of Emma Courtney* (1796), ed. Marilyn L.
Brooks (Peterborough, Ont., 2000), 224, Oct. 13, 1795, 231, Jan. 11, 1796, 236, 237; [Godwin] to
[Hays], [Feb. 2, 1796], Oxford, Bodleian, MS Abinger c. 22, fols. 18–22.

13. Philp, *Godwin's Political Justice*, 1. See Isaac Kramnick, "On Anarchism and the Real
World: William Godwin and Radical England," *American Political Science Review,* LXVI (1972),
119, 122.

in the connection of one percipient being with another." Godwin's scheme rested on the assumption that the world functioned best when its operations were natural.[14]

Godwin did not advocate a world in which there were no restraints on personal freedom. To the contrary, individuals and societies could only function morally—let alone improve themselves—when they recognized the importance of benevolence, a sense of obligation to others. They had to understand freedom, not as the power to do as they pleased, but as the ability to choose what to think and how to act as a member of a community. "The rights of one man cannot clash with or be destructive of the rights of another," wrote Godwin. "From hence it inevitably follows that men have no rights" in the sense of acting with "discretion," meaning on their own. To discover and to practice true justice, men had to consult with one another. They had to engage through books and, even better, through conversation. Ironically, the cultivation of private judgment depended on a regular exchange of ideas and feelings with other people. "To a rational being there can be but one rule of conduct, justice, and one mode of ascertaining that rule, the exercise of his understanding." Government in any form was "nothing more than a scheme for enforcing by brute violence the sense of one man or set of men upon another"; it thereby undermined the cultivation of justice. "Whenever government assumes to deliver us from the trouble of thinking for ourselves, the only consequences it produces are those of torpor and imbecility." Indeed, it institutionalized injustice in economic equality and the domination of the many by the few. Democracy in small communities most closely approximated Godwin's ideal because it, in the manner of London's literary world, was predicated on the idea that people learned through persuasion, not coercion. "To give each man a voice in the public concerns comes nearest to the admirable idea of which we should never lose sight, the uncontrolled exercise of private judgment." No one should submit to any form of power over his own mind or body except that to which his understanding, developed in conversation with other independent individuals, leads him to consent.[15]

---

14. William Godwin, *An Enquiry concerning Political Justice,* in Mark Philp et al., eds., *Political and Philosophical Writings of William Godwin,* 7 vols. (London, 1993), III, iv, 10, 15, 20, 49. See the contract between Godwin and his publisher George Robinson, Feb. 5, 1793, Oxford, Bodleian, MS Abinger c. 38, fols. 8–9; and Philp's excellent *Godwin's Political Justice,* esp. 2, and the argument that Godwin came to hold "a vision of community in which agents become progressively rational through the practices of private judgment and public discussion" (36).

15. Godwin, *Enquiry concerning Political Justice,* in Philp et al., eds., *Political and Philosophical Writings,* III, 67, 72, 92, 97, 110, 320–321.

According to Godwin, justice would flourish when individuals freely acknowledge that they need one another. "Natural independence, a freedom from all constraint except that of reason and argument presented to the understanding, is of the utmost importance to the welfare and improvement of mind." But

> moral independence is always injurious: for . . . there is no situation in which I can be placed, where it is not incumbent upon me to adopt a certain species of conduct in preference to all others, and of consequence where I shall not prove an ill member of society, if I act in any other than a particular manner. The attachment that is felt by the present race of mankind to independence in this respect, the desire to act as they please without being accountable to the principles of reason, is highly detrimental to the general welfare.

Thus "mutual communication" was the most effective way of exercising "independent judgment." Indeed, revolutions

> consist principally in a change of sentiments and dispositions in the members of those states. The true instruments for changing the opinions of men are argument and persuasion. The best security for an advantageous issue is free and unrestricted discussion. In that field truth must always prove the successful champion. If then we would improve the social institutions of mankind, we must write, we must argue, we must converse. To this business there is no close; in this pursuit there should be no pause.[16]

Like most critics, Godwin was more adept at diagnosing ills than prescribing alternatives. His vision of a more perfect world was vague. But throughout *Political Justice,* indeed throughout his career, Godwin always insisted that the dynamic process of social inquiry was the outcome he envisioned. "Every man ought to be rest upon his own centre, and consult his own understanding," wrote Godwin. If "every man ought to feel his independence, that he can assert the principles of justice and truth, without being obliged treacherously to adapt them to the peculiarities of his situation, and the errors of others," it was equally true that "mind without benevolence is a barren and cold existence." "It is in seeking the good of others, in embracing a great and expansive sphere of action, in forgetting our own individual interests, that we find our true element." People pursu-

---

16. Ibid., 98, 100, 115, 448–449.

ing their own interests would realize that their happiness depended on respecting the happiness of others.[17]

Godwin's attitude toward marriage embodied this philosophy. All relationships were consensual. Individuals should be free to come and go as they thought best. Requiring unhappy men and women to live together was to institutionalize "thwarting, bickering and unhappiness." Marriage was "a system of fraud," and property, a monopoly. Human relationships ought to function as commerce. Anything else was tyranny. "So long as two human beings are forbidden by positive institution to follow the dictates of their own mind, prejudice is alive and vigorous. So long as I seek to engross one woman to myself, and to prohibit my neighbour from proving his superior desert and reaping the fruits of it, I am guilty of the most odious of all monopolies." Moving beyond the idea that only consent made organization legitimate, Godwin insisted that consent must be understood as conditional. Just as a person could end a friendship, change residences, and leave one country for another, so, too, should he or she be free to come and go in all human relationships. No one would expect a rational person to endure a tyrant in politics or to continue a friendship that had become stale. Why expect something different from lovers? Why should not the "intercourse of the sexes . . . fall under the same system as any other species of friendship"?[18]

Many readers thought *Political Justice,* like its author, cold and impersonal, and with good reason. Godwin knew virtually nothing of love or sexuality. The prospect of children seemed not to have occurred to him. Critics cited a passage in which Godwin recommended that a person faced with the dilemma of saving a philosopher or a family member from certain death should always choose the former. He reasoned that the decision should reflect the greater good of society as a whole. Similarly, Godwin's faith in reasoned discourse and volitional community struck many as impractical, a naive dismissal of the essential tendency of flawed human beings to behave badly. The idea that people could regulate themselves was laughable. No one liked government, as his friend Thomas Paine had famously written in 1776; it was "the badge of lost innocence." Society promoted "our happiness *positively* by uniting our affections, the latter *negatively* by restraining our vices." Godwin did not deny the existence of wickedness. He, like Woll-

17. Ibid., 456.

18. Ibid., 453, 454. Godwin's reflections on marriage had many antecedents, including Daniel Defoe's *Conjugal Lewdness; or, Matrimonial Whoredom* (London, 1727) and, especially, John Milton's *Doctrine and Discipline of Divorce . . .* (London, 1644).

stonecraft, simply argued that coercion could not repress it as successfully as choices made by rational individuals in conversation with one another.[19]

The recent history of France proved the point. Yes, the Revolution had gone awry. Godwin deplored "French practices" as much as he supported "French principles." But war was not the answer. "Force will always be found the weakest of all engines in the field of theoretical controversy, and that particularly in an age of civilisation and literature." Governments could never control what men thought and felt. Great Britain might well conquer France, but it would never conquer the minds of people inspired by the principles of its revolution. After all, what differentiated "the uncultivated savage" from "the enlightened member of a civilised community" was "that the one employs force to obtain his purposes, and the other reason." "War brutifies the human species" and interrupts "the calm progress of reflexion." Like individuals, "nations are not to be dragooned into liberty and happiness, but are to be persuaded by a mild and illustrious example, and by dispassionate instruction." Godwin thus summarized his preference for natural intercourse over artificial regulation. Objecting to the existence of power in personal connections, he was seeking nothing less than a revolution in social relations.[20]

In November 1795, when writing to protest bills introduced in Parliament to outlaw mass public meetings by organizations such as the London Corresponding Society, the author of *Political Justice* argued that the struggle between liberty and order was endless. "The great problem of political knowledge, is, how to preserve to mankind the advantages of freedom, together with an authority, strong enough to controul every daring violation of general security and peace." Reason might govern local communities, but it was not enough for nations, with their endless variety in peoples and ideas. True order lay in moderation achieved through deliberation. Both radical activists and their critics were behaving impetuously. Members of Parliament were acting with "a sort of youthful alacrity," consulting, "not the coolness of philosophy[, but] the madness of passion." Rather than "reason," they "rail[ed]." "Reform must come." "It is a resistless tide," all the more dangerous when opposed. However thoughtless the actions of the London Corresponding Society, they paled in comparison with the actions of the ministry of William Pitt the Younger. Pitt seemed "determined that we shall not hear

19. Thomas Paine, *Common Sense* (1776), in Michael Foot and Isaac Kramnick, eds., *Thomas Paine Reader* (New York, 1987), 66.

20. William Godwin, "Essay against Reopening the War with France," in Philp et al., eds., *Political and Philosophical Writings*, II, 47, 50, 60–61.

the tempest, till it burst upon us in a hurricane, and level everything with the dust." In the face of extremes, Godwin persisted in his faith in social commerce.[21]

"A Solitary Walker" No More

As Godwin and Wollstonecraft progressed from being acquaintances to friends to lovers, they transformed each other, or, as important, thought they did. A cautious Wollstonecraft celebrated Godwin's divergence from Imlay. She admired his "self-government." Love with him was not a defiant surrender to emotion. With Godwin she experienced "one of those moments, when the senses are exactly tuned by the rising tenderness of the heart, and according reason entices you to live in the present moment, regardless of the past or future—It is not rapture.—It is a sublime tranquility. I have felt it in your arms." She slowly lowered her guard. Long-term happiness was found in contentment, not ecstasy. A well-considered love was a dynamic relationship in which two individuals came to know themselves better through regular intercourse. Mutuality was the foundation of everything.[22]

Wollstonecraft was manly with Godwin—and the exercise made her see herself with unprecedented clarity. She complained when he was so "full" of his "own feelings" that he "forgot" hers or did "not understand [her] character." They could not love each other if he did not accept her moodiness, or, more positively, the complexities of her emotions. She was "a painter" who "delight[ed] to view the grand scenes of nature and the various changes of the human countenance." None did she watch more avidly than her own, which was why she was inclined "to be angry" with herself when she did "not animate and please" those she loved. It was her intensity that made her so wary. Who knew what might become of their new love? She would not pretend to know where it would lead. Wollstonecraft likened herself to a sycamore tree, standing in the middle of evergreens and blossoming in the trust that spring had arrived, only to be chastised by a sudden frost. As her "living green" gave way to "a brown, melancholy hue," "a taunting neighbour whispered to her, bidding her, in future, [to] learn to distinguish feb-

---

21. A Lover of Order [William Godwin], *Considerations on Lord Grenville's and Mr. Pitt's Bills, concerning Treasonable and Seditious Practices and Unlawful Assemblies . . .* (1795), in Philp et al., eds., *Political and Philosophical Writings,* II, 125, 157, 159, 161. On Godwin's intellectual evolution, see Philp, *Godwin's Political Justice,* 103–167.

22. MW to Godwin, [Sept. 30, 1796], in Todd, ed., *Collected Letters,* 369, [Oct. 4, 1796], 371.

ruary from April." Wollstonecraft did not know whether the sycamore survived. Godwin had been warned.[23]

Unlike Imlay, Godwin did not try to sweep Wollstonecraft off her feet and into bed. Instead, he made a case for how he could help her improve the quality of her life and find a degree of contentment. As their "friendship melt[ed] into love," he strove hard to nurture an atmosphere of mutual respect. Above all, they talked, shared their feelings, reasoned together. When she rejected his physical advances in August 1796, he did more than apologize. He explained that he was being "honest." As much as he wanted Wollstonecraft "in [his] arms" and was unable to think of anything else, he needed to make sure of her "feelings." He did not want to be presumptuous. He begged her not to "hate" him or "cast [him] off." She should "not become again a *solitary walker*." No one was perfect, including Wollstonecraft. The art of living well lay in recognizing weaknesses and fighting to overcome them. Wollstonecraft's one serious "fault" was her tendency to express "the feelings of nature," to give voice to passion unmediated by reason. She must not let feelings "tyrannise" her. She must think things through carefully before she spoke. She must "estimate every thing at its just value." True friends were supportive as well as honest. As Wollstonecraft's "friend, the friend of [her] mind, the admirer of [her] excellencies," Godwin could help her find happiness. A "woman, like you, can, must, shall, shake" off "morbid madness" and "misanthropical gloom." Love did not require self-abnegation. Indeed, friendship could provide the strength that no one could summon alone.[24]

Wollstonecraft was not entirely persuaded. She was not sure that "please[d]" was the best word to describe how she felt when Godwin was happy, perhaps because it sounded too deferential. And yet in defending herself from his manly criticism she was able to make a constructive argument for the importance of passion, something Godwin seemed to have almost entirely repressed. That Imlay had wounded her "sensibility" did not make their relationship "folly." After all, the drama of her love affair had unexpected benefits. It had, for example, improved her writing. More aware of how she functioned, she was more confident about expressing herself and more perceptive about human behavior. Her prose—as in *Letters Written during a Short Residence in Sweden, Norway, and Denmark*—now contained "more of the observations of my own senses, more of the combin-

23. Ibid., [Aug. 17, 1796], 349, 350, [Aug. 19, 1796], 352.

24. Godwin, *Memoirs*, ed. Clemit and Walker, 104; [Godwin] to MW, Aug. 17, 1796, Oxford, Bodleian, MS Abinger c. 40, fols. 19–20.

ing of my own imagination—the effusions of my own feelings and passions than the cold workings of the brain on the materials procured by the senses and imaginations of other writers." Painful experience had taught her to respect the truth of her heart as well as that of her brain.[25]

By late summer, Godwin and Wollstonecraft were lovers. It was a happy experience for him and for her, too, he believed. Despite her bitter experience with Imlay, she was too generous not to regain her confidence. They did not marry because they both thought the ceremony superfluous. Why "blow a trumpet" to formalize what already existed? Half a year later, Wollstonecraft became pregnant. The couple's marriage at Saint Pancras Church on March 29, 1797, shocked everyone. After all, the newlyweds were among the most prominent critics of the institution. "The assertrix of female Rights has given her hand to the Balanciere of political Justice," commented Henry Fuseli sarcastically. Imlay had taught Wollstonecraft the value of a formal legal recognition of parenthood, however. She worried about her reputation as the mother of two illegitimate children. Godwin insisted he was not a hypocrite. He still believed that "attachment . . . between two persons of opposite sexes is right," whereas "marriage, as practiced in European countries is wrong." He married Wollstonecraft only to secure her "peace and respectability" and felt himself not "otherwise bound than [he] was before the ceremony took place." Out of respect for his wife—"Mrs. Godwin—who the devil is that?" he exclaimed to Mary Hays—he was willing to give Wollstonecraft what she needed.[26]

They quarreled, of course. Wollstonecraft objected when he was away too much or when another woman paid him too much attention. Godwin, for his part, found her moodiness and her tendency to dramatic overstatement difficult to take. Their conflicts seem less evidence of incompatibility, however, than of their commitment to negotiating their differences. "No domestic connection is fit for me, but that of a person who should habitually study my gratification and happiness—in that case I should certainly not yield the palm of affectionate attentions to my companion," Godwin later reflected. "In the only intimate connection of that kind I ever had, the partner of my

25. MW to Godwin, [Aug. 27, 1796], in Todd, ed., *Collected Letters*, 354, [Sept. 4, 1796], 357, 358.

26. Godwin, *Memoirs*, ed. Clemit and Walker, 105; Henry Fuseli to William Roscoe, May 25, 1797, in David H. Weinglass, ed., *The Collected English Letters of Henry Fuseli* (Millwood, N.Y., 1982), 170; Godwin to Thomas Wedgwood, Apr. 19, 1797, Oxford, Bodleian, MS Abinger c. 3, fols. 60–61; Godwin to Mary Hays, Apr. 10, [1797], in Clemit, ed., *Letters of Godwin*, 197. Godwin's mother took his "broken resolution" as a sign that he would soon "embrace the Gospel"; see Ann Godwin to Godwin, May 3, 1797, Oxford, Bodleian, MS Abinger c. 3, fols. 64–65.

life was too quick in [her] conceiving resentments; but they were dignified and [silent] restrained; they left no hateful and humiliating remembrances behind them; and we were as happy as is permitted to human beings." His friend Thomas Holcroft, wounded by Godwin's silence about his marriage, pronounced them "the most extraordinary married pair in existence."[27]

The marriage worked in part because Godwin and Wollstonecraft maintained different social circles and often went alone to dinners and the theater. They lived in separate spaces. After spending evenings in the same bed in Wollstonecraft's house at 29 The Polygon in Somers Town, Godwin would retreat to rented rooms at 17 Evesham Buildings in Chalton Street, some twenty doors away, to devote his days to work. They believed, recalled Godwin, "that it was possible for two persons to be too uniformly in each other's society." Their arrangement avoided "satiety." "We seemed to combine, in a considerable degree, the novelty and lively sensation of a visit, with the more delicious and heart-felt pleasures of domestic life." Wollstonecraft agreed. She wanted Godwin to "visit and dine out as formerly, and I shall do the same; in short, I still mean to be independent." She had married, she told a friend, because she "wished, while fulfilling the duty of a mother, to have some person with similar pursuits, bound to me by affection" as well as "to resign a name which seemed to disgrace me." Godwin occasionally wondered if she did not "find solitude infinitely superior to the company of a husband?" Wollstonecraft assured him that he was "a tender, affectionate creature" and that she already loved their son "William." Still, she was not "fatigued with solitude." "A husband is a convenient part of the furniture of a house." Although, she wrote, she wished Godwin "riveted in my heart . . . I do not desire to have you always at my elbow." Domestically, they found a balance that affirmed their autonomy as well as their union.[28]

On Wednesday, August 30, Wollstonecraft gave birth to a second daughter the couple named Mary. Complications arose. Wollstonecraft lost a great deal of blood and was in severe pain. Godwin fetched a male physician who removed the placenta "in pieces." In the classic pattern of puerperal fever, all seemed well immediately afterward: the baby was healthy, and Wollstonecraft was improving. Then on Sunday, September 3, she developed a

27. Godwin, "Analysis of Own Character Begun Sep 26, 1798," in Philp et al., eds., *Collected Novels and Memoirs*, I, 58; Thomas Holcroft to Godwin, Apr. 6, 1797, Oxford, Bodleian, MS Abinger c. 3, fols. 57–58.

28. Godwin, *Memoirs*, ed. Clemit and Walker, 110; MW to Amelia Alderson, [Apr. 11, 1797], in Todd, ed., *Collected Letters*, 409, to Godwin, June 6, [17]97, 416 n. 890, 417, 418. See also MW to Godwin, [Apr. 8, 1797], 406 n. 863; Marshall, *William Godwin*, 187; and St. Clair, *Godwins and Shelleys*, 173.

fever and the shivers, symptoms of a "decided mortification" caused by un-delivered pieces of tissue. The doctor's ministrations as well as Godwin's "unremitting and devoted attentions" were to no avail. She slipped in and out of consciousness. In lucid moments, they talked of Fanny and Mary. At six o'clock on Sunday morning, September 10, he was summoned to her bedside, where he watched her "expire at twenty minutes before eight." The regular precision of his diary—a meticulous record of what he was writing, what he was reading, and with whom he was talking—was broken by a short statement, "20 minutes before 8," followed by two and a half lines drawn across the page. Buried on September 15 in the yard of Saint Pancras, Mary Wollstonecraft was thirty-eight years old.[29]

Just before she died in the company of her "devoted" husband and "af-fectionate" friends, she told Godwin he was "the kindest best man in the world." "No woman," wrote Elizabeth Fenwick, who was in attendance, "was ever more happy in marriage." Fenwick and others took "consolation" in Wollstonecraft's finally finding happiness in her last months. Godwin "firmly believe[d] that there does not exist her equal in the world." They "were formed to make each other happy." He found solace in the estimation that "it is pleasing to be loved by those we feel ourselves impelled to love." Friends tried to comfort him. Joseph Johnson grieved a woman he knew "too well not to admire and love." Elizabeth Inchbald, not a fan of either Wollstonecraft or the marriage, assured Godwin that she lamented "her as a person whom you loved." Amelia Alderson confessed that the tragedy had made her realize just "how truly and warmly I esteemed you." Shortly after Wollstonecraft's death, Godwin moved his papers and books into her room and had her portrait hung in his study, where it stayed until he died in 1836. Within a fortnight, he was writing the *Memoirs of the Author of "A Vindi-cation of the Rights of Woman,"* which was published by a reluctant Joseph Johnson in 1798, along with Wollstonecraft's unedited letters to Imlay and Johnson.[30]

29. Godwin, *Memoirs,* ed. Clemit and Walker, 113, 115, 120; Eliza Fenwick to [Everina] Woll-stonecraft, Sept. 12, 1797, Oxford, Bodleian, MS Abinger b. 4, fol. 101, Godwin, Diary, Sept. 9, 1797, e. 8, fols. 1–48, esp. 25, 26.

30. Fenwick to [Everina] Wollstonecraft, Sept. 12, 1797, Oxford, Bodleian, MS Abinger b. 4, fol. 101, Godwin to Thomas Holcroft, Sept. 10, 1797, c. 22, fol. 39, Godwin to Anthony Carlisle, Sept. 19, 1797, c. 22, fols. 50–52, Joseph Johnson to Godwin, [Sept. 10–12, 1797], c. 3, fols. 97–98, Elizabeth Inchbald to [Godwin], Sept. 11, 1797, c. 3, fols. 77–78, Amelia Alderson to Godwin, Oct. 11, 1797, c. 3, fols. 99–100. See Marshall, *William Godwin,* 191. On MW's impact on Godwin, see Philp, *Godwin's Political Justice,* 169–213.

Of History and Romance

Godwin's choice to compose a memoir of his wife is hardly surprising. He was, after all, a professional writer eager to deal with his intense grief by engaging with Wollstonecraft, her friends, and a multitude of readers. What better way to manage his feelings than to continue to converse with her? The absolute worst thing he could do was to endure in solitude. As important, Godwin honored Wollstonecraft by writing manfully about how she came to be who she was. Part of the fascination of personal histories was the possibility of personal transformation. Writers such as Godwin and Wollstonecraft assumed that men and women were susceptible to persuasion and that lives were contingent processes rather than the revelation of a fixed character. Long before Godwin met Wollstonecraft, he had focused on the power of personal history to explore the challenge, posed in *Political Justice,* of seeing "how one's self fits in with everyone else's self, or to construe oneself as part of a greater whole." He did so most vividly in his novel, *Things as They Are; or, The Adventures of Caleb Williams,* one of the most influential books written in English in the 1790s.[31]

Caleb Williams is a tale of intense suspense and psychological self-analysis designed to narrate through one man's experience "'a general review of the modes of domestic and unrecorded despotism, by which man becomes the destroyer of man.'" None of the three major characters—the servant Caleb Williams, his master Fernando Falkland, or the neighbor Barrabas Tyrrel in whose murder Falkland implicates Williams—is inherently good or bad. Indeed, their behavior reflects the unstable interaction between social expectations and personal desire. The world is a prison writ large ("a theatre of calamity"). Individuals make choices within parameters imposed by their environment and their education; they are complicit to some extent in their own fate because they too often give their consent to dangerous measures. Sociability helps people navigate through a dark and mysterious world by offering support and perspective. A man alone is a man easily enslaved. It is hardly coincidental that the unhappy men in Godwin's novel have almost no sustained contact with women.[32]

---

31. Peter Howell, "Godwin, Contractarianism, and the Political Dead End of Empiricism," *Eighteenth-Century Life,* XXVIII, no. 2 (Spring 2004), 64, 71, 78. See also Jon Klancher, "Godwin and the Genre Reformers: On Necessity and Contingency in Romantic Narrative Theory," 21–38, and Gary Handwerk, "History, Trauma, and the Limits of the Liberal Imagination: William Godwin's Historical Fiction," both in Tilottama Rajan and Julia M. Wright, eds., *Romanticism, History, and the Possibilities of Genre: Re-forming Literature, 1789–1837* Cambridge, 1998).

32. Liz Bellamy, *Commerce, Morality, and the Eighteenth-Century Novel* (Cambridge, 1998),

The young Caleb Williams, like many characters in the literature of this era, is an orphan bereft of family and friends. But he is insatiably curious, perhaps in reaction to his solitary existence. A "sort of natural philosopher," Williams's particular interest in "tracing the variety of effects which might be produced from given causes" has inspired "an invincible attachment to books of narrative and romance." No amount of knowledge, however, could have prepared the young man for the twists and turns of his life. He can only make sense of them in retrospect, as the narrator of "the scattered incidents of [his] history." The "the principal agent in [that] history" is Fernando Falkland, a landed gentleman who offers Williams a position as his secretary. Caleb accepts, feeling fortunate to have an income and a patron. He immediately understands the moment as decisive. Only in hindsight will he see it as the first in a series of turning points in a narrative centered on his relationship with Falkland. The two men have much in common even after they become staunch antagonists; both are lonely figures who repeatedly make choices that exacerbate their plights.[33]

Falkland's steward, Collins, narrates much of the first section of the novel. Giving readers the story of his master's life before he and Caleb meet, Collins paints Falkland as a generous and noble man undone by "a series of adventures that seemed to take their rise in various accidents." The chief "accident" is Falkland's impulsive murder of one of his neighbors after months of simmering disputes. Barnabas Tyrrel is a rich, uneducated, selfish brute posing as a gentleman. It is a tribute to Falkland's balance of reason and passion that he works hard to overcome his disdain for his rival. He wants to "do better." Falkland expects the same of Tyrrel, urging him to develop a sense of sociability. "No man must think the world was made for him," Falkland warns Tyrrel. People must accept their differences and accommodate themselves to circumstances. In other words, they must engage with one another.[34]

166; William Godwin, *Things as They Are; or, The Adventures of Caleb Williams* (1784), ed. Maurice Hindle (London, 2005), 5. See Evan Radcliffe, "Godwin from 'Metaphysician' to Novelist: '*Political Justice,*' '*Caleb Williams,*' and the Tension between Philosophical Argument and Narrative," *Modern Philology,* XCVII (2000), 528–553, esp. 531. See also David Collings, "The Romance of the Impossible: William Godwin in the Empty Place of Reason," *ELH,* LXX (2003), 861: "No longer in thrall to an immutable reason, Caleb finds his place in the world of a mutable and progressive reason, one whose ultimate form must also be retrospective, knowable only in the future perfect tense, beyond reach from within history as it is actually lived."

33. Godwin, *Caleb Williams,* ed. Hindle, 6, 13, 124.

34. Ibid., 18, 31, 32.

An angry Tyrrel rejects Falkland's advice. Incapable of generosity, he mistreats his young cousin and ward, Emily Melville, in whom Falkland is apparently romantically interested. Tyrrel demands that Emily marry an unrefined brute in order to get rid of the financial burden she imposes on him. Emily's protest that she has a right to choose her own husband has no impact on an "insolent and unfeeling tyrant." Tyrrel keeps the defiant woman essentially imprisoned on his country estate and then has her arrested for debt. Emily dies shortly thereafter, a victim of Tyrell's brutality. Her fate causes everyone to regard her guardian "as the most diabolical wretch that had ever dishonoured the human form." When the well-respected Falkland warns Tyrrel out of a public ball, Tyrrel loses all control. He beats Falkland, humiliating him in front of the community. Later that evening, Tyrrel's corpse is found "a few yards from the assembly house" where the party was held. No one knows what happened. Suspicion falls on Falkland, but he is acquitted by a jury.[35]

Falkland is unhappy because he knows that he is in fact guilty. The murder becomes "the crisis of [his] history." A fundamentally decent man, he cannot forgive himself for his momentary loss of control, for allowing anger and shame to drive him to a Tyrell-like display of violence. Remorse turns a once-sociable man into a recluse. When Caleb Williams meets him, he is defined by "gloomy and unsociable melancholy." Everything Falkland had been, everything to which his life had been tending, was undone in a few moments of passion. He enters a prison of his own making, cuts himself off from all human beings, choosing a solitary confinement in which he can contemplate his guilt. It is a decision as self-destructive as the murder itself. Inevitably, he spirals deeper and deeper into melancholy.[36]

Caleb Williams wants to know why Falkland is miserable. His curiosity sparks him to ask the steward Collins for information; it also drives him to search through his master's private papers. Williams's "offence" is "a mistaken thirst of knowledge" that precipitates the "crisis of [his] fate." Falkland catches Williams and takes advantage of his power to confess to the murder of Tyrel. But instead of killing his now too well informed secretary, Falkland offers the young man his patronage in return for "servile submission." Caleb's acceptance of these terms effectively makes him Falkland's "prisoner." But he soon withdraws his consent. That the world is a great prison does not mean that a human being must become "a galley-slave." Falkland

35. Ibid., 65, 93, 100.
36. Ibid., 101.

refuses to accept Caleb Williams's change of mind. Having him intercepted when the secretary attempts to escape, Falkland puts him in a dungeon. Astonished at the collective failure of human beings to resist tyranny, Williams asserts: "I am an Englishman, and it is the privilege of an Englishman to be the sole judge and master of his own actions." Eventually, Williams gets away, only to fall in with thieves and spend time in jail. Government offers no protection from whimsical tyranny. Friends are few and fleeting. Entombed in a miserable prison, Williams asks what man who has seen what he has seen would "say, England has no Bastille!"[37]

Escape from prison offers illusory freedom. Caleb encounters a den of thieves that offers the appearance of independence and society. But the thieves are selfish men who misuse their energy and others' property. They are at the opposite extreme from solitude. A complete indulgence of one's passions without regard to society as a whole is as bad as prison itself. Traveling the countryside, Williams is subjected to any number of outrages in an inherently antisocial environment. Robbed of food, shelter, and clothes, the "outcast" lashes out at a world "that hates without a cause, that overwhelms innocence with calamities which ought to be spared even to guilt! Accursed world! dead to every manly sympathy; with eyes of horn, and hearts of steel! Why do I consent to live any longer?" Godwin emphasizes that suicide is a rational choice, a withdrawal of consent, an assertion of manly self-respect.[38]

Refusing to allow Williams even this degree of miserable freedom, Falkland hires one of the thieves, Gines, to follow Caleb wherever he goes. Falkland does not want Williams arrested or assassinated; he simply wants to ensure that his former secretary does not use his knowledge of Tyrrel's murder against him. "No walls could hide me from the discernment of this hated foe," complains an exhausted Williams. "Rest I had none: relief I had none; never could I count upon an instant's security; never could I wrap myself in the shroud of oblivion." What he laments most is the loss of friendship. Solitude makes his misery unbearable. Unable to find an interlocutor, Williams hits upon the idea of writing to an unknown audience. "I will unfold a tale!—I will show thee to the world for what thou art." The novel we are reading thus becomes an act of defiant resistance, an assertion of the power of sociability to triumph over tyranny. "These papers shall preserve the truth; they shall one day be published . . . He may hunt me out of the

---

37. Ibid., 139, 149, 150, 165, 188.
38. Ibid., 261.

world.—In vain! With this engine, this little pen, I defeat all his machinations; I stab him in the very point [his reputation] he was most solicitous to defend!" Writing empowers Williams; it is his best defense against Falkland's effort to destroy him.[39]

Godwin's first draft of *Caleb Williams* concluded with the hero's failing to win justice in a dramatic courtroom confrontation with a gaunt Falkland and the ever vigilant Gines. But, several days later, Godwin changed the ending, giving Williams a speech that breaks the wasted Falkland and leads him to confess his crimes. Ironically, the power of the oratory lies, not in angry rage at a monster, but in Williams's extraordinary sympathy for his exhausted persecutor. Caleb wishes he could do otherwise than accuse Falkland, an admirable man undone by an impulsive mistake. If exposing him is the right thing to do, it is also an odious act that will surely destroy a figure "worthy of affection and kindness." Falkland's excessive devotion to his reputation is as ruinous as Williams's insatiable curiosity. Godwin thus completes the parallels in the lives of two men undone by their inability to behave well at critical moments, a failure brought on by solitude. "What a train of circumstances does one error involve, how does it mix with, and poison, every source of action!" Mary Hays told Godwin in May 1796. The problem with the characters is not that they are fallible; it is that they have inured themselves against fellow feeling and therefore cannot comprehend, let alone deal with, their actions.[40]

In the end, the restoration of commerce—Williams's deployment of writing and speaking—proves decisive. Once the characters engage with one another and with society, they feel and reason more clearly. Deeply moved by Williams's courtroom speech, Falkland can do nothing but subject himself to the power of Williams's "artless and manly story." He confesses that he has "spent a life of the basest cruelty to cover one act of momentary vice." When Falkland dies a few days later, Caleb Williams eulogizes him. "A nobler spirit lived not among the sons of men." His ambition was perverted in "the corrupt wilderness of human society," a "rank and rotten soil." Yet Falkland, like Williams, was more than a powerless victim of a heartless world. He made his own bed. He failed to restrain his own weaknesses. He was the author of his own life. Despite "the purest and most laudable intentions," his passion for fame, or reputation, allowed jealousy

---

39. Ibid., 316, 325.

40. Ibid., 333, 334, 335; Hays to Godwin, [May 1796], in "Selections from Hays and Godwin Correspondence," in Hays, *Memoirs of Emma Courtney,* ed. Brooks, 252.

and competition to become a "poison" that encouraged "madness." Whatever satisfaction might exist follows from the tempering of desire through intercourse with other human beings.[41]

Caleb Williams is as much an argument for social commerce as it is an argument against tyranny. Narrative puts characters into motion, allowing them to develop understanding in dynamic relationships with other human beings. In this novel, however, Godwin highlights the opposite: the dire consequences of social isolation. Creating a retrospective narrative reveals the importance of sociability to individual happiness and human progress. Although Williams triumphs over Falkland, he is seriously disenchanted with the outcome. "I had thought that, if Falkland were dead, I should return once again to all that makes life worth possessing. I thought that if the guilt of Falkland were established, fortune and the world would smile upon my efforts. Both these events are accomplished; and it is now only that I am truly miserable." The foundation of that misery is the belated "exchange of sympathy" that led to an affirmation of "their mutual humanity."[42]

In *Political Justice,* Godwin had claimed that "'every well informed friend of mankind must look forward to the auspicious period [of] the dissolution of political government, of that brute engine which has been the only perennial cause of the vices of mankind, and which . . . has mischiefs of various sorts incorporated with its substance, and no otherwise removable than its utter annihilation!'" "'Circumstances,'" not birth, made people "'vicious.'" Rather than look to the past, people should embrace the future.

---

41. Godwin, *Caleb Williams,* ed. Hindle, 336–337.

42. Ibid., 336; Monika Fludernik, "William Godwin's *Caleb Williams:* The Tarnishing of the Sublime," *ELH,* LXVIII (2001), 857–896 (quotation on 884). Gary Handwerk, in "Of Caleb's Guilt and Godwin's Truth: Ideology and Ethics in *Caleb Williams,*" *ELH,* LX (1993), 939–960, argues that the shift to narrative led Godwin "into a much more skeptical meditation on the possibilities for political amelioration through reason" than he had discussed in *Political Justice* (940). "Benevolence and impartiality" fail "to override considerations of power" in the novel (942). Instead, Caleb triumphs through "sentimental rationalism" in his empathy for his tormentor because "he suddenly comes to understand him as the product of a corrupt political system" as well as his own "complicity," thus asserting "that social violence stems from human nature, not from circumstances or inequities of political power" (946, 948). We are all guilty, in other words, both victims and agents. I disagree with Handwerk that the sympathetic portrayal of Falkland comes from nowhere, however; in part because he wrote part 1 *after* part 3, Godwin is at great pains to show Falkland as a good man gone bad by circumstances and his own inability to control his passion in a moment of duress. And, although Handwerk is right to point out the influence of MW on Godwin, the latter wrote *Caleb Williams* long before they got to know each other well. See also Robert W. Uphaus, "*Caleb Williams:* Godwin's Epoch of Mind," *Studies in the Novel,* IX (1977), 279–296; and Radcliffe, "Godwin from 'Metaphysician' to Novelist," *Modern Philology,* XCVII (2000), 546–553.

Godwin's rejection of fixed notions of human behavior and his skepticism about any attempt to deduce motivation from outcome went to the heart of his radical faith. It was this epistemological instability that eventually raised the greatest outcry from critics on all sides who shared a conviction about the predictability of human nature. Knowing the history of both Mary Wollstonecraft and the French Revolution pushed William Godwin to think through the implications of *Caleb Williams.* In the fall of 1797, he was a man energized by grief. To contend with a depth of emotion he had never known, he brought to bear the power of the understanding he had developed in conversation with others, including Wollstonecraft.[43]

The Life of Mary Wollstonecraft

Godwin's *Memoirs of the Author of "A Vindication of the Rights of Woman"* was a self-conscious experiment in genre, an effort to blend history and literature. The author insisted that the book was accurate. He had recorded what Wollstonecraft had told him about her life. He had sought information and materials from "among the persons most intimately acquainted with her at the different periods of her life." Of course, Godwin's information was selective. Joseph Johnson and other friends cooperated, but the Wollstonecraft family and Henry Fuseli angrily denied him access to their correspondence. Eliza and Everina Wollstonecraft did not object to a sketch of their sister's life, but they doubted a longer narrative would "be even tolerably accurate." Neither Gilbert Imlay nor his letters were available for consultation. None of this stopped Godwin. To supplement the *Memoirs,* he also published in 1798 *Posthumous Works of the Author of "A Vindication of the Rights of Woman."* Godwin arranged and edited Wollstonecraft's unfinished manuscripts, including *Maria; or, The Wrongs of Woman;* more dramatically, he included his wife's private letters to Johnson and Imlay.[44]

Ironically, given the reception of the book, Godwin's stated intention was to foreclose the possibility of "malignant misrepresentation" of Wollstonecraft. He sought to cheat death by practicing social commerce in print;

---

43. Godwin, *Caleb Williams,* ed. Hindle, xvi, xvii.

44. Godwin, *Memoirs,* ed. Clemit and Walker, 44; Everina Wollstonecraft to Godwin, Nov. 24, 1797, Oxford, Bodleian, MS Abinger c. 3, fols. 104–105. See Helen M. Buss, "Memoirs Discourse and William Godwin's *Memoirs of the Author of 'A Vindication of the Rights of Woman,'"* in Helen M. Buss, D. L. Macdonald, and Anne McWhir, eds., *Mary Wollstonecraft and Mary Shelley: Writing Lives* (Waterloo, Ont., 2001), 113–126; and Tilottma Rajan, *Romantic Narrative: Shelley, Hays, Godwin, Wollstonecraft* (Baltimore, 2010).

he wanted to create sympathy (or empathy) for Wollstonecraft by making readers her friends. Unfortunately, because "the public at large" could not have been an "intimate acquaintance" with "a person of eminent merit" such as Wollstonecraft, they could not have been "the observer of those virtues which discover themselves principally in personal intercourse." The more they knew Wollstonecraft, the more they would respect and esteem her. The "more fully" readers understood "the picture and story" of people such as Mary Wollstonecraft, "with whose character the public welfare and improvement" were "intimately connected," "the more generally shall we feel in ourselves an attachment to their fate, and a sympathy in their excellencies." Thus, Godwin devoted only a few paragraphs to *A Vindication of the Rights of Woman,* a book he thought would endure as long as the English language, despite its deficiency in style and organization. The real subject of *Memoirs* was the creator of such a powerful polemic. Godwin would show the origins and consequences of *Vindication* by locating the book within the larger narrative of a life. Readers would appreciate Wollstonecraft's writing better when they knew her as a human being.[45]

Insisting on the authenticity of his memoir, Godwin deployed the techniques of a novelist to acquaint readers with his wife. Rather than compile an exhaustive record of the events of Wollstonecraft's life, he skimmed over long periods of time in order to develop at length a handful of key episodes that revealed her character and its evolution over time. Godwin regularly tells readers what Wollstonecraft was thinking or feeling, despite his devotion to evidence. The point was to create a conversation that would honor his wife by helping readers to improve themselves long after her death. Godwin constructed a story of a smart, sensitive, mercurial woman tested by innumerable disappointments and oppressions, a woman badly treated by her parents, a lonely and easily wounded woman longing for happiness away from the slings and arrows of outrageous fortune and gross inequities. Wollstonecraft's defining characteristic is her ardent sensibility. Like the women she criticized in *Vindication,* her education and her temperament combined to enslave her to her imagination, to her desire for connection with men educated to treat her badly. No wonder critics complained that Godwin's Wollstonecraft is a monument to the triumph of sensibility over rational affection.

An alternative reading suggests that the overall arc of the memoir is a monument to a stubborn woman who struggled against her education, who refused to surrender to her fate, who learned from experience, and who

---

45. Godwin, *Memoirs,* ed. Clemit and Walker, 43.

eventually achieved the ideal described in *Vindication*. Godwin is obviously an unreliable narrator. The plot of *Memoirs* leads inevitably to him. He alone loved Wollstonecraft as she needed to be loved; only their relationship fulfilled the revolutionary promise of social commerce. In Godwin's telling, all her previous love affairs—with Fanny, Fuseli, and, especially, Imlay—failed because they encouraged Wollstonecraft to indulge her imagination. If Godwin's account is self-congratulatory—and it is—he stresses that Wollstonecraft had learned from her painful education and transformed herself. That is why he fell in love with the author of the narrative of her Scandinavian journey, in which she came to terms with Imlay, and not the author of *Vindication,* which, like *Political Justice,* is more about prescription than experience.

Memoirs narrates the history of Wollstonecraft's tendency to indulge her sensibility. The pattern was set in an unhappy childhood shaped by an almost invisible mother and, foreshadowing Imlay, a restless, erratic, unhappy father unable to settle down. Instead of "humbling her," however, Ned Wollstonecraft's physical and verbal blows "roused her indignation." Mary Wollstonecraft, to her credit, "was not formed to be the contented and unresisting subject of a despot." But she could not manage her sensibility, becoming what Samuel Johnson called "'a very good hater.'" Fanny Blood rescued Mary by expanding her education and showing her the utility as well as the contentment of true friendship. Specifically, she encouraged Mary to read widely and deeply and to think of "writing as an art," awakening her "ambition to excel." Living together, "their intimacy ripened; they approached nearly to a footing of equality; and their attachment became more rooted and active." Like everyone else in *Memoirs,* Fanny matters mainly in terms of her impact on Mary's movement toward Godwin. Her major contribution lay in opening Mary to the possibilities of managing her sensibility and moving her from craving "personal independence" to seeking "usefulness." With an "expanded mind," Mary sought more than "the mere removal of personal vexations" and the enjoyment of "solitary gratifications." Alas, ardent Wollstonecraft was not yet in control of herself. "She did not sufficiently consider that, in proportion as we involve ourselves in the interests and society of others, we acquire a more exquisite sense of their defects, and are tormented with their untractableness and folly." Thanks to Fanny, Wollstonecraft realized that she had "a firmness of mind, an unconquerable greatness of soul" that allowed her, despite "a short internal struggle . . . to rise above difficulties and suffering." Fanny, on the other hand, was not a good long-term friend because she was "timid" and "irresolute" and "accustomed to yield to difficulties." She could not help

Mary deal with her strong sensibility or her arrogance. Wollstonecraft was a confident woman with a quick temper manifested in "severe and imperious" rebukes to people who disappointed her and a belief "that she saw the mind of the person with whom she had any transaction." But she struggled to understand others as well as herself. For the young Wollstonecraft, according to Godwin, social commerce was a one-way street. She demanded respect not only for what she wanted but also for her interpretation of what others wanted. As she continually told Imlay, she knew him better than he knew himself.[46]

In Godwin's telling, the French Revolution provided Wollstonecraft with the opportunity to transform her personal frustrations into a powerful indictment of a patriarchal society that badly educated men and women. It also encouraged her to indulge rather than manage her sensibility. In *Vindication* she found a cause. She aspired to be "an effectual champion . . . of one half of the human species" whose oppression had "degraded" them from "rational beings" almost "to the level of the brutes." She saw "that [women] were often attempted to be held in silken fetters, and bribed into the love of slavery." In his characteristically forthright style, Godwin pointed out that the book would endure despite its "rigid, and somewhat amazonian temper" and its "method and arrangement." The author of *Vindication* was an unruly talent in need of discipline and refinement.[47]

Godwin reinforces this point with his treatment of the Fuseli relationship. Wollstonecraft understood that the painter had seduced her by listening to her, by taking her seriously. But she did not recognize that he did not take their intimacy seriously. In fact, she did not really know the painter. Encouraging Wollstonecraft's fascination with him, Fuseli enjoyed receiving love he had no intention of returning. The couple did not become lovers because they were never really friends. Wollstonecraft learned from this relationship, Godwin suggested, but not enough. She continued to "set a great value on a mutual affection between persons of an opposite sex." "She regarded it as the principal solace of human life." Her judgment, however, was continually overwhelmed by her sensibility. Although she "regarded the manners and habits of the majority of" men when it came to physical gratification "with strong disapprobation," she was convinced that some men were capable of transcending that desire and forming friendships rooted in esteem. The key was to ensure that the imagination stimulated the senses and not the reverse. Again, Godwin's Wollstonecraft is an extraordinary per-

46. Ibid., 46, 51, 53, 55, 58, 59.
47. Ibid., 74, 75.

son with great, often noble ambition who lacks the education to attain her goal of serious friendship. Never content with "general conversation and society," she wanted "the happiness" of "domestic affection." "Alone . . . in the great mass of her species," she could not find a way to escape "comfortless solitude."[48]

The romance with Imlay occupies a central place in Godwin's narrative, comprising two of ten chapters. Given what Godwin has revealed about Wollstonecraft's imperfect understanding, which he conveniently recapitulates when she meets Imlay, readers should not be surprised by his protagonist's behavior. The education of the author of *Vindication* had not prepared her for the challenge of putting her principles into practice. Wollstonecraft was not in control of her sensibility; she could not manage either her emotions or her talent. When she met Imlay, she was transformed by love into a happy creature, free from her bouts of depression and anxiety. Entering "into that species of connection, for which her heart secretly panted," she was suddenly confident and "playful." Her demeanor became animated, her eyes brighter, her cheeks ruddier, her voice cheerful, and her temper kinder. And he would not, could not, let go of it. It is "the very essence of affection, to seek to perpetuate itself." Marriage did not matter. Their relationship was "of the most sacred nature," and they looked forward to a life in North America once they had the money to support themselves. Godwin pointed out that Wollstonecraft had reason to be happy. She was persuaded that love would cure all ills after a lifetime of being "tossed and agitated by the waves of misfortune." But Wollstonecraft had not found the right kind of love. Under the control of her sensibility, she had taken up with a man who offered her no way to manage that sensibility. In fact, he made it worse because he had the same problem.[49]

According to Godwin, the couple were doomed because they were experiencing love as wild passion rather than rational affection. If the "female Werter" found "refuge" for her "wounded and sick heart . . . in the bosom of a chosen friend," her heart "was not formed to nourish affection by halves." Trusting her overdeveloped imagination rather than her underdeveloped understanding, she put everything into a man "whose honour and principles she had the most exalted idea." Wollstonecraft was as much a speculator as Imlay. Like her lover, she invested—or gambled—on the possibilities of natural commerce. Because the relationship had begun in an indulgence of sensibility, because it had never been what she imagined it to

48. Ibid., 79, 81.
49. Ibid., 84, 86, 87, 88, 91.

be, Wollstonecraft had no strategy to manage its end. The affair was always an act of fancy. No matter what Imlay said, no matter how he behaved, she would not surrender her "glimmering of fondly cherished, expiring hope" or embrace the solitude that must follow from its loss. A blind Wollstonecraft had projected her desire onto Imlay to such an extent that she could not see his "worthlessness." Imlay was just as blind. Rather than condemn him, however, the readers (friends) of Wollstonecraft should feel "pity for the mistake of the man, who, being in possession of such a friendship and attachment as those of Mary, could hold them at a trivial price, and, 'like the base Indian, throw a pearl away, richer than all his tribe.'" Godwin's Imlay was less a cad than a naïf.[50]

In the climax toward which *Memoirs* had been building from its first sentences, William Godwin—Wollstonecraft's truest lover—does not throw her away. Instead, he embraces a Wollstonecraft who had finally learned from her experience with Imlay the danger of indulging that wanton, her imagination. They were friends who became lovers, friends who respected each other, who declined to define love as enthusiasm. With Godwin, "tranquillity" displaced "anguish." Expanding her circle of friends and interests with his encouragement, she put her mind at ease. As she tempered her ardor, people responded better to her. She listened as well as talked. She spoke openly of Imlay, whose name she used until she married Godwin, despite others' discomfort with the subject. Her second pregnancy and delayed marriage divided her true friends from those obsessed with artificial form. No matter. It said something about people that they found room for "the dull and insolent dictators, the gamblers and demireps" but not the "firmest champion" and "the greatest ornament her sex ever had to boast!"[51]

Wollstonecraft held up well. For now her countenance was serene, her manners sweet, and her pleasure greater. At last, she enjoyed "the constant and unlimited exercise of" her considerable "art of communicating happiness." She had "attained that situation, which her disposition and character imperiously demanded." Once Wollstonecraft and Godwin lived together, her anguish dissipated. A lover of "domestic life," she delighted in the growing "affection" between Godwin and Fanny (and their unborn child). Free of the discontents that had dogged her for years as well as the interference of "selfish and transitory pleasures," she found childlike happiness in "trifles" such as a ride in the country with Godwin and Fanny. As important, Wollstonecraft continued to write, but now with more discipline and less

50. Ibid., 88, 91–92.
51. Ibid., 107, 108.

haste. The love of Godwin and Wollstonecraft embodied mutual affection and improvement.[52]

If they "were as happy as is permitted to human beings," it was in no small part because he "honoured her intellectual powers and the nobleness and generosity of her propensities." "Mere tenderness would not have been adequate to produce the happiness we experienced," wrote Godwin. They learned from each other in conversation and complemented each other in their different ways of thinking and writing. His "powers" lay in "logical and metaphysical distinction," hers in "a taste for the picturesque." More spontaneous than he, she possessed a remarkable "intuition" that gave her an admirable perspicacity in matters of taste and feeling. Godwin was cautious and reserved, worried about deception and unwilling to trust first impressions. Wollstonecraft reasoned less formally and more boldly than he because she found truth by instinct rather than patient study. Godwin marveled at her quick mind, her combination of feeling and reason. He learned from her. In short, Godwin knew Wollstonecraft was as necessary to him as he was to her, a development she affirmed in her letters. Despite his construction of himself as the answer to her problems, he persuasively argued that they were happy together.[53]

Like Wollstonecraft's *Short Residence,* the *Memoirs* is a masterpiece of contingent narrative built around tensions between mind and environment, reason and passion. Writing about his dead wife allowed Godwin to channel his emotions into a story that made her life worthwhile. He also put into practice ideas about human beings and history that he had been considering for some time. Godwin's Wollstonecraft is an ardent, willful, ambitious, and impatient character who evolves over time. Godwin tells a story, not of a heroine born to greatness, not of an instrument of divine power or some vague fate, but of a mistreated girl who sometimes by accident generalized the theme of her life into a powerful indictment of gender inequality. Whatever Wollstonecraft's life says about the human condition, it does so through the unstable unfolding of concrete events in specific places and real time. Meaning lies, not in the pieces of a life, but in its whole; not in medias res, but in postfacto contemplation; not in events, but in the stories we tell about them. Like *A Short Residence, Memoirs* was a step toward a nineteenth-century Romantic sensibility that perpetuated a late-eighteenth-century sensibility about the possibilities of social commerce.

52. Ibid., 109, 110, 111.

53. Godwin, "Analysis of Own Character Begun Sep 26, 1798," in Philp et al., eds., *Collected Novels and Memoirs,* 58; Godwin, *Memoirs,* ed. Clemit and Walker, 120–122.

"And So I Dare to Hope"

Many writers were experimenting with literary forms in the late 1790s. Probably the most famous example is William Wordsworth and Samuel Taylor Coleridge's *Lyrical Ballads*. Originally published in 1798, the same year as Godwin's *Memoirs,* but much revised in succeeding editions, the collection heralded a wedding of the lyric (a highly structured form of poetry congenial to concentrated bursts of sensibility) and the ballad (a popular form often associated with plainspoken working people). *Lyrical Ballads* deployed vernacular language and manly emotion to consider the impact of deprivation, disruption, and death on rural working people during the tumultuous decade that brought a century of revolution to a close. Coleridge's "The Ancient Mariner," the first poem in the first edition, sets the tone by recounting a tale within a tale about the wanderings of a mysterious lonely man through a series of bizarre events that leaves his listener chastened, a "sadder and wiser man." At the end of the first edition, Wordsworth offered a solution to the problem of human misery detailed in the other poems. In "Lines (Written a Few Miles above Tintern Abbey)," memory, sensation, and imagination keep alive pleasure and possibility, "life and food / For future years. And so I dare to hope." Paradoxically, sympathizing with the pain of others sharpens our sense of pleasure and, ultimately, joy. Suffering serves a social purpose because it makes us aware of possibility as well as loss. In short, intense feelings of connection developed through reflection and study and crystallized in the presence of nature constitute the surest antidote to pain and despair.[54]

Writing as well as reading poetry was a social activity. A poet, Wordsworth explained in his 1802 preface, "is a man speaking to men." If he wishes "to excite rational sympathy, he must express himself as other men express themselves." He engages his readers by exciting sympathy through conjuring sensations of pleasure. Unlike the "Man of Science" who seeks a distant truth in "solitude," the poet, "singing a song in which all human beings join with him, rejoices in the presence of truth as our visible friend and hourly companion. . . . the Poet binds together by passion and knowledge the vast empire of human society, as it is spread over the whole earth, and over all

---

54. Samuel Taylor Coleridge, "The Ancient Mariner: A Poet's Reverie," 204, and William Wordsworth, "Lines (Written a Few Miles above Tintern Abbey)," 210, both in Wordsworth and Coleridge, *Lyrical Ballads,* 2d ed., ed. Michael Mason (1992; rpt. Harlow, Eng., 2007); Mason's "General Introduction," 1–31, is very useful on the publication history and arrangement of the poems.

time." Among the poet's particular gifts is the ability to experience "absent things as if they were present." As "Tintern Abbey" suggests, pleasure can be savored in the mind as well as in person, in the past and future as well as in the present. To feel was not to pursue selfish desire and follow impulses; it was to connect with other human beings through an exchange of sentiment and knowledge. Pleasure, Wordsworth explained, "derives from the perception of similitude in dissimilitude." "This principle is the great spring of the activity of our minds and their chief feeder. From this principle the direction of the sexual appetite, and all the passions connected with it, take their origin: it is the life of our ordinary conversation; and upon the accuracy with which similitude in dissimilitude, and dissimilitude in similitude are perceived, depend our taste and our moral feelings." The goal was to locate one's self with a community of people united by the bonds of affection, to understand "man and the objects that surround him as acting and reacting upon each other, so as to produce an infinite complexity of pain and pleasure."[55]

Like Wollstonecraft's *Short Residence* and Godwin's *Memoirs, Lyrical Ballads* was less a radical break with the eighteenth century than an adaptation of existing ideas about sympathy, reflection, and natural commerce. Proud of his and Coleridge's innovations, Wordsworth denied that they had ignored their predecessors. They simply believed that

> a language, arising out of repeated experience and regular feelings, is a more permanent, and a far more philosophical language, than that which is frequently substituted for it by Poets, who think that they are conferring honour upon themselves and their art, in proportion as they separate themselves from the sympathies of men, and indulge in arbitrary and capricious habits of expression, in order to furnish food for fickle tastes, and fickle appetites, of their own creation.

Wordsworth saw a poem as a product of extended reflection. If "all good Poetry is the spontaneous overflow of powerful feelings," valuable poems were the work of "a man who, being possessed of more than usual organic sensibility, had also thought long and deeply." A poet was an artisan who knew that meter helps "in tempering and restraining the passion by an intertexture of ordinary feeling." Although Wordsworth urged his readers to think for themselves, he assumed that individuals would form their opinions about poetry and all other matters through conversation and study.

---

55. William Wordsworth, "Preface (1802)," in Wordsworth and Coleridge, *Lyrical Ballads,* ed. Mason, 71, 75, 76, 77, 79, 82.

After all, "an *accurate* taste in Poetry, and in all the other arts, as Sir Joshua Reynolds has observed, is an *acquired* talent, which can only be produced by thought, and a long continued intercourse with the best models of composition."[56]

Godwin was never a poet. He lacked the talent for vivid, concise images; he could not capture a moment. But he could construct narratives that revealed the dangers of lives lived bereft of affection and intercourse. In 1796, Godwin wrote a manifesto about the need to transform existing literary genres in order to capture new perspectives. His "Essay of History and Romance" attacked artificial distinctions between history and fiction. The two genres had so much in common that it made sense to combine them. First, both histories and novels, or personal histories, were "the records of individuals." Rejecting "abstractions" of the kind found in *Political Justice,* Godwin proclaimed that the "genuine and native taste" of men "rests entirely in individualities." No one could fathom the nature of society without understanding the nature of human beings. The latter endeavor required an unending engagement with "particulars" in private as well as public life. If Godwin had only passing interest in laboring men and women, he was as concerned as Wordsworth with the quotidian and the personal. A man worth studying was worth following "into his closet." "I would see the friend and the father of a family, as well as the patriot. . . . I should rejoice to have, or be enabled to make . . . a journal of his ordinary and minutest actions." Second, Godwin denied that history differed from fiction because it was accurate and reliable. "All history bears too near a resemblance to fable. Nothing is more uncertain, more contradictory, more unsatisfying than the evidence of facts." Good history in Godwin's view was that "in which, with a scanty substratum of facts and dates, the writer interweaves a number of happy, ingenious and instructive inventions, blending them into one continuous and indiscernible mass." History was "little better than romance under a graver name."[57]

Or, rather, romance was "one of the species of history," a "nobler" version of it. Whereas historians were "confined to individual incident and individual man, and must hang upon that his invention or conjecture as he can," the novelist collects information, "generalises" it, and "selects . . . those instances" that he knows best and will best advance his case. In the end, romance was not "facts," and history was. The advantage of history was

---

56. Ibíd., 61, 62, 81, 86.

57. William Godwin, "Essay of History and Romance," in Philp et al., eds., *Political and Philosophical Writings,* V, 291, 292, 294, 297, 298.

that when done well it allowed others to "investigate the story for themselves; or, more accurately speaking, that each man, instead of resting in the inventions of another, may invent his history for himself, and possess his creed as he possesses his property, single and incommunicable." Like poetry, narrative created a dynamic relationship between writers, readers, and characters. Facts are susceptible to different interpretations given to them by different human beings. We never really know the truth. Historians conjecture about "characters," but "we never know any man's character." "My most intimate and sagacious friend continually misapprehends my motives." So what should the historian do? He must delineate "consistent, human character" through "a display of the manner in which such a character acts under successive circumstances, in showing how character increases and assimilates new substances to its own, and how it decays, together with the catastrophe into which by its own gravity it naturally declines." The historian retrospectively puts a nation, and a biographer a person, into motion and records what happens over time. As important, he understands the experience of reading as a social act—a conversation between writer and reader—that facilitates reflection and encourages multiple meanings.[58]

Three years later, Godwin elaborated on this perspective in one of his few concerted responses to a suddenly large crowd of critics. In this *apologia,* Godwin denied (and with good reason) that he had ever been as fervent a supporter of the French Revolution as many of his friends. However, he lamented the decline of democratic principles. In 1800, thanks to war, the Terror, and repression, "even the starving labourer in the alehouse is become a champion of aristocracy." Godwin had always been a man of the middle, a person who believed in moderation, however unstable. He worried about extremism in the cause of liberty in 1793, and he worried about extremism in the cause of security in 1800. Because Godwin did not believe in fixed principles or natures, he never ceased "to revise, to reconsider, or to enquire." He did not expect his ideas to remain unchallenged. "I was no man of the world; I was a mere student, connected with no party, elected into no club, exempt from every imputation of political conspiracy or cabal." What some now derisively labeled the "New Philosophy" was nothing more than faith in progress through conversation.[59]

58. Ibid., 299, 300, 301.

59. William Godwin, *Thoughts Occasioned by the Perusal of Dr. Parr's Spital Sermon, Preached at Christ Church, April 15, 1800* (1801), in Philp et al., eds., *Political and Philosophical Writings,* II, 168, 169, 171, 172.

Still, Godwin confessed that in *Political Justice* he had underestimated the importance of "our temper and social feelings." "The human intellect is a sort of barometer, directed in its variations by the atmosphere which surrounds it." Because of the inevitable fluctuations in human as well as weather conditions, a change in ideas or sentiments was rarely straightforward. It was, to the contrary, often silent "and unperceived except in its ultimate result." Godwin asserted that he and his critics wanted the same thing: human happiness. He no longer neglected the impact of "private and domestic affections." Where he persisted in being different was in his conception of the relationship between motives and judgment of those motives. Godwin concluded that people were "more the creatures of sentiment and affection, than of the understanding." "We all of us have, twisted with our very natures, the principles of parental and filial affection, of love, attachment, and friendship." Who would argue with these ideas? Nevertheless, human beings must know that even "the sentiments of love, attachment and friendship" were "liable to excess. Each must be kept within its bounds." The goal was to avoid threatening a "paramount public good" by loving too ardently, whether the object was a child or a nation. Godwin saw a "truly virtuous character" as "the combined result of regulated affections," which included subjugation to "a criterion of virtue." The basic law of morality was to act in a fashion that would increase "the greatest public sum of pleasurable sensation." A civilized man would not achieve a permanently moral life. Accepting that fact, he was ever vigilant to judge his behavior by a higher standard in conversation with friends. Godwin did not advocate perfectibility; he did advocate the pursuit of benevolence to all mankind through unceasing engagement, what he called "the progressive nature of man." He rejected the idea, associated in his mind with Christianity and government, that human beings could not improve themselves. With social intercourse, much, if not everything, was possible. His newfound emphasis on personal affection affirmed his conviction that the world would be a better place with minimal government interference. Neither history nor the future constituted grounds for despair. The key was perpetual exchange. On that everything depended.[60]

In 1800, the American novelist Charles Brockden Brown admitted that it was difficult to "reduce" to "practice" the basic distinction between history and romance, that is, "truth" and "fiction." His sense was that, whereas a historian was an "observer" who recorded "appearances" and dealt in "certainties," a "romancer" "adorn[ed] those appearances with cause and

60. Ibid., 170, 181, 182–183, 184–185, 191.

Figure 8. Charles Brockden Brown. *By William Dunlap. Watercolor on ivory, 1806. National Portrait Gallery, Smithsonian Institution; given in loving memory of Katharine Lea Hancock by her children, grandchildren, and great grandchildren*

effect" and located them in time. Men often did similar things for very different reasons. Writers could reasonably describe the former. Analysis of the latter was an indulgence in "topics of conjecture" about "probabilities." Historians were reporters of "*actions*," and romancers interpreters of "*motives*." Sometimes writers were "both . . . in the compass of the same work." That combination was necessary because of the inherent complexity of human behavior. "A voluntary action is not only connected with cause and effect, but is itself a series of motives and incidents subordinate and successive to each other. Every action differs from every other in the number and complexity of its parts, but the most simple and brief is capable of being analized into a thousand subdivisions." History as a mere connection of verifiable events accomplished very little. Writers and their readers required some sense of why people act as they do.[61]

61. Charles Brockden Brown, "The Difference between History and Romance," *Monthly Magazine and American Review,* II, no. 4 (April 1800), in Alfred Weber and Wolfgang Schäfer, eds., *Literary Essays and Reviews* (Frankfurt am Main, 1992), 83–85.

Mary Hays's attitude toward Samuel Richardson's great novel *Clarissa* reflected the turn to personal histories of ordinary people. In 1793, Hays had offered *Clarissa* as a refutation of the reputation of novels as "frivolous, if not pernicious." By 1797, she thought Clarissa "an ideal being, placed in circumstances equally ideal, far removed from common life and human feelings." Hays had not abandoned her faith in the power of a free exchange of ideas and sentiments. Novels could instruct as well as divert, if they painted life "as it really exists, mingled with imperfection, and discoloured by passion." More, she thought literature should recognize that "moralists" and "enthusiasts" were extremists. "Gradations, almost imperceptible, of light and shade, must mingle in every true portrait of the human mind. Few persons are either wholly or disinterestedly virtuous or vicious," which is why writers and readers had to know people individually and over time. He "who judges of mankind in masses, and praises or censures without discrimination, will foster innumerable prejudices, and be betrayed into perpetual mistakes: upon the most superficial appearances, he will yield himself up to excessive admiration and boundless confidence, or indulge in the bitterness of invective, and the acrimony of contempt." Hays particularly admired *Caleb Williams*. In the right hands, "fictitious histories" might "become a powerful and effective engine of truth and reform." The key, Godwin had explained, was to delineate "consistent, human character" through "a display of the manner in which such a character acts under successive circumstances, in showing how character increases and assimilates new substances to its own, and how it decays, together with the catastrophe into which by its own gravity it naturally declines." Writing history involved recovering a sensibility as well as events. Like Wordsworth, Godwin did not reject the eighteenth century so much as he sought new forms, or rather revised old forms, to contemplate the possibilities of social commerce.[62]

Knowing Mary Wollstonecraft's mind and her sensibility had transformed Godwin. Still obsessed with hearing about his "defects" and their "effects," he now knew how "pleasing [it was] to be loved by those we feel ourselves impelled to love." He accepted with "uncommon pleasure" in January 1798 Thomas Wedgwood's criticism that he lacked sympathy be-

---

62. Mary Hays, "Appendix C: On Novels and Romances: 1. Letters and Essays, Moral and Miscellaneous, London, 1793: Letter to Mrs. —— on Reading Romances, etc.," in Hays, *The Victim of Prejudice* (1793), ed. Eleanor Ty (Peterborough, Ont., 1998), 236; Hays, "Appendix C: On Novels and Romances: 2. On Novel Writing," *Monthly Magazine* (September 1797), 180–181, ibid., 240, 241, 244; Godwin, "Essay of History and Romance," in Philp et al., eds., *Political and Philosophical Writings*, V, 301.

cause his friend's letter had persuaded him that Wedgwood's "character" had "(to use an expression of Mrs Godwin's) . . . *more heart in it*" than he had previously thought. In conversation with his lover, he had become more acquainted with the value of social affection as well as the politics of gender. Virtually absent in *Political Justice* and *Caleb Williams,* women would play significant roles in his future writing, especially in terms of their ability—or lack thereof—to persuade sensible men to awaken to new possibilities. As important, Godwin was now committed to imagining the unfolding of individual lives at the unstable intersection of overlapping personal relationships. The "voluntary actions of men are under the direction of their feelings," he mused in 1798. "Reason . . . has not the smallest degree of power to put any one limb or articulation of our bodies into motion"; it only facilitates the evaluation of desires and "the most successful mode" of fulfilling them. If "the [few] benefits we can confer upon the world" are "either petty in their moment, or questionable in their results," the "benefits we can confer upon those with whom we are closely connected are of great magnitude, or continual occurrence." Godwin would not surrender his conviction that "what the heart of man is able to conceive, the hand of man is strong enough to perform." Moving from essays to fiction, from "refined and abstract speculation" to "a study and delineation of things passing in the moral world," Godwin abandoned essentialist statements about the human condition for personal histories that unfolded within people's psyches as well as in their environments. He was not alone in this endeavor. Nor was his favorite subject—the behavior of people like Wollstonecraft and Imlay, not to mention himself—idiosyncratic.[63]

---

63. Godwin to Anthony Carlisle, Sept. 15, 1797, Oxford, Bodleian, MS Abinger c. 17, fol. 53; Godwin to Thomas Wedgwood, Jan. 3, 1798, c. 3, fols. 122–123; William Godwin, "Memorandum" (1798), in C. Kegan Paul, ed., *William Godwin: His Friends and Contemporaries,* 2 vols. (London, 1876), I, 294, 295; Godwin, *Thoughts Occasioned by the Perusal of Dr. Parr's Spital Sermon,* in Philps et al., eds., *Political and Philosophical Writings,* II, 207; Godwin, *Caleb Williams,* ed. Hindle, 3.

6

Modern Philosophers

The publication of *Memoirs of the Author of "A Vindication of the Rights of Woman"* ignited a firestorm of controversy throughout the English-speaking world. Mocked as "Modern Philosophers," William Godwin, Gilbert Imlay, and Mary Wollstonecraft were derided as ineffectual egoists inhabiting a dream world disconnected from the laws of God and nature. They were all three speculators who imagined that they could find happiness by turning the world upside down. A poem entitled "A Vision of Liberty" satirized the outcome of Godwin's and Wollstonecraft's fondness for revolutionary enthusiasm. William and Mary were "mounted on a braying ass." The "husband, sans-culottes, was melancholy" because the wife "would wear the breeches— / God help poor silly men from such usurping b——s." Then he, "thinking her whoredoms were not known enough," reported "with huge delight, / How oft she cuckolded the silly clown, / And lent, O lovely piece! herself to half the town." No wonder a young woman in Maine, certain that Wollstonecraft's life was "the best comment on her writings," concluded that "her sentiments . . . will not bear analyzing." Wollstonecraft and Godwin, it would seem, had been hoist on their own petard.[1]

1. C. K[irkpatrick Sharpe], "The Vision of Liberty," *Anti-Jacobin Review and Magazine; or, Monthly Political and Literary Censor, from April to August (Inclusive) 1801 . . .* , IX (London, 1801), 518; Eliza Southgate to Moses Porter, June 1, 1801, in "Letters of Eliza Southgate to Her Cousin Moses Porter," in Gordon S. Wood, ed., *The Rising Glory of America, 1760–1820,* rev. ed. (Boston, 1990), 188. See Emerson Robert Loomis, "The New Philosophy Satirized in American Fiction," *American Quarterly,* XIV (1962), 490–495; Anna Clark, *The Struggle for the Breeches: Gender and the Making of the British Working Class* (Berkeley, Calif., 1995); and Clark, *Scandal: The Sexual Politics of the British Constitution* (Princeton, N.J., 2004), 113–136.

It is easy to see the outrage that greeted *Memoirs* as an episode in a general reaction against radicalism. In the late 1790s, at war with France or contemplating war with France, political leaders in Great Britain and the United States passed legislation equating criticism of governments with sedition. In both countries, writers and publishers, including Joseph Johnson, went to jail. Renowned avatars of revolution such as Thomas Paine were suddenly pariahs fated to die scorned and forgotten. Revulsion against the excesses of the French Revolution fueled a defense of the standing order and a backlash against the revolutionary possibilities of the late eighteenth century. This interpretation has considerable merit. Many citizens in the early nineteenth century were preoccupied with security, stability, and the regulation of political and cultural borders. But it does not follow that conversations initiated in the eighteenth century ceased. Not even ridicule guaranteed obscurity.[2]

Serious reservations about the choices Wollstonecraft, Imlay, and Godwin made often co-existed with admiration for their willingness to make choices. After all, Mary Hays argued, revolution was a long-term affair that depended on exceptional individuals risking everything to promote reform. "Vigorous minds" were animated by "a liberal curiosity" that "urges them to quit beaten paths, to explore untried ways, to burst the fetters of prescription, and to acquire wisdom by an individual experience." In the end, Hays argued, "all great changes and improvements in society" originated with "speculative and enterprising spirits." Wollstonecraft's ambition had been "the emancipation of her own sex," and that cause would not die because she had violated social convention. If "the sensibility of this extraordinary woman" had settled on "the duties of a wife and mother" earlier she might have enjoyed a quiet life. But Mary Wollstonecraft had chosen a different path, and that had made all the difference. However she might have erred and however critics maligned her, she had not "laboured in vain: the spirit of reform is silently pursuing its course. Who can mark its limits?"[3]

Hays was right. Wollstonecraft and Godwin remained influential writers. If anything, *Memoirs* and its popular reception increased their visibility. Despite, or because of, the public denunciation of Modern Philosophy, many

2. See Seth Cotlar, *Tom Paine's America: The Rise and Fall of Transatlantic Radicalism in the Early Republic* (Charlottesville, Va., 2011); Rosemarie Zagarri, *Revolutionary Backlash: Women and Politics in the Early American Republic* (Philadelphia, 2008); John Barrell, *The Spirit of Despotism: Invasions of Privacy in the 1790s* (Oxford, 2006); Clark, *The Struggle for the Breeches;* and Clark, *Scandal,* 113–136.

3. [Mary Hays], "Memoirs of Mary Wollstonecraft," *The Annual Necrology, for 1797–8; Including, Also, Various Articles of Neglected Biography* (London, 1800), 411, 412, 424, 454, 459.

NEW MORALITY; — or — The promis'd Installment of the High-Priest of the THEOPHI.

_ behold !
The Directorial LAMA, Sovereign Priest__
LE PAUX — whom Atheists worship — at whose nod
Bow their meek heads — the Men without a God :
Ere long perhaps to this astonish'd Isle
Fresh from the Shores of subjugated Nile,
Shall BUONAPARTE'S victor Fleet protect
The genuine Theo-philanthropic Sect —

The Sect of MARAT, MIRABEAU, VOLTAIRE. ...
Led by their Pontiff, good LA-REVEILLERE.
Rejoice our CLUBS shall greet him, and Install
The holy Hunch-back in thy Dome, S! PAUL, --
While countless votaries thronging in his train
Wave their Red Caps, and hymn this jocund strain:
—"Couriers and Stars, Seditions Evening Host,
" Thou Morning Chronicle, and Morning Post,

"Whether ye make the Rights of Man your theme
"Your Country libel, and your God blasphe
"Or dirt on private worth and virtue throw
"Still blasphemous and blackguard, praise LE
—"And ye five other wandering Bards that r
"In sweet accord of harmony and love,
"C__DGE and S__TH.Y, L__D and L__B and C
"Tune all your mystic harps to praise LEPAU

women and men engaged with *A Vindication of the Rights of Woman* as interlocutors rather than scolds. They developed the form as well as the content of Godwin's *Memoirs.* They continued to imagine human lives as contingent personal histories. They continued to prefer persuasion to prescription, assuming that choice was more effective than command. One group of readers insisted in essays on the universal and fixed nature of human behavior and the inexorable movement of a clockwork history beyond the control of human beings. They could not shake their fear of a society organized as a self-regulating mechanism unmoored from religion and government. The second group turned to fictitious "personal histories" to consider the predicaments of people remarkably similar to Wollstonecraft, Imlay, and Godwin. Often written by and for women, novels debated the merits of revolutionary constructions of human behavior and human history. They became, in fact, the most effective means of insuring that "il-

Figure 9.
New Morality; or, The Promis'd Installment of the High-Priest of the Theophilanthropes, with the Homage of Leviathan and His Suite. *By James Gillray, published by John Wright. Etching, published Aug. 1, 1798.* © *National Portrait Gallery, London*

liberal malice and unmanly abuse" would not "sully the treasures of mental splendour, which this illustrious woman [Wollstonecraft] has bequeathed to posterity."[4]

The Universal Laws of God and Nature

The initial assault on Wollstonecraft and Godwin was utterly merciless. *Memoirs* had exposed the author of *A Vindication of the Rights of Woman* as yet another woman who succumbs to fancy, "disregards . . . chastity,"

---

4. "Picture of London," *Literary Magazine, and American Register,* II, no. 10 (July 1804), 279. On Wollstonecraft's legacy, see Eileen Hunt Botting and Christine Carey, "Wollstonecraft's Philosophical Impact on Nineteenth-Century American Women's Rights Advocates," *American Journal of Political Science,* XLVIII (2004), 707–722.

and "becomes the dupe of some designing man . . . who . . . corrupts her mind, and debases her person." She loved Gilbert Imlay—"but he loved not her. He was leagued to her by desire." Once Imlay had satisfied his lust, he abandoned her. Others blamed Wollstonecraft for failing to control herself. The index to the *Anti-Jacobin Review* made the point succinctly: "Prostitution," "*See* Mary Wollstonecraft." No wonder friends were as horrified by the reviews as they were by the book. A few defended Godwin's decision to publish *Memoirs*. Poet Anna Seward, calling Wollstonecraft "a very extraordinary woman," suggested that to "paint the strength of her basely betrayed attachment to that villain Imlay, was surely not injury but justice to the memory of a deceased wife." Much more common was anger at Godwin for treating Wollstonecraft as cruelly in death as Imlay had in life. Robert Southey complained that Godwin had exhibited "a want of all feeling in stripping his dead wife naked." The last in a series of "men to whom she attached herself [who] were utterly unworthy of her," he had injured Wollstonecraft by reducing her life to "an extraordinary instance of the folly of departing from the established order of society." Others lamented that Godwin had given "no correct history of the formation" of her mind. "We are neither informed of her favourite books, her hours of study, nor her attainments in languages and philosophy." Instead, her husband's obsession with revealing her efforts to put her "singular opinions . . . into practice" had transformed private behavior into public scandal.[5]

No one was more surprised by the public outcry than Godwin, in part because his anxiety about his reputation exacerbated his tendency to be "nervous" in company. By his own admission, he was "bold and adventurous in opinions, not in life." Thomas Holcroft had pronounced him "too tranquil and unimpassioned" to be a writer, claiming that his mind always stood "greatly in need of stimulus and excitement." People who knew God-

5. "Biography: Mrs. Godwin," *Merrimack Miscellany*, I, no. 11 (Aug. 17, 1805), 41; "Biography: Memoirs of the Late Mrs. Godwin, Author of 'A Vindication of the Rights of Women,'" *Lady's Monitor*, I, no. 17 (Dec. 12, 1801), 130; *Anti-Jacobin Review and Magazine*, I (1798), 859 (the review of *Memoirs* is on 94–102); Anna Seward to H[umphrey] Repton, Esq., Apr. 13, 1798, in *Letters of Anna Seward, Written between the Years 1784 and 1807*, 6 vols. (Edinburgh, 1811), V, 71, 73, 74; Robert Southey to William Taylor, July 1, 1804, in J. W. Robberds, ed., *A Memoir of the Life and Writings of the Late William Taylor of Norwich . . . Containing His Correspondence of Many Years with the Late Robert Southey, Esq. . . .* (London, 1843), I, 507; Southey to Caroline Bowles, Feb. 13, 1824, in Edward Dowden, ed., *The Correspondence of Robert Southey with Caroline Bowles . . .* (Dublin, 1881), 52; "Picture of London," *Literary Magazine, and American Register* II, no. 10 (July 1804), 279; review of *Memoirs of the Author of "A Vindication of the Rights of Woman,"* by William Godwin, in *Analytical Review*, XXVII (January–June 1798) (London, 1798), 238.

win always wished he would take more chances and indulge himself more often. Affirming the success of his brief marriage to Wollstonecraft, they credited her with having enhanced his limited supply of personal warmth. After a meal in the Godwin household in December 1799, Samuel Taylor Coleridge declared that "Godwin" was "no great Things in Intellect; but in heart and manner he is all the better for having been the Husband of Mary Wollstonecraft." How would Godwin survive without his wife? The "cadaverous Silence of [the] Children" was "quite catacomb-ish," complained Coleridge, "and thinking of Mary Wolstencroft I was oppressed by it."[6]

It was hard to reconcile Godwin's "noisy fame" with his diffidence. The infamous radical was "a well behaved decent man, nothing very brilliant about him or imposing," observed Charles Lamb in 1800. He had "neither horns nor claws, quite a tame creature," although Godwin's restless interrogation of every assertion led the catty Lamb to dub him "Professor." Two years later, Bostonian William Austin described a man "of manners remarkably mild, unassuming, rather reserved; in conversation cautious, argumentative, frequently doubtful, yet modestly courting reply, more from a desire of truth, than a love of contending; in his family, affectionate, cordial, accommodating; to his friends, confidential, ready to many any sacrifice; to his enemies—you would never know from Mr Godwin that he had an enemy." The Virginian Joseph Carrington Cabell agreed when he dined with the "celebrated author" at Joseph Johnson's in 1804. Godwin was hardly intimidating. Unlike most Englishmen, "he never interrupts others." When he disagreed, he did so respectfully. "He makes no little personal attacks, and bears them from his friends with much good nature, discovering no symptom of irritation and never losing the serenity of his temper." He was, in short, "a plain, decent, modest, smiling, and agreeable little man."[7]

Godwin was surprised by the hysterical reaction to *Memoirs* because he believed it a chronicle of a life well lived. Modern Philosophy, if that is what

6. William Godwin, [1798-1799?], in C. Kegan Paul, ed., *William Godwin: His Friends and Contemporaries*, 2 vols. (London, 1876), I, 361; Godwin, "Analysis of Own Character Begun Sep 26, 1798," in Mark Philp et al., eds., *The Collected Novels and Memoirs of William Godwin*, 8 vols. (London, 1992), I, 59; Samuel Taylor Coleridge to Robert Southey, [Dec. 19, 1799], in Earl Leslie Griggs, ed., *Collected Letters of Samuel Taylor Coleridge*, 6 vols. (1956; rpt. Oxford, 1966), I, 549, [Dec. 24, 1799], 553.

7. Charles Lamb to Thomas Manning, [Feb. 18, 1800], in Edwin W. Marrs, Jr., ed., *The Letters of Charles and Mary Anne Lamb*, 3 vols. (Ithaca, N.Y., 1975), I, 185–186, [Nov. 3, 1800], 244, [Dec. 15, 1800], 258–259; William Austin, *Letters from London: Written during the Years 1802 and 1803* (Boston, 1804), 203; Joseph C. Cabell Diary, Sept. 19, 1804, Accession #2654, 107, 109, Albert and Shirley Small Special Collections Library, University of Virginia, Charlottesville, Va.

it was to be called, had not failed. Indeed, critics did not seem to understand what Wollstonecraft, Imlay, and Godwin, among others, had proposed: not anarchy, not a storm of autonomous individuals living out a Hobbesian nightmare of unrestrained desire, but a self-regulated society in which individuals worked together to manage themselves and cultivate a better world. They had imagined—and privately implemented—a revolutionary social order in which individuals achieved independence through interdependence. Escaping the confines of corrupt institutions and hoary tradition that insisted on the submission of individuals to the word of God and the laws of man, women and men could learn, grow, and change. They could experience awakenings prompted by sympathetic intercourse. History was neither the unfolding of a master plan nor an account of extraordinary men creating institutions to compensate for the essential failures of the mass of mankind. It was, rather, the sum of the stories of ordinary women and men who believed themselves competent to govern themselves. *Memoirs* was an optimistic tale. A woman acutely aware of the dangers of her enthusiastic sensibility worked hard in conversations with others to manage that "warmth," and largely succeeded. The point was clear. Everyone gave in to extremes. But anyone could recover. No fall was preordained or permanent.

Most critics valued social commerce as much as Wollstonecraft and Godwin but believed that the process had to play out within religious and political institutions developed over time to compensate for the weakness of human beings. Wollstonecraft's assertion of her independence as a historical actor, they argued, was the root of her unhappiness. Enthralled by a vision of her own power, she had ignored that history moved inexorably onward, oblivious to human understanding and subservient to predictable laws. "It is universally acknowledged," David Hume had explained in *An Enquiry concerning Human Understanding*, "that there is a great uniformity among the actions of men, in all nations and ages, and that human nature remains still the same, in its principles and operations." "The same motives always produce the same actions. The same events follow from the same causes." Thus, the "chief use" of history "is only to discover the constant and universal principles of human nature." Properly understood, a history was an aesthetically pleasing narrative of laws affirmed or violated that encouraged the cultivation of virtue, self-abnegation, and obedience.[8]

8. David Hume, *An Enquiry concerning Human Understanding* (Stilwell, Kans., 2005), 47 (section VIII, part I, paragraph 65). See also Hannah Spahn, *Thomas Jefferson, Time, and History* (Charlottesville, Va., 2011).

Wollstonecraft, Imlay, and Godwin had suffered because they asserted the power of human beings to make history rather than to live within it. They had ignored the truth that human nature was universal and fixed by arguing through the example of their personal lives that it was particular and contingent. What astonishing hubris! It was self-evident that Wollstonecraft would have been happier had she "married well in early life." "To those who are acquainted with the heart, her love to Mr. Imlay will be no problem in the science of human passion." Her exhibition of "female depravity" had happily revealed the failure of her ideas. Readers of *Vindication* would suffer the same fate as its author. Reversing the critique of marriage in *The Emigrants,* a reviewer contended that the inevitable outcome of unregulated social commerce was that homes would become brothels and wives, prostitutes. Dissenters from this conclusion were referred to "her experience, with Mr. Imlay," which surely "*must* have taught her the *imprudence* at least of disregarding the law of society regarding marriage." The challenge was to survive a world in which nature determined history more than human beings did. People had to work within the laws of nature rather than against them.[9]

Even staunch opponents of monarchy and established churches distanced themselves from Godwin, concluding that he had gone too far in his celebration of freedom. Thomas Jefferson, that self-proclaimed eternal foe of tyranny, doubted the doctrine that man "may in time be rendered so perfect that he will be able to govern himself in every circumstance so as to injure none, to do all the good he can, to leave government no occasion to exercise their powers over him, and of course to render political government useless." Jefferson's political rivals were harsher. Eager to demonstrate Aaron Burr unqualified to serve as president of the United States, Alexander Hamilton reported that Burr was "not very far from being a visionary. . . . in some instances . . . he has talked perfect *Godwinism.*" It was true. Burr admired Godwin and Wollstonecraft and continued to do so long after publication of *Memoirs.* According to Hamilton, however, mere association with Godwin was an endorsement of "the French system" of "unshackling the mind and leaving it to its natural energies." When Hamilton charged "that

9. "Memoirs of the Late Mrs. Godwin," *Lady's Monitor,* I, no. 17 (Dec. 12, 1801), 130; Review of *Memoirs of the Author of "A Vindication of the Rights of Woman,"* by William Godwin, in *The Monthly Review; or, Literary Journal, Enlarged: From September to December 1798, Inclusive,* XXVII (London, 1798), 323; Chandos Michael Brown, "Mary Wollstonecraft; or, The Female Illuminati: The Campaign against Women and 'Modern Philosophy' in the Early Republic," *Journal of the Early Republic,* XV (1995), 415.

Burr is a man of a very subtile imagination, and a mind of this make is rarely free from ingenious whimsies," he was affirming a popular judgment. Modern Philosophers followed their personal inclinations independent of respect for God, tradition, or society.[10]

The French Revolution had facilitated Wollstonecraft's self-deception. She had not married Imlay because she met him in France at a time *"when a new system of thinking on that point almost universally obtained."* What appeared "indelicate" in 1798 "would not have appeared to be so" in 1793. Then Wollstonecraft had imagined that love could organize relationships, forgetting that marriage was "the legal tie by which the laws of men compel to certain attentions and responsibilities." Her mistake was "to place confidence" when she ought "to have cherished suspicion." An uncommon person had allowed her "warmth" to lead her to unwise choices "when the cost of self-denial was a mere sensual privation." Fancying herself independent, she welcomed the attention of "the monster of insensibility, who deceived and abandoned her." The core of her problem was that she had made "personal and mental independence . . . her darling object." Her "wild and visionary scheme" to unite the joys of the "connubial life" and "a single state" was "the source of all her misfortunes." She had become, in sum, "the self-devoted victim of ungovernable sensibility." Legal institutions, not natural commerce and history, not imagination, best restrained impulses to act "out of the then wantonness of power." Without government and marriage, citizens would reenact in both public squares and bedrooms the horrors of the Terror ad infinitum.[11]

Hannah More was not surprised by the outcome of Wollstonecraft's relationship with Imlay. Left to manage themselves, women would regularly find themselves in self-constructed prisons. They had to accept the revealed truth that people are not intrinsically capable of self-government. Growing up in Bristol at midcentury, More attended a school run by her mother and her sister. At the age of twenty-two, she accepted an annuity of two hundred pounds from her fiancé when they decided not to get married. Able to support herself, she remained single for the rest of her life. More went to Lon-

10. Thomas Jefferson to Bishop James Madison, Jan. 31, 1800, in Julian P. Boyd et al., eds., *The Papers of Thomas Jefferson,* 36 vols. to date (Princeton, N.J., 1950–), XXXI, 350; Alexander Hamilton to James A. Bayard, Jan. 16, 1801, in Harold C. Syrett et al., eds., *The Papers of Alexander Hamilton,* 27 vols. (New York, 1961–1987), XXV, 321.

11. Review of *Memoirs of the Author of "A Vindication of the Rights of Woman,"* by Godwin, in *Analytical Review,* XXVII (January–June 1798), 239; "Reflections on the Character of Mary Wollstonecraft Godwin," *Monthly Magazine, and American Review,* I, no. 5 (August 1799), 330, 332, 334, 335.

don in the 1770s and became a successful playwright and a witty member of literary circles. Late in the 1780s, she took a turn to evangelical religion and devoted herself to philanthropy and antislavery. Until her death in 1833 at the age of eighty-eight, she wrote enormously popular books and tracts in praise of British political and religious institutions. A committed Christian who trusted in an omnipotent God, not in imperfect man, she doubted that either men or women could fight the "natural corruption of the heart" on their own.[12]

More was a strong advocate of a Christian education for females. Abhorring the arts of decoration, display, and diversion, she wanted girls to read and think. Women "will not content themselves with polishing, when they are able to reform; with entertaining, when they may awaken; and with captivating for a day, when they may bring into action powers of which the effects may be commensurate with eternity." But a Christian education would teach a young woman to accept "the subordinate station she is called to fill in life." She would learn to respect the word of God in "an age when inversion is the character of the day." The "modern idea of improvement" was an "indefinite rage for radical reform." The *"Female Werter,"* Wollstonecraft—and other well-meaning radicals—had wrongly characterized "marriage as an unjust infringement on liberty, and a tyrannical deduction from general happiness." Modern Philosophy would increase the misery of the weaker sex by leaving them vulnerable to the likes of Imlay. In a world governed by imagination, a "popular libertine" could easily persuade "delicate women" to join him in "criminal commerce." Imlay's inconstant behavior was as predictable as the course of the French Revolution.[13]

"Heathen perfectionists," as More labeled Modern Philosophers, had forgotten that the fallen state of human beings necessitated their voluntary subordination to divine will. After all, the "history of the world" was "little else than the history of the crimes of the human race." To expect individuals to improve themselves without God was to defy reality. "The Gospel *can* have nothing to do with a system in which sin is reduced to a little human imperfection, and Old Bailey crimes are softened down into a few engaging weaknesses; and in which the turpitude of all the vices a man himself commits is done away by his *candour* in tolerating all the vices committed by others." Education and conversation had enormous social value if they

---

12. Hannah More, *Strictures on the Modern System of Female Education* . . . (1799), vol. V of *The Works of Hannah More*, new ed., 11 vols. (London, 1830), xv. See Colin Wells, *The Devil and Doctor Dwight: Satire and Theology in the Early American Republic* (Chapel Hill, N.C., 2002).

13. More, *Strictures*, 3, 15, 16, 19, 26, 32, 226, 237.

led individuals to confront that revolutions could not overcome the tendencies of human nature to undermine the progress they promised. Instead of secular commerce fueled by visions of an earthly paradise, women should engage in "holy commerce" that amounted to an exchange of prayers in "'the communion of saints.'" True reformation involved a decision to obey the word of God and the institutions designed to protect individuals from one another. Where, More fretted, would this invocation of human power end? Discussions of the *"rights of man,"* which had led to discussions of "the *rights of woman"* would encourage discussions of "the *rights of youth,* the *rights of children,* the *rights of babies!"* Revolution was the triumph of the darkest of tyrants: an "ungoverned sensibility" that fueled anarchy and corroded civilization.[14]

If Hannah More worried that Modern Philosophy outlined the path to perdition, Thomas Robert Malthus warned that it justified behavior that was literally destroying human society. Malthus extended an argument with his father over *Political Justice* into *An Essay on the Principle of Population,* first published by the redoubtable Joseph Johnson in 1798 and republished in a much longer and fuller edition in 1803. The book was so persuasive that a reviewer incorrectly credited Malthus with leading Godwin to renounce "his former principles of policy and government." Malthus had studied at Jesus College, Cambridge, before obtaining a living as a minister. His father was a devotee of Rousseau and optimistic about human progress. The son was not. The younger Malthus's position was a straightforward statement of the law of unanticipated consequences. Human beings were too little aware of the natural outcome of their failure to control desire.[15]

Famously afraid that human beings were having far more children than they could possibly feed, Malthus warned that a "too rapid increase of population" was causing "poverty and misery" all over the world. The problem with Modern Philosophy lay in its apparent endorsement of the pursuit of fleeting pleasure at the expense of social stability. Godwin and Wollstonecraft's vision of progress was a recipe for disaster. Their endorsement of "unshackled intercourse" would leave virtually every woman pregnant by the time she was twenty-three, adding to an exploding number of hungry people and putting pressure on lagging resources. The institution of marriage, the practice of sexual restraint, and the secondary status of women were more than issues of religious morality; they were the well-established

14. Ibid., 26, 109, 110, 145, 294, 391, 438, 439.

15. "Godwin and Malthus," *Literary Magazine and American Register,* II, no. 11 (August 1804), 361.

MODERN PHILOSOPHERS / 193

means through which human beings respected the workings of the natural world set in motion by God.[16]

Wollstonecraft, Imlay, and Godwin's revolution amounted to an act of temerity. Like More, Malthus wanted human beings to accept their powerlessness, to recognize themselves as creatures whose behavior was predictable. In human society, romantic love was never a match for sexual instinct. "The mighty law of self-preservation," wrote Malthus, "expels all the softer and more exalted emotions of the soul." "The temptations to evil are too strong for human nature to resist." Human beings thus needed to rest "contented with that mode of improvement which is dictated by the course of nature, and of not obstructing the advances which would otherwise be made in this way."[17]

Like More, Malthus favored education and sociability as ways to avoid that collective fate. He believed that men and women were historical agents to the extent that they could and should make choices. But they had to act within borders. Plants and other animals followed their instinct to reproduce without any check on their activities except those provided by the world God had created. Once they outran available resources, they died from violence, disease, and starvation. Man, however, had the cognitive capacity to predict the results of his behavior and to act to prevent disaster. "Reason interrupts his career," wrote Malthus, "and asks him whether he may not bring beings into the world for whom he cannot provide the means of support." Reason taught the deleterious effects of unrestrained physical gratification, including "promiscuous intercourse, unnatural passions, violations of the marriage bed, and improper arts to conceal" any of the above. Not only did vice "degrade the female character," it also poisoned "the springs of domestic happiness."[18]

Like Wollstonecraft and Godwin, Malthus wanted to manage passions, not extinguish them. Doubting the efficacy of coercion as much as Godwin and company did—the British Poor Laws only exacerbated the situation— Malthus preferred to encourage voluntary celibacy. Force and prescription would not get men to delay marriage and avoid "irregular gratifications." Perhaps persuasion could, by showing European males that it was in their

16. T[homas] R[obert] Malthus, *An Essay on the Principle of Population; or, A View of Its Past and Present Effects on Human Happiness . . .* (1798), 2 vols. (Cambridge, 1989), I, 1, 319.

17. Ibid., 321, II, 199. Godwin and Malthus were cordial. Godwin did not respond in print until *Of Population: An Enquiry concerning the Power of Increase in the Numbers of Mankind, Being an Answer to Mr. Malthus's Essay on That Subject* (London, 1820).

18. Malthus, *Essay on Population,* I, 10, 18.

interest not to have sex until their late twenties. Malthus hoped, in advice as idealistic as anything Godwin ever wrote, that they would accept what he politely termed "a certain degree of temporary unhappiness" in order to avert a larger social crisis. They should refrain from sexual intercourse with women until they were capable of supporting a family. If tens of thousands of men delayed sexual activity until they married in their late twenties, families would be smaller and demographic catastrophe averted.[19]

Following the logic of Adam Smith, Malthus argued that prolonged abstinence would cultivate gentility among men and improve their treatment of women. God had created "natural and moral evil" as "instruments" to guide individuals to prudence. A man's desire for regular access to a woman's body stimulates his "benevolence and pity" and restrains his temper and his tendency to enslave her, especially when that desire had been thwarted over a period of time. "Passion is stronger, and its general effects in producing gentleness, kindness, and suavity of manners, much more powerful, where obstacles are thrown in the way of very early and universal gratification." Romantic attachment served society as long as it flowed within the bounds of the institution of marriage. "The passion of love," Malthus concluded, "is a powerful stimulus in the formation of character, and often prompts to the most noble and generous exertions; but this is only when the affections are centred in one object; and generally, when full gratification is delayed by difficulties." Sexual abstinence until a late marriage was a reasonable choice that satisfied the demands of both individual desire and the survival of the species. Without it, Malthus could not predict human survival, let alone progress. Nature, in the end, would do as it wished.[20]

Neither More nor Malthus objected to love or social commerce. They simply saw them as the means by which human beings could choose to subordinate themselves rather than to declare their independence from God and nature. More and Malthus were no more cold tribunes of self-denial than Godwin and Wollstonecraft were wild-eyed anarchists. Both images are caricatures of thoughtful people whose books circled similar issues.

Imagined Histories

"Of the numbers who study, or at least who read history, how few derive any advantage from their labours!" wrote Maria Edgeworth in the preface to her

19. Ibid., 17, 18, 304.
20. Ibid., II, 88, 91, 92, 98.

1800 novel, *Castle Rackrent.* "The heroes of history are so decked out by the finc fancy of the professed historian; they talk in such measured prose, and act from such sublime or such diabolical motives, that few have sufficient taste, wickedness, or heroism, to sympathize in their fate." Instead, Edgeworth chose to enter into what her friend Godwin called people's closets to understand who they were and why they behaved as they did. "We cannot judge either of the feelings or of the characters of men with perfect accuracy, from their actions or their appearance in public." Rather, "it is from their careless conversations, their half-finished sentences, that we may hope with the greatest probability of success to discover their real characters." To capture the exchange of perceptions as well as information about a specific topic between two or more people was to reveal the dynamism and contingency of human behavior, to see individuals making choices and justifying them. And there was no more effective medium to do that than fictional histories, or novels.[21]

Revolving around dilemmas familiar to the middling people, especially women, who created and consumed them, novels elaborated on the notion that social commerce was more likely to promote morality and progress than institutions. Independent people who chose interdependence were more likely to live useful lives than those who practiced obedience to the laws of God and nature. Imagining the present was preferable to honoring the past. In the hands of someone like Hannah More, fiction did illustrate the unfolding of a universal history in which individuals behaved in predictable ways.[22] But most novels invited readers to follow characters' efforts to make sense of what was happening to them and why. Plots developed,

21. Maria Edgeworth, *Castle Rackrent and Ennui* (1800) (Lexington, Ky., 2008), 5. See Elizabeth Kowaleski-Wallace, *Their Fathers' Daughters: Hannah More, Maria Edgeworth, and Patriarchal Complicity* (New York, 1991), on the role of Edgeworth's father in her writing; Edgeworth was "a particularly strong example of a male-centered woman" (96). See also Marilyn Butler, *Romantics, Rebels, and Reactionaries: English Literature and Its Background, 1760–1830* (Oxford, 1981). On the influence of Godwin's *Memoirs*, see Helen M. Buss, "Memoirs Discourse and William Godwin's *Memoirs of the Author of 'A Vindication of the Rights of Woman,'*" in Buss, D. L. Macdonald, and Anne McWhir, eds., *Mary Wollstonecraft and Mary Shelley: Writing Lives* (Waterloo, Ont., 2001), 113–126; Jon Klancher, "Godwin and the Genre Reformers: On Necessity and Contingency in Romantic Narrative Theory," 21–38, and Gary Handwerk, "History, Trauma, and the Limits of the Liberal Imagination: William Godwin's Historical Fiction," 64–85, both in Tilottama Rajan and Julia M. Wright, eds., *Romanticism, History, and the Possibilities of Genre: Re-forming Literature, 1789–1837* (Cambridge, 1998). The next few paragraphs draw on Andrew Cayton, "The Authority of the Imagination in an Age of Wonder," *JER*, XXXIII (2013), 1–27.

22. See, for example, Hannah More, *Coelebs in Search of a Wife* (1809) (Charleston, S.C., 2010).

as in *Caleb Williams,* as quests for information; resolutions occurred when the heroine or hero acquires the confidence, usually through social commerce, to make an informed choice. Both the Gothic novel (in its emphasis on ambiguous environments) and the Jacobin novel (in its emphasis on ambiguous personalities) stressed not simply the mysteries of life but also the ability of human beings to construct meaning. Especially in sentimental novels, meaning emerged from a dynamic conversation among author, characters, and readers about the sustainability of love as the organizing principle of any human society.[23]

How marvelous it would have been if reason could make sense of everything! How wonderful if human beings could predict outcomes and adjust their behavior accordingly, as Malthus urged them to do. But the world was not so transparent or accessible. In his *Lectures on Astronomy,* Adam Smith had noted the pleasure the mind takes in observing the resemblances among different objects that allows it "to reduce them to one common class, and to call them by one general name." Individuals comprehended occurrences by putting them into familiar categories until the fateful moment when "something quite new and singular [was] presented." Anomalies defeated categorization and produced "uncertain and undetermined" "thought," a state of bewilderment that "constitute[s] the sentiment properly called *Wonder.*" Agitated people demand to know: "What sort of a thing can that be? What is that like?" Lacking answers, they "are quite at a loss." Neither revealed truth nor natural laws explained everything.[24]

Human beings could not make sense of their world by relying on their own judgment. They needed one another, as Wollstonecraft, Imlay, and Godwin had argued at length. The cornerstone of understanding was sympathy. To understand someone else, an individual had to put himself in the other's situation. "As we have no immediate experience of what other men feel," Smith argued, "we can form no idea of the manner in which they are

23. See Gary Kelly, *The English Jacobin Novel, 1780–1805* (Oxford, 1976); Kelly, *English Fiction of the Romantic Period, 1789–1830* (New York, 1989). See also Cathy N. Davidson, *Revolution and the Word: The Rise of the Novel in America* (New York, 1986); R[ussell] B. N[ye], "Historical Essay," in Charles Brockden Brown, *Ormond; or, The Secret Witness,* vol. II of *The Novels and Related Works of Charles Brockden Brown,* Bicentennial ed., ed. Sydney J. Krause et al. (Kent, Ohio, 1982), 295–341; Stephen Shapiro, "'Man to Man I Needed Not to Dread His Encounter': *Edgar Huntly*'s End of Erotic Pessimism," in Philip Barnard, Mark Kamrath, and Shapiro, eds., *Revising Charles Brockden Brown: Culture, Politics, and Sexuality in the Early Republic* (Knoxville, Tenn., 2004), 238; and Steven Hamelman, "Secret to the Last: Charles Brockden Brown's *Ormond," LIT: Literature Interpretation Theory,* XI (2000), 305–326.

24. Adam Smith, "The History of Astronomy" (1795), in W. P. D. Wightman, J. P. Bryce, and I. S. Ross, eds., *Adam Smith: Essays on Philosophical Subjects* (New York, 1980), 38, 39.

affected, but by conceiving what we ourselves should feel in the like situation." Sympathy achieved through an exercise of imagination—becoming "in some measure" one with another person—was the first step toward dealing with wonder. Because the senses cannot "carry us beyond our own persons," it was "by the imagination only that we can form any conception of what are his sensations." Why should anyone care? As always, Smith insisted that they would when they saw that it was in their self-interest to do so. Extended imagined scenarios allowed human beings to understand themselves as well as others. Individuals "sympathize even with the dead," despite their inability to affect the dead. The point of imagining "our own living souls in their inanimated bodies" was to put to good use suffering on their behalf. Self-understanding commenced with imagining others' understanding of similar situations, which in turn encouraged self-restraint and promoted benevolence. Individuals who isolated themselves, who did not listen to others, who defined themselves as independent of their relationships with other men and women, were dangers to everyone, most especially themselves. That was why friends were so often called monitors. "Our sentiments," Smith explained, must "have always some secret reference, either to what are, or to what upon a certain condition would be, or to what we imagine ought to be the sentiments of others." Acquaintances were mirrors through which individuals saw themselves as others saw them. A healthy person divided himself in half in order to evaluate his conduct. He was an agent in his desire to merit approbation by practicing virtue and to avoid censure by shunning vice. And he was a spectator in his need to evaluate himself continually.[25]

When literary critics refer to the importance of "social minds"—that is, "joint, group, shared, or collective thought, as opposed to . . . private, individual thought"—in nineteenth-century literature, they are invoking the very eighteenth-century idea that understanding emerges through dynamic interaction with other people, through what Edgeworth called careless conversation and half-finished sentences. More than a lack of craft was responsible for the shaggy, rambling character of much of contemporary fiction. Novels were all about seeing people in medias res, in specific situations at a specific time. Authors implicitly assumed that human behavior was neither universal nor predictable, that the linear logic of histories and treatises could not reveal the development of self-awareness. In real

25. Adam Smith, *The Theory of Moral Sentiments,* 2d ed. (London, 1761), 2, 8, 9, 10, 198, 199, 202. See E. M. Dadlez, *Mirrors to One Another: Emotion and Value in Jane Austen and David Hume* (Malden, Mass., 2009).

life, people stopped, started, listened, spoke, interrupted, laughed, smiled, got angry, scowled, grimaced, changed their minds, misconstrued intention, and ignored consequences. Differentiating impulse from judgment or desire from duty was hardly clear-cut. Novels were psychologically astute, as Godwin and Edgeworth suggested, because they traced inner personal stories over time. More than anything else, they were an exercise in cultivating self-knowledge.[26]

Reading novels was as much a social act as writing them. Identifying with characters, their dilemmas, and their choices had the potential to prompt individual transformation. Far from passive, readers of novels were "side-participants" in imagined conversations. They engaged in the same manner as they did while listening to friends, watching a play, or enjoying a concert. A key dimension of the social power of fiction lay in the physical distance between readers and characters. In the controlled laboratory of the imagination, readers could wonder exactly when the indulgence of desire became antisocial or where restraint moved into repression. They could put a book aside if it bored or disturbed them. They could reflect, reread, evaluate, and make judgments in ways rarely possible in ordinary life. A novel allows "a person to relive some patterns of experience" and "to think about its implications." It invites "readers to adopt perspectives and commitments they would not entertain in their actual worlds," to distinguish and then integrate "several, often-divergent perspectives of multiple characters," and to reflect on the possibility that "more than one path is possible." Reading fiction does not necessarily lead to emulation of characters, as late-eighteenth-century critics feared. The genius of *Anna Karenina*, for example, lies in Leo Tolstoy's ability to persuade his readers to empathize with Anna's dilemma even when they do not agree with her choice. After all, Tolstoy himself did not approve of her decision for reasons similar to those of the critics of Wollstonecraft and Imlay: Anna selfishly indulges her desire without regard to the impact of her adultery on her family, especially her son, and society in general. But Tolstoy makes Anna's dilemma real by stressing both her ambivalence and the ambiguity of her situation.[27]

26. Alan Palmer, *Social Minds in the Novel* (Columbus, Ohio, 2010), 4; Frank Ankersmit, "Truth in History and Literature," *Narrative*, XVIII (2010), 36; Keith Oatley, "Emotions and the Story Worlds of Fiction," in Melanie C. Green, Jeffrey J. Strange, and Timothy C. Brock, eds., *Narrative Impact: Social and Cognitive Foundations* (Mahwah, N.J., 2002), 41. See Eric Slauter, "History, Literature, and the Atlantic World," *Early American Literature*, XLIII (2005), 153.

27. Oatley, "Emotions and the Story Worlds of Fiction," in Green, Strange, and Brock, eds., *Narrative Impact*, 75; Gary Saul Morson, *"Anna Karenina" in Our Time: Seeing More Wisely* (New Haven, Conn., 2007), 65, 281.

Nineteenth-century novelists often wrote with a sensibility similar to that of *Memoirs of the Author of "A Vindication of the Rights of Woman."* A useful life was a social life, defined by mistakes and turning points understood best through careless conversation and retrospective narration. The decisive acts of Dorothea Brooke's life, explains George Eliot at the end of *Middlemarch,* "were the mixed result of a young and noble impulse struggling amidst the conditions of an imperfect social state, in which great feelings will often take the aspect of error, and great faith the aspect of illusion." "For there is no creature whose inward being is so strong that it is not greatly determined by what lies outside it." Like *Memoirs,* novels were personal histories in which individual behavior mattered not only because nothing was fixed or predictable but also because meaning was created through sympathy and imagination.[28]

Sentimental fiction, to be sure, was a discourse of liberalism that deflected attention away from the structures of patriarchy, colonialism, and market capitalism to revel in the personal problems of individuals. Why worry about love affairs in the middle of commercial and industrial revolutions (not to mention global warfare) that were radically reorganizing life around the world? Worse, why encourage young women to imagine that they could change a man, as Elizabeth Bennett famously transformed Fitzwilliam Darcy? How could romantic love be subversive in a world in which women had virtually no political or economic power? But sentimental fiction flourished in a context where "the opportunity to influence one's own outcome to even a limited degree" was a major development for many women. By making problems personal rather than structural, sentimental discourse revealed desire to be both the "will's fundamental impulse and a potential obstacle to its exercise." Fiction taught that "mistakes need not be expunged but could rather be incorporated into the social fabric." The challenge was to move between "self-abnegation and self-approval," "passive acceptance and intellectual assertion," and "reasoned moderation and fervent outcry."[29]

Mary Hays was one of many writers in the English language at the turn of the nineteenth century who thought of novels in these terms. Observing the attacks on Wollstonecraft's reputation that followed the appearance of *Memoirs,* Hays argued for a genre of fiction influenced by biography rather

---

28. George Eliot, *Middlemarch* (1871–1872) (New York, 1992), 765–766. This paragraph reflects my understanding of Morson's argument *("Anna Karenina" in Our Time).*

29. Marion Rust, *Prodigal Daughters: Susanna Rowson's Early American Women* (Chapel Hill, N.C., 2008), 43, 70, 102–103.

than the other way around. Here was a way for women to talk about the dilemmas encountered by Wollstonecraft without having to endure public scandal. Hays wanted novels to reveal life "as it really exists, mingled with imperfection, and discoloured by passion." In the right hands, "fictitious histories" might "become a powerful and effective engine of truth and reform." Narrating a version of her own life—and her struggle to control her romantic imagination—in her 1796 novel, *The Memoirs of Emma Courtney*, Hays had sought "to represent [Emma], as a human being, loving virtue while enslaved by passion, liable to the mistakes and weaknesses of our fragile nature." Emma is not concerned with whether her story is true, but whether it is "altogether improbable" and whether it persuades her adopted son to "exercise [his] understanding, think freely, investigate every opinion, disdain the rust of antiquity, raise systems, invent hypotheses, and, by the absurdities they involve, seize on the clue of truth." Attempting "a work of fiction, to engage my mind, to sluice off its impressions," Hays designed *The Memoirs of Emma Courtney* to show from her own example "the possible effects of the present system of things, and the contradictory principles which have bewilder'd mankind, upon private character, and private happiness."[30]

Emma Courtney loves a man of sympathy, Augustus Harley, with whom she reads, converses, and grows. But he does not—or will not—love her. Hays shows the danger of enthusiasm. Emma's infatuation with Harley takes over her life. "Every morning dawned with expectation, and every evening closed in disappointment." Emma races to the post office and returns "dejected, spiritless." The *"Hope"* of one hour gives way in the next to "pale *despair.*" Unable to persuade Harley to love her, a desperate Emma offers to have sex with him. *"My friend—I would give myself to you."* After Harley refuses, Emma finally learns that he has a rich wife. He does love Emma, but he will not violate his wedding vows. Left alone, Emma settles for a marriage of convenience with a man who betrays her with a servant and then kills himself.[31]

We could dismiss Emma's passion for Harley as the wild desire of a woman out of touch with reality. She thought it "a memento of [her] own

---

30. Mary Hays, "On Novel Writing," *Monthly Magazine* (September 1797), 180–181, in Hays, *The Victim of Prejudice,* ed. Eleanor Ty (Peterborough, Ont., 1998), 241, 244; Mary Hays, *Memoirs of Emma Courtney* (1796), ed. Marilyn L. Brooks (Peterborough, Ont., 2000), 36, 37, 42, Hays to William Godwin, Feb. 6, 1796, in "Appendix A—Selections from the Mary Hays and William Godwin Correspondence," 245, May 11, 1796, 255.

31. Hays, *Memoirs of Emma Courtney,* ed. Brooks, 114, 155.

folly or madness, call it which you please!" Why should a man have to love her simply because she loves him? And in fact Godwin criticized the novel in manuscript because Emma was so self-interested. But Hays—and Wollstonecraft with Imlay—were not suggesting that a man should do whatever a woman wanted. They were pointing out an unjust situation. Men had a greater range of choices than women. "Men pursue interest, honor, pleasure," comments Emma, while women "remain insulated beings, and must be content tamely to look on, without taking any part in the great, though often absurd and tragical, drama of life." Their "strong feelings, and strong energies" were the "the struggles, of an ardent spirit, denied a scope for its exertions!" She and Wollstonecraft loved men they hoped would help them achieve their intertwined personal and professional ambitions. But that they made a choice, that they exercised some degree of self-determination, did not eliminate inequality, and nothing revealed that more than a man's decision to withdraw or withhold his affection. Not for nothing did Emma Courtney address her memoirs to the son of the deceased Harley, whom she has raised as her own child.[32]

In 1799, Hays published *The Victim of Prejudice*, a novel that vividly highlights the divergence in the consequences for women and men in imagining themselves as independent actors. The central character, Mary, announces at the outset of her narrative that she is "a child of misfortune, a wretched outcast from my fellow-beings, driven with ignominy from social intercourse, cut off from human sympathy, [and] immured in the gloomy walls of a prison." Raised by a benevolent paternal figure in rural England, Mary has suffered through a series of familiar crises—the revelation of her illegitimate birth, desertion by her lover, the death of her benefactor, horrific experiences in London, and a brutal rape at the hands of her relentless pursuer, Sir Peter Osborne. Mary's education moves from an idyllic early life of mutual friendship to a shocking existence at the hands of preda-

---

32. Ibid., 116, Hays to Godwin, May 11, 1796, in "Apendix A—Selections from Hays and Godwin Correspondence," 255. See Tilottama Rajan, "Autonarration and Genotext in Mary Hays' *Memoirs of Emma Courtney,*" in Rajan and Wright, eds., *Romanticism,* 213–239; and Liz Bellamy, *Commerce, Morality, and the Eighteenth-Century Novel* (Cambridge, 1998), 170–175. See also Gillian Brown, "Consent, Coquetry, and Consequences," *American Literary History,* IX (1997), 625–652. Brown's reading of Hannah Foster's novel, *The Coquette,* leads her to conclude, "Women as well as men are agents" in a sentimental novel. But "gender defines and maintains different spheres of agency" (627–628). Like Wollstonecraft, Foster "found the novel a useful format in which to analyze and reformulate masculinist accounts of femininity. . . . Women in eighteenth-century novels so often suffer so much [because] they bear the consequences of consent" (634).

tory men more interested in sex than love—a life, she learns, similar to her mother's.[33]

The Victim of Prejudice imagines the dilemma of women who would seek independence in a patriarchal society. Young Mary knows young William, someone she has loved and who has loved her since childhood as his equal "in courage, in spirit, in dexterity, and resource." Their "mutual display of congenial qualities and an interchange of kindness" has left them "thoroughly impressed with affection for each other." William and Mary cannot marry, however, because she is a bastard. Hays denounces this custom as profoundly antisocial. It divides two people whose "association has been a reciprocal source of moral and mental improvement." But Hays does not support the opposite extreme: defiance of social conventions. She does not approve when William, trying to persuade a reluctant Mary to marry him in defiance of his family, "gave a loose to all the impetuosity of his passions; and abandoned himself to the most frantic excesses."[34]

Disconsolate, William and Mary go off into the world separately. William makes mistakes but eventually marries a respectable woman. Mary makes mistakes and pays for them. In London, she accepts the hospitality of Sir Peter Osborne, who imprisons and then brutally rapes her. Mary demands her liberty. "No one has a right to control me." Osborne scoffs at her protest and outlines the sexual double standard. Her reputation is already in tatters because she has been living in his house for more than a week. Mary could take him to court and become "the sport of ribaldry, the theme of obscene jesters." The supremely confident Osborne releases her, assuming she will have no choice but to return to him. Mary runs into the married William who generously offers to make her his mistress. Why not? They love each other, and Mary, thanks to Osborne, is no longer a virgin. Mary boldly refuses. Eventually, she returns to the rural neighborhood of her youth with James, one of her guardian's old servants, with whom she enjoys a "cordial friendship." Mary and James manage a dairy farm in contentment until Osborne unexpectedly appears, seeking forgiveness and offering marriage. When she declines, he arranges to send her to prison. But, of course, for a woman the whole world is a prison.[35]

Tradition, institutions, and law not only fail to protect Mary, they also put her in harm's way. "*Happiness*," she concludes in a rejoinder to the likes of More and Malthus, is "only to be found in the real solid pleasures of nature

33. Hays, *Victim of Prejudice*, ed. Ty, 3, 6. Ty's introduction is excellent.
34. Ibid., 9–10, 31, 83.
35. Ibid., 118, 119, 157, 164.

and social affection." Finding her voice as a writer, she narrates her story so that others will learn from her experience. All is not lost if "the story of my sorrows should kindle in the heart of man, in behalf of my oppressed sex, the sacred claims of humanity and justice." The larger point is the one Wollstonecraft made about the French Revolution. Social commerce cannot have failed because it was never actually tried. Avoiding extremes is tough work. Progress is not linear or without obstacles. The middle ground between duty and desire is not moderation in all things; it is a state of continual evaluation by people doubling as actors and spectators. Mary will narrate her story so that others will learn from her experience. As with Wollstonecraft, Hays, and Emma Courtney, the act of writing for Mary is an act of defiance, a gesture of endurance. In a society in which women have little power, they can at least tell their own stories. If neither Harley nor William fully grasps the dilemma of women, perhaps their sons may, through imaginative identification with Emma and Mary, develop a better understanding of both women and themselves.[36]

Women were not the only ones to turn to fiction to come to terms with the possibilities as well as the perils of Modern Philosophy. Born into a Quaker family in Birmingham in 1775, Charles Lloyd was never comfortable with his father's career as a banker and left home in 1794 for Edinburgh and a career as a doctor. There he embraced a literary life, publishing poetry and reading Godwin's *Political Justice* and other radical texts. Returning to Birmingham, Lloyd became close friends with Samuel Taylor Coleridge, an admirer of Godwin and Wollstonecraft whom Lloyd's father had hired as a tutor. The son of an Anglican minister and his wife, Coleridge was born in 1772 and educated at Christ Hospital's in London and Jesus College, Cambridge. Among his friends were the essayist Charles Lamb and the poet Robert Southey.

This circle of friends put a very male spin on Modern Philosophy. Reading *Political Justice* focused their radical energy. Disillusioned with Great Britain and the French Revolution, several planned a settlement in the Susquehannah Valley of Pennsylvania that "comprised all that is good in Godwin." Twelve men and twelve women would spend two or three hours a day working and the rest talking, writing, and making love free from government and marriage. They would enjoy equal political participation (termed "Pantisocracy") and share their property in common. Although the women would have to bear and nurse children, the men would help with the washing and cleaning. Their wives were less than enthusiastic about this scheme,

36. Ibid., 47, 168, 174.

which was wise, given Coleridge's blithe assertion that infants required little attention because they were always sleeping. Nevertheless, Coleridge kept his eye on the prize. "The leading Idea of Pantisocracy," he reminded Southey, was "to make men *necessarily* virtuous by removing all Motives to Evil." The vision, like many of Coleridge's plans, was never realized. A critic of both marriage and free love, Coleridge sought to root relationships in affection rather than law. Property was the "real source of inconstancy, depravity, and prostitution."[37]

Lloyd suffered from mental instability. According to Coleridge, the young man had an alarming "distemper (which may with equal propriety be named either Somnambulism, or frightful Reverie, or *Epilepsy from accumulated feelings*)." Apparently, the enthusiastic Lloyd lost touch with reality and went into a kind of trance. Whatever "he perceives and hears he perverts into the substance of his delirious Vision." Coleridge sent Lloyd home. In 1797, events repeated themselves. Lloyd went to live with Coleridge and his wife only to be dispatched back to Birmingham. Again surrendering to impulse, Lloyd became obsessed with marrying his Birmingham neighbor Sophia Pemberton against the wishes of her jeweler father. In addition to his disappointment about Pemberton, Lloyd was upset by his volatile friendship with Mary Hays. It is hard to imagine a woman with a more ungovernable sensibility than Lloyd. And like others, men as well as women, he found a way through his dilemma in fiction.[38]

Satirical and didactic, *Edmund Oliver* offers an ambiguous response to Modern Philosophy. Lloyd had reacted to Wollstonecraft's death with sympathy for her "undeserved sufferings," although he dissented from "almost all her moral speculations." She had been wrong to seek the cause of the world's problems in institutions when their source lay "in the brute turbulencies of human nature." In his novel, he sought to expose "modern philosophers'" idea of "cohabitation" as "a mad spirit of experiment, that would eradicate all the valuable feelings of man's nature." Marriage, or "domestic connections," was "the necessary means of disciplining Beings . . . to a

---

37. Coleridge to Southey, Oct. 21, [1794], in Griggs, ed., *Collected Letters of Coleridge*, I, 114–115, to John Thelwall, May 13, 1796, I, 214, to John Thelwall, Feb. 6, 1797, 306. See Nicola Trott, "The Coleridge Circle and the 'Answer to Godwin,'" *Review of English Studies*, n.s., XLI, no. 162 (May 1990), 212–229.

38. Coleridge to Thomas Poole, Nov. 15, 1796, in Griggs, ed., *Collected Letters of Coleridge*, I, 155. See Philip Cox's introduction in *Charles Lloyd, Edmund Oliver (1798)*, ed. Cox (hereafter cited as Lloyd, *Edmund Oliver*), vol. II of *Anti-Jacobin Novels*, ed. W. M. Verhoeven (London, 2005), vii–xxi; and Trott, "The Coleridge Circle," *Review of English Studies*, n.s., XLI, no. 162 (May 1990), 212–229.

rational and enlarged benevolence." But Lloyd endorses the value of social commerce, especially in helping him turn his "excessive sensibility" and "impetuous desires" into "evenness of temper, and subduedness of will."[39]

The son of a Glasgow merchant, Edmund lives a life of tortured navigation between the extremes of enthusiasm and repression. The former is represented by his cousin Gertrude, "a woman of warm affections, strong passions, and energetic intellect" who, like Wollstonecraft and Hays, has "yield[ed] herself" to Modern Philosophy. Despite her attachment to Edmund, Gertrude falls in love with Edward D'Oyley. Devotees of Godwin and Wollstonecraft, the couple advocates the attainment of "human perfection" through the pursuit of "the sacred spark of truth" in the "collision" of conversation. Wedding vows are nothing but "Promises," "Snares!" and "fetters for the mind! . . . The soul should ever be its own arbitrator and disposer." Gertrude's foil in Oliver's life is Charles Maurice, a man who revels in a simple country life and claims that "nothing more tends to fritter away genius, and level down the sublimity of original thought than the constant habit of attack and defence, of intellectual gladiatorship, adopted in literary and argumentative circles." Charles insists on the importance of religion and "definite laws" and scoffs at D'Oyley, a "man who wills not to *do right,* but finds that all is right which *he wills.*" Charles warns Edmund about his unrequited love for Gertrude. Romantic love "can never *last.*" To imagine otherwise is to be "emasculated." Marriages must follow from "well grounded esteem, and not from love." Life was not the stuff of "rapturous agitations, and debilitating day-dreams!"[40]

After D'Oyley sleeps with Gertrude, he deserts her for a wealthy older woman. Furious and distraught, Gertrude wonders why she and Edward had "laughed at the forms of men?—is it for this that we have abandoned all institutions, and positive rules"? Like Wollstonecraft, she pays a higher price than her lover. But Gertrude is responsible for her predicament. Her pregnancy, explains Charles, is the "horrible effect of playing with human passions, and throwing down wantonly the barriers which religion and morality have erected—and of adopting a method of cold and generalizing calculation in conduct, which stands aloof from nature and human sympathies." Once she gives birth to her illegitimate child, Gertrude kills herself. The suicide devastates Edmund. He grieves until he recovers his inheritance and makes a happy marriage with a sensible woman in an idyllic

39. Charles Lloyd, "Lines to Mary Wollstonecraft Godwin," in *Blank Verse by Charles Lloyd and Charles Lamb* (London, 1798), 64, 65; Lloyd, *Edmund Oliver,* 3.

40. Lloyd, *Edmund Oliver,* 3, 17, 21, 24, 31, 39, 67.

rural community with Charles and other friends who "have banished the words *mine* and *thine.*" Working together on property they own together, they try in their nightly meetings "by means of reading or conversation . . . to approximate to a common identity." As in the Pantisocratic experiment, the women who "always join in these sweet associations of love" are clearly junior partners. It is the men who benefit the most. Having converted his "passions and appetites to affections and aspirations after purity," he now compares "romantic passion" to "habit[s] of devotion." True love is contentment.[41]

Edmund Oliver embraces Modern Philosophy even as it mocks it. With the exception of D'Oyley, the characters learn to temper their behavior through conversation with friends of both sexes. Gender matters. Gertrude, like all women, cannot escape punishment for indulging desire. Edmund, on the other hand, does. Overcoming "the severest and bitterest sufferings," he becomes "a settled and useful character." Social commerce properly practiced transforms enthusiastic men into models of Christian domesticity and reinforces complementary gender differences. Although unequal domesticity was not what Wollstonecraft, Imlay, Godwin, and others had in mind, Edmund learns to contemplate marriage as "a relation that affords an everlasting opportunity, nay, even implies the constant duty of making another happy." Marriage "calls each soul out of itself—makes it necessarily extend its compass of hopes, and fears; creates the duties of a parent, and evermore presents objects for the tenderest feelings, and most interesting sympathies." Conjugal love, sanctioned by God, was a dynamic path to personal contentment and social utility.[42]

Elizabeth Hamilton's satirical novel, *Memoirs of Modern Philosophers,* published in 1800, was an equally complicated response to the social dilemma embodied by the romance of Wollstonecraft and Imlay. A native of Belfast, Ireland, Hamilton was born in 1758 and grew up in an aunt's middle-class family in Stirling, Scotland. Her parents, both of whom died when she was young, were less important than her siblings, one of whom served as an army officer in India. The deaths of her aunt and uncle when Elizabeth was thirty precipitated a move to London, where through her brother she met a wide group of writers and in 1796 published a well-received novel, *Letters of a Hindoo Rajah.*

The title of *Memoirs of Modern Philosophers* establishes the tone for the novel, the purpose of which is to expose the consequences of the Godwinian

41. Ibid., 126, 130, 156, 159, 208, 209.
42. Ibid., 205, 207.

"new philosophy" by mocking it. The novel is overpopulated, garrulous, and limited by a thoroughly conventional romantic plot and subplots in which young women put desire before duty and listen to lovers rather than fathers. Hamilton's attitudes were complex, however, and frequently ambiguous or ambivalent. Although wanting women to live pious lives in accordance with the wisdom of older (especially male) relatives, she was sympathetic to the plight of vulnerable women in a patriarchal society.[43]

The central female characters in *Memoirs of Modern Philosophers* reduce the choices available to women to three. Bridgetina Brotherim (a vicious caricature of Mary Hays) is a devotee of Godwin's *Political Justice* and an impulsive narcissist who talks incessantly. Bridgetina loves dutiful Henry, but Henry marries dutiful Harriet Orwell. Harriet and Henry are so well suited that Hamilton apologizes to her readers for bringing Henry and Harriet together: "There is nothing interesting in their story" because "competence in middle life is quite a bore." Quoting Godwin incessantly (and mindlessly), Bridgetina assumes that Henry loves her because it would be irrational not to love her. After all, she has "investigated the subject." "Why should there be any distinction of sex?" "Are not women formed with powers and energies capable of perfectibility?" How terrible that a woman should be condemned to the "unjust and odious tyranny" of taking "care of her family!" Thankfully, "the time shall come when the mind of woman will be too enlightened to submit to the slavish talk!"[44]

The epitome of Bridgetina's nonsense is her support of a scheme to live among Hottentots in the interior of Africa. Consciously or not, Hamilton mocks the plot of Gilbert Imlay's *The Emigrants*. Disgusted with the slow progress of improvement in "the corrupt societies of Europe," modern philosophers will journey to live with people who have "no trade, no commerce, no distinctions of rank, no laws, no coercion, no government; . . . NO GOD!" The Hottentots believe that marriage is a transient state founded on mutual consent; men and women come together in mutual passion and part in mutual indifference. Clearly, Europe is savage and corrupt, whereas Africa is civilized and free. The Hottentots exemplify "the Age of Reason" and offer "proof sufficient of the perfectibility of man!" They are "the very perfection of modern philosophy." Bridgetina knows that in Africa Henry's emancipated mind will "expand in all the energy of affection, and give a loose to the soul-touching tenderness of love." Reason will support whatever its ad-

43. Claire Grogan, "Introduction," in Elizabeth Hamilton, *Memoirs of Modern Philosophers,* ed. Grogan (Peterborough, Ont., 2000), 9–26.

44. Hamilton, *Memoirs,* ed. Grogan, 101–102, 385.

herents want because it blinds them to the wishes of other people, including those they love.[45]

Like Charles and Gertrude in *Edmund Oliver,* Harriet and Bridgetina are foils. Harriet is self-destructive because she covets self-abnegation. Obeying her father, Harriet subscribes to the tenets of the philosopher "JESUS CHRIST," who "invariably treated the female sex as beings who were to be taught the performance of duty, not by arbitrary regulations confined to particular parts of conduct, but by the knowledge of principles which enlighten the understanding and improve the heart." Harriet is as pessimistic as Bridgetina is optimistic. The world, she has been taught, is "a dangerous ocean, where hidden rocks and quicksands may shipwreck your hopes." All individuals can do to survive is to put their faith in God, accept their fate, and restrain their imagination. History is "beyond our reach." People who claim to understand the workings of divine Providence are sowing the seeds of their own undoing. Godwin's greatest flaw was his arrogant assertion of the ability of human beings to understand themselves and thereby improve the world. Harriet asserts "the immutability of the ALL-PERFECT" and its "tendency to *fix* as well as to exalt our notions of virtue." Human beings are too passionate and prejudiced to rely on their own unstable judgments. Trusting in "the judgment of a Being whose moral attributes are unchangeable," they should venerate "unchangeable principles of morality" rather than "speculative opinions."[46]

Cold Harriet and impulsive Bridgetina highlight the dilemma of the lovely Julia Delmond. Her virtue and loyalty to her father scarcely contain her desire for a charming Frenchman, an obvious fraud named Vallaton. Vacillating between Bridgetina and Harriet, she knows that "*importunate sensibility*" dominates her character. Emotional and easily swayed, she has an "open and susceptible heart." Because she learned more from literature than Christianity, she has little sense of the dangers of the world. She falls in love with Vallaton despite her friends' insistence that he is "a London hair-dresser, a common friseur" rather than a philosopher whose "writings have enlightened the world" and whose "virtues are the most illustrious comment on the glorious doctrine of perfectibility." She endangers herself because she has learned from the philosophers that "there was nothing so pernicious as *fixed principle.*" Julia rejects "immoral and slavish deference" to her father and embraces "the first rights of humanity—the right of fol-

45. Ibid., 142, 143, 144, 159.
46. Ibid., 103, 111, 164, 185.

lowing [her] own inclination." Falling for Vallaton's argument that mutual consent is all that is required for a happy relationship, Julia suffers the same fate as Wollstonecraft. "She finally consented to set an example of moral rectitude, by throwing off the ignoble chains of filial duty, and to contribute her share to the general weal, by promoting the happiness of one of the most zealous of its advocates." That is, she goes to bed with Vallaton, fatally confusing emotion with reason and liberty with license.[47]

Months later, Harriet and the rest find a pregnant Julia in an asylum. Her father has died. Like Imlay, Vallaton, having satisfied his lust, has run off to Paris with another woman. Arrested as a Royalist spy, he is guillotined. Happy to be safe within the walls of an asylum, Julia realizes that Modern Philosophy is a dangerous illusion. "Intoxicated with the idea" that she was pointing out to women "a new and nobler path to glory than the quiet duties of domestic life," she had made a serious mistake from which there was no recovery. There was no profit in "a gloomy and querulous discontent against the present order of things." But that advice is not the same as an affirmation of the status quo. Like many interlocutors of Godwin and Wollstonecraft, Hamilton was sensitive to the plight of women and the possibilities of social commerce even as she feared the consequences of abandoning tradition and defying institutions such as marriage. Faith in love alone as a way to organize relationships was a chimera that obscured the reality of gender inequality as well as the lessons of Christianity and history. But love within traditional institutions was socially useful and worth pursuing.[48]

Memoirs of the Author of "A Vindication of the Rights of Woman" and its revelations about Wollstonecraft's private life sharply focused a discussion about the viability of a revolution taking place in the minds and hearts of individuals as well as on streets, battlefields, and the floors of Parliament and Congress. In March 1799, a young Englishwoman named Rachel Prescott thanked Godwin for his work and that of his wife. Mary Wollstonecraft had "first induced [her] to think," and his writings had encouraged her to persist. Prescott was optimistic about the future. Someday all who sought "to perpetuate benevolence in the place of oppression" would be Godwin's "neighbor." Among other things, they would continue to inquire into "the individual, or reciprocal claims founded in marriage," and wonder whether a marriage "erroneously made" was *irrevocable.* Much more was at stake

47. Ibid., 88, 133, 175, 182, 234, 236.
48. Ibid., 372, 383.

in the Wollstonecraft-Imlay-Godwin scandal than the problems of three people. At issue was the question of whether human beings were capable of realizing the future they were able to imagine. Neither *Memoirs* nor its reception resolved anything in that regard. In fact, the conversation had scarcely begun.[49]

49. Rachel Prescott to Godwin, Mar. 10, 1799, Oxford, Bodleian, MS Abinger c. 4, fols. 88–89, Apr. 12, 1799, c. 4, fols. 100–103, Godwin to Prescott, Apr. 17, 1799, c. 22, fols. 107–110.

7

American Commerce

"What are the mutual influences of beings on beings: how far is the well-being of each, consistent with that of every other," asked Elihu Hubbard Smith, a young man living in New York City in the mid-1790s. Like many admirers of William Godwin and Mary Wollstonecraft, Smith hoped that Americans would ponder exactly how they could exercise their newfound liberty without infringing on the liberty of others. The dilemma was acute in the vast, diverse, and loosely organized Republic because so many American men saw the pursuit of self-interest as their birthright. They wanted to make their fortunes, not discuss limits on their independence. Instead of love for one another, the "*love of gain* peculiarly characterizes the inhabitants of the United States," lamented theologian Samuel Miller. Education was "superficial," and wealth "the principal test of influence." Was it folly to speculate about the role of sociability in shaping the future of such a nation?[1]

A small but influential number of Americans did not think so. Men and women of letters were eager participants in a cosmopolitan discourse that promoted conversation among friends as a major source of authority and

---

1. Elihu Hubbard Smith, "Notes from Recollections of My Life from My Birth till the Age of Eleven," in James E. Cronin, ed., *The Diary of Elihu Hubbard Smith (1771–1798)* (Philadelphia, 1973), 27, Smith to Idea Strong, July 22, 1796, 188; Samuel Miller, *A Brief Retrospect of the Eighteenth Century . . .* , 2 vols. (New York, 1803), II, 407. See Gilbert Chinard, "A Landmark in American Intellectual History, Samuel Miller's *A Brief Retrospect of the Eighteenth Century*," *Princeton University Library Chronicle*, XIV, no. 2 (Winter 1953), 55–71. More generally, see Linda K. Kerber, *Federalists in Dissent: Imagery and Ideology in Jeffersonian America* (Ithaca, N.Y., 1970); and Rachel Hope Cleves, *The Reign of Terror in America: Visions of Violence from Anti-Jacobinism to Antislavery* (New York, 2009).

the most effective engine of progress. Reading books published in Great Britain, they discussed their contents and then wrote their own books, some of which were read on both sides of the Atlantic. Their preferred genre consisted of novels that meditated on the power of conjugal love to transform selfish individuals and create affectionate marriages that institutionalized mutuality. If imagining the perils of romantic entanglements was to confront power at the very core of human existence, imagining its possibilities was to sustain the radical conviction that human beings in commerce with one another could improve as well as govern themselves.[2]

American writers operated within an American context. Literary radicals in London called for free-floating communities as a revolutionary alternative to a well-entrenched patriarchal social order unexpectedly reinforced by the exigencies of a global war against France. Their American counterparts focused on affectionate marriages as a means of redirecting a democratic social order that seemed to put a premium on personal independence at the expense of mutuality. But men and women on both sides of the Atlantic were concerned about a world in which too many people were suddenly imagining themselves as completely independent historical actors. An enthusiasm for liberty as the right to pursue self-interest without regard for the interests of others amounted to enslaving one's self to the tyranny of desire. Well aware of the power of that impulse, American writers rejected institutional restraint in favor of persuasion through romantic love as the most effective means of managing it. No matter how hard the struggle, they preferred to consider what human beings might become rather than to accept that they would always remain the same.

2. This chapter reflects the influence of Michael O'Brien, *Conjectures of Order: Intellectual Life and the American South, 1810–1860*, 2 vols. (Chapel Hill, N.C., 2004), and Leonard Tennenhouse's provocative *The Importance of Feeling English: American Literature and the British Disapora, 1750–1850* (Princeton, N.J., 2007). See also Edward Watts, *Writing and Postcolonialism in the Early Republic* (Charlottesville, Va., 1998); Richard Gravil, *Romantic Dialogues: Anglo-American Continuities, 1776–1862* (New York, 2000); Paul Giles, *Transatlantic Insurrections: British Culture and the Formation of American Literature, 1730–1860* (Philadelphia, 2001); Michael Scrivener, *The Cosmopolitan Ideal in the Age of Revolution and Reaction, 1776–1832* (London, 2007); Elizabeth Barnes, "Novels," in Robert A. Gross and Mary Kelley, eds., *An Extensive Republic: Print, Culture, and Society in the New Nation, 1790–1840*, vol. II of David D. Hall, ed., *A History of the Book in America* (Chapel Hill, N.C., 2010), 440–449; and Sandra M. Gustafson and Gordon Hutner, "Projecting Early American Literary Studies," *American Literary History,* XXII (2010), 245–249.

Transatlantic Conversations

The decentralized structure of the book trade in the United States, which worked against the development of a national literary culture, facilitated transatlantic intellectual conversation in the early Republic. American printers, many of them Scottish and Irish émigrés, were a pragmatic bunch eager to expand their business by supplying local markets with products demanded, primarily Bibles, religious tracts, sermons, and children's books. Rather than invest in American authors, they followed the Irish and Scottish custom of producing several hundred copies of books that had already appeared in England. The combination of imported books and local reprints meant that residents of Philadelphia, New York, Boston, and Charleston had access to most titles published in London, Dublin, and Edinburgh within a couple of years, if not months, of their original publication.[3]

American readers thus had the opportunity to engage with Wollstonecraft and Godwin long before *Memoirs of the Author of "A Vindication of the Rights of Woman"* appeared in an American edition in Philadelphia in 1799. Readers on one end of the spectrum were enthusiastic disciples, such as the Connecticut-born Yale graduate, physician, and aspiring writer Elihu Hubbard Smith. In 1795, Smith helped organize the New York Friendly Club, "a small association of men . . . connected by mutual esteem, and habits of unrestricted communication." Member Charles Brockden Brown urged his colleagues to seek knowledge "for its own sake mainly." He needed only "one or two friends whom I can wholly love, and who enjoy like me the conveniences of life and leisure, with whom I may eat drink study converse travel, and whose dispositions are congenial and affection mutual." Smith was more explicit about the social value of the club. Conversation counteracted the "avarice and ambition, envy and heedlessness, speculation and ignorance, audacity and cowardice, superstition, and credulity, [that] have leagued together to betray, corrupt, and destroy mankind." Spoken like a true student of Godwin and Wollstonecraft![4]

3. Robert A. Gross, "Introduction: An Extensive Republic," 1–50, James N. Green, "The Rise of Book Publishing," 75–127, and Kenneth E. Carpenter, "Libraries," 273–286, all in Gross and Kelley, eds., *Extensive Republic.* On the absence of a national print culture, see Trish Loughran, *The Republic in Print: Print Culture in the Age of U.S. Nation-Building, 1770–1870* (New York, 2007). On efforts to develop broader markets for books, see Rosalind Remer, *Printers and Men of Capital: Philadelphia Book Publishers in the New Republic* (Philadelphia, 1996).

4. Smith to John Aikin, Apr. 14, 1798, in Cronin, ed., *Diary,* 438; Charles Brockden Brown to Joseph Bringhurst, July 29, 1793, Charles Brockden Brown Papers, George J. Mitchell Department of Special Collections and Archives, Bowdoin College Library, New Brunswick, Maine;

Smith also embraced the British radicals' fondness for personal histories. In 1794, at the advanced age of twenty-three, he "commenced the history of [his] own life." Like all people, he required "an acquaintance with himself." Narrative was critical to that process. "Man is so variable a being, susceptible of such infinite changes, and capable of such wonderful diversities, that, in no other way, than by composing an actual history of himself, can he come to a thorough knowledge of his true nature and absolute constitution." To develop "a connected view of [his] actions, feelings, and opinions," he had to "delineate the progress, of all those connections with my fellow-beings, which have been to me such fertile sources of delight and grief." Like Maria Edgeworth and Godwin, he would find truth in quotidian moments.[5]

Godwin and Wollstonecraft were never far from Smith's mind. In his hometown of Litchfield, Connecticut, in November 1795, he talked with a group of men and women about *Caleb Williams*. One person admired "the style," but not "the plan." Smith's response was to suggest that his friend's principles "had *retrograded*." Others thought Godwin a celebrity. Theatrical impresario William Dunlap rushed to show Smith a nice letter he had received from Godwin. Smith, meanwhile, decided he had to reread *Political Justice*. He also recommended Mary Hays's *Emma Courtney*, "a fine exhibition of the miseries of an improper indulgence of love in a mind not otherwise far remote from what it ought to be."[6]

Smith's lifelong relationship with Susan Bull Tracy illustrated the difficulties of putting ideas about friendship into practice. She was briefly his teacher in Litchfield, Connecticut, when he was five years old and "a particular favorite, often admitted to sit on her lap, receive her caresses." Bull married Uriah Tracy, a Yale graduate and schoolmaster who was reading

---

Elihu Hubbard Smith, Journal, Oct. 17, 1795, in Cronin, ed., *Diary*, 74. See James E. Cronin, "Elihu Hubbard Smith and the New York Friendly Club, 1795-1798," *PMLA*, LXIV (1949), 471–479; Thomas Bender, *New York Intellect: A History of Intellectual Life in New York City, from 1750 to the Beginnings of Our Own Time* (Baltimore, 1987), 9–45; Fredrika J. Teute, "A 'Republic of Intellect': Conversation and Criticism among the Sexes in 1790s New York," in Philip Barnard, Mark L. Kamrath, and Stephen Shapiro, eds., *Revising Charles Brockden Brown: Culture, Politics, and Sexuality in the Early Republic* (Knoxville, Tenn., 2004), 149–181; Bryan Waterman, *Republic of Intellect: The Friendly Club of New York City and the Making of American Literature* (Baltimore, 2007); and Catherine O'Donnell Kaplan, *Men of Letters in the Early Republic: Cultivating Forums of Citizenship* (Chapel Hill, N.C., 2008).

5. Smith, Journal, Dec. 11, 1795, in Cronin, ed., *Diary*, 99–100, Smith to Idea Strong, July 22, 1796, 188.

6. Smith, Journal, Nov. 5, 1796, ibid., 85, Mar. 24, 1796, 143, Smith to Charles Brocken Brown, Aug. 25, 1797, 349, Sept. 16, 1797, 364.

Figure 10. Elihu Hubbard Smith. *By James Sharples. Pastel, 1797. Accession #1833.1. Collection of The New-York Historical Society*

law and who became a member of Congress and a U.S. senator. Her marriage did not inhibit Smith. During a November 1795 visit to Litchfield, he talked with her about Godwin and Wollstonecraft. She promised to read the copy of *Political Justice* that had just arrived in Litchfield and gave him a letter in which she reflected on Wollstonecraft's *Vindication of the Rights of Woman*. Tracy agreed that women should be "so educated that they can *think* for themselves." At the very least, women should have practical training and be allowed to manage property, for they often did these things anyway. But Tracy's religious faith made her wary of Modern Philosophy.[7]

Back in New York City, Smith responded forcefully to Tracy's skepticism. Unconcerned that he had read less than half of one volume of *Political Justice,* he insisted that the book should not be "condemned" because it "is imperfect." Echoing Godwin, Smith asserted his duty "to examine, candidly and attentively, the *arguments,* of all" with the recognition that he had "no right to *substitute the convictions of another, for those of my own mind.*" Whatever the consequences, he had to decide for himself. And so did Tracy. They should correspond regularly, not simply for "mutual pleasure" but also to make themselves "better members of the great society of mankind." In late summer 1796, Smith recommended Wollstonecraft's account of her journey in Scandinavia, although it was difficult to engage with "the soul of this admirable woman" when she "appears wounded, afflicted, desolate," the victim of "ridiculous stories." As Tracy withdrew, in part because her husband had forbidden her to read Godwin, Smith insisted that she share the "revolutions" in her "mind." In the meantime, she should look at *Caleb Williams.*[8]

The Smith-Tracy relationship underscored the challenges faced by devotées of Modern Philosophy in America. Smith's headlong embrace of ideas he got from books could not overcome the obstacles presented by Tracy's marriage and religious conviction. However innocent Smith thought the relationship, it was clear that others, including Uriah Tracy, constructed it differently. Like Wollstonecraft with Henry Fuseli, Smith struggled until his sudden death in 1798 to recognize that what he wanted from their friend-

7. Smith, "Notes from Recollections," ibid., 17, 18, Smith, Journal, Nov. 9, 1797, 87, June 6, 1797, 448, S[usan] T[racy] to James Morris, Jan. 25, 1794, 109, 110.

8. Smith to Tracy, Dec. 15, 1795, ibid., 103, 104, 105, Jan. 18, 1796, 123–124, Sept. 11, 1796, 210, 211, Feb. 16, 1797, 294, 295, 296. See Catherine Kaplan, "Elihu Hubbard Smith's 'The Institutions of the Republic of Utopia,'" *Early American Literature,* XXXV (2000), 294–308. Kaplan notes that, although Smith explicitly excluded women from suffrage, he envisioned a world in which the circulation of information and ideas would essentially displace politics and reasonable people would defer to the wishes of their more enlightened neighbors.

ship was not what Tracy wanted and, moreover, that his enthusiasm put her in a difficult position with her family and friends.

The publication of Godwin's *Memoirs* of Wollstonecraft prompted American critics to elaborate on religious objections to Modern Philosophy. Yale Professor Benjamin Silliman's *Oration, Delivered at Hartford* denounced a "NEW ERA" of a "bold and impious philosophy." Godwin and Wollstonecraft, "the Camilla of modern philosophy" and leader of "its Amazonian legions," were urging people "to abandon every principle which we have learned, every habit which has been sanctioned by experience, and every institution which we have derived from our fathers." Samuel Miller, a former member of the Friendly Club and an ordained minister who later taught ecclesiastical history and church history at Princeton Theological Seminary, joined the conversation in 1804. Agreeing that man was "always variable, and never consistent," Miller celebrated a revolution in education, particularly for women. But he thought Wollstonecraft had gone too far. Reason was against the equality of the sexes, for women's bodies were so obviously intended for different purposes. Morality was against it, for promiscuous education "would convert society into hordes of seducers and prostitutes," as Wollstonecraft herself had demonstrated. Most important, revelation was against it, for equality of the sexes violated the word of God. Women were "rational beings . . . made not to be the servants, but the companions of men." They should learn "to shine not only in the routine of domestic employments, but also in the social circle, and in the literary conversation." The problem lay in insisting "that there should be *no difference* in their education and pursuits." Miller particularly censured fiction for making it difficult to "distinguish between *revolution* and *improvement.*" Living in an *"Age of Novels,"* he understood the value of narratives of "ordinary scenes of social and domestic intercourse." But too many trumpeted "the omnipotence of *love* over all obligations and all duties."[9]

The most influential opponent of Modern Philosophy was Yale president Timothy Dwight, the grandson of Jonathan Edwards and a powerful figure politically as well as spiritually. Dwight mocked Godwin and Wollstonecraft

---

9. Benjamin Silliman, *An Oration, Delivered at Hartford on the 6th of July, A.D., 1802 . . . to Celebrate the Anniversary of American Independence* (Hartford, Conn., 1802), 4–5, 22; Miller, *Brief Retrospect*, I, 3, II, 287, 292, 373, 374, 393. See Chandos Michael Brown, "Mary Wollstonecraft; or, The Female Illuminati: The Campaign against Women and 'Modern Philosophy' in the Early Republic," *Journal of the Early Republic*, XV (1995), 389–424; and Lawrence J. Friedman, *Inventors of the Promised Land* (New York, 1975), 111–144. On the general reaction against European radicalism, see Seth Cotlar, *Tom Paine's America: The Rise and Fall of Transatlantic Radicalism in the Early Republic* (Charlottesville, Va., 2011).

in a series of essays in 1801 and 1802 entitled "Morpheus." He had laid out the general case in a 1797 lecture at Yale, which was printed in New Haven and then in Bristol and London. After the usual salacious list of the sins of British radicals, he identified the core of the problem as a crisis of authority. Persuasion was replacing revelation. Modern Philosophy amounted to perpetual revolution practiced by speculators. Like Imlay, its advocates seduced the innocent away from obedience and virtue. The task was all too easy. Christianity told people what they needed to know, not what they wanted to hear. A recognition of the essential character of sin, religion was "a system of restraint on every passion, and every appetite." Philosophy, on the other hand, offered "a general license to every passion and appetite." In the face of such a powerful challenge, the faithful must persist. Rational liberty depended on unwavering commitment to the idea that truth was "at all times, and with respect to all things, of an unchangeable nature." Americans should look to the Bible, not the imagination.[10]

Dwight's attack on Modern Philosophy may seem as out of proportion as Elihu Hubbard Smith's naive acceptance of it. To the extent that the majority of Americans had the time or inclination for books, they read the Bible, religious tracts, sermons, and poetry. That the president of Yale College worried about the impact of a few writers suggests the depth of his fear about the extent of their influence. Dwight was a poet who celebrated in *Greenfield Hill* and other writings the virtues of an imagined social order not unlike the interdependence imagined by Godwin and Wollstonecraft. Like others, he entered into a transatlantic conversation by writing for periodicals and in books published in Britain as well America. Religious truth and human progress were hardly incompatible; choices overlapped, and people lived in ambiguity. What ultimately disturbed Dwight was the argument that individuals could make their own history and improve themselves in conversation with one another rather than with God. Dwight was concerned not just that Modern Philosophers would persuade Americans to imagine the

---

10. [Timothy Dwight], "Morpheus," *Mercury and New-England Palladium*, Nov. 24, Dec. 8, 11, 1801, "Morpheus, Part 2," Mar. 5, 9, 1802; Dwight, *The Nature and Danger of Infidel Philosophy, Exhibited in Two Discourses, Addressed to the Candidates for the Baccalaureate, in Yale College . . .* (1798) (New Haven, Conn., 1799), 47, 59, 62. See Colin Wells, *The Devil and Doctor Dwight: Satire and Theology in the Early American Republic* (Chapel Hill, N.C., 2002). On books in rural areas, see William J. Gilmore, *Reading Becomes a Necessity of Life: Material and Cultural Life in Rural New England, 1780–1835* (Knoxville, Tenn., 1992); Rosalind Remer, "Preachers, Peddlers, and Publishers: Philadelphia's Backcountry Book Trade, 1800–1830," *JER*, XIV (1994), 497–522; and Ann Smart Martin, *Buying into the World of Goods: Early Consumers in Backcountry Virginia* (Baltimore, 2008).

benefits of abandoning church and family but also that imagination would become the source of all authority in a culture untethered from revelation and reality.

The Rights of Woman in America

As in Great Britain, American critics of Godwin and Wollstonecraft misrepresented their ideas. The English radicals were advocating neither human perfection nor anarchy but the cultivation of a middle ground by imperfect human beings acutely aware of their dependence on one another. Understanding this position, many American readers sought something in between the enthusiastic embrace of Elihu Hubbard Smith and the enthusiastic denunciation of Benjamin Silliman. They did not see imagination and religion as incompatible. They did not advocate the abolition of the institution of marriage or the pursuit of free love. What fascinated them were the mysteries of romantic love and their power to create egalitarian marriages between strong women who were neither dolls nor Amazons and empathetic men who were neither patriarchs nor libertines.

These men and women of letters tended to congregate in areas closely tied with the interrelated trade networks that extended throughout the Atlantic and into the Caribbean and Mediterranean seas. Built around the production, transportation, sale, and consumption of commodities, these networks became arteries of intellectual and cultural exchanges. Women as well as men, poor as well as wealthy were consumers of goods from all over the world in cities that boasted an abundance of social libraries, voluntary societies, and educational institutions. By the early nineteenth century, these networks extended well into the interior of North America. Many of the critics of male independence lived in places well integrated into global commerce. What they read and wrote reflected lives spent in environments shaped by commerce with people from the West Indies to Scotland.[11]

11. On Atlantic commerce, see David Hancock, *Oceans of Wine: Madeira and the Emergence of American Trade and Taste* (New Haven, Conn., 2009); and Ellen Hartigan-O'Connor, *The Ties That Buy: Women and Commerce in Revolutionary America* (Philadelphia, 2009). On the participation of women, see Mary Kelley, *Learning to Stand and Speak: Women, Education, and Public Life in America's Republic* (Chapel Hill, N.C., 2006); Margaret A. Nash, "Rethinking Republican Motherhood: Benjamin Rush and the Young Ladies' Academy of Philadelphia," *JER*, XVII (1997), 171–191; Susan Branson, *These Fiery Frenchified Dames: Women and Political Culture in Early National Philadelphia* (Philadelphia, 2001); Catherine Kerrison, *Claiming the Pen: Women and Intellectual Life in the Early American South* (Ithaca, N.Y., 2006); and A. Kristen Foster, "'A Few Thoughts in Vindication of Female Eloquence': The Case for the Education of

The Ladies' Monitor, later *The Lady's Monitor,* the very name of which honored the social role of friendship, was one of several periodicals that briefly facilitated this culture. It appeared weekly in New York City in 1801 and 1802. Confident of his prospects for making the journal "an interesting and agreeable companion," the editor argued that his desire "to instruct and amuse the fair sex" would depend on women's willingness to contribute "their share of literary materials." In the meantime, he would reprint articles "from the latest London publications." There would be nothing on battles, demagogues, monarchs, or duels. Over the next few months, he published excerpts from Wollstonecraft's *Vindication of the Rights of Woman, Mary,* and *A Short Residence* as well as from Godwin's *Memoirs of the Author of "A Vindication of the Rights of Woman"* and Elizabeth Inchbald's memoirs.[12]

Readers of *The Lady's Monitor* responded with articles that endorsed the rights of woman within patriarchal institutions. The challenge facing a new generation of Americans was to locate the proper balance between obedience to parents and independent choices and to make marriages carefully considered alliances between friends. Marriages formed in haste or for financial considerations forged "chains which are lasting as life; fetters which remorse, disappointment, or sorrow cannot remove." Love, on the other hand, was the practice of empathy and mutuality. In one dialogue, a woman agreed with a friendly male rather than a spirited young woman that, because "the sensibility of women is livelier, and their enthusiasm more ardent than that of men, they are less qualified to decide on the affairs of government." Women were more socially useful when they cultivated domestic virtues and literary talent. They should use their exquisite sensibility "to tranquillize [their husbands'] passions, and to turn the impetuous current of [their] feelings into a more orderly channel." But they, not their fathers, should choose their husbands, men who would be susceptible to conversation. Domesticity in retrospect seemed to limit the options of young women. But in the early nineteenth century the ability not only

Republican Women," in James Marten, ed., *Children and Youth in a New Nation* (New York, 2009), 129–148. On the relationship between commerce and novels, see Stephen Shapiro, *The Culture and Commerce of the Early American Novel: Reading the Atlantic World-System* (University Park, Pa., 2008).

12. P. Heard, "To the Patrons of *The Lady's Monitor*," *Lady's Monitor*, I, no. 10 (Oct. 10, 1801), 73. See also "To Our Patrons," no. 20 (Jan. 2, 1802), 158. On the general issue, see Linda K. Kerber, *Women of the Republic: Intellect and Ideology in Revolutionary America* (Chapel Hill, N.C., 1980); and Jan Lewis, "The Republican Wife: Virtue and Seduction in the Early Republic," *William and Mary Quarterly,* 3d Ser., XLIV (1987), 689–721.

to choose husbands but also to influence and change them was a source of unprecedented power. Advocates of what we would call a middle-class nuclear family organized around affection and choice thought they were inventing something new under the sun, not the bastion of a stable social order that it became later in the nineteenth century. Families might function as revolutionary cells and companionate marriages as a model of all human relationships, just as Wollstonecraft and Godwin had imagined they might.[13]

Martha Meredith Read, about whose life we know very little other than that she exemplified the kind of woman likely to write in the early Republic, was the daughter of a Philadelphia merchant who served as treasurer of the United States from 1789 until 1801. She married the son of George Read, a signer of the Declaration of Independence and a Federalist U.S. senator from Delaware in the early 1790s. In 1797, she gave birth to her first child, John M. Read, who became a lawyer in Philadelphia and whose opposition to the expansion of slavery cost him an appointment to the U.S. Supreme Court. Installments of "A Second Vindication of the Rights of Women," all attributed to Read under the pseudonyms of an "An American Lady" and "A Lady of Philadelphia," appeared in *The Ladies' Monitor*.[14]

Focusing on relationships between fathers and daughters, Read upheld patriarchy while she demanded reform of abuses rooted in a distorted education. Fathers had to take their daughters seriously and prepare them for useful lives. Too many women invited men's scorn because they did not behave reasonably. But their behavior was a product of an education dictated by men, not nature. Why, then, were women "under subjection to the government of men, when from men we may trace every source that has long since conducted to the perversion of the female character"? Like Wollstonecraft, Read argued that, "if women would learn to respect themselves, the respect of man would follow as a natural consequence." Absent self-esteem, "wanton seduction" traduces "artless" girls. Parents who love their daughters would ensure that they were "taught to respect themselves" and "to promote virtue, religion, and morality." Fathers must endure "corroding anxieties for daughters until a reformation takes place in the conduct

13. Observer, "New-York: Hints to the Ladies," *Lady's Monitor*, I, no. 26 (Feb. 13, 1802), 206, "On Sensibility," no. 24 (Jan. 30, 1802), 185, "Essays: Remarks on Female Politicians," no. 41 (May 29, 1802), 324.

14. See Joseph Fichtelberg, "Friendless in Philadelphia: The Feminist Critique of Martha Meredith Read," *EAL*, XXXII (1997), 205–221; and Fichtelberg, "Lovers and Citizens," in *Critical Fictions: Sentiment and the American Market, 1780-1870* (Athens, Ga., 2003), 72–116.

of husbands towards their wives." As a poet warned, men would be happier if they married out of respect for their partner's intelligence and character. Good marriages would be a negotiated blend of reason and sentiment, an affirmation that "love is the most powerful passion of the human breast."[15]

These ideas were not new. They echoed the writings of the most prominent eighteenth-century American advocate of a revolution in the status of women, Judith Sargent Stevens Murray, a deeply religious woman with strong connections to English Dissenters and Atlantic trade. Born in 1751 in the port town of Gloucester, Massachusetts, she wrote poems, plays, novels, and essays, usually under the pseudonym of Constantia, with the encouragement of her husband, John Murray, an English-born Universalist minister. Like Wollstonecraft, Murray advocated female education; unlike Wollstonecraft, she never questioned marriage or domesticity. Writing in the 1780s and 1790s as Constantia, Murray argued that a girl who knew she was "a rational being" capable of an "intellectual existence" would be a successful wife and mother. But a girl convinced she was inferior to men would "probably, throw herself away upon the first who approaches her with tenders of love, however indifferent may be her chance for happiness." Educated women would demonstrate to the "lordly . . . haughty sex" that "our souls are by nature *equal* to yours; the same breath of God animates, enlivens, and invigorates us." Constantia urged women to "commence immediate war" on those who held "a most contemptible opinion of the sex." A husband who was an "equal, a sensible friend," would receive from a devoted wife "the hand of amity" and the cultivation of conjugal happiness. She would teach their children by playing on "the pleasure which they derive from her smiles, her approbation, and her society." In the United States, "'the Rights of Women' begin to be understood," wrote Murray in the late 1790s, "and, improving on the opinions of a Wollstonecraft, we are ready to contend for the *quantity,* as well as *quality,* of mind." But they would do so largely within the confines of marriage.[16]

---

15. "A Second Vindication of the Rights of Women . . . ," *Ladies' Monitor* (Aug. 22, 1801), 1, Charity, "To the Author of the Lines, 'Address to a Young Lady,'" I, no. 7 (Sept. 19, 1801), 56, "A Second Vindication of the Rights of Women . . . ," no. 5 (Sept. 5, 1801), 34.

16. Constantia, "Desultory Thoughts upon the Utility of Encouraging a Degree of Self-Complacency, Especially in Female Bosoms," *Gentleman and Lady's Town and Country Magazine,* VI (October 1784), 251; [Constantia], "On the Equality of the Sexes," *Massachusetts Magazine; or Monthly Museum . . . ,* II, no. 3 (March 1790), 132, Constantia, "On the Equality of the Sexes . . . ," no. 4 (April 1790), 223, Constantia, "On the Domestic Education of Children," no. 5 (May 1790), 275; Judith Sargent Murray, "LXXXVIII: Observations on Female Abilities," in Murray, *The Gleaner . . . ,* ed. Nina Baym (Schenectady, N.Y., 1992), 703, 705. See Sheila L.

Young white women from comfortable families in the northeast imbibed these and other ideas in schools such as the Young Ladies' Academy in Philadelphia. Many read, and some occasionally wrote, histories, biographies, travel books, and novels. They filled their journals and letters with information, questions, and reflections. Their education encouraged a sense of themselves as women with the authority to engage in social commerce with one another and with men. When they thought about marriage, they insisted on the importance of love and mutuality as the foundation of healthy lifelong relationships between friends. In so doing, they were following Wollstonecraft's advice. Murray exulted in 1798 that her "confidence in THE SEX" was such that she expected "to see our young women forming a new era in female history." At the very least, they were asserting themselves by reflecting and writing. Love within marriage constituted, not a retreat from revolution, but a radical means of ensuring its success.[17]

Drawing on British models, a handful of American authors at the turn of the nineteenth century wrote novels that contemplated the social power of romantic love. Most sought a middle ground between obedience and freedom, rights and obligations, rarely advocating one extreme or the other. As important, they investigated the nature of men as well as women. Because men were more powerful than women, the revolution in the name of conjugal love required their cooperation. Was that possible? Could love transform men into more empathetic creatures? In terms of the numbers produced and read, these books should not have given Timothy Dwight the slightest pause. What worried him was what they represented: the growing insistence of human beings that they could manage themselves, that the imagination was a source of authority for social revolution. A future readers could imagine was a future they might achieve.[18]

Even novels that seemed in line with Dwight's thinking were ambivalent about the principles of Wollstonecraft and Godwin. *The Coquette* by Hannah Webster Foster was one of several American novels that appeared after the success of the English-American Susannah Haswell Rowson's

Skemp, *First Lady of Letters: Judith Sargent Murray and the Struggle for Female Independence* (Philadelphia, 2009).

17. Murray, "Observations on Female Abilities," in Murray, *The Gleaner,* ed. Baym, 703. For these ideas in practice, see Timothy Kenslea, *The Sedgwicks in Love: Courtship, Engagement, and Marriage in the Early Republic* (Boston, 2006); and Martha Tomhave Blauvelt, *The Work of the Heart: Young Women and Emotion, 1780–1830* (Charlottesville, Va., 2007).

18. Tennenhouse, *Importance of Feeling English,* 43–93. For models of manhood, see J. M. Opal, *Beyond the Farm: National Ambitions in Rural New England* (Philadelphia, 2008); Thomas A. Foster, ed., *New Men: Manliness in Early America* (New York, 2011).

Charlotte Temple; or, A Tale of Truth (1791). Born in 1758, Foster grew up in an affluent Boston merchant family. Like Murray, she married a minister. Unlike the Dissenting John Murray, John Foster was a member of the established Congregational Church and led First Church in Brighton, Massachusetts. Like Murray, Foster was both a mother and a writer and a deeply religious woman who was very familiar with British literature. *The Coquette* was inspired by the life of John Foster's relative Elizabeth Whitman, with whom Joel Barlow had a serious flirtation in the 1780s. But Foster's reimagining of Whitman's story was a subtle exploration of the possibilities as well as the perils of romantic love. She was all for women's choosing husbands, if they did so in conversation with others. A series of letters between the principal figures and their family and friends, the format of the novel affirms the importance of as well as different perspectives on the practice of mixed-gender sociability.[19]

Eliza Wharton is a stock figure in late-eighteenth-century sentimental novels: an enthusiastic young woman who defies the advice of friends and family, sleeps with a married man who claims to love her, and dies in disgrace giving birth to an illegitimate child. But Foster's mix of respect for piety and parents with empathy for social experimentation produced an ambiguous American variation on a familiar theme. If in the end Eliza pays the ultimate price for indulging desire, her experience reveals the range of options open to American women. She calls Eliza a coquette, a pejorative term for a woman whose "highest ambition was to ensnare" a sensible man, to defeat "all his boasted reason" and "play upon his passions" in order to experience "the most exquisite pleasure." But Eliza is neither cruel nor instrumental. Her challenge is to manage her lively spirit, not squash it.[20]

19. Susanna Rowson, *Charlotte Temple* (1791), ed. Cathy N. Davidson (New York, 1986), 5, 82. Here as elsewhere I learned much from Marion Rust, *Prodigal Daughters: Susanna Rowson's Early American Women* (Chapel Hill, N.C., 2008).

20. "History of a Coquette," *Rural Magazine . . .* , I, no. 42 (Dec. 1, 1798), 2; "The Limner," *Dessert to the True American*, II, no. 3 (July 22, 1799), 7. See Bryan Waterman, "Elizabeth Whitman's Disappearance and Her 'Disappointment,'" *WMQ*, 3d Ser., LXVI (2009), 325–364. For discussions of the novel, see Walter P. Wenska, Jr., "*The Coquette* and the American Dream of Freedom," *EAL*, XII (1977–1978), 243–255; Carroll Smith-Rosenberg, "Domesticating 'Virtue': Coquettes and Revolutionaries in Young America," in Elaine Scarry, ed., *Literature and the Body: Essays on Population and Persons* (Baltimore, 1988), 160–184; Kristie Hamilton, "An Assault on the Will: Republican Virtue and the City in Hannah Webster Foster's *The Coquette*," *EAL*, XXIV (1989), 135–151; John Paul Tassoni, "'I Can Step Out of Myself a Little': Feminine Virtue and Female Friendship in Hannah Foster's *The Coquette*," in Janet Doubler Ward and JoAnna Stephens Mink, eds., *Communication and Women's Friendships: Parallels and Intersections in Literature and Life* (Bowling Green, Ohio, 1993); Sharon M. Harris, "Hannah Webster

In no hurry to get married after the death of a boring fiancé, Eliza dismisses her friends' warning that she is behaving badly by flirting with men. Fearing that "'marriage is the tomb of friendship,'" Eliza wants "to gratify [her] natural disposition in a participation of those pleasures which youth and innocence afford." Her two suitors—the dull, upright Reverend Boyer and the handsome, lively Major Sanford—embody the extremes of mind and body, tradition and revolution. Boyer prides himself on being "a reasonable creature" who will not be "misled by the operations of a blind passion." He wants a good woman as a domestic partner. Sanford, on the other hand, is intrigued by the challenge of conquering a woman like Eliza.[21]

Contemplating these men, Eliza comes to know herself. Her "fancy" and her "judgment" are at odds: "Sometimes one preponderates, sometimes the other. Which will finally outweigh, time alone can reveal." Aware that Boyer would be a good husband, she recognizes that her "natural volatility" is incompatible with "the duties of domestic life." On the other hand, she agrees with her mother and her friends that Sanford is a rake and not to be trusted. Both men are trying to seduce her from the independence she enjoys as a single woman. If Sanford's intention is sensual and Boyer's is domestic, ruin awaits her in both cases. No wonder Eliza thinks she would be happiest without either of them. Circumstances combine to make that desire reality. Boyer indignantly abandons Eliza because of her flirtation with Sanford. Sanford then deserts Eliza to marry a wealthy woman. Unable to woo Boyer back, Eliza pines over lost opportunity.[22]

Sanford reappears, having realized he loves Eliza and claiming he would have married her if she had enough money to support him. Overwhelmed by desire, the couple has sex. Eliza soon regrets her choice. Her "delusive dream of sensual gratification" awakens "a most poignant sense of [Sanford's] baseness and of [her] own crime and misery." Running away from home, she dies

Foster's The Coquette: Critiquing Franklin's America," in Harris, ed., Redefining the Political Novel: American Women Writers, 1797–1901 (Knoxville, Tenn., 1995); Gillian Brown, "Consent, Coquetry, and Consequences," American Literary History, IX (1997), 625–652; Brown, The Consent of the Governed: The Lockean Legacy in Early American Culture (Cambridge, 2001); Laura Hanft Korobkin, "'Can Your Volatile Daughter Ever Acquire Your Wisdom?': Luxury and False Ideals in the The Coquette," EAL, XLI (2006), 79–107; and Ivy Schweitzer, "Hannah Webster Foster's Coquette: Resurrecting Friendship from the Tomb of Marriage," Perfecting Friendship: Politics and Affiliation in Early American Literature (Chapel Hill, N.C., 2007), 103–132. I want to acknowledge the enormous influence of Cathy N. Davidson, Revolution and the Word: The Rise of the Novel in America (New York, 1986).

21. Hannah Webster Foster, The Coquette (1797), ed. Cathy N. Davidson (New York, 1986), 5, 13, 17, 24.

22. Ibid., 29, 51, 53.

in childbirth "among strangers." Sanford also experiences remorse. Declining to abandon Eliza when she becomes pregnant, he arranges her departure and gives her money. Her death then shocks him into realizing that he will feel forever "the disgraceful, and torturing effects of [his] guilt in seducing her." After his wife divorces him for his infidelity, he flees the United States, penniless and scorned. Foster's judgment is complex. Unwilling to absolve Eliza of responsibility, Foster sympathizes with her unwillingness to accept a loveless marriage. Excoriating Sanford as "the monster, whose detestable arts have blasted one of the fairest flowers in creation," she recognizes he, too, was constrained by interest from enjoying love.[23]

Whereas Foster explored the mysteries of love within the confines of a sentimental plot, Charles Brockden Brown imagined a dialogue that embodies mixed-gender sociability. *Alcuin* consists largely of a conversation unfolding in real time between a man and a woman about men and women that succeeds mainly in identifying the limits of a revolution in sentiments. Brown was born into a Quaker family in Philadelphia in January 1771. His childhood was tumultuous, in part because of the American War of Independence and in part because of his father's erratic mercantile career and refusal to swear allegiance to the new Republic. Domestic instability and the impact of anti-Quaker mobs defined his early life. Trained as a lawyer, Brown set out to become "a visionary writer" and eagerly devoured the works of Jean-Jacques Rousseau and Johann Wolfgang von Goethe, among others. In 1795, Brown moved to New York City, where he joined the Friendly Club. Brown and Smith were good friends until the latter's sudden death in 1798. Smith complained that Brown's fiction was too "mysterious." He "made ambiguity [his] delight." Occasionally, truth broke through: "*Godwin came, and all was light.*" But even "the Sun himself" could not always brighten a man consumed by despair and "self-love."[24]

Alcuin, which was published in two parts, the first in 1798 and the second after Brown's death, narrates two exchanges between Mrs. Carter, a married woman, and Alcuin, a young unmarried man, recorded by him. Mrs. Carter presides over a salon in her brother's Philadelphia home. It is "a lyceum open at stated hours, and to particular persons, who enjoyed, gratis, the benefits of rational discourse, and agreeable repasts." Alcuin, an insecure schoolteacher with literary ambitions, has taken the name of the

23. Ibid., 23, 145, 162, 165, 167.

24. Peter Kafer, *Charles Brockden Brown's Revolution and the Birth of American Gothic* (Philadelphia, 2004), 56; Smith, Journal, Oct. 17, 1795, in Cronin, ed., *Diary,* 74, Smith to Brown, May 27, 1796, 170, 171.

eighth-century English monk who became the teacher of Charlemagne and a central figure in an intellectual renaissance at his court. He admires "conversation, careless and unfettered, . . . sometimes abrupt and sententious, sometimes fugitive and brilliant, and sometimes copious and declamatory" because it combines "utility and pleasure" far better than "any other method of instruction." The conversation in the novella, however, questions conversation as a means of revolution. Whatever power women find in personal relationships cannot compensate for the tyranny of the patriarchal structures in which they live.[25]

One evening in Mrs. Carter's salon, Alcuin invites his host to comment on contemporary politics. Although he seems prepared to take her seriously, she is wary. Why does he ask? she inquires. Because, Alcuin says, well-educated women ought to have opinions about "all commerce with the world." Mrs. Carter is not reassured. Education, she replies, does not guarantee legal and economic independence. Even in the American Republic, women are "subject to the controul of others who are guided by established prejudices, and are careful to remember that we are women." True, mixed-gender conversation might allow men and women to work through their "different systems of morality, different languages, or, at least, the same words with a different set of meanings." But the fact remains that she and Alcuin live under a government that perpetuates the tyranny of men. Of course, Alcuin rejoins, any advocate of liberty generally "intends only freedom to himself, and subjection to all others." But Mrs. Carter will not be diverted from her objection. As a woman, she "cannot celebrate the equity of that scheme of government which classes me with dogs and swine." Alcuin hopes that men will use their power wisely. In any case, excluding dependent people from full citizenship is necessary in a well-ordered republic. "Want of property, youth, and servile condition, may possibly be well founded objections," replies Mrs. Carter, but not sex, which is "purely physical" and a permanent liability because it is impossible to change. The conversation ends in an impasse.[26]

In the second half of the novella, Mrs. Carter and her guest meet in her salon a week later. This conversation is edgier. Alcuin tells Mrs. Carter of a journey he has taken to "the paradise of women," a marvelous place filled with people like Americans but without distinctions of gender in manners,

25. Charles Brockden Brown, *Alcuin: A Dialogue* (1798), ed. Sydney J. Krause (Kent, Ohio, 1987), 3, 4, 5, and see R[obert] D. A[rner]'s "Historical Essay," 273–298; Kafer, *Charles Brockden Brown's Revolution*, 94–100.

26. Brown, *Alcuin*, ed. Krause, 9, 16, 18, 21, 24, 25, 28, 29.

dress, or public life. They do not marry. Alcuin assumes women would de-
nounce critics of marriage as "odious and selfish" men whose real design is
sexual. Mrs. Carter rejoins that her support for "an equality of conditions"
does not mean she objects to marriage. Without the institution, women would
be victims of merely "sensual impulse[s]." Alcuin's protest that he is not "the
champion of sensuality" prompts a sharp reminder of the difference in their
power. In a world in which "words are arbitrary," Mrs. Carter concludes, men
"are at liberty to annex to words what meaning they think proper."[27]

Committed to the importance of romantic love in marriage, the interlocutors conclude with a discussion of divorce. "Shall this contract subsist
no longer than suits the wishes of either party?" Yes, replies Mrs. Carter.
She wishes this "liberty . . . of conjugal choice" above all others. Trivial indeed is the disappointment of being forbidden to marry someone you love
compared to "the controul and the nauseous caresses of one whom I hate,
or despise." Women must have the right to "revoke [their] choice" when
a husband is a tyrant. Failed marriages "are peculiarly severe upon the
female." Should a woman continue to live with a man who no longer loves
her only because the law requires it? Mrs. Carter asks. A marriage is a "union
founded on free and mutual consent. It cannot exist without friendship. It
cannot exist without personal fidelity. As soon as the union ceases to be
spontaneous, it ceases to be just."[28]

Alcuin is both a performance of and a commentary on mixed-gender social commerce. If men and women were ever going to work together rather
than at cross-purposes, they had to talk at length in a manly fashion, no
matter how fluid the conversation. But they must approach it carefully. A
woman sharing her story with a man simultaneously affirmed her faith in
conversation and put herself at risk. A man might revise himself in response
to a woman. But she had no means to ensure that he would not shift again
in response to another woman or another opportunity. In this case, mixed-
gender conversation revealed the stark differences in the status of men and

27. Ibid., 34, 45, 51, 54.

28. Ibid., 57, 58, 59, 64, 65, 67. See Bruce Burgett, "Between Speculation and Population:
The Problem of 'Sex' in Thomas Malthus's Essay on the Principle of Population and Charles
Brockden Brown's *Alcuin*," in Barnard, Kamrath, and Shapiro, eds., *Revising Charles Brockden
Brown*, 122–148, esp. 138 ("marriage becomes for both Alcuin and Carter a word signifying indi-
viduals' rights to consensual relations within civil society, regardless of the status categories
that would soon come to regulate those relations: gender, class, race, age, and number"). See
also Burgett, *Sentimental Bodies: Sex, Gender, and Citizenship in the Early Republic* (Princeton,
N.J., 1998), 125–127; Stephen Shapiro, "'Man to Man I Needed Not to Dread His Encounter':
Edgar Huntly's End of Erotic Pessimism," in Barnard, Kamrath, and Shapiro, eds., *Revising
Charles Brockden Brown*, 216–251.

women. In the end, men held all the cards no matter how much they invited women to play. Or did they?

The Power of Love

The handful of novels written in the United States around the turn of the nineteenth century directly addressed the issues debated by Alcuin and Mrs. Carter. These fictional personal histories were not all about young women like Eliza Wharton. They also imagined the behavior of a wide range of men to provoke discussion about whether the conversation of lovers could awaken men to the value of mutuality and respect. They continued, in short, to believe in the power of love to awaken speculators to their true selves. Mrs. Carter lacked the political rights enjoyed by Alcuin. But politics was not everything. Women could assert themselves in print as well as in person. To write was to assert one's right to participate in larger cultural conversations. To write a novel was to assert the power of the imagination to describe behavior that might yet exist. Vulgarity, violence, and male privilege were omnipresent in Gothic scenarios about young women alone and in danger. But they did not preclude the existence of strong women or the potential of awakening at least some men to the possibilities of romantic love understood as mutuality rather than desire.

Martha Meredith Read's *Margaretta; or, The Intricacies of the Heart,* originally published in installments in *The Lady's Monitor* and then in book form in Charleston, South Carolina, in 1807, exemplifies the challenges faced by young women with nothing and no one to guide them. A virtuous, well-read girl of sixteen bereft of parents, Margaretta Wilmot lives with a cottager and his wife in a Maryland village. Local residents are provincial and narrow, proud of their simple lives and resentful of people who consider themselves superior. "How well it was that I was born in America!" exclaims a woman. She despises people who pretend "to be something more than us." The beautiful Margaretta attracts the attention of many men. Her surrogate father has agreed she should marry the son of a neighbor in order to unite their property. There are also more worldly men who have traveled around the Atlantic mainly to benefit themselves at the expense of others. Their interest in Margaretta is entirely sexual.[29]

The most important of her would-be lovers is a gentleman from the West Indies, William de Burling. After denouncing marriage as "a perversion of

29. [Martha Meredith Read], *Margaretta; or, The Intricacies of the Heart: A Novel* (Charleston, S.C., 1807), 6.

every thing that is noble in man," he is surprised to learn that Margaretta has doubts about the institution herself. No matter how much she wishes to obey her guardian, she cannot live with a man she does not love. The more William knows Margaretta—her simplicity, her benevolence, her love of books, and her virtue—the more he values her friendship. Talking with her, he realizes that his hostility to marriage lies in his father's demand that he marry an heiress named Arabella Roulant. Like Margaretta, he will marry, if marry he must, for love, not money. Falling in love starts a revolution in sentiments within William. "Oh! woman," he announces, "how great your sway over man, when your powers are properly directed!" Persuaded that he is "not hardened enough" to take her on any terms other "than those of WIFE," William decides he will marry the poor girl in defiance of his father and good sense.[30]

William's transformation, however, is incomplete. He does not yet grasp that mutuality is the essence of love. Instead of dealing directly with Margaretta, he imagines that she must be falling in love with him. He exults: She "is mine! . . . This is a conquest I glory in." A gentlewoman who has taken Margaretta under her wing in her home in Philadelphia and knows that William is pledged to Arabella is shocked but not surprised by his egoistic attitude. She denounces him as either "a finished rake, or, like all your sex, inconstant, and faithless to vows which relate to matrimonial connections, and with every new face, change your system of thinking, absorb your honour by new fancies, and thus characterize yourselves as MEN." But William's blind passion leaves him oblivious to social obligations and the wishes of others. He must be with Margaretta. If they cannot marry, they should live together like brother and sister with his wife Arabella. William insists to Margaretta that he wants only "your presence, your conversation, your friendship." But William does not really know Margaretta. He does not take her seriously as an independent person. All that matters is what he wants. He will do whatever is required to possess her. "You are mine, Margaretta, by the fiat of God himself.—*He* has implanted that sympathy in our nature which we call love; 'tis the tie of soul and soul: we will live to love, and have our affections transmitted with us, beyond this transitory existence." When Margaretta declines his offer, William secretly signs over £150,000 to Arabella as compensation for breaking their engagement. He is ready to work to support his father and the woman he loves.[31]

William's ardent pursuit confuses Margaretta. She rejects him because

30. Ibid., 13–14, 18, 31.
31. Ibid., 88, 93–94, 98, 101, 102, 141.

of lies invented by Arabella. But she is not sure what she actually thinks of him. Overwhelmed by a swarm of young men whose interest in her is totally sexual, Margaretta relies on the friendship of the deceitful Arabella. Eager to get her rival away from Philadelphia and William, Arabella easily persuades Margaretta to seek refuge in her father's home in Saint Domingue. The destination is a reasonable one given the commercial ties between Philadelphia and the West Indies. But it takes Margaretta into what many white Americans considered the heart of darkness. In 1804, Saint Domingue became Haiti, and no place in the world was more associated with revolution transformed into anarchy. Traveling by herself, Margaretta accepts that she has no home. Everyone is a stranger, and she a vagrant, "unconnected, unprotected, and uninvited."[32]

In Saint Domingue, Margaretta finds herself in a Gothic nightmare. Women are even more at risk in the West Indies than they are in the United States. Law and religion are nonexistent. Hispaniola is populated by selfish people who care only about indulging their immediate desires. Slavery is a symptom of a larger cultural problem. If "human nature is all over the same," it is particularly unrestrained in the Caribbean. Imprisoned by Arabella's father, Benjamin Roulant, who wants to marry her, Margaretta has to fend off a host of aggressive men obsessed with enjoying her body, with or without her consent. Beguiled by Margaretta's combination of innocence and independence, most men want to possess her in order to demonstrate their sexual prowess. Defying their contention that she is a slave of sensibility, a child incapable of deciding what is best for herself, Margaretta survives, aware of "how greatly" she has been "the sport of wicked people!"[33]

Eventually, Margaretta escapes and sails for England with a new female friend and a more genteel suitor. Great Britain is stable and orderly, a world away from Hispaniola. Lacking options, Margaretta agrees to marry the man even though she does not love him. Just in time to avoid committing incest (another manifestation of social anarchy common in contemporary literature), she learns that he is her father. He believed that his wife and daughter were lost at sea years ago. With her family reconstituted, well born, and wealthy, Margaretta is suddenly an attractive heiress with a stable of boring suitors whose interest in her is entirely financial.

The plot resolves itself with a return to America to establish a household sustained by love. William de Burling arrives in England having finally learned to "love Margaretta for herself." She accepts his proposal, and they

32. Ibid., 106, 195.
33. Ibid., 178, 260, 392.

are wed. The newlyweds then depart for the United States with her parents. Margaretta's father and husband bond over their "enthusiastic zeal for equal rights and equal liberties between man and man." But their embrace of freedom is tempered by a sense of humility and an acceptance of mutuality. In a conclusion that recalls that of *The Emigrants,* somewhere along the Susquehanna River, "warmed with a noble enthusiasm for the rights and liberties of the citizens of Columbia," the parents become plain "Mr. and Mrs. Warren, laying their title on the altar of liberty, as a sacrifice to equality, peace and independence." Margaretta imagines her marriage as one of many in which intelligent, strong women will be allied with empathetic, strong men.[34]

Read's imagined personal history illustrates the resourcefulness of young women and the malleability of at least some men. No matter what evil she faces, the well-read and virtuous Margaretta perseveres. Nor are all the men she encounters brutes. Sympathetic men help her on occasion. As important, the practice of romantic love through social commerce awakens William to the kind of man he might be. All of this serves the will of God as well as the happiness of human beings. The "human heart, as it comes from the hand of its Creator, *is* good," Read maintains. God made man free, establishing "no limits to his actions, but such as reason would point out, as necessary to his present happiness." Ambition has to be regulated by men and women together, through mutual consent, not by history or institutions. Neither chaotic Hispaniola nor artificial Great Britain is the future. There is still hope in the United States for people to govern themselves.[35]

The author of *Alcuin* was not so sure about the transformative impact of romantic love on self-interested men. Charles Brockden Brown was not even confident of the ability of human beings to understand themselves at all. Believing that "human society is powerfully modified by individual members," he also contended that "actions and motives cannot be truly described." "We can only make approaches to the truth. The more attentively we observe mankind, and study ourselves, the greater will this uncertainty appear, and the farther shall we find ourselves from truth." It was in this frame of mind that he wrote *Ormond; or, The Secret Witness,* which was published in early 1799.[36]

34. Ibid., 395, 398, 404, 417.

35. Ibid., 417–418.

36. Charles Brockden Brown, "Walstein's School of History," *Monthly Magazine, and American Review,* I, no. 5 (August 1799), and I, no. 6 (September 1799), in Brown, *Literary Essays and Reviews,* ed. Alfred Weber and Wolfgang Schäfer with John R. Holmes (Frankfurt, 1992), 32, 33.

Sophia Courtland Westyn narrates the personal history of Constantia Dudley, a woman who perseveres in the face of a host of obstacles created by weak men, including her father, or untrustworthy men, most notably her suitor Ormond. The book is also the personal history of a man who is a most unlikely candidate for transformation by his love for a woman. The mysterious, often "contradictory or unintelligible" Ormond was a soldier in the service of the Russian Romanovs and attempted to foment revolution in Germany. At eighteen, he had kidnapped a young girl, killed a competitor for her body, raped and murdered her, and massacred five Turkish soldiers the next morning in expiation for the murder of his rival. Sophia, who is more cosmopolitan and religious than Constantia, knows that Ormond is a master of deception, a man unto himself who acts only for himself.[37]

Motherless, Constantia grows up in a dysfunctional male household. Circumstances force her from a comfortable life as the daughter of a New York City apothecary to the destitute condition of a woman whose income consists of what she can earn from her needle in disease-ridden Philadelphia. One night on her way home, two men accost Constantia. They quarrel over the order in which they will rape her—"First come, first served"—as if she were their "property." Luckily, a decent man named Balfour rescues her. Unluckily, he starts to court her, not because he loves her, but because he admires her economy and equanimity. Constantia will not consent to marry a man she does not love, however, even for material comfort. Or, rather, notwithstanding the advantages of the match pointed out by her father, she will not go to bed with a man she does not love. Balfour refuses to credit her objections, considers himself "unjustly treated," and gives in to resentment. His sister and her friends stop giving Constantia work, leaving the Dudley family in truly dire straits. Balfour saves Constantia only to destroy her livelihood. What role could love possibly have in such a world? That, in fact, is the problem that underlies the entire novel.[38]

See also "Remarks on *Wieland* and *Ormond:* Two Original American Novels," *Weekly Museum,* XIII, no. 36 (June 20, 1801), 36; Paul Allen, *The Life of Charles Brockden Brown . . .* (1815), intro. Charles E. Bennett (Delmar, N.Y., 1975), I, 258; Paul C. Rodgers, Jr., "Brown's *Ormond:* The Fruits of Improvisation," *American Quarterly,* XXVI (1974), 4–22; Sydney J. Krause, "*Ormond:* How Rapidly and How Well 'Composed, Arranged, and Delivered,'" *EAL,* XIII (1978–1979), 238–249; Russell B. Nye, "Historical Essay," in Charles Brockden Brown, *Ormond; or, The Secret Witness,* ed. Sydney J. Krause (Kent, Ohio, 1982), 295–341; Steven Hamelman, "Secret to the Last: Charles Brockden Brown's *Ormond,*" *LIT: Literature Interpretation Theory,* XI (2000), 305–326; Shapiro, "'Man to Man I Needed Not to Dread His Encounter,'" in Barnard, Kamrath, and Shapiro, eds., *Revising Charles Brockden Brown,* 238.

37. Brown, *Ormond,* ed. Krause, 3, 264.

38. Ibid., 82, 84, 87, 136. See Julia Stern, "The State of 'Women' in *Ormond; or, Patricide in*

Just as Constantia is an educated, strong woman capable in the tradition of Wollstonecraft of thinking and acting on her own, so is Ormond a variation on the kind of man Imlay represented in the narrative constructed by Godwin and his critics. Indeed, Ormond defends selfishness and autonomy. Individuals should not "attempt . . . so chimerical an enterprize as that of promoting the happiness of mankind." Even the most well-intentioned motives lead to actions that tend "to the production of evil." Concludes Ormond: "Virtue and duty . . . require us to promote our own happiness and not the happiness of others." A man may "hope to accomplish his end, when he proposes nothing but his own good." Ormond has no use for either religion or philosophy. He is a self-aware shape-shifter who deploys his considerable talent for mimicry and deception because the "treachery of mankind compelled him to resort to it." He is insincere because the mass of mankind is insincere.[39]

Ormond is "superior" to love. All of his relationships are instrumental. His mistress is Helena Cleves, the orphaned daughter of a New York merchant remarkable for her beauty and singing voice. Calling marriage "absurd" and prostitution "detestable," Ormond proposes to keep Helena in an elegant mansion in Philadelphia. Helena consents. Leading a solitary life, except for her lover's visits, she soon regrets her decision. Sophia is at pains to show that Helena had few other options. Her father is dead, and she has no other protectors or advisers. Nor is she wealthy enough to live independently. Constantia had opted for a different path, of course, choosing poverty over marriage to a man she did not love. But the cost Constantia paid was higher than most women could afford. Growing bored with the melancholy, doll-like Helena, who, Sophia reminds us, he had molded "nearly into the creature that he wished," Ormond sets his sights on Constantia, a woman like Wollstonecraft. Impressed by her intelligence, competence, and independence, Ormond takes her seriously.[40]

Helena and Constantia discuss the situation in a dialogue between two very different women narrated by another woman, all imagined by a man. Helena takes responsibility for her predicament. After all, Ormond had not forced her to live with him. A woman like Constantia would have resisted. But Helena cannot leave Ormond because she loves him, because she is a ruined woman, and, above all, because she cannot stand up to him.

the New Nation," in Barnard, Kamrath, and Shapiro, eds., *Revising Charles Brockden Brown*, 182–215; and Steven Watts, *The Romance of Real Life: Charles Brockden Brown and the Origins of American Culture* (Baltimore, 1994).

39. Brown, *Ormond*, ed. Krause, 112–113, 115, 116.

40. Ibid., 117, 122, 123, 124, 138, 140.

She can only hope that Ormond will decide to marry her. In conversation with Helena, Constantia reflects on herself and her own uncertain future. Stronger and better educated, Constantia is neither rash nor naive. She accepts that everyone, including herself, sometimes acts out of "sinister and selfish motives." She has unaccountably fallen in love with Ormond and is jealous of Helena. Was that why she opposed a marriage between the two? Why should not she also follow her inclination? Why should she put loyalty to Helena above the choice of her heart?[41]

Constantia's impact on Ormond is profound. He informs Helena that he is finished with her. Such is Constantia's hold on him that he comes to regret his treatment of Helena even as he drives her to commit suicide. Like Imlay, Sanford, and de Burling, Ormond is susceptible to change through a relationship with a woman he loves. His passion for Constantia mixes lust and love; he wants both her "person and affections." To get them, he is willing to make major changes in his life, including marriage to an autonomous, intelligent woman who will scrutinize him closely. All too closely, in fact, for Constantia is too smart to surrender to Ormond, no matter how much she imagines she loves him. Her refusal to marry him drives him mad. Exhausted with "well-doing" and "unattainable good," Ormond wants "to possess" what he "crave[s]." Trapping her in an isolated farmhouse in New Jersey, Ormond attempts to rape her, and she kills him in self-defense. With no other option, she destroys him before he destroys her. Evil is evil, and it can be kept at bay only through coercion and violence.[42]

After the mixed reception of a series of dark novels like *Ormond,* Brown wrote two sentimental tales that end in happy marriages. Once considered a pragmatic move to win over female readers, Brown's shift away from the Gothic to the sentimental now seems less of a radical departure.[43] Despite

---

41. Ibid., 139, 140, 157, 158.

42. Ibid., 168, 170–171, 178, 181, 282.

43. Kafer, *Charles Brockden Brown's Revolution,* 166; Donald A. Ringe, "Historical Essay," in Charles Brockden Brown, *"Clara Howard in a Series of Letters" and "Jane Talbot, A Novel,"* ed. Sydney J. Krause, S. W. Reid, and Ringe (Kent, Ohio, 1986), 433–436. In *Sentimental Bodies,* Bruce Burgett argues that, in *Clara Howard,* Brown moves toward an essentialist notion of reason (embodied subversively in the female) and emotion (embodied in the male). The novel highlights the contradictory implications of eighteenth-century sentimental literature: "that love consists of a reciprocal passion between selves and others that are implicitly gendered male and female; [and] that such a passion ought to be unmediated by any such impersonal concerns." Yet mutability gives way to prescription in the wake of the fading of "the eighteenth-century counter-possibility of ungendered sentimental citizenship" (129, 133). See also Paul Witherington, "Brockden Brown's Other Novels: *Clara Howard* and *Jane Talbot,*" *Nineteenth-Century Fiction,* XXIX (1974), 257–272.

the change of genres, Brown continued to explore the problem of male behavior. *Clara Howard* and *Jane Talbot* unfold as a series of misperceptions and accidents embodied in different perspectives presented in the letters human beings write, forge, and read at different points in time. Because characters do not grasp either "their fundamental interdependence" or "the interdependence of the present and the future," "neither the self nor the present is in possession of itself" in either novel. Having escaped patriarchal authority and marriages founded on interest, the young couples in love seem ill equipped to prosper in the new Republic. In their own way, these two novels are as dark as *Ormond.* Clara Howard and Jane Talbot are strong women who find sensible men willing to participate in egalitarian marriages grounded in affectionate friendship. The problem is that their prospective husbands are too sensible, too eager to defer to the wishes of their prospective wives. Weak and passive, they are the antithesis of Ormond.[44]

Clara, the daughter of a British man and an American woman, loves Edward Hartley, a man without family or property. To support his sisters and establish himself on land in the Ohio Valley, Edward has agreed to marry wealthy Mary Wilmot. He honors his commitment even when Mary disappears and he learns she has no fortune. He tracks her across North America until he finds her happily in love with a good man of means. Having discharged his obligation to Mary, he is free to marry Clara. The novel consists of the letters collected by Edward to detail his progress from lonely obscurity to a happy marriage.[45]

Despite its conventional plot, *Clara Howard* inverts readers' expectations about gender. The female characters dominate the males. Edward admires Clara's intelligence, and with good reason. She is a rational figure who makes tough choices and sticks by them. When Edward tells Clara about his commitment to Mary, she defines the terms of their relationship. "I love

---

44. Michelle Burnham, "Epistolarity, Anticipation, and Revolution in *Clara Howard*," 271, and Mark L. Kamrath, "American Exceptionalism and Radicalism in the 'Annals of Europe and America,'" 377, both in Barnard, Kamrath, and Shapiro, eds., *Revising Charles Brockden Brown.* See James M. Decker, "Reassessing Charles Brockden Brown's *Clara Howard*," Missouri Philological Association, *Publications,* XIX (1994), 28–36; Witherington, "Brockden Brown's Other Novels," *Nineteenth-Century Fiction,* XXIX (1974), 257–272; W. B. Berthoff, "'A Lesson on Concealment': Brockden Brown's Method in Fiction," *Philological Quarterly,* XXXVII (1958), 55; and Erica Burleigh, "Incommensurate Equivalences: Genre, Representation, and Equity in Clara Howard and Jane Talbot," *Early American Studies: An Interdisciplinary Journal,* IX (2011), 748–780.

45. Brown, *Clara Howard,* ed. Krause, Reid, and Ringe, 3. My analysis draws on Tennenhouse, *Importance of Feeling English,* 73–93. Hartley's name is a possible reference to Harley, the main character in Henry MacKenzie's *Man of Feeling.*

you, Edward, as I ought to love you. . . [but] while Mary lives, and is not bound to another, I will never be to you any thing but Your friend." If men are free to ignore obligations, if they can flit from woman to woman in the manner of Imlay, then society will disintegrate entirely. But Edward eagerly complies. His ambition is to garner Clara's approval, not assert himself. "So far from wishing to rule others," he announces, "it is my glory and my boast to submit to one whom I deem unerring and divine. Clara's will is my law." Unable to manage his body, Edward confesses his "palpitations increased" whenever Clara is near; for we are never "so intense and vivid . . . as when we are on the eve of some anticipated revolution, momentous to our happiness." Although Clara and Edward are in love, their future is uncertain. Clueless Edward is almost as unsuitable a companion as Ormond. Surely there was something in between these extremes.[46]

Jane Talbot addresses this issue even more ambiguously than *Clara Howard.* Jane had married a much older man in obedience to her father, brother, and Mrs. Fielder (the obligatory substitute for her dead mother). Now a widow, Jane has fallen in love with Henry Colden. Mrs. Fielder doubts Henry's suitability because of his character, not his lack of property. Her suspicions are confirmed by a forged letter implying that Jane slept with Henry while her first husband was alive. In fact, Jane had allowed Henry to spend the night in her home in a separate room. Confronted by an indignant Mrs. Fielder, Jane is utterly distraught. Should she forsake Henry to satisfy a "groundless prejudice?" All she could attain from him was a "blasted reputation, poverty: contempt." Henry is sensible but no real help. He advises her to "to seek [her] own good."[47]

Mrs. Fielder locates Jane's and Henry's behavior in a broad cultural context. Jane, she insists, does not know men. Reading novels has nurtured a "wayward heart" and left her a slave to her imagination. Now she cannot be content with a hardworking, frugal man. All Jane knows of Henry comes from "his conversation" during his "*very* frequent visits" and their "*very* long walks." If he has no "gross or enormous vices," he is "contemplative and bookish and . . . somewhat visionary and romantic." In short, Henry is a follower of Godwin. The latter was "a scoffer at promises; the despiser of revelation, of providence and a future state; an opponent of marriage, and . . . one who denied (shocking!) that any thing but mere habit and positive law, stood in the way . . . of intercourse without marriage, between brother and sister, parent and child!" Henry was too weak to resist the blandishments

46. Brown, *Clara Howard,* ed. Krause, Reid, and Ringe, 63, 64–65, 90, 109, 111, 113.
47. Brown, *Jane Talbot,* ed. Krause, Reid, and Ringe, 234, 235, 241, 249, 258–259.

of *Political Justice,* whose author "has the art of the grand deceiver." Like Edward, Henry barely qualifies as a man.[48]

Henry benefits somewhat in comparison with Jane's brother Frank, the very model of an American male obsessed with making money and treating women badly. Admitting to a youthful infatuation with Godwin, Henry denies that he is a seducer and a villain. But he is too smart to deny Mrs. Fielder's doubts. A poor man whose "chief goods" are "affection" and "company," he would likely fail as a husband and a father and eventually kill himself. Frank, on the other hand, grew up preferring "frolics and carousals" to "books and study." Devoted to "the indefatigable pursuit of gain," he indulges in "numerous excursions, a French girl whom he maintained in expensive lodgings, his horses, dogs, and *friends.*" After he cheats his cousin, he denounces Jane's plans to reimburse his victim. Then he tries to get hold of Jane's income, cajoling her until she loans him five hundred dollars. Frank is heartless and selfish, a prosaic version of *Ormond.* Both Frank and Henry get what they desire. Frank lives well but in virtual solitude. Henry gets Jane when Mrs. Fielder conveniently falls ill and blesses their marriage on her deathbed, but he is ill equipped to survive in the world beyond his imagination.[49]

Clara Howard and *Jane Talbot* reflect a predicament Brown knew all too well. A sensible man who lived much of his life through his imagination, he married a Presbyterian woman in 1804 after a long courtship opposed by their parents on religious grounds. Trying to support his family as a writer until his death from tuberculosis in 1810, Brown stopped writing fiction because it did not sell. But his novels were hardly ephemeral. The Minerva Press in England published several of them, including *Ormond* in 1800, *Jane Talbot* in 1804, and *Clara Howard* in 1806 under the title *Philip Stanley; or, The Enthusiasm of Love.* Jane Austen might have read Brown's work. William Godwin certainly did, and so did his and Wollstonecraft's daughter, Mary, and her lover Percy Shelley. It is easy to see why. American writers were not the only ones struggling to sustain both their literary careers and their faith in the transformative power of romantic love in a world far removed from the heady days in the summer of 1793 when Mary Wollstonecraft and Gilbert Imlay made love and imagined a life together in North America.[50]

48. Ibid., 222, 223, 225, 227, 228.
49. Ibid., 157, 158, 160, 173, 266, 267.
50. Tennenhouse, *Importance of Feeling English,* 74–75, 83–91.

8

The New Man of Feeling

Like Charles Brockden Brown, William Godwin was struggling to survive as a man of letters in a nation suddenly overrun with speculators, bankers, lawyers, and soldiers. By the early nineteenth century, the eighteenth-century blend of intellectual, social, and economic speculation uneasily embodied in the person of Gilbert Imlay had fractured. *Commerce,* which had signified, according to the *Oxford English Dictionary,* "intercourse in the affairs of life," became strictly economic, the business of exchanging commodities and capital. *Intercourse* acquired its modern meaning when Thomas Malthus linked it to sexuality; it connoted male penetration of the female body, nothing more. *Society* became a synonym for public life.

Godwin denounced these changes, and not only because he was personally uncomfortable with them. Social commerce was as important to a healthy society as economic commerce. "The genuine wealth of man is leisure, when it meets with a disposition to improve it," Godwin claimed. "All other riches are of petty and inconsiderable value." In a just world, "each man's share of labour would be light, and his portion of leisure would be ample." Selfish individuals mistaking isolation for autonomy were suddenly the most alarming impediments to natural commerce. The worst of the lot was a "trader or merchant" obsessed with "the desire of gain" from morning to night. He deploys "all the arts of the male coquette; not that he wishes his fair visitor to fall in love with his person, but that he may induce her to take off his goods." A "supple, fawning, cringing creature, [a] systematic, cold-hearted liar," he "has the audacity to call himself a man." A tradesman, in short, was an antisocial creature whose behavior subverted revolution.[1]

Godwin's indignation reflected the depth of his alienation. All around him, the revolutionary argument that independent men and women could organize themselves through social commerce was being perverted into a dangerous definition of freedom as the ability to act as one pleased without regard to the interests of others. The problem remained: How did men and women enjoy liberty without infringing on the liberty of others? Literary radicals in the 1790s had offered the dynamic mutuality of friendship turning into love. Godwin persisted in advocating this idea, although with mixed results. The single man of letters who had married Mary Wollstonecraft and attracted attention around the Atlantic would become an awkward husband, an uncomfortable father, and an obscure novelist. His fiction reflected his sense that revolution had gone awry, especially in the emergence of new men whose inability to sustain rational affection was isolating them in prisons of their own devising. It was a fate Godwin hoped to avoid. Unfortunately, his clumsy efforts to find a new life and to be a good father suggest the enormity of the challenge. Love in its myriad forms was never easy, even for one of its most persistent advocates.

William in Search of a Wife

By early 1798, a few months after the death of Mary Wollstonecraft, William Godwin was enjoying a life similar to the one he had before meeting her. In addition to attending the theater regularly, he systematically made his way through Samuel Richardson's *Clarissa;* Jean-Jacques Rousseau's *Julie;* and Ovid's poetry. He dined with old friends, including Joseph Johnson, Henry Fuseli, George Dyson, Eliza Fenwick, Maria Reveley, and Rebecca Christie, the widow of Thomas Christie, who had died in Surinam in 1796. Godwin's sister Hannah urged him to reflect on how Wollstonecraft "loved you" and how his love had helped heal her "wounds." He could look forward to the pleasure of seeing his infant daughter Mary reveal "that she will be as like her poor Mamma as Fanny promises to be—or else like her father." As was his habit, Godwin rarely referred in his diary to public events. He did not mention the outrage that greeted *Memoirs,* although he produced a revised version pruned of some of its more controversial statements. Then he com-

---

1. William Godwin, *The Enquirer: Reflections on Education, Manners, and Literature* (1797), in Mark Philp et al., eds., *Political and Philosophical Writings of William Godwin,* 7 vols. (London, 1993), V, 153, 155, 156, 172, 173, 174, 175.

pounded the problem by publishing Wollstonecraft's private correspondence with Imlay.[2]

Godwin devoted himself to acquiring a new wife. Wollstonecraft had awakened him to the pleasures of sex, among other things. Exposed to the joy of intimacy, he wanted more. Godwin also accepted responsibility for its consequences: Fanny and Mary. In the short term, he depended on a wet nurse and housekeeper, Louisa Jones. Fanny was making astonishing progress, according to Jones. She was a smart young girl who had "a great many things to tell *Somebody*" and was "gloriously happy" playing games. She sent a kiss and a handshake to her "Pappa." Meanwhile, Mary would not allow Jones to nurse her and write "at the same time." Godwin never considered personally caring for Fanny and Mary any more than he contemplated cooking his meals or washing his clothes. Eager to find a new lover, he was equally committed to finding a domestic partner.[3]

In March 1798, Godwin left the girls with Jones and sought diversion in Bristol and Bath. The latter was a bustling resort town famed for its healing waters and public assemblies. There Godwin met Harriet Lee, a teacher who, with her sister Sophia, had published the popular *Canterbury Tales* in 1797. Godwin's awkward courtship of Harriet reveals a desperate man slipping into self-delusion. Only half a year after the death of Wollstonecraft, Godwin was sure that Lee was in love with him. He was wrong. Enthusiasm made it impossible for him to comprehend her reluctance to spend time with him, let alone marry him. When Lee did not reply to an invitation to visit him and, worse, when she came to London and left without telling him, Godwin was perplexed. He could not grasp that Lee, who found him vain and presumptuous, was being polite when she encouraged their correspondence. Trying to persuade Lee to embrace him, he only drove her away.

Godwin was at cross-purposes. He wanted a lover and a housekeeper. He wanted to be a father and have plenty of time to write and socialize with his friends. Now when Godwin valorized social commerce, he increasingly did so in domestic terms. Conjugal sexuality, he informed Lee, cured the ill effects of solitude. "Celibacy contracts and palsies the mind, and shuts us out from the most valuable topics of experience." More generally, a family organized around affection was the most sociable of institutions, a source of happiness, and the key to the general progress of mankind. "The senti-

2. William Godwin to Mary Hays, Oct. 27, 1797, Oxford, Bodleian, MS Abinger c. 22, fols. 78–79, [Hannah Godwin] to Godwin, Feb. 5, 1798, c. 4, fols. 4–5, William Godwin, Diary, December 1797–July 1798, e. 8, fols. 1–48.

3. Louisa Jones to Godwin, Mar. 9, 1798, Oxford, Bodleian, MS Abinger c. 4, fols. 8–9.

ments of mutual and equal affection, and of parental love, and these only, are competent to unlock the heart and expand its sentiments—they are the Promethean fire, with which, if we have never been touched, we have scarcely attained the semblance of what we are capable to be." Reinforcing her perception of his imperious vanity, Godwin assured Lee that life as a wife and mother would make her a better person because she would know him. In any case, scruples about his atheism should not matter more than "liberal . . . sentiments." Lee refused to take her suitor seriously, however, because she did not love him. As important, she worried about her reputation if she married such a notorious radical.[4]

A year later, Godwin turned to someone more likely to be a variation on Wollstonecraft. Although he talked less about domesticity within marriage, making it clear that he wanted physical and emotional intimacy, the relationship progressed from social experimentation to something more conventional. Both Godwin and his prospective wife sought to balance their desire for intimacy and mutuality with their need for stability and security. The key issue, as in virtually all relationships, was to make sure they understood each other. Too many romances foundered, as did Godwin's with Harriet Lee, on a rock of misunderstanding, each partner imagining the other wanted the same thing.

Maria James Reveley was a married woman with whom Godwin had long enjoyed a flirtatious relationship. Like most of his female friends, Reveley was intelligent, artistic (especially in drawing and music), and somewhat exotic (she had spent time in Constantinople and Rome). Reveley and Godwin had met in 1793 and become fast friends. In January 1795, Reveley, who led a life largely independent of her husband, might well have proposed a greater degree of intimacy, which Godwin apparently rejected. Three years later, Reveley's husband was barely dead of a sudden stroke when Godwin was importuning Reveley to abandon her respect for "ceremony." Like Lee, she should ignore the wishes of the world and see their love as an honest expression of rational feeling; they were behaving "with propriety and a generous confidence in the rectitude of the[ir] sentiment" in their plan "to see each other freely and honestly as friends; to lay down no beggarly rules about married and unmarried men." Reveley rebuffed the overture. Godwin was again seriously flummoxed by a woman who did not understand what he understood. Why had she told him she loved him when they were both

---

4. [Godwin] to [Harriet Lee] [drafts], [Mar.–June 1798], Oxford, Bodleian, MS Abinger c. 17, Harriet Lee to Godwin, July 31, 1798, c. 4, fols. 35–36. See William St. Clair, *The Godwins and the Shelleys: The Biography of a Family* (New York, 1989), 201–205.

married? Why, now that their spouses were dead, did she decline to exercise her "power to give [him] new life, a new interest in existence, to raise [him] from the grave in which [his] heart [lay] buried[?]" He was, after all, inviting her "to form the sole happiness of one of the most known men of the age." Reveley chose not to live with such vanity, knowing that Godwin was oblivious to the difficulty of balancing intimacy and domesticity over time.[5]

An indignant Godwin made matters worse by proclaiming his qualifications. Most men did not understand love, he conceded. But he was not an ordinary man. He, William Godwin, exemplified "the man of real powers [who] will infallibly, at least when he loves, be affectionate, attentive, familiar, and totally incapable of all questions of competition or ideas of superiority." He was not "the man of meaner or middling understanding [who] may almost always be expected to be jealous of rivalship, obstinate, self-willed, and puffed with the imaginary superiority he ascribes to himself." So, too, men were "different" in "structure" from women and "still more different in [their] education." A healthy relationship celebrated those differences and, as important, put them to work for the common good. Reveley had in Godwin a promising collaborator. A man of sensibility, he possessed the courage to defend her, the "constancy to inspire her with firmness," and the "science and information to furnish to her resources of amusement, and materials for studying." In return, she should emulate wives who contributed "the softness of their natures, the delicacy of their sentiments, and that peculiar and instantaneous sensibility by which they are qualified to guide our tastes and to correct our skepticism."[6]

Godwin was a long way from Wollstonecraft. He and his ideal wife, it seemed, were people who strayed not too far from assigned gender roles. Godwin could not imagine "domestic happiness . . . without this disparity of character," and, therefore, he would never "marry a man in female form." There were limits to the idea of marriage as a collaboration of equals. The widower of Wollstonecraft was suddenly the champion of male prerogative. Reveley ought to defer to Godwin's judgment because "the superiority of education" gave men "the privilege" to decide; "your sex, though feeling both exquisitely and admirably, are often in danger of deciding from a partial view of the subject." Qualifying some of the more radical dimensions of mixed-gender sociability, he was channeling what remained into pater-

5. Godwin to [Maria Reveley], [Aug. 18, 1799], Oxford, Bodleian, MS Abinger c. 22, fols. 117–118; Godwin to Maria Reveley, August 1799, in C. Kegan Paul, ed., *William Godwin: His Friends and Contemporaries*, 2 vols. (London, 1876), I, 335; St. Clair, *Godwins and Shelleys*, 155–200.

6. Godwin to Maria Reveley, [1799], Oxford, Bodleian, MS Abinger c. 17, fols. 92–94.

nalistic marriage. Reveley rejected Godwin's advice and married a man she thought would support her desire to maintain her independence. He was John Gisborne, a merchant with the sensibility of an artist. The couple moved to Italy, a place alienated English men and women increasingly identified as a refuge from the changes transforming Great Britain.[7]

Ambition versus Sensibility

Godwin confronted new realities in his professional as well as in his personal life. By the late 1790s, for reasons that only peripherally involved the scandal that greeted *Memoirs of the Author of "A Vindication of the Rights of Woman,"* the celebrated author of *Political Justice* and *Caleb Williams* was suddenly yesterday's news to a new generation of writers more interested in poetry than in prose. Their admiration for Godwin's ideas was qualified by their criticism of his character. Godwin responded to the challenge posed by poet Samuel Taylor Coleridge and others by trying to speak their language and master their forms. "I feel myself a purer a simpler, a more unreserved and natural being in your company than in that of almost any creature," Godwin told Coleridge in September 1800. The younger man demurred, crediting the older man's embrace of his "poetic and physiopathic feelings" to "dear little Fanny and Mary." But there is no doubting the impact of Coleridge's advice to Godwin to "seek for sympathy and love, not for detection or censure. Dismiss, my dear fellow, your theory of Collision of Ideas, and take up that of mutual Propulsions." Shocked and inspired by the direct emotional celebration of ordinary English life in William Wordsworth and Coleridge's *Lyrical Ballads,* Godwin considered becoming a poet. He also tried his hand at playwriting. But he had no aptitude for either verse or drama. At the end of the day, he was most effective as a narrator of fictional personal histories that ruminated on contemporary cultural dilemmas.[8]

In his 1799 novel *St. Leon: A Tale of the Sixteenth Century,* Godwin considered why a sensible man transformed by love found it so difficult to sustain intimacy. St. Leon resembles the kind of man Godwin imagined Gilbert Imlay to be, and his wife a projected version of Wollstonecraft. Perhaps Godwin was identifying with Imlay, or at least the extent to which he

---

7. Ibid.

8. Godwin to Samuel Taylor Coleridge, Sept. 5, 1800, Pierpont Morgan Library Department of Literary and Historical Manuscripts, New York; Coleridge to Godwin, May 21, 1800, in Earl Leslie Griggs, ed., *Collected Letters of Samuel Taylor Coleridge,* 6 vols. (1956; rpt. Oxford, 1966), I, 588, Oct. 13, 1800, 636, Apr. 28, 1801, II, 724–725.

imagined his wife's lover had modeled the attributes of selfish tradesmen. In any case, St. Leon regularly sacrifices private happiness in a relentless quest to do good. Like Imlay, he struggles to be both a man of feeling and a man of action. Unfortunately, he never grasps the extent to which love and family might promote human progress more effectively than wealth or public power. Mixing "human feelings and passions with incredible situations," Godwin was trying to remind readers that "domestic and private affections [were] inseparable from the nature of man, and from what may be styled the culture of the heart." He was "fully persuaded that they are not incompatible with a profound and active sense of justice in the mind of him that cherishes them." Men could change the world by loving and being loved by women who were also their best friends. To promote revolution from personal conviction alone was to invite failure, for it was to confuse reform with a projection of personal interest.[9]

A sixteenth-century French nobleman, St. Leon tells his story retrospectively, looking for clues to where he went wrong, just as Godwin turns to the distant past to consider the endless conflict between self-interest and benevolence. Raised by an ambitious mother, he fights against the Holy Roman Emperor in northern Italy and comes to love the military fraternity. Defeat in battle destroys this charmed life, however, just as it destroys "the reign of chivalry" and inaugurates an era of "dissimulation, corruption, and commerce." Like his peers, St. Leon channels his "suppressed ambition" in a "sordid and inglorious passion for gaming" and a string of mistresses. Redemption appears in the form of a woman. Nineteen-year-old noblewoman Marguerite Louise Isabeau de Damville is a person of intelligence, "uncommon prudence," and "unalterable amiableness."[10]

Falling in love with Marguerite transforms St. Leon. "Ashamed of [his] own degradation" "in pleasures mean and sensual," he declares himself "a new man." Rescued by her father from financial ruin, St. Leon marries Marguerite. They retire to a rural estate where they enjoy "perfect happiness." Mutual love—"the transcendent enjoyment and nameless delights which, wherever the heart is pure and the soul is refined, wait on the attachment of two persons of opposite sexes"—brings St. Leon unimaginable happiness. Over the next decade, he and Marguerite enjoy the kind of socially useful

9. William Godwin, *St. Leon: A Tale of the Sixteenth Century* (1799), ed. William D. Brewer (Peterborough, Ont., 2006), 51, 52 (Godwin deleted the reference to Mary Wollstonecraft in a later edition [52n]). See David Collings, "The Romance of the Impossible: William Godwin in the Empty Place of Reason," *ELH*, LXX (2003), 847–874.

10. Godwin, *St. Leon*, ed. Brewer, 74, 75, 79, 80, 81.

intimacy Wollstonecraft had imagined she would find with Imlay and that Godwin thought she had found with him. They talk, read, travel, share ideas and feelings, create five children (four of whom survive), and respect their "separate pursuits." St. Leon and Marguerite are affectionate friends who realize that they complement and improve each other. "To feel that we are loved by one whose love we have deserved, to be employed in the mutual interchange of the marks of this love, habitually to study the happiness of one by whom our happiness is studied in return, this is the most desirable, as it is the genuine and unadulterated condition of human nature." St. Leon and Marguerite rejoice "in this reciprocation of benefits. . . . Mutual esteem was incessantly kept alive, and mutual esteem is the only substantial basis of love."[11]

As in Wollstonecraft's relationship with her sensible American, the cause of the ruin of this Eden is, not Marguerite, whom St. Leon acknowledges as his moral superior. It is, rather, "the original vice of [St. Leon's] mind," his insatiable need for the "gestures of worship and the voices of applause" in the company of other men. The story of his life turns on his inability to accept that intimacy with Marguerite is sufficient. He ignores the dying advice of his father-in-law to "live in the midst of [his] family; cultivate domestic affection; be the solace and joy of [his] wife; [and] watch for the present and future welfare of [his] children." By himself on a trip to Paris to arrange for the education of their son, Charles, St. Leon resumes gambling. His passion becomes ungovernable, and he loses his entire fortune in one long night.[12]

The long-suffering Marguerite sustains her family as they endure a life of poverty in Switzerland. She sees to the education of her children and helps St. Leon deal with a profound depression that has brought him to the brink of suicide. In yet another example of the power of sociability, Marguerite's steadfast love and remarkable example pull her husband out of his downward spiral. St. Leon proclaims himself "cured of [his] folly." He has "learned to value [his] domestic blessings." The essential truth of life is simple: "He that loves, and is loved by, a race of pure and virtuous creatures, and that lives continually in the midst of them, is an idiot, if he does not think himself happy."[13]

Unfortunately, St. Leon—like the ever restless Imlay—cannot sustain that thought. When a mysterious stranger offers him the secrets of immor-

11. Ibid., 82, 85–86, 87.
12. Ibid., 84 85, 88, 93, 97.
13. Ibid., 121, 130.

tality and inexhaustible wealth on the condition that he not tell Marguerite, he agrees. But the wife immediately senses the change in her husband, and the marriage disintegrates. St. Leon rationalizes his choice by claiming that he can do more good with money and perpetual youth than he can with his family. If he neglected the truism that "no man stands alone in the world" and created "a permanent difference and separation between [him] and [his] family," so be it. St. Leon's decision alienates his son Charles and breaks Marguerite's heart. Too late, he asks her to become his director, admitting that he has "never been wise or virtuous but when [he has] been implicitly guided by [her]!" She will have none of it because she thinks him lost to her forever. "A consort should be a human being and an equal," Marguerite says. "But to this equality and simple humanity it is no longer in your power to return." A man without love is a "monster" living "the solitary, joyless tenant of a prison, the materials of which are emeralds and rubies! . . . How weak and ignoble the man that voluntarily accepts these laws of existence!" When Marguerite dies after giving birth to a stillborn child, her foolish husband is left to mourn what might have been.[14]

St. Leon's life becomes an unending series of adventures in which he uses his power to create wealth to try to right wrongs. His strange circumstances attract the attention of the Inquisition in Spain, and he spends a dozen years in a prison. Once he escapes, he disguises himself to seek out his daughters. When he finds them, they have forgotten him. St. Leon moves on to Hungary, where he intends to help Christians repulse the Muslim Turks. Initially, people are grateful for his money and leadership, but they turn against him when prices rise. Suddenly, his "interference" is met "with contempt and execration," leaving him to realize that his enlightened "design" to develop Hungary had produced "unruliness [in] those for whose benefit it had been planned." St. Leon meets with a local Ottoman official who is aghast at what the Christian Frenchman has wrought in Hungary. He is "one of those busy-bodies, who never see an evil without imagining they are the persons to correct it, intruding into every thing, and subverting every thing." Only those chosen by Mahomet could deal with the "mystery" of the "superintendence of the public welfare." St. Leon once again understands the truth of Marguerite's advice about the power of love. He is in trouble because only money—"the coarsest, the meanest, the least flattering, and the most brittle" of all connections—ties him to other people. St. Leon is rescued by a Christian army whose leader Charles does not rec-

14. Ibid., 157, 192, 193, 194, 224, 225, 226, 227, 297.

ognize him. They become friends until the father interferes with his son's romance.[15]

St. Leon has the means to satisfy the most basic desires of human beings. Forever rich and forever young, he is an attractive and powerful man who can have whatever he wants, go wherever he wants, and do whatever he wants. None of these attributes, however, makes him happy. None permits him to improve either himself or mankind. Over and over again, his efforts at reform backfire, producing conflict and chaos. St. Leon's problem is similar to Ormond's, an exaggerated version of what Godwin thought was ruining so many of his contemporaries. "Utterly alone," he is imprisoned in "true solitude." Reuniting Charles and his lover, Godwin suggests that the son has learned what the father never did: that real happiness and real progress begin and end in a social life centered on a family defined by rational affection. This "busy and anxious world of ours yet contains something in its stores that is worth living for," Godwin concluded. Staying true to Wollstonecraft, he insisted that not every man had to suffer the fate of Imlay or St. Leon. The question now was whether he was one who would.[16]

"A Philosophic Coxcomb"

Critics marveled at how personal experience had transformed the author of *Political Justice.* Harping on Godwin's embrace of domesticity, one commented that love, marriage, and children had made him "the fervent eulogist of what he formerly despised, or at least treated dubiously and blamefully." The writer's friend Ralph Fell found the novel compelling and realistic as long as Marguerite and her daughters were present to incite his sympathy, but he lost interest as St. Leon became more and more obsessed with money and his supernatural gifts. Elizabeth Inchbald celebrated Godwin's "brilliant imagination" and "grand conception" (as well as his happier attitude toward marriage) but concluded that he had "failed in the execution of this vast design." Others were even less kind. Edward Du Bois published a popular satire of the novel in which St. Godwin, a man who "followed the dictates of [his] passions," wanders around Europe in a series of misadventures, all the while spouting absurd parodies of Godwin's ideas. "I hate the man who presumes to think he has a *right to monopolize any woman!*" exclaims the benighted narrator. "Women, like air, were by nature intended as a common advantage, and should be free and open to every man that

15. Ibid., 369, 371, 376, 381.
16. Ibid., 439, 440, 450.

breathes." After languishing in the Bastille from 1612 until 1789, he becomes a Jacobin and advocates "what nobody could understand; namely, The *absoluteness of necessity,* the *perfectibility of man,* and *the omnipotence of truth.*" He "opposed all political and moral order, and endeavoured to overturn every system that time and experience had sanctioned and approved." Stung by such ridicule, Godwin nonetheless persevered, not only as a writer, but as a suitor.[17]

In the spring of 1801, Godwin met Mary Jane Clairmont, a decidedly unconventional woman with whom he ultimately forged a successful domestic partnership. Clairmont was a thirty-year-old Roman Catholic widow supporting herself as a translator. She had a five-year-old son, Charles, and a three-year-old daughter, Jane, who later called herself Claire. According to family lore, Clairmont initiated a relationship with Godwin after several weeks of residence at Number 27 Paragon in London by calling from her balcony to his: "Is it possible that I behold the immortal Godwin?" Whatever Mary Jane's words, the privately rejected and publicly scorned Godwin welcomed the attention. The couple became intimate physically as well as emotionally in short order. In October, Mary Jane was supervising Godwin's daughters when he was away: "Kiss Fanny and Mary. Tell them to remember me, and to love me," he reminded her. A pregnant Mary Jane and Godwin married in December. (The child died at birth the following June.) Thomas Holcroft was happy for his old friend. "There is not anything on earth so requisite, as well to the every day as to the exquisite happiness of man," he wrote, "as the love and friendship of woman."[18]

Privately, the reaction of Godwin's friends to his marriage was not so high-minded. Many thought him a fool manipulated by a scheming woman. Charles Lamb could barely contain himself when reporting news of the impending wedding. He smirked that a widow "with green spectacles" had brought out the "juvenile" in the lonely writer. "You never saw such a philosophic coxcomb," hooted Lamb. No one had ever played "the Romeo so unnaturally." Months later, Lamb gleefully announced that the "Professor

17. "Remarks on Godwin's 'St. Leon,'" *Monthly Magazine, and American Review,* II, no. 6 (June 1800), 405; Ralph Fell to Godwin, Dec. 6, 1799, Oxford, Bodleian, MS Abinger c. 5, fols. 31–32, Elizabeth Inchbald to Godwin, Dec. 24, [1799], c. 5, fols. 44–47 (see Thomas Holcroft's mixed review in Holcroft to Godwin, Sept. 9, 1800, c. 6, fols. 45–46); Edward Du Bois, *St. Godwin: A Tale of the Sixteenth, Seventeenth, and Eighteenth Centuries* (1800), ed. Gina Luria (New York, 1974), 203, 233.

18. Originally reported in Paul, ed., *William Godwin,* II, 58; Godwin to Mary Jane Godwin, Oct. 9, 1801, Oxford, Bodleian, MS Abinger c. 42, fols. 1–2, Holcroft to Godwin, Jan. 1, 1802, c. 7, fols. 80–81.

Figure 11. Thomas Holcroft; William Godwin. *By Thomas Lawrence. Pencil with black and red chalk, 1794.* © *National Portrait Gallery, London*

has not done making Love to his new Spouse." These and similar comments from others, including the Godwin children, have contributed to an image of Mary Jane Clairmont as a scheming shrew. She did not help her cause by hiding details that Godwin discovered after he was in love with her. Her name was not Clairmont. Years earlier, she had run away to France, where she had given birth to her two children by two men, neither of whom she married.[19]

Mary Jane Clairmont could not escape the shadow of Mary Wollstonecraft. Most people, including her stepdaughter Mary and her own daughter Claire, thought her mercurial and willful. But then many people thought the same of Wollstonecraft. Some people actually liked Mary Jane Godwin. Aaron Burr, the former vice president of the United States in the midst of an extended European sojourn following his acquittal on a charge of treason, enjoyed the time he spent dining, talking, and playing whist with this "sensible, amiable woman." And in fact Mary Jane was smart and well read. Godwin loved her, as he had loved Wollstonecraft, despite—or perhaps because of—her moodiness. His "dear love" needed to manage her "temper." But she should not strive to eliminate all her "faults," for he loved "some of them." "I love what is human, what gives softness, and an agreeable air of frailty and pliability to the whole." Godwin almost always defended her, even when his oldest friends, including Thomas Holcroft, criticized her behavior. He needed stimulation, and he got an abundance of it from his second wife as well as from his first. She, in turn, no doubt hoped for more financial stability and minor celebrity than she received from her "ever dear dear Godwin," a man who when she was away likely went to bed without "thinking of me!!!"[20]

Knowing that Godwin was susceptible to persuasion, fancying himself the very model of conjugal mutuality, Mary Jane Clairmont asserted herself

19. Charles Lamb to Thomas Manning, Apr. 23, 1802, in Edwin W. Marrs, Jr., ed., *The Letters of Charles and Mary Anne Lamb,* 3 vols. (Ithaca, N.Y., 1975), II, 61, to John Rickman, early December 1801, 40, Sept. 16, 1801, 22, to Thomas Manning, Apr. 23, 1802, 61. See St. Clair, *Godwins and Shelleys,* 238–254.

20. Aaron Burr to Theodosia, Nov. 21, 1808, in Matthew L. Davis, ed., *The Private Journal of Aaron Burr* (1838), 2 vols. (Upper Saddle River, N.J., 1970), I, 99 (see also Mar. 15, 1812, II, 350); Godwin to Mary Jane Godwin, Oct. 9, 1801, Oxford, Bodleian, MS Abinger c. 42, fols. 1–2, Godwin to Holcroft, Sept. 2, 1803, c. 18, fol. 25, [Mary Jane Godwin] to Godwin, June 2, 18[06], c. 9, fols. 105–106. See Miranda Seymour, *Mary Shelley* (New York, 2000), 45–48. On middle-class women, see Margaret Hunt, *The Middling Sort: Commerce, Gender, and the Family in England, 1680–1780* (Berkeley, Calif., 1996); Amanda Vickery, *The Gentleman's Daughter: Women's Lives in Georgian England* (New Haven, Conn., 1998); and Harriet Guest, *Small Change: Women, Learning, Patriotism, 1650–1810* (Chicago, 2000).

in the coquettish manner Wollstonecraft had denounced in *A Vindication of the Rights of Woman*. On one occasion, she scolded Godwin for thinking she ignored him. If he "could be a woman," he would understand how busy she was. And still she had time to let him rest in "more than half our bed," keep "the cup of coffee all ready," walk with him into town, devote idle hours to him, and offer him bliss. Mary Jane's ambition was confined to the household. She wanted to be the wife of a respectable man, the mother of his children, the doyenne of his household, and a partner in a bookstore she encouraged him to open. Like most women, she negotiated a role within the confines of a culture that assumed her deference to the needs of her husband. Once, while traveling on her own, she returned from "a solitary walk in such sweet gardens" persuaded that life in such a beautiful environment would make her "tender, generous, serene and happy. Here I could, I feel I could, be a better wife, a better mother, a better human being." The inscriptions on the obelisk in the graveyard of Saint Pancras Church reflect the two women's self-images. One side reads, "Mary Wollstonecraft Godwin, author of A Vindication of the Rights of Woman," and the other, "Mary Jane, second wife of William Godwin."[21]

The husband labored to support his family. Most of the 400 guineas he earned for *St. Leon* were already encumbered when he received them. An ardent foray into playwriting produced three unmitigated disasters entitled *Antonio; or, The Soldier's Return* (1800), *Abbas, an Historical Tragedy* (1801), and *Faulkener* (1807). By 1804, a new publisher, Richard Phillips, was encouraging Godwin to write history and religious stories. His *Life of Geoffrey Chaucer* (1803) was not a success. Children's books, for which there was a growing market, seemed a more likely bet. In 1805, at the instigation of his wife, Godwin borrowed money from a friend and opened a children's bookshop on Tottenham Court Road under the name of Hodgkins, the man he hired to manage it. The City French and English Juvenile Library offered a range of toys, maps, games, paints, and stationery as well as books. In 1807, Godwin borrowed more money and leased a five-story house at 41 Skinner Street on Snow Hill for £150 per year in order to put his Juvenile Library and his family under one roof. The squalid neighborhood featured prisons and warehouses. Rarely leaving his study, Godwin entrusted the bookstore (renamed M. J. Godwin and Company) to the management of his wife

21. Mary Jane Godwin to Godwin, September 1805, Oxford, Bodleian, MS Abinger c. 9, fol. 44, Mary Jane Godwin to Godwin, [June 1806], c. 9, fols. 114–115, Godwin to [Dr.] Ash, May 21, 1808, MS Abinger c. 10, fols. 64–65. See Mary Jane Godwin to Godwin, June 7, 1806, c. 9, fols. 109–110.

and their daughters. At no time did the operation generate enough income to cover the family's mounting debts. The more Godwin tried to solve his financial woes, the more he fell behind. Suffering from "sick-headaches," he lamented the tyranny of his erratic moods. Man was "a miserable creature" because of his "elasticity"; an evening walk was sufficient to replace "despair" with "serenity." Similarly, marriage and his "little establishment" had made him "less independent" than he had hoped it would. Those who thought life with Mary Jane a trial might have considered life with her husband.[22]

Mary Jane and William Godwin's version of affectionate sociability was different from that of Mary Wollstonecraft and Godwin. His second wife was not an intellectual. To be sure, they engaged with each other. They were friends and lovers, in their own way. When Godwin was far from home, he regretted leaving a place "where we understood each other by looks, where we needed but few words, and words were often volumes." Yet there was no confusion about where power lay in the Godwin household. When Godwin sought to reform his wife, he spoke with condescension, even if he was trying to persuade rather than command. Mary Jane Godwin reacted to her husband's lectures in a manner familiar to readers of *A Vindication of the Rights of Woman.* She behaved like a child, indulging what he paternalistically termed "the excesses of that baby-sullenness for every trifle." Occasionally, she raised the stakes by threatening a separation, often in response to one too many instances of thoughtless neglect by a self-absorbed, tactless husband. Once, she lost her temper over having to provide dinner for a friend of his who failed to appear on three successive nights. On another occasion, she fell out with Thomas Holcroft because she thought he was avoiding her. (Godwin and Holcroft completely fell out themselves shortly thereafter.) The pattern of their fights was clear. When Mary Jane concluded that Godwin had heard her, she recovered her equilibrium and sought reconciliation, reminding him of what she had sacrificed for him. Godwin then reinforced her withdrawals by affirming their success. After one particularly intense spat, he proclaimed his admiration for the endurance of his "dearest love." How he wished he behaved better! Experience had taught him "that where I meant to beget effects of the kindest sort, the result has been the reverse." A grateful Godwin thanked his wife for putting aside his faults

---

22. [Godwin] to Mary Jane Godwin, June 2, 1806, Oxford, Bodleian, MS Abinger c. 42, fols. 21–22, Godwin to John Rickman, June 27, 1808, c. 10, fols. 69–72 (a long letter narrating Godwin's efforts to find some regular income). See St. Clair, *Godwins and Shelleys,* 232–237, 289–295.

and applying herself "to plans for the common benefit and support of our united family" with grace and "chearfulness." All things considered, Clairmont's life was not "the worst."[23]

The Godwin marriage exemplified a social reorganization taking place throughout the English-speaking world. Like many of their friends, the Godwins had been unhappy children whose relationships with their parents, if they existed at all, were fraught with tension. A major part of their quest for personal independence was the replacement of the artificial tyranny of birth families with the natural freedom of volitional families. If parents and children could not choose one another in the manner of friends and spouses, they could and should cultivate ties of affection rather than accept the bonds of genetic slavery. Authority within the family as in the larger society should follow from persuasion and consent. Successful parents would abandon coercion in favor of modeling good behavior and convincing children through conversation. Like lovers, family members would manage their sensibilities and exercise their understanding through collaboration. Children would develop sympathy, practice benevolence, and do their duty out of mutual esteem and enlightened self-interest. The dangers of a failure to educate children in the value of social commerce, Wollstonecraft had argued in *A Vindication of the Rights of Woman,* was obvious: parents who treated daughters and sons as dolls and masters produced slaves and tyrants.

Here as elsewhere, Wollstonecraft, Godwin, and their friends were imagining—*speculating,* if you will—that a society of friends would produce natural harmony, that parents and children who loved one another would respect one another. Once again, the practice of domestic love, like the practice of romantic love, was more complicated than the vision. Engaging in social commerce within what we would call a middle-class family, Godwin encouraged intellectual independence and free inquiry in his children. At the same time, his personal limitations and the inevitable logic of his ideals compromised his project. Incapable of restraining his manly opinions or expressing love easily, Godwin nurtured children uncertain about exactly where they stood with him in part because his second wife enabled

---

23. Godwin to Mary Jane Godwin, Oct. 9, 1801, Oxford, Bodleian, MS Abinger c. 42, fols. 1–2, [Godwin] to [Mary Jane Godwin], Oct. 28, 1803, c. 42, fol. 5, Holcroft to Mary Jane Godwin, Nov. 24, 1803, c. 42, fols. 6–7, Mary Jane Godwin to [Godwin], Aug. 14, 1811, c. 11, fol. 50, Godwin to Mary Jane Godwin, July 10, 1815, c. 42, fols. 87–88; Godwin to Mary Jane Godwin, Sept. 24, 1812, in Marion Kingston Stocking, ed., *The Clairmont Correspondence: Letters of Claire Clairmont, Charles Clairmont, and Fanny Imlay Godwin,* 2 vols. (Baltimore, 1995), II, 643, 644.

rather than challenged his emotional reserve, vanity, and self-absorption. Above all, Godwin was not prepared to deal with outcomes he had not anticipated, especially the tendency of his children and young disciples to cultivate understandings of his and Wollstonecraft's ideas that led them to make choices of which he could not approve.

"Vigorous Little Girl[s]"

In *Thoughts on the Education of Daughters,* which sold more copies in her lifetime than any of her books, Wollstonecraft had urged well-educated mothers to employ their reason to "cultivate and govern those instincts" of infants, "for if they are not governed they will run wild; and strengthen the passions which are ever endeavouring to obtain dominion—I mean vanity and self-love." In *Original Stories from Real Life,* she called for education through persuasion. Knowledge was to be "gradually imparted" more by example than instruction.[24]

These ideas about education were commonplace among middling English-speaking peoples at the turn of the nineteenth century. Wollstonecraft and her contemporaries started with John Locke's premise that individuals were born "blank slates" and evolved perpetually in response to external stimuli. They accepted the notion (originating with Anthony Ashley Cooper, third earl of Shaftesbury, and refined by Scots such as Francis Hutcheson, David Hume, and Adam Smith) that education ought to promote affectionate benevolence rather than egocentric selfishness. Thus, children required attention from mothers (and fathers) who would discipline rather than indulge them within an atmosphere of mutual respect and affection. No longer adults in miniature, children were malleable creatures who acquired obligations and liberties at "the age of consent," that is, the age at which society deemed them capable of understanding. People of good character were respectable citizens who worked together to govern themselves.[25]

24. MW, *Thoughts on the Education of Daughters,* in Janet Todd and Marilyn Butler, eds., *The Works of Mary Wollstonecraft,* 7 vols. (New York, 1989), IV, 7, MW, *Original Stories from Real Life,* 359.

25. Holly Brewer, *By Birth or Consent: Children, Law, and the Anglo-American Revolution in Authority* (Chapel Hill, N.C., 2005), 314. See also Jacqueline S. Reinier, *From Virtue to Character: American Childhood, 1775-1850* (New York, 1996); and Mary Waldron, "Childhood and Child Rearing in Late Eighteenth- and Early Nineteenth-Century Fiction: A Quiet Revolution," in Carolyn D. Williams, Angela Escott, and Louise Duckling, eds., *Woman to Woman: Female Negotiations during the Long Eighteenth Century* (Newark, Del., 2010), 49–62.

In Great Britain and the United States, respectable people were almost exclusively white and middle or upper class. Resisting the democratizing tendency of education, many argued that biology limited the human capacity to develop reason. The bodies of people with different skin colors who originated in regions far from Europe and eastern North America disqualified them from participation in social as well as political networks. With a few exceptions, they were assumed to be irredeemably enslaved to their passions and therefore permanently relegated to the status of children. White middling women complicated this argument. Their sex nullified, or at least reduced, the possibilities accorded them by their race and class. Wollstonecraft and her peers, writing almost exclusively about people like them, never confronted these issues because they shared the prejudices of their larger cohort. They generalized from their own experience in a largely unconscious imperialism. The implications of their contribution extended well beyond their particular case, however. Asserting that properly educated women could reason as well as properly educated men, they challenged essentialist arguments that justified the power of any group of people. If patriarchal structures had developed over time in reaction to specific historical circumstances, they could certainly change over time in reaction to new historical circumstances. And nothing demonstrated this argument more conclusively than their public performance as authors capable of persuading readers.

Wollstonecraft regularly rested her claims to public authority on her private role as a mother. "I feel great pleasure at being a mother," she exclaimed shortly after the birth of Fanny. Wollstonecraft characteristically linked affection and duty. To love was to engage; to feel sympathy was to accept responsibility. From the moment of Fanny's birth, she loved her "vigorous little Girl" and sought to develop her obvious intelligence and talent. As middling white women such as Wollstonecraft sought to limit the number of children they bore by experimenting with birth control, pregnancy became "an obligation, a duty, that women undertook voluntarily for rational, sentimental, and instrumental purposes: to welcome a stranger and to secure a marriage by expressing romantic love." Fewer children meant that women could develop other parts of their lives. A mother could also engage with friends in conversation and the broader world in print.[26]

---

26. MW to Ruth Barlow, May 20, 1794, in Janet Todd, ed., *The Collected Letters of Mary Wollstonecraft* (New York, 2003), 253; Susan E. Klepp, "Revolutionary Bodies: Women and the Fertility Transition in the Mid-Atlantic Region, 1760–1820," *Journal of American History,* LXXXV (1998), 928. See Sarah Moss, "The Maternal Aliment: Feeding Daughters in the Works of Mary

Wollstonecraft had no intention of sacrificing either her literary career or her personal liberty to devote herself to Fanny, any more than she would have done for Imlay or Godwin. Like many of her contemporaries, she understood the roles of mother and author as complementary. A mother cultivated the understanding of children as much as a writer cultivated the understanding of readers. Both constituted critical work in the cultivation of persuadable human beings. Mothers read books, pamphlets, and articles designed to help them do cultural work—and increasingly they wrote them, too, rejecting the advice of paternalistic men such as the Reverend James Fordyce.[27]

Wollstonecraft not only took pride in becoming a mother, she contextualized it within her larger philosophy. Her labor with Fanny in May 1794 was "not smooth work." The French midwife, while praising Wollstonecraft's behavior in the end, worried that an agitated mother would kill herself as well as her child. Wollstonecraft ascribed her behavior to a lack of education. This "struggle of nature," like so much of female experience, was "rendered much more cruel by the ignorance and affectation of women." Learning from the birth of Fanny, Wollstonecraft prepared for the birth of Mary by employing a midwife who, according to Godwin, understood that her "proper business . . . in the instance of a natural labour, is to sit by and wait for the operations of nature, which seldom, in these affairs, demand the interposition of art." The world, as always, unfolded best with a minimum of artificial intervention in the workings of natural commerce. Ever committed to truth, Wollstonecraft (and Godwin) shared details of her daughters' births as socially useful information.[28]

Women of Wollstonecraft's generation increasingly believed that to give birth was to meet a new person created in the physical intimacy of mother and father. Mother and child formed an emotional bond that affirmed the

Wollstonecraft," in *Spilling the Beans: Eating, Cooking, Reading, and Writing in British Women's Fiction, 1770–1830* (Manchester, 2009), 82–121; Susan C. Greenfield, *Mothering Daughters: Novels and the Politics of Family Romance from Frances Burney to Jane Austen* (Detroit, 2002); and Angela Keane, *Women Writers and the English Nation in the 1790s: Romantic Belongings* (Cambridge, 2000). See also Joanna Goldsworthy and Marie Mulvey-Roberts, "Revolutionary Mothers and Revolting Daughters: Mary Wollstonecraft and Mary Shelley, Anna Wheeler and Rosina Bulwer Lytton," in Williams, Escott, and Duckling, eds., *Woman to Woman*, 62–78; and, especially, Susan E. Klepp, *Revolutionary Conceptions: Women, Fertility, and Family Limitation in America, 1760–1820* (Chapel Hill, N.C., 2009).

27. Moss, "Maternal Aliment," in *Spilling the Beans*, 82, 83.

28. MW to Ruth Barlow, May 20, 1794, in Todd, ed., *Collected Letters*, 252; Godwin, *Memoirs of the Author of "A Vindication of the Rights of Woman"* (1798), ed. Paula Clemit and Gina Luria Walker (Peterborough, Ont., 2001), 112.

emotional bond between mother and father. Breast-feeding not only linked mother and child, it was "a natural way of cementing the matrimonial tie, and twisting esteem with fonder recollections." Wollstonecraft assumed that sensible men would "delight" in seeing their wives breast-feed, even if it entailed curtailment of conjugal sexuality. As always, love followed from natural connections more than "artful wanton tricks." Good parenting required the participation of both parents. Thus Imlay's reaction to Fanny's birth, like Godwin's to Mary's, mattered to Wollstonecraft. "The constant tenderness of my most affectionate companion makes me regard a fresh tie as a blessing." Perhaps at no other moment had Wollstonecraft been more confident that she and Imlay were cultivating an emotional intimacy that would sustain them long after desire had cooled or become irregular.[29]

Wollstonecraft directly described the workings of her ideal family. In the *Posthumous Works of the Author of "A Vindication of the Rights of Woman,"* Godwin published an unfinished manuscript entitled *Lessons,* which was written to Fanny in October 1795 at the height of Wollstonecraft's despair about Imlay. Godwin noted "the agonizing and painful sentiment with which the author originally bequeathed these papers, as a legacy for the benefit of her child." *Lessons* was the "first book of a series" Wollstonecraft had planned to write "for my unfortunate girl." Godwin included the work in part because of its parallel with the relationship between Maria and her child in Wollstonecraft's unfinished novel, *Maria; or, The Wrongs of Woman.* The manuscript details Wollstonecraft's sense of mothers as the primary shapers of their children in collaboration with affectionate but more distant fathers. The narrator and her tales encourage female agency even as they demonstrate that, although mothers could advocate specific humanitarian reforms (including antislavery), their overall purpose was to show "how girl and parent readers can reform themselves to help reform the world."[30]

Lessons is a story of collaborative parenting that exemplifies the child-rearing notions of Wollstonecraft and her friends. Over the course of ten lessons, a mother—the central figure and the source of authority—encourages the development of her daughter. The girl learns the difference between

---

29. MW, *A Vindication of the Rights of Woman* (1792), ed. Carol H. Poston (New York, 1988), 142; MW to Ruth Barlow, May 20, 1794, in Todd, ed., *Collected Letters,* 253. See Marylynn Salmon, "The Cultural Significance of Breastfeeding and Infant Care in Early Modern England and America," *Journal of Social History,* XXVIII (1994), 247–269.

30. MW, *Lessons,* in William Godwin, ed., *Posthumous Works of the Author of "A Vindication of the Rights of Woman"* (1798), 2 vols. (Clifton, N.J., 1972), II, 174, 175; Mitzi Myers, "'Impeccable Governesses': Rational Dames and Moral Mothers: Mary Wollstonecraft and the Female Tradition in Georgian Children's Books," *Children's Literature,* XIV (1986), 43.

nouns and verbs; the mother progresses from simple sentences to more complex expressions of complicated thoughts and feelings that impart lessons drawn from ordinary life. The discussion focuses on the quotidian and the personal rather than on the heroic and the public. The unnamed girl has a younger brother, William, whom the mother uses to show her daughter how and, as important, why she treated her as she did when she was an infant. To know is to observe ("Look at him.") and to empathize ("How did you do when you were a baby like him?"). The daughter also benefits from the attention of a playful but distant father and a cooperative servant. Maturity was about cultivating sense rather than sensibility, growing "older and wiser at the same time." Children became adults through conversation with their parents. The mother persuades by example, not prescription. "I have lived a long time" she avers, "I know what is good; I do not want my body to tell me." The family portrait is affectionate. Father and mother treat each other well because they "love" each other. All this the child absorbs, slowly but surely, until she begins to understand.[31]

The content of the lessons is about discipline—learning to take care of the body and regulate behavior. The means to that end is sociability. An early paragraph begins with commands about personal cleanliness. "Hide your face. Wipe your nose. Wash your hands. Dirty hands." It then moves immediately to empathy—"Why do you cry?"—and engagement—"Shake hands. I love you. Kiss me now. Good girl." The mother constantly talks with her daughter, invites her participation in the raising of her younger brother. She discusses breast-feeding, how the infant girl sucked even after she had teeth that hurt her mother. When the mother can no longer stand the pain, she enlists the father in teaching the child how to eat solid food. "Come to me," he says, "and I will teach you, my little dear, for you must not hurt poor mamma, who has given you her milk, when you could not take any thing else."[32]

Godwin shared many of these ideas. The only book he published while he and Wollstonecraft were together—he wrote it between August 1796 and January 1797—was largely about education. *The Enquirer: Reflections on Education, Manners, and Literature,* Godwin explained, was "principally the result of conversations" with Wollstonecraft. She had transformed him by teaching him to temper his "ardent . . . passion for innovation." He had become less "imperious . . . impatient and impetuous." Now he investigated "the humbler walks of private life," believing that "the cause of political re-

---

31. MW, *Lessons,* in Godwin, ed., *Posthumous Works,* II, 180, 189, 191, 194–196.
32. Ibid., 178, 182.

form, and the cause of intellectual and literary refinement, are inseparably connected." Written in the same year as *Memoirs, The Enquirer* celebrated the possibilities of emotion, especially love, which many had found lacking in his earlier writing.[33]

The goal of pedagogy was to nurture "habits of intellectual activity." Genius, observed Godwin, was "generated subsequent to birth." Thus, the major responsibility of a teacher (or parent) was to awaken curiosity and inspire perseverance until the moment when, "in the intercourse of our companions, or in our commerce with nature," something "makes its way directly to the heart, and becomes the fruitful parent of a thousand projects and contemplations." Godwin wanted to be a revolutionary kind of father, one who shaped his children without controlling them. The challenge was to encourage them to cultivate their fancies without surrendering to their sensibilities. Neither personal nor public improvement was possible if individuals did not consider possibilities. When the atheist Godwin wrote *Bible Stories* in 1802 to make money, he highlighted that neglected but "most essential branch of human nature the imagination." Children's education in general was too mechanical, complained Godwin. "Every thing is studied and attended to, except those things which open the heart, which insensibly initiate the learner in the relations and generous offices of society, and enable him to put himself in imagination into the place of his neighbour, to feel his feelings, and to wish his wishes." Only with empathy achieved through imagination would people become benevolent. Sentiment was more persuasive than reason. "It is the heart which most deserves to be cultivated, . . . the pulses which beat with sympathy, and qualify us for the habits of charity, reverence, and attachment."[34]

Imagining an affectionate family was as empowering as imagining romantic love. Both were enthusiasms, the letting loose of sensibility in ways Wollstonecraft had warned against and struggled with for years. Godwin was not Imlay. He was a responsible man who sincerely wanted to do well by Wollstonecraft's daughters, "the two poor animals left under [his] protection." In Ireland in the summer of 1800, his first extended trip since the death of their mother, he longed to hear news of them. He fretted about Fanny's "improvement" in spelling and reading. Mary was not to worry that he would "give her away, as she shall be nobody's little girl but papa's." He looked forward to both girls greeting his coach when he returned to London. In the meantime, he hoped they would not forget him. He thought of

33. Godwin, *Enquirer,* in Philp et al., eds., *Political and Philosophical Writings,* V, 78, 79.
34. Ibid., 83, 85, 89, William Scolfield [William Godwin], *Bible Stories . . .* (1802), 313, 314.

them every day and sent them kisses on a fair wind from Dublin. Reporting a visit to their aunts (he loved Eliza as much as he hated Everina), he offered Fanny as the eldest her choice of their presents to the girls. After several weeks, Godwin longed to hold his daughters. "Will not Fanny be glad to see papa . . . ? Will not Mary"? He would not, he resolved, leave them again for "a long, long while."[35]

Godwin kept in touch with his mother, his siblings, and occasionally with Wollstonecraft's sisters and brothers, although Everina complained that he kept Fanny at a distance from her aunts. But his major focus was on his household of five children, only one of whom was the child of William and Mary Jane Godwin. Fanny was the oldest, followed by Charles Clairmont, Jane (Claire) Clairmont, and Mary. William Godwin, Jr., was born the year after the marriage of William and Mary Jane Godwin. Until 1811, with the exception of Charles, who was sent to the nearby Charterhouse School, the Godwin children were taught at home by a governess, Maria Smith; a tutor, Mr. Burton; and their parents. While Smith and Burton focused on geography, mathematics, and chemistry, the Godwins supervised reading and writing. The children studied the literature and history of England, Greece, Rome, Italy, and France. Above all, Godwin wanted them to cultivate their imagination. For "without imagination there can be no genuine ardour in any pursuit," no morality, no empathy. Still, Godwin later admitted that Wollstonecraft's daughters were not "brought up with an exclusive attention to the system and theories of their mother." Neither he nor Mary Jane had the leisure to reduce "novel theories of education to practice." Godwin had a much higher opinion of his "own daughter" than he did of her "quiet, modest," and indolent ("her greatest fault") sister. If Fanny was "disposed to exercise her own thoughts and follow her own judgment," Mary was "the reverse of her in many particulars. She is singularly bold, somewhat imperious and active of mind." Mary was also "very pretty," whereas Fanny was "by no means handsome."[36]

35. [Godwin] to [Anthony] Carlisle, Sept. 15, 1797, Oxford, Bodleian, MS Abinger c. 17, fol. 53, [Godwin] to James Marshall, July 11, 1800, c. 6, fols. 18–19, [Godwin] to Marshall, Aug. 6, 1800, c. 6, fols. 26–27, [Godwin] to Marshall, August 1800, c. 6, fols. 36–37. For an analysis of the infant Mary's "physiognomy," see William Nicholson to Godwin, Sept. 18, 1797, c. 3, fols. 91–92.

36. Godwin, *Enquirer,* in Philp et al., eds., *Political and Philosophical Writings,* 238–289; Everina Wollstonecraft to Godwin, July 17, 1807, Oxford, Bodleian, MS Abinger c. 10, fol. 48, Godwin to William Cole, Mar. 2, 1802, c. 7, fols. 97–98, [Godwin] to E. Fordham, Nov. 13, 1811, c. 19, fols. 32–33. Everina Wollstonecraft to Godwin, Feb. 24, 1806, c. 9, fols. 86–87, is typical of the correspondence between Godwin and his first wife's family. It deals with questions of money and the fate of siblings.

The Godwin children benefited from desultory reading in the many books accumulated by a writer and bookseller. In addition to access to their father's library, Fanny, Mary, and Claire worked from an early age in the Juvenile Library. The children read many of their father's works in manuscript, including his histories of England and Rome. As important were his books for children, including a biography of Lady Jane Grey that celebrated the breadth of her erudition. More popular, in part because Godwin used a pseudonym, were *Bible Stories* (later called *Sacred Histories*), published in 1802, and *Fables, Ancient and Modern,* which appeared in 1805. Bible stories were useful parables of human conduct. Historical tales inspired by Christianity might lead thoughtful people to question "the greater mysteries of religion." Godwin characteristically contended that children could decide for themselves about religion. He did not object to his wife's taking the children to Saint Paul's for Sunday services as long as he quizzed them about what they had heard when they returned. The popular writer Maria Edgeworth also urged parents to encourage children to think for themselves. They should grow up confident of their ability to gather information, analyze situations, and reach conclusions. Instrumental in "an innovative emphasis on the individual child's life of the mind," Edgeworth, like Godwin, hoped stories would prompt conversation rather than inculcate dogma.[37]

Godwin wanted his children to envision possibilities. In one of his many restatements of his commitment to social commerce, he asserted to a young male admirer in 1811 that the "great advantage" of a human being was the ability "to open himself" to others. "It takes away the savageness of our nature; it smooths down the ruggedness of our intellectual surface, and makes man the confederate and coadjutor of man." Too many individuals saw the world from only their limited perspective. People ought to strive for "*the religious feeling*" that acknowledges "that there may be something right which we do not comprehend, and something good that we do not perfectly see to be such." "It is built upon a sober and perfect conviction of our weakness, our ignorance, and the errors to which we are perpetually liable." Godwin insisted that his children exercise their imagination through writing as a

37. Scolfield [Godwin], *Bible Stories,* in Philp et al., eds., *Political and Philosophical Writings,* V, 315; Claire Clairmont to Edward John Trelawny, May 30 1875, in Stocking, ed., *Clairmont Correspondence,* II, 627; Mitzi Myers, "Canonical 'Orphans' and Critical *Ennui:* Rereading Edgeworth's Cross-Writing," *Children's Literature: Annual of the Modern Language Association Division on Children's Literature,* XXV (1997), 126; Clíona ÓGallchoir, "Introductory Note," in Elizabeth Eger and ÓGallchoir, eds., *The Parent's Assistant: Moral Tales for Young People,* vol. 10 of Marilyn Butler and Mitzi Myers, eds., *The Novels and Selected Works of Maria Edgeworth* (London, 2003), ix.

major means of improving themselves. In retrospect, his daughter Mary believed she did exactly that. In 1831, she recalled that her "favourite pastime" as a child had been "to 'write stories'" that she shared with a companion. None of this was surprising, given that her parents were of "distinguished literary celebrity." More "fantastic and agreeable" was her indulgence "in waking dreams." A source of "refuge," they belonged to her alone.[38]

Mary and her sisters might well have thought they needed a refuge. For all the intellectual stimulation and occasional visitors, the Godwins lived a tense life always on the edge of financial ruin. The children had a well-intentioned father who wanted to be attentive and affectionate, and often was. Godwin and Mary were particularly close, begetting a tempestuous relationship that lasted until his death in 1836. She later referred to "my excessive and romantic attachment to my father," about which she was decidedly ambivalent, as even the most cursory reading of her novels makes clear. Godwin doted on her in the extreme. Father and daughter resented rivals for each other's affection.[39]

Fanny Imlay Godwin was never one of them. Early on she seems to have realized that, although she was in the Godwin family, she would never be quite of it. Her early life had shaped her to accept marginality as a norm. Her father was an infrequent presence who completely ignored her after she was three. Her mother was volatile, to say the least. Godwin, who adopted her upon Wollstonecraft's death, was affectionate but remote. Apparently, he did not tell her about the circumstances of her birth until February 1806. A brief entry in his diary—*"Explanation w. Fanny"*—stands out in its stark contrast with usual entries about his reading, writing, and visits with friends. Less attractive and not as smart as Mary, or so we are told, Fanny gravitated toward the role of household factotum. She took responsibility for shopping and dealing with creditors and worked hard to smooth over domestic tensions. Almost no one thought Fanny happy. Coleridge observed a decided preference for "dear meek little Mary" over her older sister. The smiling child Wollstonecraft had watched in Sweden had become a gloomy girl. No wonder Charles predicted rain on her birthday.[40]

38. Godwin to Proctor Patrickson, June 20, 1811, Oxford, Bodleian, MS Abinger c. 11, fols. 35–36, Godwin to Proctor Patrickson, Apr. 1, 1812, c. 11, fols. 83–84; Mary W. Shelley, "Introduction to the *1831* Edition," in Mary Wollstonecraft Shelley (with Percy Bysshe Shelley), *Frankenstein; or, The Modern Prometheus: The Original Two-Volume Novel of 1816–1817 from the Bodleian Library Manuscripts,* ed. Charles E. Robinson (2008; rpt. New York, 2009), 437.

39. Mary Wollstonecraft Shelley to Maria Gisborne, Oct. 30–Nov. 17, [1834], in Betty T. Bennett, ed., *The Letters of Mary Wollstonecraft Shelley,* 3 vols. (Baltimore, 1980–1988), I, 215.

40. Godwin, Diary, Feb. 8, 1803, Oxford, Bodleian, MS Abinger e. 11, fols. 1–48, esp. 14; Cole-

The Godwin household was as volatile emotionally as it was financially. Fanny and especially Mary thought Mary Jane Godwin a shrew who manipulated their father. Mary Jane, for her part, had little patience with the girls' daydreams. Mary's and Fanny's relationships with their siblings were less fraught. Claire, who also disliked her mother, became a boon companion for both of her sisters. The boys were less important in their lives, perhaps because Charles was not often at home and William was so young. Under their stepmother's eye, the Godwin children behaved respectably. Aaron Burr lamented in 1808 that, although Fanny and Mary were "very fine children," they showed "scarcely a discernible trace of the mother," that "able advocate" whose *Vindication* was "a work of genius." Below the surface, however, were stirrings of rebellion nurtured by the absence of a mother they revered, a stepmother they perceived as an unimaginative tyrant, and a father who insisted on free thinking without respect to consequences.[41]

Whether by temperament or training or a blend of the two, the Godwin children grew into assertive young people who would do and think as they thought best. In many ways, they seemed more in touch with their imagination than they were with navigating through the world in which they lived. Even the Godwins were frequently nonplussed by their willful behavior. When Charles Clairmont nearly fell while wandering carelessly on a cliff, the shock caused him to confront his weakness as well as the existence of God. His subsequent conversion experience was entirely Godwinian, even if the paterfamilias himself would not cooperate. Charles wanted to start his existential exploration with Thomas Paine's *Age of Reason.* Godwin refused to send him a copy, calling it a burlesque and substituting a book by the eighteenth-century minister Anthony Collins. Charles stubbornly announced to a friend that, although he would dutifully read Collins, he would turn to Paine immediately afterward. This reaction was typical of the Godwin children. In the spirit of Fanny's and Mary's long-dead mother, they were in the habit of challenging convention, imagining possibilities, and following inquiries wherever they led.[42]

---

ridge to Godwin, May 21, 1800, in Griggs, ed., *Collected Letters of Coleridge,* I, 588, 589. See St. Clair, *Godwins and Shelleys,* 296.

41. Burr to Theodosia, Nov. 21, 1808, in Davis, ed., *Private Journal,* I, 99, Feb. 16, 1793, 363.

42. Charles Clairmont to [Thomas Turner?], [May 25, 1811?], in Stocking, ed., *Clairmont Correspondence,* I, 7.

He Who "Feels Absolutely and Exclusively for . . . Himself"

Fanny, Mary, and Claire would eventually continue their education through relationships outside their family. In the meantime, their father developed his sense of a kind of man they would likely encounter in his 1805 novel *Fleetwood; or, The New Man of Feeling*. It was not a pretty picture. Unable to engage successfully with other people, particularly women, Casimir Fleetwood suffers from the delusion that he can function effectively on his own. Privy to no perspective other than his own, he is a slave to sensibility, flailing around as he tries unsuccessfully to figure out how to behave. Looking back on his life, he regrets the misanthropy that underlay his "train of follies" and feels "inexpressible sorrow" that his sense of being "alone in the world" had fueled "perpetual disappointments." Readers of his memoir should know that he "felt what man ought to be" and kept that "model" always in his mind. His tragedy lies in his inability to become what he imagined he could be.[43]

The tragedy of *Fleetwood* the novel was that it baffled the handful of people who read it. Elizabeth Inchbald saw "a Master's hand" at work in the early chapters and praised the novel as a whole. Most readers sharply disagreed. *Fleetwood* struck them as a failed attempt to update the model of sensibility personified by Harley, the hero of Henry MacKenzie's 1771 novel *The Man of Feeling*. If a man of feeling is "generally understood a man of warm and active benevolence, whose heart is exquisitely sensible," wrote a critic, Fleetwood did not qualify. He was "a most disgusting egotist." Reviewer Walter Scott was aghast. Far from a "man of sentiment," Fleetwood was "a determined egotist" who when irritated becomes "a frantic madman." He "feels absolutely and exclusively for one individual, and that individual is himself." Godwin would have agreed with the essence of this judgment. But he tried so hard to create empathy for his deeply flawed character that he frustrated his outraged readers.[44]

43. William Godwin, *Fleetwood; or, The New Man of Feeling* (1805), ed. Gary Handwerk and A. A. Markley (Peterborough, Ont., 2001), 116; on the history of the novel, see Handwerk and Markley's "Introduction," 9–39. See also Gary Kelley, *The English Jacobin Novel, 1780–1805* (Oxford, 1976); Mona Scheuermann, "The Study of Mind: The Later Novels of William Godwin," *Forum for Modern Language Studies,* XIX (1983), 16–30; Steven Bruhm, "William Godwin's *Fleetwood:* The Epistemology of the Tortured Body," *Eighteenth-Century Life,* XVI (1992), 25–43; Pamela Clemit, *The Godwinian Novel: The Rational Fictions of Godwin, Brockden Brown, Mary Shelley* (Oxford, 1993); and Gary Handwerk, "Historical Trauma: Political Theory and Novelistic Practice in William Godwin's Fiction," *Comparative Criticism,* XVI (1994), 71–92.

44. [Inchbald] to Godwin, Mar. 1, [1805], Oxford, Bodleian, MS Abinger c. 8, fols. 104–105,

Godwin located the source of Fleetwood's failure in his education. He never becomes an adult male psychologically. The only child of a gentleman who retired to Wales upon the death of his wife, Fleetwood grows up "a solitary savage" uncomfortable with women, unfamiliar with love, and unable to manage his desire. He is a "spoiled child." The homosocial world of Oxford University reinforces his preference for immediate gratification. Lacking any core conviction, he is easily "seduced" by men "whose applauses [he] sought, whose ridicule awed [him], and whose judgment [he] looked to for the standard of [his] actions." Fleetwood then travels to Paris where he indulges in a life of sensual pleasure with a succession of aristocratic married women. Lacking true friends, he is an impulsive creature mindlessly mimicking others. "I was in Paris," he offers as explanation for his behavior, "and I did as people of fashion in Paris were accustomed to do."[45]

Rejected by his mistresses, Fleetwood leaves Paris for Switzerland. There he meets a family friend named Ruffigny, who convinces him of the antisocial character of his behavior. Traveling to England for the funeral of his father, Fleetwood realizes how destructive his behavior has become. "Woe to the man who is always busy,—hurried in a turmoil of engagements, from occupation to occupation, and with no seasons interposed, of recollection, contemplation, and repose!" he concludes in a Godwinian burst of indignation. "Such a man must inevitably be gross and vulgar, and hard and indelicate,—the sort of man with whom no generous spirit would desire to hold intercourse." But it is easier to call for better behavior in others than to practice it himself. In London, Fleetwood, reverting to form, becomes infatuated with an "alluring" woman he has no intention of marrying. Ruffigny calls the relationship a sacrifice of honor "to the tumult of the lowest passions in man." Moved by the sympathetic indictment of his "admirable monitor," Fleetwood escapes "delusion" and renounces the life of a libertine. He decides to commit himself to doing good in the world. Elected to Parliament, he is quickly disillusioned. Behaving like shopkeepers, members are men more interested in place than progress, servants of "a commercial and arithmetical nation" with an empire that empowered "contractors, directors, and upstarts." Unable to control their ambition and their

---

[Inchbald] to [Godwin], Mar. 7, [1805], c. 8, fols. 106–109; "Original Criticism: *Fleetwood, or, The New Man of Feeling,*" *Anti-Jacobin Review and Magazine,* XXI, no. 86 (August 1805), 339; Walter Scott, "Review of *Fleetwood . . . ,*" *Edinburgh Review, or Critical Journal,* VI (April 1805), 182–193, esp. 192, 193. A self-proclaimed "schoolboy" enjoyed the novel so much he wrote to Godwin to tell him so. See William Parker to Godwin, Feb. 23, 1806, Oxford, Bodleian, MS Abinger c. 9, fol. 85.

45. Godwin, *Fleetwood,* ed. Handwerk and Markley, 54, 70, 90, 100, 110.

desire, new men of feeling have distorted revolution into an orgy of selfish gratification.[46]

Well into his forties, Fleetwood at long last identifies the source of his unhappiness as his isolation. Contentment is elusive. He wanted "something," but he "knew not what." He "sought it in solitude and in crowds, in travel and at home, in ambition and in independence." If only he could find a friend, someone to assure him that he does "not stand alone in the world," a friend "who is to me as another self, who joys in all my joys, and grieves in all my sorrows, not with a joy or grief that like compliment, not with a sympathy that changes into smiles when I am not longer present." His ideal friend is male. Fleetwood thinks in terms of a brother because he distrusts women. Happily, he eventually meets some neighbors named McNeil who demonstrate the value of a happy family operating as a circle of sympathetic friends. Unhappily, McNeil encourages Fleetwood to imagine a successful marriage as a union between a man in search of a companion and a woman in need of a protector. He should court a young woman who is "all pliancy, accommodation, and good humour" so that he can "form her to [his] mind; educate her [him]self."[47]

When most of the McNeils are lost in a shipwreck, Fleetwood dutifully marries the surviving daughter, Mary. Because they are not friends, they are unable to manage the tensions in their relationship. The husband cannot see the wife as an independent actor. Nor can he imagine himself as she experiences him. Mary wants a marriage between friends, something for which Fleetwood is ill prepared. Despite her explicit submission to his authority, Mary refuses to "promise to sink [her] being and individuality in [his]." She wishes him to respect her "distinct propensities and preferences" and to win her consent "with kindness." That Fleetwood will not do. Panting "for a friend" who will give him "value in [his] own eyes," he bristles every time Mary asserts herself. Unable to comprehend how his staunch defense of his independence violates her independence, he cannot fathom why she wants "things . . . abhorrent" to him.[48]

Like all new men of feeling, Fleetwood values others only to the extent that they facilitate or frustrate his desire. Ironically, this sensibility makes him easy prey for people who would play upon his passions to get what they want. A young male relative hoping to inherit the older man's property persuades Fleetwood that Mary has been unfaithful and that he is not the

46. Ibid., 203–204, 205, 211, 212, 214, 226, 227.
47. Ibid., 223, 229–230, 254.
48. Ibid., 281, 285, 287, 311.

father of the baby in her womb. Brushing aside his wife's denials, refusing, indeed, to talk with her, Fleetwood initiates divorce proceedings and plans to declare the child illegitimate only to discover that his Iago-like relative has deceived him. A remorseful Fleetwood improbably wins Mary back, and the marriage begins again on a foundation of mutual respect. His memoir is evidence that he has learned the value of engagement with perspectives other than his own. To write "the record of my errors," he proclaims, "is the act of my penitence and humiliation." But what rational reader would bet on the permanence of his conversion?[49]

St. Leon and *Fleetwood* narrate ambiguous stories that bear more than a passing resemblance to the history of Wollstonecraft and Imlay. Marguerite and Mary are smart, competent individuals who understand the importance of enduring friendship. Women do not need to be persuaded that they will improve themselves and their world through the mutuality of romantic love. Men are the problem. St. Leon and Fleetwood are slaves to insatiable ambition, egotists acting under the delusion that they can master themselves and their worlds. St. Leon's efforts to promote progress are counterproductive; Fleetwood is so self-absorbed he barely tries. Every time each man proclaims himself transformed by love, he lapses back into the fantasy that he can manage on his own. *St. Leon* and *Fleetwood* reverse the process outlined in *Memoirs of the Author of "A Vindication of the Rights of Woman":* romantic love does not transform St. Leon and Fleetwood as it did Mary Wollstonecraft. The pain of these novels lies in the exquisite sensitivity of the two men to the consequences of their failure. Knowing all too well how they benefit from embracing women as their equals within affectionate marriages, they suffer from the curse of being unable to do so.

Godwin confounds the expectations of many readers because he suggests a historical rather than an essentialist explanation of this behavior. Defying his critics' contention that human beings are born with an intractable nature that necessitates their restraint by legal and religious institutions, Godwin suggests that St. Leon and Fleetwood have been crippled and distorted by an education that encourages the pursuit of ambition and sensuality in homosocial settings. Men trained to be egotists will act like egotists, just as women trained to be dolls will behave like dolls. Godwin indicts the nature of education, not the nature of men. Neither St. Leon nor Fleetwood exhaust the possibilities of male behavior nor invalidate the promise of mixed-gender sociability.

49. Ibid., 59.

Rather than give up on his ideas, Godwin had identified a new obstacle to their realization. He was now less worried about the state and the church enslaving human beings than about badly educated free people enslaving themselves. Until something changed, women, in particular, would have to be on alert. In a world where every stranger was a potential Ormond and every husband a potential Fleetwood, the need for social engagement was stronger than ever. Or so warned a father whose daughter Mary, educated in the spirit of her mother to assert herself and to question authority, was about to embark on one of the most famous romances of the nineteenth century with a man who proudly defined himself against society rather than within it.

9

Love's "very essence is liberty"

Their runaway romance became famous because they became famous. Percy Bysshe Shelley was twenty-one in the early summer of 1814. Although he could not have known it, he had already lived two-thirds of his life. In the eight years that remained before he drowned in a storm off the coast of Italy, he would write some of the most celebrated poems in the English language. Sixteen-year-old Mary Godwin would survive her husband by twenty-nine years. A professional writer whose novels mimicked, commented on, and revised the forms and content of her parents' works, Mary was best known, until recently, as the author of *Frankenstein* and the steward of her husband's reputation. Percy was not widely appreciated until later in the nineteenth century. Controversial in life, he became a signature Romantic artist in death: a creative genius whose transcendent poetry excused, if it did not depend upon, unconventional behavior, an iconoclastic rebel who refused to kowtow to social expectations.[1]

---

1. I use the first names of the younger generation in this chapter so that readers can keep the players straight. I have also called Mary Jane Godwin's daughter, Mary Jane Clairmont—known as Jane in her youth—Claire, the name she adopted as an adult. My narrative bears the influence of many other writers. See, especially, Richard Holmes, *Shelley: The Pursuit* (1974; rpt. New York, 1994); William St. Clair, *The Godwins and the Shelleys: The Biography of a Family* (New York, 1989); Emily W. Sunstein, *Mary Shelley: Romance and Reality* (Baltimore, 1989); Robert Gittings and Jo Manton, *Claire Clairmont and the Shelleys, 1798–1879* (New York, 1992); Miranda Seymour, *Mary Shelley* (London, 2000); James Bieri, *Percy Bysshe Shelley*, 2 vols. (Newark, Del., 2004–2005); Janet Todd, *Death and the Maidens: Fanny Wollstonecraft and the Shelley Circle* (Berkeley, Calif., 2007); and Daisy Hay, *Young Romantics: The Tangled Lives of English Poetry's Greatest Generation* (New York, 2010).

In 1814, however, Mary and Percy's affair was neither unique nor as straightforward as it appears in retrospect. It was only one of multiple liaisons involving disciples and children of Mary Wollstonecraft and William Godwin. In reprising the romance of Wollstonecraft and Gilbert Imlay or the romance of Imlay with the unknown woman for whom he left Wollstonecraft, Percy and Mary thought they were honoring the legacy of her parents. They were wrong, and they were right, sometimes simultaneously. Unlike Wollstonecraft and Godwin, Mary and Percy celebrated love as rare, fleeting, and available only to sensitive souls like them. More important, they seemed, at least initially, to make love a source of authority in and of itself. Shocked by the impact of their choices on friends and relatives, they were mystified by the misery and anger they provoked. Surely they were free to act as they thought best for themselves. The dominion of the imagination made anything possible, any liaison discussable, any desire plausible. But the defiant young lovers were also thoughtful people who reflected on what they were doing and how people were reacting to them, adapting to others' expectations more than their collective reputation suggests. Eventually, they, too, confronted the conundrum highlighted in the 1790s: the more individuals exercised their freedom, the more they restricted the freedom not only of others but of themselves.

To those who would think through the logic of revolution, Wollstonecraft's and Godwin's writings provided more questions than answers. Their personal lives charted erratic courses that too often slipped into misery, confusion, and dead ends. But they also delineated a strategy of long-term progress in their celebration of the possibilities of mixed-gender sociability. Wollstonecraft and Godwin were nothing if not remarkably persistent. Refusing to succumb to despair about the human condition, they insisted that human beings in conversation with one another could eventually make the world a better place. Mary, Percy, and their friends and relatives initially struggled to come to terms with a parental (and cultural) legacy that amounted to more than a defiance of patriarchal power. Unmediated individual authority was counterproductive, they learned; that wanton, the imagination, created prisons as well as nurtured possibilities. Like the older generation, the younger generation made mistakes, contradicted themselves, and wounded others. In the end, they neither fulfilled nor repudiated the radicalism of the 1790s so much as they entered into a continuing conversation. To love, Mary at least eventually concluded, was not to enjoy a state of perpetual bliss; it was to engage in negotiating and renegotiating the unstable borders of imagination and reason, desire and responsibility, self and society. It was to celebrate a paradox: personal happiness depended, not on defying authority and asserting desire, but on constructing authority and tempering desire in collaboration with friends and family. The more individuals located themselves within webs of personal relationships, the more they considered not just what they wanted but also what others wanted, the more likely they were to find the satisfaction they craved.

Living "the Godwinian Plan"

Mary Wollstonecraft's daughters were unhappy as they grew older. Family circumstances exacerbated their predisposition to melancholy. Their father's obsession with his career intensified his emotional distance and reinforced his reluctance to challenge his wife's management of their household. Mary Jane's relationships with Fanny and Mary deteriorated into cold pragmatism punctuated by occasional outbursts on all sides. Perhaps because Godwin frequently remarked on his particular attachment to Mary, stepmother and stepdaughter struggled to control their resentment of each other. Godwin later protested that he had done well by "the children, with whom I have voluntarily, or by the laws of society, been concerned." In them, he had sown "seeds of intellect and knowledge, seeds of moral judgement and conduct." If they seemed ungrateful on occasion, Godwin believed that at "the moment, when it was of the most importance, they unfolded themselves to the delight of every beholder."[2]

In early summer 1812, Godwin accepted an arranged invitation from his friend William Thomas Baxter for Mary to spend time with his family in Dundee, Scotland. Stepbrother Charles was already working for Archibald Constable's publishing firm in Edinburgh. Mary was eager to go. Her health was not good. Nor was her relationship with Mary Jane Godwin. Her stepmother wanted to get Mary out of the family bookstore where, except for a brief 1811 sojourn at Miss Petman's Ladies School in Ramsgate, Kent, she spent much of her time clerking. Mary arrived in Scotland in June. Godwin hoped the change in environment would rejuvenate her spirits and strengthen her character. Mary spent the majority of the next two years in the Scottish countryside reading books and exercising her imagination on long walks. Communing "with the creatures of my fancy," she conjured

---

2. William Godwin to Percy Bysshe Shelley (PBS), Mar. 30, 1812, in Mark Philp et al., eds., *The Collected Novels and Memoirs of William Godwin*, 8 vols. (London, 1992), I, 77. See Katherine C. Hill-Miller, *"My Hideous Progeny": Mary Shelley, William Godwin, and the Father-Daughter Relationship* (Newark, Del., 1995).

all kinds of possibilities far from crowded London and the tense Godwin household. She returned home in the spring of 1814 a more confident young woman. Her father was happy to see her. So, too, was his new friend, Percy Bysshe Shelley, an ardent disciple of her parents and the husband of Harriet Westbrook.[3]

More than half a century later, Claire Clairmont, Mary's stepsister, re-called Percy's fine lips and beautiful forehead, his small shoulders and long legs, and his high, childlike voice. No less memorable was his charisma. Percy treated his interlocutors, women as well as men, with respect, invit-ing everyone to join in rambling conversations about any and all subjects. Mary shared Percy's fondness for ruminating on intractable problems. Many of her acquaintances thought her "reserved," as cold as her father. Not Percy. He saw the "wildness and sublimity of her feelings," an ability to be "pathetic" and "gentle" as well as capable "of ardent indignation and hatred." Mary's blend of intelligence and sensibility, defiance and vulnera-bility inspired "an ardent passion to posess [sic] this inestimable treasure."[4]

Born on August 4, 1792, the year before Wollstonecraft met Imlay, Percy was the oldest son of a minor baronet and his wife. Educated at home and at Eton and Oxford, Percy required stimulation. School was a "prison." At fifteen he devoted dull winter days to reading "Novels and Romances" until he imagined himself "a Character." He delighted in being "the wild-est, most delirious of enthusiasm's offspring." His hatred of orthodoxy led him to write a pamphlet attacking Christianity that got him sent down from Oxford. Percy antagonized his father and lost most of his living by marry-ing his cousin Harriet Westbrook, despite his denunciation of the institu-tion. He then toyed with revolution in Ireland, wrote poems, made and lost

3. Mary Wollstonecraft Shelley (MWS), "Appendix C: Introduction to the *1831* Edition," in MWS (with PBS), *Frankenstein; or, The Modern Prometheus: The Original Two-Volume Novel of 1816–1817 from the Bodleian Library Manuscripts,* ed. Charles E. Robinson (2008; rpt. New York, 2009), 438. See MWS to Maria Gisborne, Oct. 30–Nov. 17, [1834], in Betty T. Bennett, ed., *The Letters of Mary Wollstonecraft Shelley,* 3 vols. (Baltimore, 1980–1988), II, 215; Godwin to [William Thomas] Baxter, June 8, 1812, in Mrs. Julian Marshall, *The Life and Letters of Mary Wollstonecraft Shelley,* 2 vols. (London, 1889), I, 29.

4. Claire Clairmont to Edward John Trelawny, Aug. 30, 1875, in Marion Kingston Stocking, ed., *The Clairmont Correspondence: Letters of Claire Clairmont, Charles Clairmont, and Fanny Imlay Godwin,* 2 vols. (Baltimore, 1995), II, 631; Paula R. Feldman and Diana Scott-Kilvert, eds., "Introduction," in *The Journals of Mary Shelley, 1814–1844,* 2 vols. (Oxford, 1987), I, xv; PBS to Thomas Jefferson Hogg, Oct. 3 [for 4], 1814, in Frederick L. Jones, ed., *The Letters of Percy Bysshe Shelley,* 2 vols. (Oxford, 1964), I, 402, 403. See "Edward Augustus Silsbee," in Stocking, ed., *Clair-mont Correspondence,* II, 657.

Figure 12. Percy Bysshe Shelley. *By Amelia Curran. Oil on canvas, 1819.*
© *National Portrait Gallery, London*

friends, and lived on the edge of ruin—all before he was twenty-one. Eventually dismissing "general reform" as "impracticable," Percy decided that
"human nature taken in the mass . . . is corrupt beyond all hope." Even personal conversion was available only to a limited number of men "capable of
exalted notions of virtue" who felt "the passions of soft tenderness *the object
of whose regard is distinct from* selfish desire." Percy rejected the notion that
a "world which wallows in selfishness and every hateful passion" should re-

strict "superior" "souls." Setting himself and his peers apart, Percy asserted his right to act "in noble violation of the laws of a prejudiced society."[5]

Stunned to learn in early 1812 that William Godwin was still alive, Percy proposed a friendship. With characteristic hyperbole, he exclaimed that the writings of Godwin, "a luminary too dazzling for the darkness which surrounds him," had helped him cultivate a refined sensibility. *Political Justice* had "materially influenced my character." He "rose from its perusal a wiser and a better man" aware that he "had duties to perform" in a world in which there "was enough to excite the interest of the heart, enough to employ the discussions of Reason." Now happily "married to a woman whose views are similar to my own," Percy had resolved "to lose no opportunity to disseminate truth and happiness." To that end, he was drafting "'an inquiry into the causes of the failure of the French revolution to benefit mankind.'" Would Godwin consent to become his mentor? Percy wanted to learn from a "veteran in persecution and independence." Godwin, as unsettled as he was flattered by his correspondent's enthusiasm, was wary. But Percy would not countenance caution. He could not wait to talk at length. The more open-ended their commerce, the more salutary it would be for both of them. They should have no set agenda. Topics ought to emerge from conversation, assuming "a definite form in consequence of the method that grows out of the induced train of thought."[6]

Young Percy wanted Godwin to know that he saw an embrace of love as an expression of individual freedom. He had fallen in love with Harriet in part because she was an "isolated and friendless" victim of a "system of domestic oppressions." Now she was his partner in "thoughts and feelings." In the summer of 1811, he had urged her to stand up to her father and run off with him. When his small inheritance was exhausted, they would depend "upon love." Harriet balked, and Percy had agreed to marry her. The institution, he explained to Godwin in a rationale familiar to the older man, accorded women a necessary degree of legal protection. His decision to marry Harriet, however, did not compromise his commitment to the power of love, which, he explained in his notes to *Queen Mab: A Philosophical Poem* (1813), was an expression of the right to think, feel, and act without reference to anyone else. Love "withers under constraint; its very essence

5. PBS to Hogg, Dec. 20, 1810, in Jones, ed., *Letters of Shelley*, I, 28, 29, May 9, 1811, 81, May 12, 1811, 83, to James T. T. Tisdall, Jan. 10, 1808, 2.

6. PBS to Godwin, Jan. 3, 1811 [1812], ibid., 220, Jan. 10, 1812, 227, 228, 229, Jan. 16, 1812, 229, to Elizabeth Hitchener, Jan. 16, 1812, 232, to Godwin, Jan. 26, 1812, 241, Feb. 24, 1812, 259. On Godwin, see PBS to Hitchener, Jan. 7, 1812, 221.

is liberty: it is compatible neither with obedience, jealousy, nor fear." Love was dynamic because lovers changed their minds. "Love is free." Percy proclaimed, "To promise for ever to love the same woman" was as "absurd" as "to promise to believe the same creed." No one should be persecuted for following his heart. Thus, the abolition of marriage would "be natural and right, because choice and change will be exempted from restraint." The perspective echoed Wollstonecraft, Imlay, and Godwin. But Percy diverged in his insistence that love was sensibility unmediated by social engagement. He would act on his own authority.[7]

Percy did not believe that everyone should—or could—behave as he did. When he did not like the choices others made, he saw the value of tempering internal authority through conversation with friends. He did not react well when Thomas Jefferson Hogg announced he was in love with Percy's sister, a woman he had never met her and would see just once in his life. Born in 1792, Hogg had met Percy at Oxford and left the university when his friend was expelled. Preparing for a legal career, Hogg lived off and on with Percy, even after the latter's marriage. His sexual attraction to virtually every woman associated with Percy suggests the depth of his romantic attachment to his friend.[8]

Percy reacted to Hogg's declaration of love for his sister by invoking the power of reason. He would help his friend see the folly of acting on raw desire. Reason was a process of thinking through the consequences of an uncritical acceptance of possibilities conjured by the imagination. Percy warned Hogg that a "thousand barriers oppose any more intimate connexion, barriers which altho unnatural and fettering to the virtuous mind, are nevertheless unconquerable." Yes, agony was the "too constant attendant" of love, a state of being that flourished "independent of volition." Human beings inevitably suffered from "the despair which springs from disappointed hope." That was why friendship mattered. Social intercourse offered more than consolation. An exchange of perspectives was the essence of reason, the means by which free men (and women) worked

7. PBS to Godwin, Jan. 26, 1812, ibid., 242, to Hogg, Aug. 3, 1811, 131, Aug. 15, 1811, 135; PBS, "May 1813: To Harriet," in Donald H. Reiman and Neil Fraistat, eds., *The Complete Poetry of Percy Bysshe Shelley*, 2 vols. (Baltimore, 2000–2004), I, 154, PBS, "Note 9 [to *Queen Mab*]," II, 251, 252, 253, 254, 255.

8. Thomas Jefferson Hogg, *The Memoirs of Prince Alexy Haimatoff* (1813) (London, 1952), is suggestive about Hogg's sensibility with regard to love and sexuality. More generally, see Sharon Marcus, *Between Women: Friendship, Desire, and Marriage in Victorian England* (Princeton, N.J., 2007); Judith Butler, "Is Kinship Always Already Heterosexual?" *Differences: A Journal of Feminist Cultural Studies*, XIII, no. 1 (Spring 2002), 14–44.

through the challenge of seeing how their exercise of liberty constituted tyranny for another, even someone they loved. Once Hogg accepted that his attachment to Percy's sister was "an idea in your own mind which had no real existence," he would become himself again. Percy confessed that he often indulged similar madness, only to realize that he was happy honoring *"reason,* exerted . . . under discouraging circumstances."[9]

Elizabeth Hitchener, a twenty-nine-year-old woman supporting herself as a teacher, might well have disputed that claim. Welcoming friendship with Percy, she was taken aback by his unbridled enthusiasm. She declined Percy's invitation to live with him, Harriet, and Hogg, even though he was "the Brother of my soul." Percy insisted his interest was entirely platonic. Yet he also admitted that his passion was making it difficult to control his body. He would not give her up no matter what the "world might demand." Their relationship was more than a transitory sensation. Trying to reconcile what he was feeling for Hitchener with his advice to Hogg, Percy argued that love was not "a *ball* an *apple* a *plaything* which must be taken from one to be given to another." True love was disinterested. It was a "friend- ship" that sought "the good of all" by choice. It promoted "the happiness of others *not* from the obligation of fearing Hell or desiring Heaven, but for pure simple unsophisticated Virtue." Harriet laughed at Hitchener's scruples, or so Percy said. With Hitchener, he told Hogg, "passion [was] preferable to reason," or at least "the great, aspiring Passions of disinter- ested friendship, Philanthropy." She, like he, would maintain her "individu- ality, reason for [her]self, *compare* and *discuss*" with him. Although Percy eventually persuaded Hitchener to join the household, the arrangement disintegrated quickly. The Harriet who spoke for herself rather than the one Percy imagined was no more excited by the arrival of her husband's friend than Fuseli's wife had been by Wollstonecraft's similar proposal. As the tri- angle fell apart, another one emerged. Percy assumed Harriet's proposed role: a lover asked to tolerate a lover's intimacy with another person.[10]

Thomas Jefferson Hogg had decided he was in love with Harriet. Rebuff- ing his advance, she delayed several days before telling her husband about the incident. Percy was deeply shaken. In principle, he celebrated the close bond between his wife and his friend. In practice, he was profoundly dis- turbed. Unable to forbid love, he reminded Hogg of his failure to consider

9. PBS to Hogg, Dec. 23, 1810, in Jones, ed., *Letters of Shelley,* I, 29–30, Dec. 28, 1810, 33, Jan. 1, 1811, 34, December [for Jan.] 3, 1811, 36, Apr. 26, 1811, 68, June 2, 1811, 94, 95, June 23, 1811, 113.

10. PBS to Hitchener, June 11, 1811, ibid., 99, Oct. 8, 1811, 144, Hitchener to PBS, Oct. 11, 1811, 145n, PBS to Hitchener, Nov. 11, 1811, 173, Nov. 14, 1811, 182, 183, Nov. 23, 1811, 188, 189, 190.

the impact of his action. If Hogg, a man with a gaze so transfixing that Percy had "fancied the world could be reformed by gazing too," could behave so selfishly, then anyone could. But what was so selfish about falling in love anyway? Was it a rational choice? Could it be controlled? Attributing Hogg's attempted seduction of his wife to "self-centred, self-possessing" "vanity," Percy admitted his jealousy was just as self-absorbed and tinged with self-pity to boot. Mixing empathy with petulance he demanded to know why he should suffer so that Hogg could enjoy his freedom. "Stand you alone preeminent in suffering. . . . And what am I?—nothing! a speck in an Universe." Like Wollstonecraft with Imlay, Percy warned Hogg he was "*not* him whom I love." "Become yourself," he repeated. "Bear pain." They could help each other if they talked honestly. "Dearest, dearest friend, reason with me." Percy advocated to his friend what Wollstonecraft and Godwin had advocated to each other: to sustain the strength they have as a couple—a strength that they could never muster as isolated individuals—and to see love as a means of negotiating mutuality. Their intense friendship would buttress rather than threaten their separate relationships with Harriet.[11]

And what did Harriet want? Percy professed respect for her opinion, at least in part as a means of dissuading Hogg, although he described her refusal as an expression of narrow prejudice. He would have it both ways. He could accept Hogg's "possession of Harriet's person, or the attainment of her love." But his wife "does not think so," and therefore it would not happen. The dynamics of a male friendship flirting with the homoerotic thus ironically protected a marriage and elevated a wife to a position of equal power within a triad of lovers. "If *she* was convinced of [the] innocence [of Hogg's proposal], would I be so sottish a slave to opinion as to endeavour to monopolize what if participated would give my friend pleasure without diminishing my own?" Empowering a wife—"on her opinions of right and wrong alone does the morality of the present case depend"—was convenient for a husband eager to retain sole possession of her body. Her would-be lover risked making a fool of himself by pining over her refusal. Hogg was surrendering to the "wildest reveries of ungratified desire." He had become "the sport of a womans whim." "Assert yourself," Percy urged, "be what you were[.] Love[.] Adore!" Above all, Hogg should regain control of himself. Do "not love one who *cannot* return it, who if she *could ought* to stifle her desire to do so—Love is not a whirlwind that it is unvanguishable." Man-

11. PBS to Hogg, Nov. 6, 1811, ibid., 167, Hitchener to PBS, Nov. 12, 1811, 170n, PBS to Hogg, [circa Nov. 10, 1811], 171, 172. On the ways in which same-sex intimacy complemented heterosexual relationships, and vice versa, see Marcus, *Between Women*.

aging desire was a display of masculine fortitude achieved through social commerce with other men.[12]

In a larger sense, conversations that created scenarios about love and its consequences enacted the disruptive force of individual authority legitimized by revolution. The problem was that the exercise of individual liberty so frequently came at the expense of someone else's liberty. Wollstonecraft and company had argued that the most viable solution to this dilemma lay in mutuality developed through rational affection and social commerce. Percy and company sought to implement these principles. In a "terrible world where Nature seems to own no monster in her works but man!" Percy could offer no hope save "the Godwinian plan." Institutions that coerced human beings perverted human connections. What would we think of laws to "compel" us to listen to certain music or to be friends with "a particular person?" "Liberty [was] the very soul of friendship." More and more, Percy followed Godwin: "to discuss, to be skeptical," to introduce "Virtue to Usefulness."[13]

No wonder Percy was delighted that Godwin accepted his offer of friendship. Ignored, depressed, and beset by financial woes, Godwin welcomed someone eager to join him in venerating free "discussion, reading, inquiry, perpetual communication" as the best "methods for the improvement of mankind." The relationship proved to be one of the most complicated of Godwin's life. Indeed, identifying exactly who held the upper hand was difficult. Percy arranged to loan Godwin £2,240 borrowed against his inheritance to revive the struggling M. J. Godwin and Company. In July 1814, however, he delivered only half the promised amount. He had to reserve the other half, he informed Godwin. Percy was leaving his wife to take up with his mentor's daughter. He and Mary Godwin had fallen in love. Courting beside the grave of her mother and reading books written by her parents, they were blissfully unaware that they were provoking a cultural as well as a domestic crisis. Percy and Mary, it seemed, had abandoned reason for the pleasures of the imagination.[14]

"Our Own Perceptions Are the World"

The romance of Godwin and Wollstonecraft's child and disciple reflected the impact of individual will unleashed during the time of revolution. Claire

12. PBS to Hogg, [circa Nov. 16, 1811], in Jones, ed., *Letters of Shelley*, I, 184, [circa Nov. 12, 1811], 175, 176, Nov. 14, 1811, 178, 179, 180, 181.

13. PBS to Hogg, [circa Nov. 16, 1811], ibid., 184, to Hitchener, Nov. 26, 1811, 194, 195.

14. Godwin to PBS, Mar. 4, 1812, ibid., 261n.

retrospectively constructed Mary's romance with Percy as a tale of a reluctant innocent overwhelmed by a desperate man. She claimed that in late June 1814, when the sisters ran into Harriet in Chapel Street, Mary assured Percy's wife that "she would not yield to Shelley's entreaties." When she did yield, shortly thereafter, it was only because Percy threatened suicide if she declined to become the "Partner of his Life." Harriet told a different story. Mary, she complained to a friend, was "to blame." "She heated his imagination by talking of her mother, and going to her grave with him every day, till at last she told him she was dying in love for him, accompanied with the most violent gestures and vehement expostulations." Percy accepted Mary's proposition that the three of them live together, "I [Harriet] as his sister, she as his wife." Percy "has become profligate and sensual, owing entirely to Godwin's *Political Justice*." The father had provided a rationale, and the daughter had engineered the seduction. Harriet believed she had helped her husband strengthen his character—and he hers—through mutual exchange. Mary, on the other hand, had destroyed Percy. Encouraging him to indulge his imagination, she had demonstrated herself an unfit partner by making her lover into an antisocial egotist. The man Harriet "once loved is dead." "This is a vampire. His character is blasted for ever. Nothing can save him now." Percy and Mary had become what critics of Modern Philosophy had feared: individuals who acted solely on their own authority. From Harriet's perspective, they were monsters, heartless creatures whose lack of sympathy was unnatural and fearful.[15]

Mary thought the reverse, of course. Godwin had raised the daughter of Wollstonecraft to speak her mind and to follow her heart. Mary and Percy were in love. To hide or deny their feelings was unmanly, unreasonable, and irresponsible. Others simply had to understand the logic of their passion. The first Shelley marriage was a fragile union that could not survive Percy's withdrawal. A relationship in which only one person loved or wanted love was a shell of what it might once have been, amounting to form without substance, a connection that satisfied neither partner and caused the world more harm than good. On June 26, shortly after meeting Harriet, Mary told Percy she loved him, announcing her decision on the grave of her mother outside Saint Pancras Church. It was, Percy wrote, a "sublime and rapturous moment when she confessed herself mine." Believing that Harriet shared

15. Clairmont to Edward John Trelawny, [April 1871?], in Stocking, ed., *Clairmont Correspondence*, II, 615; Harriet Westbrook Shelley to Catherine Nugent, Nov. 20, [1814], in Jones, ed., *Letters of Shelley*, I, 421n.

what Percy later called the "pure and liberal principles of which [she] used to boast that [she was] a disciple," Mary and Percy assumed that she would accept their relationship.[16]

On July 13 or 14, Percy informed Harriet in an exhausting "interview" that he was leaving her, all the while insisting that he and Mary were above reproach. A "violent and lasting passion for another leads me to prefer her society to yours," he later explained. There was no way he and Mary could "overcome" their "attachments." Percy worried that "the shock might inflict" on Harriet "some incurable unhappiness." He was therefore grateful for her "assurances" that it had not. He wanted her understanding, if not her explicit consent. "I repeat (and believe me, for I am sincere) that my attachment to you is unimpaired. . . . Friendship was its basis, and on this basis it has enlarged and strengthened." He hoped that she would "find a lover as passionate and faithful, as I shall ever be a friend affectionate and sincere." Perhaps Harriet might even muster some compassion for Mary, who suffered from "tyranny," presumably the disapproval of her father and stepmother. Harriet's equanimity was temporary, and she would soon experience a profound sense of injury. William and Mary Jane Godwin, on the other hand, refused to countenance the relationship from the start.[17]

Baffled and hurt, Percy and Mary ran away. A sympathetic Claire accompanied them. Leaving the Godwin house on Skinner Street before the sun had risen on the morning of July 28 was a sublime experience. As four horses pulled their carriage toward Dover, they thrilled to the "danger" and the "terror" of their expedition. Percy and Mary fretted over every minor separation. Time spent eating, hiring a boat, and talking over plans was time wasted. By evening, they had reached the Channel and arranged passage to Calais. It was a rough crossing. Squalls tossed their vessel about as lightning lit up the dark skies. A seasick Mary rested quietly between Percy's knees while he "had time in that moment to reflect and even to reason upon death," anxious that the storm might threaten their happiness. As morning at last arrived, Percy awakened his lover: "Mary look. the sun rises over France." Safely on the Continent, the couple secured rooms in an inn. "Mary was there," wrote Percy later that day. "Shelley was also with me," added Mary. Later that day, Mary Jane, who had pursued the lovers, arrived in Calais. Claire prevailed upon her mother to return to London. Soon

16. PBS to Hogg, Oct. 3 [4], 1814, in Jones, ed., *Letters of Shelley,* I, 402, 403, to Harriet Westbrook Shelley, Sept. 26, 1814, 397.

17. PBS to Harriet Westbrook Shelley, Sept. 15, 1814, ibid., 394, 395, July 14, 1814, 389, 390.

thereafter, Percy, Mary, and Claire departed for Paris, arriving in the French capital on August 2.[18]

Twenty-one years earlier, Mary Wollstonecraft and Gilbert Imlay had met and fallen in love in the same city in a similar whirlwind romance. Paris was then the epicenter of revolution, bursting with plots and plans and possibilities; now, drained of energy, it was suffused with the somber stillness of surrender. In March, the allies arrayed against France had occupied Paris. A month later, the Treaty of Fontainebleau had sent Emperor Napoleon Bonaparte into exile on the island of Elba and made Louis XVIII king of France. Low on funds, Percy, Mary, and Claire toured the Louvre and Notre Dame; tried unsuccessfully to locate potential allies, including Wollstonecraft's old friend, Helena Maria Williams; and fended off con men patrolling the streets of Paris like vultures hovering over choice carrion. Percy and Mary, insisting that "love would alone suffice to resist the invasions of calamity," were "prisoners in Paris," the home of the wounded soldiers, grasping aristocrats, and scheming parvenus that would populate Honoré de Balzac's *La Comédie Humaine*.[19]

More than Paris had changed since 1793. Mary and Percy were less interested in love as a means of transforming the world than as a way of surviving a world transformed by war. Turning their gaze inward, they sought comfort in small circles of friends. Percy had once explained to Hogg that reason was managing the imagination's ability to conjure possibilities. Social commerce helped individuals negotiate the elusive border between liberty and license. But reason could scarcely function when love affirmed rather than monitored personal authority. Taking refuge in their shared passion, the lovers were indifferent to what others thought. What mattered was what they felt. Their "own perceptions" were "the world," wrote Percy. This intoxicating notion revised the older generation's notions about love as a social activity that changed individuals through empathy. Love was now an enthusiasm that separated lovers from society.[20]

Abandoning Paris after a week's residence, Mary, Percy, and Claire set their sights on Switzerland, more specifically, the town of Uri on Lake Lucerne. A remote location in the mountains offered an ideal setting for their exercise of liberty. Wollstonecraft had canceled a trip to Switzerland in the summer of 1793 in order to be with Imlay. Now in the company of her lover and half-sister, her daughter rode a mule across France toward

---

18. July 28 and 29, 1814, in Feldman and Scott-Kilvert, eds., *Journals of Mary Shelley*, I, 6, 7.
19. Aug. 7, 1814, ibid., 11.
20. Aug. 3, 1814, ibid., 9.

a Swiss oasis. But where the travelers imagined serenity, they found anarchy. The countryside was even more dangerous than Paris. The trio journeyed through a region recently overrun by invading Russian and Austrian troops. Cultivated areas around the capital soon gave way to scenes of destruction. In one town, the "houses were redu[c]ed to heaps of white ruins, and the bridge was destroyed." Fields lacked crops, an ominous sight in late summer. One night they slept in a "wretched" hovel, ate "sour bread," and mingled with dirty, stinking people. Rats scurrying about the bed kept Claire awake. Even more alarming was the eagerness of their host to have sex with her; only Percy's shouted threats dissuaded him. The next day the road was no safer. They met a man who claimed Russians had murdered one of his children.[21]

Percy wrote to Harriet that, although they had not seen any of the thieves Parisians had warned them about, they had encountered "frightful desolation." War had produced "filth, misery and famine everywhere." Not even the "inhospitable and unaccomodating" inhabitants deserved such an awful fate. Keeping to themselves, they shared books, conversation, and admiration for the shifting landscape. Mary and Percy had sex regularly (she was pregnant by October). Sometimes they even forgot that they "were in France or in the world." Mary's mother was much on her mind. At Mort, perched on some rocks, the couple read Wollstonecraft's *Mary.* By the end of the year, Mary had also perused Wollstonecraft's letters from Scandinavia, her history of the French Revolution, and *Maria; or, The Wrongs of Woman* as well as her father's *Caleb Williams* and *Political Justice.* Also on the list were Voltaire's *Candide* and Charles Brockden Brown's *Edgar Huntly.* In addition to composing letters, the couple kept a joint journal, largely a report of their daily activities. Percy would drop out of the collaboration over the next year, and Mary's entries became more introspective. But the joint record embodied their general union. In Lucerne, they leased a house for six months. Shortly thereafter, reality intruded. Short of money and aware that sooner or later they would have to deal with the anger and pain their happiness had created, they decided to go home. In late August, they took a boat to Cologne, traveled overland to Rotterdam, and secured passage to London. Arriving on the evening of September 13, they took lodgings at the Stratford Hotel in Oxford Street.[22]

21. Aug. 11, 1814, ibid., 12, Aug. 12, 1814, 13. On the condition of postwar Europe, see Michael O'Brien, *Mrs. Adams in Winter: A Journey in the Last Days of Napoleon* (New York, 2010).

22. PBS to Harriet Westbrook Shelley, Aug. 13, 1814, in Jones, ed., *Letters of Shelley,* I, 392; Aug. 14, 1814, in Feldman and Scott-Kilvert, eds., *Journals of Mary Shelley,* I, 14, Aug. 16, 1814,

Percy and Mary celebrated their love as a turning point in their personal histories. Percy was a new man. He was "wonderfully . . . changed." He was happy. "Not a disembodied spirit can have undergone a stranger revolution!" wrote Percy. "Contentment" was no longer an "unmeaning abstraction." He now considered himself "as an whole accurately united rather than an assemblage of inconsistent and discordant portions." He was "deeply persuaded that thus ennobled, [he would] become a more true and constant friend, a more useful lover of mankind, a more ardent asserter of truth and virtue—above all more consistent, more intelligible more true." All this happiness flowed from engagement with his lover. Away from Mary, he felt "a solitariness and a desolation of heart." For her part, Mary reveled in the quotidian. Weeks of separation necessitated by Percy's need to hide to avoid debtor's prison were almost unbearable. Daily meetings only intensified her longing. She lived to see him. That was "the hope that" carried her "through the day." Longing for him to "press" her to him and hug his "own Mary to [his] heart," she protested the "dreary life" of "a poor widowed deserted thing no one cares for." "Ah love is not that enough?" she wondered. Until her father accepted them, her lover must "be every thing" to her. They had no one but each other.[23]

A Circle of Monsters

Suddenly Mary, Percy, and Claire no longer recognized William and Mary Jane Godwin and Harriet. The latter, in turn, no longer seemed to know Mary, Percy, and Claire. Mary and Percy thought their families and friends "selfish and unfeeling." Harriet and the Godwins entertained roughly the same opinion of Mary and Percy. Everyone thought everyone was behaving like Fleetwood, isolating themselves and surrendering to sensibility. No one was being reasonable, meaning no one was engaging, considering alternative perspectives, or mediating their perceptions through conversation.[24]

15; Mary Jean Corbett, "Reading Mary Shelley's *Journals:* Romantic Subjectivity and Feminist Criticism," in Audrey A. Fisch, Anne K. Mellor, and Esther H. Schor, eds., *The Other Mary Shelley: Beyond Frankenstein* (New York, 1993), 74, 78–79. See Eleanor Sickels, "Shelley and Charles Brockden Brown," *PMLA*, XLV (1930), 1116–1128.

23. PBS to Hogg, Oct. 3 [4], 1814, in Jones, ed., *Letters of Shelley*, I, 402, 403, to Mary Godwin, Oct. 24, 1814, 407; Feldman and Scott-Kilvert, "Introduction," in Feldman and Scott-Kilvert, eds., *Journals of Mary Shelley*, I, xvii; Mary Godwin to PBS, Oct. 28, 1814, in Bennett, ed., *Letters of Mary Wollstonecraft Shelley*, I, 1.

24. Mary Godwin to PBS, Nov. 3, 1814, in Bennett, ed., *Letters of Mary Wollstonecraft Shelley,* I, 4.

Harriet took a while to get angry with her husband and his new lover. Once she recovered from the initial shock, she flew into a rage. In September, when Mary and Percy returned to London, Harriet reproached him severely for deserting her and their one-year-old child, Eliza Ianthe. Percy had blamed the end of his marriage on a mutual cooling of interest that had started a year earlier. Some evidence to the contrary arrived at the end of November 1814 when Harriet gave birth to a son, Charles Bysshe Shelley. Percy visited mother and son as soon as he heard the news, according to Harriet, albeit without any of his former "tenderness." He was happy to have a boy, she bitterly explained, because boys were cheaper. See "how the noble soul is debased. Money now, not philosophy, is the grand spring of his actions." The author of *St. Leon* could not have said it better.[25]

Stunned by Harriet's rage, Percy pronounced himself wounded "with reproach and blame." He had tried to behave responsibly. He had told her about Mary; he had promised friendship and support; he had written to her from France and Switzerland. And now she was angry because "a violent and lasting passion for another leads me to prefer her society to yours"? It was impossible for him and Mary to "overcome" their "attachment." He had been "an idiot to expect greatness or generosity" from Harriet. So much for all their reading and talking! "The pure and liberal principles of which you used to boast that you were a disciple, served only for display," he exclaimed. She had become an ungrateful monster seeking "to injure an innocent man struggling with distress."[26]

Percy would not apologize for his relationship with Mary. Only she "waken[ed]" his thoughts "to energy." His mind without hers was "dead and cold as the dark midnight river when the moon is down." She shielded him from "impurity and vice." Without her company, he would "shudder with horror" at himself, for his "understanding" became "undisciplined" without her. The love of Percy and Mary fulfilled, at least in their minds, all the expectations of a culture of mixed-gender social commerce. But their relationship seemed less like rational friendship between two independent individuals than a total subordination of self to a grand passion. "How divinely sweet a task it is to imitate each others excellencies—and each moment to become wiser in this surpassing love—so that constituting but one being, all real knowledge may be comprised in the maxim γνωθι σεαντον (know thyself) with infinitely more justice than in its narrow and common

25. Harriet Westbrook Shelley to Mrs. Nugent, Dec. 11, 1814, in Jones, ed., *Letters of Shelley,* I, 422n.

26. PBS to Harriet Westbrook Shelley, Sept. 15 [14], 1814, ibid., 394, 395, Sept. 26, 1814, 397.

application." Perhaps they were protesting too much that they were not indulging in self-love or disrupting the revolutionary vision of her parents.[27]

Godwin dealt with the pain of his daughter's desertion and his friend's
betrayal by constructing his own version of the elopement. Its major purpose was to mollify creditors. In an August 27 letter to John Taylor, to whom
he owed money, Godwin recounted "a story . . . of the deepest melancholy,"
which was in reality all about his suffering at the hands of a monster. A
"married man, has run away with my daughter." "I cannot conceive of an
event of more accumulated horror." Percy, while lodging temporarily in
Fleet Street, had exploited his friendship with Godwin to insinuate himself
into his household. Determined to seduce Mary, Percy was soon "playing
the traitor to me and deserting his wife." On July 6, he "had the madness" to
inform Godwin and "to ask [his] consent." Godwin exploded. Percy backed
down, promising "to give up his licentious love, and return to virtue." Then
the father turned to his daughter. "Mary could only be withheld from ruin
by her mind." So Godwin talked with her, summoning "a sense of honour
and natural affection." He thought he had succeeded, as he thought he had
with Percy. But he was wrong in both cases. "They both deceived me." In
Godwin's narrative, he—the unyielding tyrant of the Percy-Mary narrative—became the pawn of willful liars. Finding a letter on his dressing table
announcing the departure of the lovers and Claire, he had readily agreed
to let Mary Jane pursue them. His wife, after all, had a much greater appetite for confrontation. Mary Jane's failure to persuade even Claire to come
home left him "at once without children, and without resources, in a situation calculated to fill the strongest mind with despair." Surely, "these unworthy children" would soon "again seek the protection and aid of their
father."[28]

By mid-autumn 1814, the full extent of the upheaval provoked by Percy
and Mary's choice was clear. The Godwins, the lovers, and their siblings
indulged in multiple expressions of outrage and self-justification. Mary
and Percy were frustrated by their families' refusal to affirm their passion.
Harriet was angry that Percy had ended their relationship without her consent. Mary Jane was furious that her stepdaughter had brought disgrace
upon the Godwin household. And Godwin cast himself as the victim of
selfish children. His concern for the reputation of his daughters—"I had
a thousand times rather remain unvindicated, than publish the tale to a

27. PBS to Mary Godwin, Oct. 28, 1814, ibid., 413–414.
28. Godwin to John Taylor, Aug. 27, 1814, in H. Buxton Forman, ed., *The Elopement of Percy
Bysshe Shelley and Mary Wollstonecraft Godwin* (Boston, 1911), 9, 10, 11, 12, 13.

single human creature to whom it might remain unknown"—scarcely concealed his contempt for their choices. Claire was guilty of "indiscretion," Mary of a "crime."[29]

Percy's complaint that "Godwin's cold injustice" "shocked and staggered" him suggests more than naïveté. It also reveals the depth of the young lovers' devotion to their reading of the works of her parents. Of all people, Percy and Mary believed, Godwin should have been exempt from "the perfidy and wickedness and hard heartedness of mankind." How could they feel anything but "despair" when confronted by "how cold and worldly Godwin [had] become"? They genuinely thought they were behaving as responsible individuals ought to behave in a free society held together by commerce and consent. And yet their manly admission had prompted hostility, not sympathy. The practice of the Godwinian plan in Godwin's own household had failed.[30]

Among the principal players in the melodrama of 1814, only twenty-one-year-old Fanny Imlay Godwin seemed more concerned with the feelings of others than with her own, a reflection, perhaps, of her peripheral role in the events transpiring around her. Although Godwin had raised Fanny as his daughter—not even telling her of Gilbert Imlay until she was twelve years old—his affection scarcely obscured his preference for Mary. Although Fanny was "disposed to exercise her own thoughts and follow her own judgment," Mary ("my daughter") was more like her mother: "singularly bold, somewhat imperious, and active of mind" and possessing more than her share of "curiosity, perseverance, and beauty." No wonder Fanny seemed tentative. An illegitimate child, abandoned by a father she did not know about until she was a teenager, loved deeply by a mercurial mother who died when she was three, and raised more out of obligation than affection by her stepparents, Fanny had reason enough to distrust anyone. No one seemed comfortable with her, in no small part because she was not comfortable with them.[31]

An extended visit with relatives in Wales had kept Fanny from witnessing the events of the summer of 1814. Back in London, she was eager to broker a settlement. While the Godwins fretted and Harriet raged at Percy's cruelty, Fanny took up the role of disinterested intermediary. Accompanied by Mary Jane, she called on Mary and Claire, although she would not enter

29. Ibid., 15, 16.

30. PBS to Mary Godwin, Oct. 24, 1814, in Jones, ed., *Letters of Shelley*, I, 408.

31. [Godwin] to E. Fordham, Nov. 13, 1811, Oxford, Bodleian, MS Abinger c. 19, fols. 32–33; Peter H. Marshall, *William Godwin* (New Haven, Conn., 1984), 195.

their residence or speak to Percy. A few weeks later, she returned to warn Mary that a bailiff knew their address, but she would not talk to Claire or Percy. Three days later, she met with Claire in the home of a mutual friend to tell her that their stepfather wished her to rejoin his household, apparently without punishment. The offer had some appeal. Claire wavered for a while, and then declined. The failure of the attempted reconciliation prompted Fanny to write a "doleful" letter to Mary. In mid-November, Fanny again implored Claire to meet her at a neutral site. When Claire demurred, Fanny went directly to her sisters' lodging. Mary, whom she refused to greet, heard her sisters' conversation and learned the full extent of the Godwins' emotional blackmail. "Papa tells Fanny if she sees me he will never speak to her again—a blessed degree of liberty this," Mary told Percy. Worse, Fanny said that Mary Jane thought she was dying. With this news, Claire agreed to go home. Two acrimonious days later—Mary Jane was perfectly healthy—she returned to Mary and Percy.[32]

Fanny's inability to stand up to her stepmother made her, in her sister's eyes, complicit in her own subjugation. Mary referred to an incident in December when Mary Jane had reportedly refused to "allow Fanny to come down to dinner on her receiving a lock of my hair." Fanny had "of course behave[d] slavishly." More than her sister's refusal to choose her side annoyed Mary. She could not fathom why Fanny did not rebel against the tyranny of their parents. But Fanny had her own reasons for trying to maintain good relations with everyone. Percy and the Godwins were fighting over Mary because they felt strongly about her. No one except Mary Wollstonecraft had ever had that level of attachment to Fanny.[33]

The real monster, Mary suspected, was Mary Jane. Fanny's docility was merely annoying. Godwin's recalcitrance baffled as well as hurt. Surely the author of *Political Justice* must sympathize with the choice made by her and Percy? Surely the author of *Caleb Williams* would not tyrannize honest lovers? The only explanation for his behavior was the willful interference of her stepmother. Struggling to control her emotions when she got back to London, Mary had crossed out a reference in her diary to "Mamma" and substituted "Mrs G." Mary Jane was a barbaric woman incapable of recognizing genuine love or engaging in honest conversation. Without sup-

32. Sept. 16, 1814, in Feldman and Scott-Kilvert, eds., *Journals of Mary Shelley,* I, 26, Oct. 22, 1814, 38, Oct. 25, 1814, 38–39, Oct. 27, 1814, 40, Nov. 13, 1814, 44; Mary Godwin to PBS, Oct. 25, 1814, in Bennett, ed., *Letters of Mary Wollstonecraft Shelley,* I, 1 ("perhaps as it is so rainy a day Fanny will not be allowed to come at all—").

33. Dec. 17, 1814, in Feldman and Scott-Kilvert, eds., *Journals of Mary Shelley,* I, 53.

port from his wife, Godwin could not reason his way through this storm of emotion. Mary Jane, Mary told Percy, "plagues my father out of his life and then—well no matter—why will not Godwin follow the obvious bent of his affections and be reconciled to us—no his prejudices the world and she—do you not hate her my love—all these forbid it—what am I to do trust to time of course—for what else can I do."[34]

Mary's current reading—at Percy's suggestion, she was working her way through the novels of Charles Brockden Brown—reinforced her anger. *Wieland* bothered her because the author had "most detestable opinions—he is one of those men who alter all their opinions when they are about 40 and then thinking that it will be the same with every one think themselves the only proper monitors of youth." Just as transparent was her reaction to *Jane Talbot*. It was a "very stupid book," mainly because "the old woman in it is so abominable" and "the young woman so weak." Fanny was not the only real life example of a woman who refused to challenge authority. The husband of Mary's good friend Isabella Booth, anxious to avoid attention to his own marriage to his deceased wife's sister, forbade any communication between the two women. Mary was disappointed. Isabella was a woman of "unexampled frankness and sweetness of character," "perfectly unprejudiced," who "adore[d] the shade of my mother." But Isabella, like Fanny with her father, could not "resist" her husband's "opinions." Could no one understand that Harriet was "selfish and unfeeling" or that Godwin "might be happy if he chose"?[35]

The more alienation they experienced, the more Mary and Percy constructed themselves as different, as inhabiting a place that the mass of mankind could not imagine. They were happy together, apart from all but a handful of true companions. They took pride in their difficult course. It was easier to defer to the world, as Fanny seemed to do, or to vacillate, as Percy thought Claire did, than to stand up in the spirit of *manly* independence and say directly what you thought and felt, like Caleb Williams, no matter the consequences. Mary and Percy knew they were not unique. Accounts of adulterous liaisons among the rich and famous filled the columns of newspapers from London to Philadelphia. When Percy talked of their perceptions being their world, he meant that lovers succeed when they summon

34. Sept. 16, 1814, ibid., 26; Mary Godwin to PBS, Oct. 28, 1814, in Bennett, ed., *Letters of Mary Wollstonecraft Shelley*, I, 3.

35. Dec. 7, 1814, in Feldman and Scott-Kilvert, eds., *Journals of Mary Shelley*, I, 51, Dec. 15, 1814, 53; Mary Godwin to PBS, Nov. 3, 1814, in Bennett, ed., *Letters of Mary Wollstonecraft Shelley*, I, 4.

the strength together to resist efforts to force them to conform to social expectations. If this attitude reflected the influence of Wollstonecraft and Godwin, it diverged from them in both its celebration of sensibility and its restriction of the possibilities of true love to certain kinds of people. Percy and Mary's relationship was only for those souls capable of following the intertwined logic of their minds and bodies. Away from Mary, Percy felt "degraded to the level of the vulgar and impure" and enervated by the "vacant stiff eyeballs" that stared at him. A "*moments* bliss" with each other was compensation enough, however, because it reflected the "exalted and buoyant" rather than "prudence."[36]

This all-consuming obsession with themselves undermined Mary's and Percy's ability to empathize with people they had hurt. The strength they found together to endure criticism flirted with a mutually reinforcing egotism that justified a rejection of alternative perceptions as manifestations of tyranny. Soon enough, however, the invocation of personal authority that legitimized their runaway romance was allowing them to contemplate new relationships and new permutations on the themes of desire, consent, and family. Once let loose, imagination governed everything.

"The Most Dreadful Convulsions"

On an evening in early October 1814, Percy and Claire talked long after Mary had gone to bed about "oppression and reform" and women. They drifted into a lengthy discussion of the complex personal relationships among "Hogg Harriet Miss Hitchener etc." and Percy. Around one in the morning, their conversation devolved into silence. Overcome with emotion, Percy could not control "an expression in his countenance." The couple exchanged good nights, and Claire went to her room. Shortly thereafter, she came back down the stairs, claiming that a pillow had somehow migrated from her bed to a chair. Was a supernatural force at work? Percy and Claire considered the possibility. Suddenly, "the most dreadful convulsions" overwhelmed Claire, and she "shr[i]eked and writhed on the floor" until she fell asleep. Perhaps the mysteries of mutual attraction were as responsible as the mysteries of ghosts. Two people attracted to each other found it impossible to restrain their imagination or govern their sensibilities. Percy was frustrated by Claire's erratic (or indecisive?) behavior and her refusal to honor her feelings. Persuaded of her "insensibility and incapacity for the slightest degree of friendship," he castigated her (and himself) for their flir-

<hr/>

36. PBS to Mary Godwin, Oct. 24, 1814, in Jones, ed., *Letters of Shelley,* I, 408, Oct. 27, 1814, 412.

tation with intimacy. He should have known better than to surrender to "trivial sympathies." In the future, he told her, he would content himself with "one great affection, with a single mighty hope: let the rest of mankind be the subjects of your benevolence your justice: and as human beings of your sensibility."[37]

A few days later, Percy expressed sympathy for Claire's unsettled situation and her willingness to make "concessions." He recognized that he had behaved badly in rushing to condemn her. After all, "the most exalted philosophy, the truest virtue consists in an habitual contempt of self: a subduing of all angry feelings: a sacrifize of pride and selfishness." He would work hard to refrain from impugning the motives of his critics as well as his friends. But promises of personal reform did not resolve a situation fraught with tension. Claire had a harder time working through her attraction to her sister's lover. She walked in her sleep, groaned frequently, and grew despondent. The two thwarted lovers talked a good deal about themselves. She later reported that he described "two Clare's— . . . the nervous Clare is reserved and melancholy and more sarcastic than violent; the good Clare is gentle yet cheerful; and to me the most engaging of human creatures." Most of all, she was "as easily managed by the person [she] love[d] (and he) as the reed is by the wind." It was her "weak side." It is highly unlikely that Percy and Claire had sex, and that might have affected Percy's construction of Claire as indecisive.[38]

Claire's volatility is understandable. Loving Percy had its advantages. How many attractive men seemed eager for mutuality with a smart woman? But the price of considering her options was a strained relationship with a sister who had begun to see her as an insensitive rival. A pregnant Mary resented Claire and Percy's regular walks and conversations and encouraged Claire to leave. In May 1815, several weeks after the birth and death of the baby, Mary celebrated her half-sister's departure by beginning a new journal. Claire, for her part, made the most of her solitude in the valleys and hills near Lynmouth. "After so much discontent, such violent scenes, such a turmoil of passion and hatred," referring as much to her parents as to her sister, she professed herself happy.[39]

37. Oct. 7, 1814, in Feldman and Scott-Kilvert, eds., *Journals of Mary Shelley*, I, 32, 33, Oct. 14, 1814, 35–36.

38. Oct. 14, 1814, ibid., 35–36; Clairmont to Lord Byron, [Apr. 18, 1816], in Stocking, ed., *Clairmont Correspondence*, I, 38.

39. May 13, 1815, in Feldman and Scott-Kilvert, eds., *Journals of Mary Shelley*, I, 78–79; Clairmont to Fanny Imlay Godwin, May 28, 1815, in Stocking, ed., *Clairmont Correspondence*, I, 9–10.

Eighteen months later, away from her sister and her lover and anxious about her immediate future (should she become a writer? an actress?), Claire acted decisively. Whether she had learned from the impasse with Percy and Mary or whether she felt less inhibited because her family was not involved, she behaved very differently. The object of her ardor was Lord Byron. Claire had become infatuated with him through his poetry. Writing as an "utter stranger," she requested a meeting, explaining what Byron might think "an impudent imposture" as an invitation to make love. Claire's rhetoric echoed that of Wollstonecraft. Her fear of rejection and ridicule surfaced in a plea for his sympathy; after all, a "moment of passion, or an impulse of pride often destroys our own happiness and that of others." Claire was well aware of the pain that the exercise of liberty might inflict on another human being. Byron should not let his freedom to decide obscure "how much [his choice] may injure another." If, in the end, Byron had to do what was best for Byron, he nonetheless owed her consideration. Hers was "a delicate case"; her "feet [were] on the edge of a precipice"; and she had nothing to rely on but hope. Byron should think seriously about the folly of rejecting the "fond affection and unbounded devotion" of a woman of good reputation "without either guardian or husband to control" her. Claire's advance was an exercise of liberty by an autonomous woman. Her overtures reflected, "not the results of momentary temptation, the impulses of passion" but the "decision" of her "judgement." As "erroneous" as it might be, it was her only "guide."[40]

Byron also acted on his own unmediated authority. But his gender exempted him from the penalties Claire paid for indulging her desire. Already a renowned monster, especially with women, Byron encouraged Claire without taking her terribly seriously. He invited her to call on him but was not at home when she did. At their first meeting, Claire abandoned any pretense of restraint. Drawn in by "the gentleness of [his] manners and the wild originality of [his] countenance," she offered to spend a night with him some ten to twelve miles outside London where they "shall be free and unknown." Byron accepted her invitation but insisted on a house in the city. Shortly after they had sex, Byron left for the Continent. He had no scruples about taking up with this "odd-headed girl" again when she caught up with him in Geneva. Months later, Byron was blunt in his appraisal of their relationship and essentialist in his attitude about gender and sexuality. He "never loved nor pretended to love her—but a man is a man—and if a girl

---

40. [Clairmont] to [Lord Byron], [March or April 1816], in Stocking, ed., *Clairmont Correspondence*, I, 24, 25, 27.

of eighteen [actually, seventeen] comes prancing to you at all hours—there is but one way."[41]

This assessment was precipitated by Claire's announcement that she had given birth to his daughter. Byron claimed the "brat" because he had "reason to think . . . she had *not lived* with" Percy while he was having sex with her. Claire thanked him for his kindness. She was confident that, although he might "trifle" with some women and "amuse" himself with others, he would "never find one who loved [him] with more serious[ness] or treated [him] with more gentle affection" than she did. The feeling was hardly mutual. Byron wanted nothing to do with Claire and dealt with her and her daughter Allegra largely through Percy, Mary, and other go-betweens. After a bitter custody fight, Byron placed the girl in a convent at Bagnacavallo near Ravenna, Italy. Claire finally became so angry with her former lover that she dreamed that an autopsy would reveal the growth of a large capital *I* on his heart. Byron was a monster, a selfish egotist whose talk of romance was a sham designed to lure women into satisfying his lust. Claire had practiced restraint with Percy and indulged herself with Byron. No matter her choice, she ended up alone in large part because she so often acted alone. She never fully recovered, living the rest of her life with bitter longings for what might have been.[42]

Mary, the sister who endured Percy and Claire's flirtation during the winter of 1814–1815, was hardly an innocent herself. On November 14, Thomas Jefferson Hogg, Shelley's old friend and would-be seducer of his sister and his first wife, visited Mary and Percy. They were delighted to see him, in no small part because so few people wanted anything to do with them. Unsurprisingly, Hogg soon decided he was in love with his friend's lover, and he said so. Mary was not displeased. No doubt she enjoyed the opportunity to turn the tables on Percy. But she generally liked her new friend and encouraged his attention. Although they had not known each other long enough for her to think of loving him, that might "come in time" and make them "happier." Over the next few days, her "affection" for Hogg, although "not now exactly as [he] would wish," grew. Mary's pregnancy conveniently delayed a physical consummation of their passion. Hogg should not despair, however, for Percy "will be subject" to the same constraints. Come summer, she

41. Clairmont to [Lord Byron], [Apr. 16, 1816?], ibid., 36, Lord Byron to Douglas Kinnaird, Jan. 20, 1817, 39 n. 4.

42. Lord Byron to Kinnaird, Jan. 20, 1817, ibid., 39 n. 4, Clairmont to [Lord Byron], [Apr. 21, 1816], 40. See Fiona MacCarthy, *Byron: Life and Legend* (New York, 2002), 271–272, 296–298, 324–346, 418–419, 519–520.

promised, they would "pass the time" with "exquisite pleasure." Hogg would teach her Italian, and they would read many books together. Their "greater happiness" would follow from being themselves and making Percy happy.[43]

Mary and Hogg did become quite good friends. She wrote to him almost immediately upon the death of her infant baby to ask him to come to her bedside. She valued his calm presence. Even in less traumatic moments, Hogg provided her with companionship. They had pet names for each other. Sharing experiences and ideas, dealing with each other directly and honestly, they found in friendship the strength to behave as they thought best. As in all these relationships, mutual love was far more promising than the gloom of solitude. In this context, Mary could easily understand the love she shared with Hogg as contributing to the love she shared with Percy. Friendship, even intense friendship, need not threaten another romantic relationship. "To turn perpetually upon one's own pivot is the real definition of selfishness," declared Claire to Mary decades later, "generosity is to allow one's circumference some point in it, to become the centre of another's circle."[44]

Percy certainly was more generous with Hogg and Mary than he had been with Hogg and Harriet, thus affirming his assertion that the real issue was the consent of the woman. Percy knew about Hogg and Mary from the beginning. He even went out on January 1 so that they could enjoy some privacy. In mid-April, he jocularly wrote to Hogg expressing a desire to see him and "to give [Hogg his] share of our common treasure of which you have been cheated for several days." Mary knew "how highly" Hogg prized "this exquisite possession." Hogg should not fear. "We will not again be deprived of this participated pleasure." The conclusion that Mary and Hogg consummated their relationship ignores her pregnancy and the death of her child in early March after a difficult birth. In no condition to have sex with anyone, she was in need of a friend.[45]

"Never . . . to Be a Disgrace to Such a Mother"

So was her older sister, whose lifelong quest for intimacy was nearing its conclusion. Fanny had continued to visit her sisters and Percy occasion-

43. PBS, Nov. 14, 1814, in Feldman and Scott-Kilvert, eds., *Journals of Mary Shelley*, I, 45; Mary Godwin to Hogg, Jan. 1, 1815, in Bennett, ed., *Letters of Mary Wollstonecraft Shelley*, I, 6, Jan. 7, 1815, 8, Jan. 24, 1815, 9.

44. Mary Godwin to Hogg, Mar. 6, 1815, in Bennett, ed., *Letters of Mary Wollstonecraft Shelley*, I, 10; Clairmont to MWS, June 2, 1835, in Stocking, ed., *Clairmont Correspondence*, II, 322.

45. PBS to Hogg, Jan. 1, 1815, in Jones, ed., *Letters of Shelley*, I, 423, [Apr. 26, 1815?], 426.

ally. Percy specifically requested Fanny's presence after Mary gave birth in March. Fanny came, but only because the Godwins were not home. Then, ignoring Claire's pleas, she delayed calling on Mary for a week after the death of the infant. When she did visit, no one was home but Mary. Soaked from walking in the rain, Fanny stayed for supper. The conversation diverted a lonely Mary from contemplating the idea that she "was a mother and am so no longer."[46]

Fanny's erratic behavior was more than likely the product of her desire to please everyone, a surefire recipe for a sense of powerlessness leading to melancholy. She was plaintive and more than a little annoying because she had no serious friends. Claire, writing about her new life away from Mary and Percy, urged Fanny "not [to] be melancholy—for heaven's sake be cheerful." She should just be "a good Fanny." Percy had written to Fanny in a similar vein two years earlier, mocking her concern about whether it was proper for her to write to him. True, he was "one of those formidable and long clawed animals called a *Man*." But he was "one of the most inoffensive of [his] species" and did not bite any more. He hoped she would become "an interesting and valuable correspondent." Like Claire, Percy did not take Fanny entirely seriously. And she knew it.[47]

Fanny jumped at every opportunity to connect with another human being. A letter from Aunt Everina Wollstonecraft in early 1816 prompted an immediate response. She had found the letter "a greater source of delight than [she had] experienced [in] a long time," wishing that her "conduct and character" would secure her aunt's affection "through life, even under the greatest misfortunes." Then in May, Fanny met George Blood, the brother of Fanny Blood, Mary Wollstonecraft's friend, after whom she had been named. Blood's memories of her mother increased Fanny's "love and admiration of her memory" and her "hope that her daughters were not unworthy of her." Meeting Blood, she wrote, "roused me from my torpor—I have determined never to live to be a disgrace to *such a mother*." Unfortunately, the energy soon dissipated.[48]

Fanny lacked the confidence to assert her authority in a family specializing in self-authorized behavior. The meaningful social intercourse she

46. Feb. 23, 26, Mar. 8, 13, 1815, in Feldman and Scott-Kilvert, eds., *Journals of Mary Shelley*, I, 65, 66, 68, 69.

47. Clairmont to Fanny Imlay Godwin, May 28, 1815, in Stocking, ed., *Clairmont Correspondence*, I, 10; PBS to Fanny Imlay Godwin, Dec. 10, 1812, in Jones, ed., *Letters of Shelley*, I, 337, 338.

48. Fanny Imlay Godwin to Everina Wollstonecraft, Apr. 9, 1816, in Stocking, ed., *Clairmont Correspondence*, I, 23, to Mary Godwin and PBS, May 29, 1816, 48, 49.

craved eluded her. Her parents and siblings depended on her but rarely exhibited strong feelings about her. Fanny was just *there,* almost invisible. Understanding that she was "a dependant being in every sense of the word but most particularly in money," she had no idea how she would support herself if she did not marry. Her loneliness ensured her empathy with Mary and Percy, although, unlike them, she felt more ignored than rejected. She understood that feeling; she knew what it was like to be ignored and rejected. Refusing to be "*sordid* or vulgar," Fanny insisted she loved her sister and her lover for "*[them]selves alone.*" In return, she wanted to reveal her "real character" to them. The restless child of restless parents, she lacked Mary's "calm contented disposition."[49]

Over the summer, Fanny began to lose her struggle with melancholy. In late July, she experienced "ill humour" brought on by "a variety [of] trying circumstance's," including the financial and emotional distress in the Godwin household. "Sick, at heart" about "the misery I see my fellow beings suffering," she did not want "to live to see the extinction of all genius, talent, and elevated generous feeling in [G]reat Britain." The human dilemma, as Fanny understood it, was to find a way to "make man plain, and simple, in manners, and mode of life, and at the same time a *poet* a painter and a philosopher." Fanny denied that she was "wise enough, philosophical enough, or historian enough" to offer guidance on the subject. But she continued to consider it. Rarely did anyone more succinctly summarize the value of social commerce. She granted that "it is impossible to tell the good that poets do there fellow creatures—(at least those that can feel)." But "whilst I read I am a poet—I am inspired with good feeling's, feeling that create[s] perhaps a more permanent good in me" and tells "us there is something yet in the world to aspire to—something by which succeeding ages may be made happy, or perhaps better." Mary Wollstonecraft and Gilbert Imlay's daughter could imagine a future but she could not imagine a place for herself in it.[50]

On October 8, Fanny left the Godwin household headed for Wales, or at least to "the spot from which [she] hope[d] never to remove." The next day, she wrote to Godwin and Percy from Swansea, asking them to come bury her. Percy, who was in Bath, read the letter and "started up," quite "distracted." Godwin and Percy rushed separately to Bristol. Percy alone followed Fanny's trail to the Mackworth Arms in Swansea. He arrived too

49. Fanny Imlay Godwin to Mary Godwin and PBS, May 29, 1816, in Stocking, ed., *Clairmont Correspondence,* I, 48, 49, to Mary Godwin, July 29, Aug. 1, 1816, 56, Sept. 26, 1816, 74.

50. Fanny Imlay Godwin to Mary Godwin, July 29, Aug. 1, 1816, ibid., 54, 56, 57. See Fanny Imlay Godwin to Mary Godwin, Sept. 26, 1816, 74–75, Oct. 3, 1816, 80–82.

late: Fanny had committed suicide during the night of October 9–10. A local
newspaper reported that a "most respectable-looking female" had taken tea
and gone to her room without a maid. The staff of the inn broke into Fanny's
room the next morning when she failed to appear for breakfast and found "a
corpse, with the remains of a bottle of laudanum on the table, and a note."
Her possessions were few: a French gold watch, a handkerchief, a necklace,
a purse, and the white dress with blue-striped skirt she was wearing. Under
the dress were stockings marked with the letter G and stays inscribed with
the letters "M. W." The note read:

> I have long determined that the best thing I could do was to put an end
> to the existence of a being whose birth was unfortunate, and whose
> life has only been a series of pain to those persons who have hurt their
> health in endeavouring to promote her welfare. Perhaps to hear of my
> death will give you pain, but you will soon have the blessing of forget-
> ting that such a creature ever existed as [Fanny Imlay Godwin].

The daughter had succeeded where the mother had failed. It was the most
decisive act of a young woman who had long suffered from what amounted
to social death. Extraordinarily sensitive to her impact on others and theirs
on her, Fanny correctly anticipated the consequences of her decision. Her
suicide stunned her family. But the pain it caused would, like Fanny's memory, prove fleeting. No one except her mother had ever loved her enough to
mourn her for long.[51]

Fanny Imlay Godwin was not the only young woman to seek peace in the
fall of 1816. Harriet Westbrook Shelley had tried to come to terms with her
husband's choice to leave her for Mary Godwin and with the repercussions
economically and socially as well as emotionally. From late 1814 until 1816,
Harriet, a young woman with two children, lived with her parents. Percy
later charged that her father threw her out when he discovered that she was
sleeping with his groom, who then abandoned her when she became pregnant. In any case, Harriet, who was living by herself at 7 Elizabeth Street,
Hans Place, had had enough by the fall of 1816. She disappeared in the late
afternoon of November 7; her body was found in the Serpentine River in
Hyde Park on December 10. A jury attributed the death of "Harriet Smith"
to drowning. But everyone knew what had happened.[52]

51. Fanny Imlay Godwin to Godwin, [Oct. 8, 1816], ibid., 85, Clairmont to Trelawny, May 30,
1875, II, 629, Fanny Imlay Godwin to Godwin and PBS, Oct. 9, 1816, I, 86 (for the details, see
86–87 n. 2).

52. PBS to Mary Godwin, Dec. 16, 1816, in Jones, ed., *Letters of Shelley*, I, 520, 521. See also

The day before she left her rooms, Harriet told her sister that she was no longer "an inhabitant of this miserable world." Eliza should "not regard the loss of one who could never be anything but a source of vexation and misery to you [and] all belonging to me." "Too wretched to exert myself, lowered in the opinion of everyone, why should I drag on a miserable existence?" "Embittered by past recollections and not one ray of hope to rest on for the future," she had acted in the best interests of all concerned. Like Fanny, Harriet claimed to be doing everyone a favor. She indicted herself for her predicament. She had failed to assert herself. How could she have done otherwise bereft of family, friends, and a lover? Self-assertion did not, could not, survive social isolation. The ability of individuals to achieve a sense of autonomy was largely dependent on regular interaction with other individuals. Love was the foundation of independence. When Percy left her, he had done more than wound her emotionally and leave her vulnerable financially. Alone, she was defenseless. If Percy had stayed with her, she "might have lived." But he had chosen otherwise. She "freely" forgave him and wished him the "happiness" he had denied her. That he and her sister enjoy "all happiness" was "the last wish of her who loved [them] more than all others." Harriet would not play the monster in death.[53]

A shocked Claire told Byron that she and Percy spent "such wretched hours" dealing with the misery prompted by Fanny's and Harriet's suicides. Mary lamented that her older sister would have found in her home "a proper asylum." But as she and others groped to deal with their sadness and mild guilt, they seemed not to miss Fanny *as* Fanny. The Godwins and the Shelleys repeated the experience several weeks later when Harriet's body was found. Percy's friend Leigh Hunt helped him work through the news. More important was Mary. Through her he could "entertain without despair the recollection of the horrors unutterable villainy that led to this dark dreadful death." Percy was attributing Harriet's desperation to mistreatment at the hands of all the men in her life, except him, of course. Everyone reassured Percy, who protested far too much, that his conduct toward Harriet had been upright and liberal.[54]

Feldman and Scott-Kilvert, eds., *Journals of Mary Shelley,* I, 150–152; Thomas Hookham to PBS, Dec. 13, 1816, in Jones, ed., *Letters of Shelley,* I, 519 n. 1.

53. Harriet Westbrook Shelley to Eliza Westbrook, [Nov. 9, 1816], in Jones, ed., *Letters of Shelley,* I, 520 n. 1.

54. Ibid.; Clairmont to Lord Byron, Oct. 27, Nov. 19, 1816, in Stocking, ed., *Clairmont Correspondence,* I, 89; Mary Godwin to PBS, Dec. 17, 1816, in Bennett, ed., *Letters of Mary Wollstonecraft Shelley,* I, 24; PBS to Mary Godwin, Dec. 16, 1816, in Jones, ed., *Letters of Shelley,* I,

Almost overnight, Harriet's death accomplished what Fanny had been unable to achieve: the reconciliation of the Godwin family. As soon as he heard the news, William Godwin contacted Percy and Mary. Suddenly, they were welcome in his household again because they were now free to get married. Sympathy restored and monsters forgotten, Godwin accompanied Percy to get the license. He and Mary Jane entertained the couple at their home in Skinner Street on the wedding eve, the first time the couple had been there since July 1814. Decades later, Claire claimed that Percy had resisted marriage until Mary threatened suicide. Mary Jane and Claire liked to think that the shades of Harriet and Fanny had "forced him to the conclusion he came to." Percy never said anything that supports this interpretation of his motives. He described the ceremony, held on December 30, 1816, at Saint Mildred's Church in London, as "magical in its effects." Surely his new parents-in-law were thrilled. Mary was once again respectable, not to mention married to the son of a baronet who still might come into a good deal of money.[55]

520, 521. See also Dec. 15, 1816, in Feldman and Scott-Kilvert, eds., *Journals of Mary Shelley,* I, 150–152 n. 2.

55. PBS to Clairmont, Dec. 30, 1816, in Jones, ed., *Letters of Shelley,* I, 525, Godwin to Hull Godwin, Feb. 21, 1817, 525 n. 3; [Clairmont] to [Trelawny], [April 1871], in Stocking, ed., *Clairmont Correspondence,* II, 617.

IO

"The True Key of the Universe is Love"

In May 1846, Thomas Medwin informed Mary Shelley that he was writing a biography of his second cousin Percy Shelley, who had drowned off the coast of Italy almost a quarter century earlier. Medwin implied that he would mine the records of the 1817 Chancery suit in which Percy had lost guardianship of his children by Harriet Westbrook to detail the poet's desertion of his first wife and her subsequent suicide. An appalled Mary Shelley urged Medwin to give up the project entirely. At stake were the reputations of innocent people. "In modern society," she protested, "there is no injury so great as dragging private names and private life before the world." Medwin's book "would wound and injure the living," Percy Shelley's daughter in particular. "In these publishing, inquisitive, scandal-mongering days," she concluded, "one feels called upon for a double exercise of delicacy, forbearance—and reserve." Hardly qualities Mary had honored as a young woman, they reflected the values of a bourgeois culture that flourished by her death in 1851.[1]

No one knew better than Mary Shelley the power of a public narrative of a private life. The memoir of her mother written by her father in the aftermath of her birth was arguably the ur-text of the genre. Now aging acquaintances of literary figures were feeding a market suddenly hungry for tales

---

1. T[homas] Medwin to Mary Wollstonecraft Shelley (MWS), May 17, 1846, in Betty T. Bennet, ed., *The Letters of Mary Wollstonecraft Shelley,* 3 vols. (Baltimore, 1980–1988), III, 285, MWS to Medwin, May 13–16, 1846, 284.

Figure 13. Mary Wollstonecraft Shelley. *By Richard Rothwell. Oil on canvas, exhibited 1840.* © *National Portrait Gallery, London*

of famous people behaving badly. Largely ignored in his lifetime, Percy in death was one of several Romantic poets who fascinated a growing number of middle-class Britons and Americans as true men of feeling. In the popular imagination, they were the foils of respectable men: sensitive souls who slept with multiple partners of both sexes and experimented with unconventional living arrangements in warm Mediterranean climates. Appropriated as entertainment with a moral, their lives cautioned as they thrilled.

Readers could empathize with a defiance of social norms still under construction when Mary and Percy eloped. They could contemplate alternative paths, explore alternative worlds, and reject all of them, certain of their far more prosaic choices.

Mary Shelley scarcely objected to exercising the imagination. After all, she supported herself and her son by writing fiction. What bothered her was the mercenary approach of Medwin and others like him, including Thomas Jefferson Hogg and Edward John Trelawny, the latter a good friend in the last year of Percy's life. They were ghouls scavenging the lives of the dead for sensational gossip to make money and achieve notoriety through association with a celebrity. In acting by and for themselves in utter disregard of the wishes and feelings of others, they were behaving like inhuman monsters. Self-love had long fascinated Mary Shelley. She knew all too well the often grievous consequences of choices made by individuals who imagined themselves as independent actors, who failed to comprehend how the exercise of their liberty might constrain or even destroy the liberty of others.

Mary repeatedly returned to this cultural dilemma in her fiction, particularly as it played out within affectionate families. Like her mother, she wanted to understand why so many fathers, husbands, lovers, friends, and sons acted like monsters and what mothers, wives, lovers, friends, and daughters might do about it. Like her father, she wanted to explore the consequences, often unintended, of self-love, especially male insistence on confusing feeling with unmediated desire. Her particular concern was with the antisocial character of self-love and the unreliability of unmediated individual perception. Understanding required exchange. No one could comprehend anything on their own. "Our several minds, in reflecting to our judgments the occurrences of life," observes the narrator in one of her novels, "are like mirrors of various shapes and hues, so that we none of us perceive passing objects with exactly similar optics; and while all pretend to regulate themselves by the quadrant of justice, the deceptive medium through which the reality is viewed, causes our ideas of it to be at once various and false." Without social commerce, "self-love magnifies, and passion obscures, the glass through which we look upon others and ourselves." This "strange distortion of vision" blinds men and women "to the truth, which experience so perpetually teaches us, that the consequences of our actions *never die.*"[2]

2. Mary Shelley, *Lodore* (1835), ed. Lisa Vargo (Peterborough, Ont., 1997), 123, 156.

"The Want of a Friend"

The genesis of *Frankenstein; or, The Modern Prometheus* is one of the most charming stories in British literature. A group of friends whiling away the summer of 1816 together near Geneva, Switzerland, challenged one another one night to compose some kind of Gothic tale. Only twenty-one-year-old Mary Godwin completed the assignment, writing from late summer through the early spring, partly with the help of her collaborator, Percy. He contributed at least four thousand to five thousand of the seventy-two-thousand-word total in the first edition of *Frankenstein,* none of which changed the conception, plot, or argument. Mary recalled that he "was from the first, very anxious that I should prove myself worthy of my parentage, and enrol myself on the page of fame," although he "with his far more cultivated mind" reserved the right to judge the quality of her writing. Percy the critic of patriarchy could not shake the instinct of a paternalist. As important, neither Mary nor Percy could entirely shake the sense of dark crisis that, despite their marriage in December, enveloped them in the wake of the suicides of Fanny and Harriet, the pregnancy of Claire, and the March 1817 judgment of the Chancery Court that gave custody of Harriet's children to her parents rather than their father.[3]

No wonder *Frankenstein* begins in the cold Arctic, a place uncongenial to human society. A young man we know as Walton fights loneliness by writing a letter to his sister. His expedition to the polar region is the fulfillment of a long-standing ambition. But Walton is sad because there is no one with whom he can share his successes and his disappointments. He can write letters, "it is true: but that is a poor medium for the communication of feeling." Walton "feel[s] the want of a friend" who would not mock his dreams and offer "affection enough for [him] to endeavour to regulate [his] mind." He is therefore delighted when the crew picks up a man named Victor Frankenstein. Most impressive about the determined Frankenstein

---

3. MWS, "Introduction to the *1831* Edition," in MWS (with Percy Bysshe Shelley [PBS]), *Frankenstein; or, The Modern Prometheus: The Original Two-Volume Novel of 1816–1817 from the Bodleian Library Manuscripts,* ed. Charles E. Robinson (2008; rpt. New York, 2009), 438. I have used the original 1818 edition rather than the much revised 1831 version: Mary Shelley, *Frankenstein,* ed. J. Paul Hunter (New York, 1996) (see the essays in this volume). See Pamela Clemit, "*Frankenstein, Mathilda,* and the Legacies of Godwin and Wollstonecraft," 26–44, and Diane Long Hoeveler, "*Frankenstein,* Feminism, and Literary Theory," 45–62, both in Esther H. Schor, ed., *The Cambridge Companion to Mary Shelley* (Cambridge, 2003); and Isabelle Bour, "Sensibility as Epistemology in *Caleb Williams, Waverly,* and *Frankenstein,*" *Studies in English Literature, 1500–1900,* XLV (2005), 813–827.

is "the interest he instinctively takes in the welfare of those who surround him." Indeed, he rewards Walton for his generous hospitality by telling him the story of his life. "Learn from me," Frankenstein implores Walton, "if not by my precepts, at least by my example, how dangerous is the acquirement of knowledge, and how much happier that man is who believes his native town to be the world, than he who aspires to become greater than his nature will allow." Mary had read John Milton and Jean-Jacques Rousseau as well as Godwin and Wollstonecraft. Her novel investigates not only the social costs of the failure of educated, good men to resist the allure of ambition but also the deleterious impact of their choices on women and children. *Frankenstein,* like *St. Leon* and *Fleetwood,* investigates the tragic inability of men to sustain mutual domesticity—or the bourgeois family—as an institution for social good.[4]

Frankenstein tells Walton of his idyllic youth in Switzerland, where he had grown up in a happy family with an antipatriarchal father. Not "command" but "mutual affection engaged us all to comply with and obey the slightest desire of each other." In this virtual Eden, Frankenstein had enjoyed the mixed-gender company of his cousin Elizabeth Lavenza and his good friend Henry Clerval. As he grew older, however, his ambition had slowly but surely gathered the force of a "torrent" that had "swept away all [his] hopes and joys." Eventually, Frankenstein conceives a desire to create a human being. Human knowledge has reached a point where a mortal man can do what once was assumed to be the province of eternal God: breathe life into a man assembled from the body parts of dead people. Consumed by hubris, Frankenstein can imagine no limits on his ambition. He does not consider the possible consequences of his action for his family, friends, the new man, and, especially, himself.[5]

Frankenstein's uneducated creature almost immediately wreaks havoc in his clumsy efforts to make connections with other human beings. When Frankenstein's younger brother William is murdered, he blames the creature—and himself. The subsequent arrest and execution of Justine Moritz, an innocent servant of the Frankensteins, exacerbate his self-loathing and guilt. Elizabeth, the woman he loves, says that men now "appear . . . as monsters thirsting for each other's blood." Withdrawal is antisocial because, his father tells him, it "prevents improvement or enjoyment." Without company, the world is a barren place full of miserable and useless creatures. No one understands this better than the creature. Blaming his maker for his fall

4. MWS, *Frankenstein,* ed. Hunter, 10, 16, 31.
5. Ibid., 21, 24.

from grace, he knows how to set things right. Frankenstein ought to provide him with a female companion. In so doing, he would atone for his original sin: the failure to recognize that human beings alone cannot manage their bodies themselves. Society requires an authority that emerges from human intercourse, more specifically, love.[6]

Frankenstein's new man wants a lover. More than physical pleasure, he craves connection; he seeks habits of intimacy. Narrating his own story, he describes his relationship with a couple of young people and a blind old man in a cottage far from the villagers who despise him. As the creature, undetected, watches the family, he is moved by their kindness. From them, he learns not only how to talk but also the power of language, the ways in which persuasion happens, how words produce "pleasure or pain, smiles or sadness." He starts to empathize with his new friends. "When they were unhappy, I felt depressed; when they rejoiced, I sympathized in their joys." Hearing them talk about history and religion, the creature grows curious. He starts to read books, including Milton's *Paradise Lost* and Johann Wolfgang von Goethe's *Sorrows of Werther*. In a few short weeks in a paradise obviously indebted to Rousseau, Frankenstein's creature learns about the importance of empathy and engagement, the value of reading and talking, the idea that life can be more than nasty, brutish, and short. Cultivating an understanding that merges passion and reason, autonomy and society is a recipe for individual and collective happiness. But that attitude cannot exist, let alone thrive, in the absence of regular communication. Isolated men and women become monsters or victims of monsters. Unable to assert themselves and unable to engage, they lack the strength and the authority to resist inevitable disappointments and dangers. Only through human connection can they learn that their perceptions constitute a limited and distorted perspective.[7]

Frankenstein's creature knows that his education will be incomplete and his life unfulfilled if he does not have friends. Eager to experience love, he summons the courage to knock on the cottage door when the blind old man is home alone. Fearfully, he informs the man that he is an outcast without friends, a monster whom people shun. "Do not despair," is the reply of a man who cannot see him, who knows him only by his words and his voice. People are capable of love. But just as the creature announces his desire to be friends, the other members of the family suddenly return. In their horror, they faint or run away. The kind young man drives away the creature with a

6. Ibid., 59, 61, 66.
7. Ibid., 75, 86–87.

stick. The realization that irrational fear precludes any opportunity to enjoy the benefits of company drives the creature to murder and revenge. The source of his antisocial behavior—like the suicides of Fanny and Harriet—are products of an imposed social isolation. Alone, although the creature can think and feel, he cannot cultivate a reliable understanding of himself as a member of a larger community.[8]

Frankenstein is just as tortured by the unanticipated consequence of his relentless ambition. Contemplating the creature's request for a companion forces him to weigh the impact of his choice. Their best interests are mutually exclusive. Whatever Frankenstein does, he will produce both misery and happiness. To acquiesce in the creature's demand would be socially irresponsible: it would let loose another person who would frighten people and produce more innocent victims. And yet Frankenstein empathizes with his new man. Flooded with remorse, he acknowledges that he created "a rational creature" in a "fit of enthusiastic madness." Does he not owe him a companion? Is not that the most likely way to tame his antisocial behavior? Frankenstein finally consents and travels with his friend Henry Clerval to the Orkney Islands, off the coast of Scotland, to create a new woman. Interrupted by his all too eager male, Frankenstein abandons the project in revulsion and throws the parts into a lake. In revenge, the creature kills Clerval and then strangles Elizabeth on her and Frankenstein's wedding night. If the creation cannot have a friend and a lover, neither will the creator.[9]

In the end, the flummoxed Frankenstein flees. Running to the far edge of the world, beyond Scandinavia, to the frozen Arctic, he finds temporary sanctuary on Walton's ship, where he desperately narrates the story of his life. In his hubris, he sought—like St. Leon—to be God. But from the moment the creature breathed, Frankenstein's life had become a terror of misunderstandings, tragedies, and injuries, none of which he seemed to be able to influence, let alone control. The creator had become the victim of his own creation. Like the protodetective in *Caleb Williams,* the new man relentlessly pursues Frankenstein. In the daughter's novel, there is no redemption, no out, and no obvious opportunity to undo the long string of calamities that has become Frankenstein's personal history. His tale told, Frankenstein dies at the hand of the man he made.

The killer finds no solace in his act, for his curse is to live when he knows that the life of the unloved is not worth living—either for the individual or society. How might his life have been different had he had friends, relatives,

8. Ibid., 90–91.
9. Ibid., 151.

a lover? As the creature explains to Walton before he disappears into the darkness, he has a heart "fashioned to be susceptible of love and sympathy." Without them, he is a demon, "the slave, not the master of an impulse." Unable to enjoy the "love and fellowship" all people require, he sees no escape from misery but death. But even that relief is denied him. We leave him scurrying across the ice, fading into darkness, his ultimate fate, like that of Gilbert Imlay, as inevitable as the details are unknown.[10]

"My Daughter, I Love You!"

Mary Shelley composed her second novel, *Matilda,* in a six-month period between August 1819 and February 1820. Beyond its obvious echo of her relationships with her parents, the book reflected a serious depression prompted by the recent deaths of her three-year-old son William and an infant daughter named Clara. *Matilda* remained unpublished until 1959, mainly because William Godwin was so disgusted with its theme of incest. The novel is more than a sensational variation on the author's own life, however. Like *Frankenstein, Matilda* imagines the consequences of the choices of a well-intentioned man on his family, particularly his daughter. This time, Mary Shelley tells the story entirely from the perspective of a young woman. *Matilda* is about women, not men; it is about consequences, not intentions.

Twenty-year-old Matilda begins her narrative in the dead of winter somewhere in the north of Great Britain, acutely aware that death is imminent. Addressing Woodville, a sympathetic poet she had only met recently, she emphasizes her isolation. "I live in a lone cottage on a solitary, wide heath; . . . I am alone—quite alone—in the world." Like Frankenstein, she writes to explain how she ended up in such desperate circumstances. As always, the answer involves the absence of relatives or friends. *Matilda* grapples with the Romantic theme of the deterioration of patriarchal authority and the disintegration of all institutions, including the family. Father and daughter come close to an incestuous relationship because they, like the characters in *Frankenstein,* do not understand love as sympathy. Thinking themselves autonomous and in control of their own destinies, they are blind to their dependence on other human beings.[11]

---

10. Ibid., 153, 154.

11. MWS, *Matilda,* ed., Janet Todd (1959; rpt. New York, 2004), 151. See Audra Dibert Himes, "'Knew Shame, and Knew Desire': Ambivalence as Structure in Mary Shelley's *Mathilda,*" 115–129, and Ranita Chatterjee, "*Mathilda:* Mary Shelley, William Godwin, and the Ideologies

The difficulty of creating a family, let alone sustaining one, affects all the characters. Matilda's father was a selfish boy. His education, which included reading novels, had encouraged him to indulge desire without calculating his impact on other people. The turning point in his life occurs when he meets Matilda's mother. Their friendship and then their love—their mutual esteem—transform him into a useful man. Recognizing that his wife is necessary to his emotional and intellectual as well as physical happiness, he understands he "had received a new and better soul." "She was his monitress as he learned . . . the true ends of life." Like Mary Shelley's parents, the couple enjoys fifteen months of intimacy until she dies giving birth to Matilda. Her father, surrendering to "the deepest melancholy," flees England to become, like Frankenstein, "a wanderer, a miserable outcast alone!" Matilda suffers from the absence of family. Raised on the shores of Loch Lomond by an aunt, "an unsocial being" who never touches her, Matilda "had no companion." To relieve her solitude, she communes with nature and books in a perversion of a childhood idealized by Rousseau. Her senses provide her with stimulation; the sights and sounds of nature join with books to take "the place of human intercourse." So, too, do her fancies of "affections and intimacies," none of which is an adequate substitute for real people.[12]

When Matilda is sixteen, her father suddenly reappears. Two lonely people craving connection, they immediately nurture an intense intimacy. "And now I began to live," Matilda exults. Father and daughter "were for ever together; and the subjects of our conversations were inexhaustible." On some level, they were still children innocent of the ways of the world. After all, it "is intercourse with civilized society; it is the disappointment of cherished hopes, the falsehood of friends, or the perpetual clash of mean passions that changes the heart and damps the ardour of youthful feelings." Neither father nor daughter knows how to behave; neither understands the need to temper their sensibilities or be wary of unexpected complications.

---

of Incest," 130–149, both in Syndy M. Conger, Frederick S. Frank, and Gregory O'Dea, eds., *Iconoclastic Departures: Mary Shelley after "Frankenstein": Essays in Honor of the Bicentenary of Mary Shelley's Birth* (Madison, N.J., 1997); Anne-Lise François and Daniel Mozes, "'Don't Say 'I Love You': Agency, Gender, and Romanticism in Mary Shelley's *Mathilda*," in Michael Eberle-Sinatra and Nora Crook, eds., *Mary Shelley's Fictions: From "Frankenstein" to "Falkner"* (New York, 2000), 57–74; Pamela Clemit, "From *The Fields of Fancy* to *Matilda*: Mary Shelley's Changing Conception of Her Novella," 64–75, and Charles E. Robinson, "Mathilda as Dramatic Actress," 76–87, both in Betty T. Bennett and Stuart Curran, eds., *Mary Shelley in Her Times* (Baltimore, 2000).

12. MWS, *Matilda*, ed. Todd, 155, 156, 157, 158, 159.

Matilda and her father continue their friendship after the death of the aunt and their removal to London. All is well until a young man begins to court Matilda. Abruptly, the father becomes silent and distant, and her mood shifts from "happiness to despair." She follows him when he leaves for his estate in York. Two months pass. He ignores her. Eventually, she concludes that he was nursing "melancholy as an antidote to wilder passion." But at the time she is simply hurt and bewildered.[13]

Matilda impulsively decides to confront her father and demand the truth in a strategy worthy of Wollstonecraft's with Imlay and Godwin's with Wollstonecraft's life story. Honest conversation will make things right. In retrospect, Matilda decries her "rashness" and takes full responsibility for the consequences. "I alone was the cause of his defeat and justly did I pay the fearful penalty. I said to myself, let him receive sympathy and these struggles will cease. Let him confide his misery to another heart and half the weight of it will be lightened. I will win him to me. . . . Half I accomplished; I gained his secret and we were both lost forever." On a walk, the daughter, rejecting her father's protests, asserts her right to know why he has changed. "You must tell me. . . . I beseech you; by your former love for me now lost, I adjure you to answer that one question. Am I the cause of your grief?" The father demurs repeatedly, warning of the dangers of "a word." But the daughter persuades him to relent. "You are my light, my only one, my life.—My daughter, I love you," he exclaims. Shocked at his own behavior, he declares himself a "Monster." Horrified by his confession and her reaction, Matilda retreats to her room, where she cries for hours without anyone to offer comfort, let alone advice.[14]

In the morning, Matilda finds her father gone, leaving only a letter full of remorse for having "made your innocent heart acquainted with the looks and language of unlawful and monstrous passion. I must expiate these crimes." He will kill himself because he has failed to manage himself. Frantically pursuing her father, Matilda contemplates her ambivalence about whether he "was her lover." A long journey in a violent storm ends in her discovery of his drowned corpse in a cottage on the beach. Nothing can console the bereft Matilda. She has no friends. The support of her "female relations" matters little because "they were nearly all . . . strangers to me." Emotionally numb, unable to grieve or love, she flees to a life of solitude in the north of England. Telling the truth, she concludes, is counterproductive. Rather than reveal the secret about her father, she will lie. Like many

13. Ibid., 161, 164, 169.
14. Ibid., 169, 171, 172, 173.

of Mary Shelley's characters, Matilda seems resigned to her fate. Whatever personal issues inform this behavior, it reflects Matilda's bafflement about how to proceed. Her dilemma is the dilemma of the many women like her.[15]

Two years of solitary communion with nature and books, except for occasional visits from a female servant, cannot shake Matilda's need for social commerce. Like the new man in *Frankenstein,* she needs "one friend to love me." She desires, not "sympathy and aid in ambition or wisdom, but sweet and mutual affection." She finds it when she meets the admirable Woodville, a handsome poet recovering from the death of his fiancée. Gradually, "an intimacy grew between us." Unfortunately, Matilda concludes that her unresolved guilt about her father and her extended solitude have made her "unfit for any intercourse, even with Woodville, the most gentle and sympathizing creature that existed." More than her parents, Mary Shelley appreciated irony. "It is a strange circumstance but it often occurs that blessings by their use turn to curses; and that I who in solitude had desired sympathy as the only relief I could enjoy now found it an additional torture to me." She who had been patient and affectionate had become "arrogant, peevish, and above all suspicious." Woodville tries to help her out of her depression. Although we "know not what all this wide world means; its strange mixture of good and evil," he believes "there is some good beyond us that we must seek." Friendship matters. "You can bestow happiness on another; if you can give one person only one hour of joy ought you not live to do it?" But Matilda cannot be persuaded. An "outcast from human feeling," she cannot overcome her "withering fear" that she is "a marked creature, a pariah, only fit for death." Lying down in wet grass, she falls asleep. When she awakens feeling ill, she is ready to experience a death that will link her to her "father . . . in eternal mental union." Incest is no longer a problem when sex is no longer possible.[16]

The theme of incest that pervaded eighteenth- and nineteenth-century British and American literature is often taken to represent the dangerous consequences of organizing society around love rather than patriarchal institutions. Certainly contemporaries thought so. A father wanting to sleep with his daughter and a daughter surprised by her ambivalence about his desire was yet another example of the social anarchy encouraged by Modern Philosophy. Absolutely anything was now possible. Admitting incestuous feelings did not equate with indulging them. Confronting them, *Matilda* suggested, was better than denying or ignoring them. Mary Shelley's in-

---

15. Ibid., 177, 181, 184, 185.
16. Ibid., 190, 195, 198, 199, 202, 203, 204, 208.

tense relationship with William Godwin was hardly unique in a society that increasingly encouraged a culture of affection within families. Fathers and daughters who were now supposed to love each other were understandably confused about how their behavior ought to differ from that with strangers or spouses. Intimacy took many forms, and fiction allowed writers and readers to think through a broad range of rapidly changing human relationships and their potential to cause both pleasure and pain.[17]

"The Beauty of the Object Resides in His Eyes Instead of in Her Mind"

Contending with men fixated on themselves defined much of Mary Shelley's life. Starting with her father and her husband, she struggled to maintain her independence within the context of social relationships she believed necessary to her happiness. It was a lifelong challenge, one she shared with growing numbers of middle-class women in Great Britain and the United States. In her fiction, she consistently imagined daughters struggling to deal with the deleterious impact of their fathers' and potential lovers' self-love. The revolution her mother had called for in *A Vindication of the Rights of Woman* was succeeding more with women than with men. Well-educated, strong women abounded by the 1820s and 1830s. Like Mary Shelley, they imagined a wide range of social and professional possibilities. The major obstacle to the realization of these dreams was the stubborn refusal of men to imagine happiness as a shared negotiation of desire between two individuals who respected each other. The men in Mary's life and fiction were less rational and more enslaved than women to a runaway sensibility that blinded them to social complexity. Like her mother and many of her peers, Mary continued to advocate for the transformative potential of romantic love. Men might yet be persuaded of the value of multiple perspectives and the importance of obligations.

Unlike Mary Wollstonecraft, Mary Shelley established herself as a professional writer with the help of her husband and father instead of friends such as Joseph Johnson. Rejected by the major publishers in London, probably out of fear that it would offend readers, *Frankenstein* was accepted by Lackington, a small house specializing in horror, on the condition that the

17. See Ellen Pollak, *Incest and the English Novel, 1684–1814* (Baltimore, 2003); and, especially, Mary Jean Corbett, *Family Likeness: Sex, Marriage, and Incest from Jane Austen to Virginia Woolf* (Ithaca, N.Y., 2008). On the United States, see Brian Connolly, "'Every Family Become a School of Abominable Impurity': Incest and Theology in the Early Republic," *Journal of the Early Republic*, XXX (2010), 413–442. See also Katherine C. Hill-Miller, *"My Hideous Progeny": Mary Shelley, William Godwin, and the Father-Daughter Relationship* (Newark, Del., 1995).

publisher would retain all profits from the first edition. Percy Shelley arranged for his wife to receive one-third of the net profits. Lackington expected to sell most of its run of five hundred copies of the three-volume 1818 edition to circulating libraries, whose members would rent the volumes separately. The book earned the publisher around a 300 percent profit, and its author made more money than her husband's oeuvre garnered in his lifetime. When pirated dramatic productions in the 1820s made *Frankenstein* a popular sensation, William Godwin arranged for the publication of a new edition that he presumed to edit. Desperate for income, Mary sold the copyright in 1831 to Richard Bentley for six hundred shillings. Bentley was a speculator who printed cheap one-volume editions of out-of-print fiction. In the first year, he sold more than three thousand copies of a revised edition of *Frankenstein,* replete with an introduction by the author refuting claims that her husband had written the work. Mary never made money from the book again.[18]

Despite this financial fiasco, Mary successfully supported herself and members of her family. In the nearly three decades from the death of Percy in 1822 until her death in 1851, she produced a remarkable number of novels, short stories, essays, reviews, and biographies. She negotiated with publishers and kept a close eye on her manuscripts as they became books. Although her novels never sold more than a few hundred copies, her writing as a whole was a significant source of income.[19]

Mary needed the money. Percy Shelley's father could have provided his daughter-in-law and his grandson with a comfortable income. But he chose not to do so. In November 1823, almost a year and a half after Percy's death, a lawyer informed Mary that her father-in-law would grant her an annual loan of two hundred pounds on the condition that she not make public his son's writings or information about his life. Only the legal requirements of entail ensured that her son, Percy Florence, inherited his grandfather's title and property. Almost three years older than William Godwin, Sir Timothy Shelley was eighty when he died in 1844. His long life was a source of considerable frustration to Mary. Her father, in the meantime, was a financial liability. Declaring bankruptcy in 1825, Godwin gave up selling books, if not writing them. Eight years later, the government granted the author of *Politi-*

---

18. William St. Clair, "The Impact of *Frankenstein,*" in Bennett and Curran, eds., *Mary Shelley in Her Times,* 38–63.

19. Betty T. Bennett, "Feminism and Editing Mary Wollstonecraft Shelley: The Editor And? / Or? the Text," in George Bornstein and Ralph G. Williams, eds., *Palimpsest: Editorial Theory in the Humanities* (Ann Arbor, Mich., 1993), 67–96.

cal Justice an annual income of two hundred pounds and a small house in return for perfunctory performance of a minor post. Upon her father's death in 1836, Mary took responsibility for her stepmother. Mary Jane died in 1841.

Mary mourned Percy as long as she breathed. Declining to enjoy intimacy with another man, she idealized her relationship with her husband as a realization of what her mother had sought with Imlay. In retrospect, their marriage was not a partnership between a man and a woman who complemented each other through a division of household tasks; it was an honest friendship between two individuals who helped each other to manage their passions and live useful lives. The memory of what she had lost underscored Mary's commitment to the possibilities of love. She missed Percy acutely when she wondered whether she had "the talent" to capture the "thoughts and feelings that as a tempest hurry me along." She was "alone," she wrote, and therefore "my voice can with none assume its natural modulation." Her life was *"unnatural"* because it was void of "love, friendship, society, ambition." She could not be happy. Nor could she improve herself. Worried that she was overly sensitive "with my fellow creatures, and yet their victim and dupe," too, she had no monitor, no one with whom she could see herself better, no one with whom she could develop her reason. Social isolation destroyed "the spring of my mind," drained "all strength from my character," and made her "who by nature am too much so—timid."[20]

A dozen years after her husband's death, Mary could not control her self-pity. Fate had been unkind to her. She was cursed with "ill fortune." "*One* Adversity, blotted and sprinkled by *many* adversities" had made her life "a dark ground with sad figures painted on it." Self-doubt even overshadowed the strength she found in the "memory of my Mother." Mary Wollstonecraft was "always . . . the pride and delight of my life" and others' "admiration" for her "the cause of most of [my] happiness," she wrote in 1827. But her mother's "greatness of soul and my father['s] high talents have perpetually reminded me that I ought to degenerate as little as I could from those from who I derived my being." Mary Shelley shrank from "publicity" because she had suffered from "too much of it." Seeking only to be "forgotten," she was "a silly goose—who far from wishing to stand forward to assert myself in any way, now tha[t] I am alone in the world, have but the desire to wrap night and the obscurity of insignificance around me." Every woman who emerged from privacy regretted it. "This is weakness," she knew, but she could not

20. Oct. 2, 1822, Paula R. Feldman and Diana Scott-Kilvert, eds., *The Journals of Mary Shelley, 1814–1822*, 2 vols. (Oxford, 1987), II, 429; MWS to Maria [Reveley] Gisborne, Oct. 30–Nov. 17, [1834], in Bennett, ed., *Letters of Mary Wollstonecraft Shelley*, II, 214.

face being "in print—the subject of *men's* observations—of the bitter hard world's commentaries." She struggled to overcome her timidity by engaging with her parents and husband as she imagined them to have been. "Many men have [Percy Shelley's] opinions," she admitted, but "none fearlessly and conscientiously act on them, as he did—it is his act that marks him." Similarly, if her parents had chosen the path of delicacy—if her mother had not challenged women and men to do better, if her father had not written so honestly of her mother—would they be so worthy of her respect? Like her sister Fanny, Mary did not want to disgrace *"such a mother."* Unlike Fanny, she found her voice, imagining dilemmas that reflected both personal experience and cultural expectations.[21]

Mary's tendency to feel sorry for herself was hardly unwarranted. She had known grief as much or more than affection. The births and deaths of children preoccupied Mary and Percy during their relatively short marriage. A son, William Godwin, was born in early 1816. Later that year, the suicides of Fanny and Harriet likely left both of them more attuned to social obligation. Percy sought custody of the daughter and son he had fathered with Harriet despite the objections of her family. In March 1817 the lord chancellor denied his petition on the grounds he would teach them immorality and placed Eliza Ianthe and Charles Bysshe with foster parents. That disappointment was followed by the birth in September of Clara Everina. Percy and Mary left England for Italy in March 1818. Grief followed them. Clara died in Venice in September, and William the next June in Rome. By then Mary was pregnant with Percy Florence, who would be born in Florence in November 1819 and would die in 1889. The Shelleys also adopted a young girl (Elena Adelaide) who might have been Percy's child; in any case, she died in 1820 at the age of two. And then there was intermittent responsibility for Allegra, the daughter of Claire and Byron, until her death at the age of five in 1822. No wonder Mary fell into a deep depression in 1819 and the writings of both husband and wife turned dark.

Percy Florence survived to become his mother's only real companion. By the time Percy was fifteen, Mary's relationship with him reflected her general ambivalence about men. Taking a friend's advice to cultivate his affection, she admitted he was "a blessing." He gave her reason to live, although

21. MWS to Gisborne, Oct. 30–Nov. 17, [1834], in Bennett, ed., *Letters of Mary Wollstonecraft Shelley,* II, 214, to Frances Wright, Sept. 12, 1827, 3–4, to Edward John Trelawny, April 1[829], 72; Fanny Imlay Godwin to Mary Godwin, May 29, 1816, in Marion Kingston Stocking, ed., *The Clairmont Correspondence: Letters of Claire Clairmont, Charles Clairmont, and Fanny Imlay Godwin,* 2 vols. (Baltimore, 1995), I, 49, July 29, Aug. 1, 1816, 56.

there "is no sympathy in a child," and he would eventually marry and leave her entirely alone. Mary had enrolled Percy at Harrow to ensure he would receive the public education his father had wanted him to have, but her "poverty" required him to live with her rather than his peers. If Percy lacked "ambition" and "transcendant" talent, she was proud of her "fine, spirited, clever Boy." He and his friends enjoyed "liberty to the verge of licence," but they rarely indulged it beyond breaking a few windows. Her son benefited from living with his mother because she encouraged more attention to "the cultivation of the affections." Still, he who yielded "either to persuasion or rebuke" at home with her was "very haughty . . . with his Boys—their utmost violence can never make him give in a jot—he can say *No,* which I cannot do—and has lively spirits." Mary's sketch of her son as "a strange mixture of Shelley and I" reflected her uncertainty about male susceptibility to transformation through love.[22]

Men, even sensible men, her experience suggested, performed as much, or more, for other men than they did for women. In London in 1816, the couple had become friends with the writer and critic Leigh Hunt and his wife Marianne. Through them, they met the poet John Keats, among others. While in Italy, Percy and Mary renewed their relationships with the Hunts and Keatses as well as Byron, Hogg, and Medwin. They met the restless Edward John Trelawny, who was with the couple in the last few months of Percy's life. The Shelleys were close with Maria Reveley Gisborne—the woman who two decades earlier William Godwin had asked to become Mary's stepmother—and her husband John Gisborne. Even closer was their relationship with Jane and Edward Williams, with whom they were living in San Terenzo in the late spring of 1822. The Williamses were not married; in fact, Jane was still legally married to the abusive and absent husband from whom Edward had rescued her in London in 1818. Percy and Jane shared an intense friendship, although its extent remains unclear. Edward Williams, who never complained about the relationship between his lover and his friend, died with Percy.[23]

Multiple configurations of romantic love flourished within circles of English writers and their admirers in Italy, some homosocial, if not homosexual. The tendency of Percy's male friends to fall in love with the women Percy loved reflected their strong attraction to him. Shortly after the deaths

22. MWS to Gisborne, Oct. 30–Nov. 17, [1834], in Bennett, ed., *Letters of Mary Wollstonecraft Shelley,* II, 214, 215.

23. Jeffrey N. Cox, *Poetry and Politics in the Cockney School: Keats, Shelley, Hunt, and Their Circle* (New York, 1998).

of Percy and Edward Williams, a devastated Thomas Jefferson Hogg decided he was in love with Jane Williams. Married to one man, living with another, and flirting heavily with yet another, Jane was no stranger to multiple possibilities. In any case, Percy's interest in Jane ensured Hogg's interest in Jane. Suddenly on her own with two sons to support, Jane could hardly decline Hogg's protestations of eternal love. Never married, Jane and Hogg had two daughters, one in 1827 and another in 1838. Hogg supported his family by writing and working as a lawyer. He died in 1862, leaving behind a self-serving and inaccurate biography of Percy, whose friendship was his only claim to fame. Trelawny behaved in a similar fashion. Having divorced his wife for infidelity with an older man, Trelawny fell in love with Claire Clairmont when he met her in Italy. Twice she refused his offer of marriage. The second time was in 1828 after Mary Shelley had turned him down. Living with a succession of mistresses, Trelawny marketed imagined, exaggerated, and self-serving memories of his time among the poets in Italy. He died in England in 1881. His ashes were taken to Rome and buried next to the grave of Percy. On his tombstone was an epitaph typical of Trelawny's gift for embellishment. A relationship that had lasted a matter of months in 1822 became a story of "two friends whose lives were undivided" and whose "two hearts in life were single hearted." These were Percy Shelley's words in a poem entitled "Epitaph." But the friendship Percy was invoking was the one he had enjoyed with Edward Williams.[24]

The Shelley marriage remained affectionate despite the loss of children and the tensions engendered by liaisons that were emotional, if not physical, affairs. When Mary returned with her son to London after Percy's death, she reestablished an equally fraught relationship with her father. Mary often experienced William Godwin's love as controlling, as an extension of his regard for himself. Certainly he constructed himself as a rival of her lover. In 1819, when she was seriously depressed, he pointedly reminded her that she had a husband "of your choice, to whom you seem to be unalterably attached." Percy was "a man of high intellectual endowments" and low "morality." A jealous Godwin wanted his "dearest Mary" to remain close to him. No wonder Mary wrote *Matilda.* In the spring of 1822, Godwin tried unsuccessfully in the wake of one of their long-distance fights to break with her entirely, entreating her "to forget that you have a father in existence" because of the pain their many misunderstandings caused each other. Then Percy died. As soon as he heard the news, a compassion-

24. The most recent account of these relationships is Daisy Hay, *Young Romantics: The Tangled Lives of English Poetry's Greatest Generation* (New York, 2010), 311.

ate Godwin was offering her self-serving paternal advice about what to do with her life. She was "the best judge," of course. But she should return to England where, having lost her "closest friend," she would find solace with her "earliest friend." Father and daughter could be "a great support to each other" in a world of endless trials now that the source of their contention (Percy, that is) was gone. Until Godwin's death, Mary would struggle, as she had with Percy, to sustain her sense of independence within a relationship she believed necessary to her happiness. The challenge did not evaporate when he was gone. Agreeing to compose "Memoirs and Correspondence of the Late William Godwin" for her stepmother, she worked on it only sporadically, perhaps because it was easier (and less painful for herself and her son) to contemplate her father in fiction. In the fragments she wrote, she idealized her parents' marriage, stressed the piety of Godwin's memoir of Wollstonecraft, and sanitized her father's relationships with other women as a quest to fill a hole created by her mother's death.[25]

Mary Shelley never gave up on the value of cultivating "sympathy and companionship" with other individuals. "To be loved is indeed necessary," she argued, especially for people who saw themselves as members of a middle class. Unlike the overworked poor and the diverted rich, middling people had to contend with "ennui," "listlessness and weariness." Nothing—not "books, operas, concerts, hunting, shooting, balls, picture-dealing, building, planting, travelling, fanciful changes of dress, [or] gambling," not "professions, trades, nor ambition," not "wisdom" or "science"—could "take the sting from life" and change "its burthen to gladness: this miracle is left for the affections; and the best form of affection, from the excess of its sympathy, is Love." Love was the enemy of "satiety" and "sorrow" because it was the practice of intimacy, the ultimate form of commerce. Mary quoted Percy's description of love as "that powerful attraction towards all we conceive, or fear, or hope beyond ourselves." It was the "meeting with an understanding capable of clearly estimating our own, an imagination which should enter into . . . a frame whose nerves, like the chords of two exquisite lyres strung to the accompaniment of one delightful voice, vibrate with the vibrations of our own."[26]

25. William Godwin to MWS, Sept. 9, 1819, Oxford, Bodleian, MS Abinger c. 45, fol. 18, [Godwin] to MWS, Apr. 19, 1822, c. 45, fols. 122–123, Godwin to MWS, Aug. 9, 1822, c. 45, fols. 135–136. See also Godwin to MWS, May 3, 1822, c. 45, fol. 128, and Godwin to MWS, Aug. 6, 1822, c. 45, fols. 131–132. See Hill-Miller, *"My Hideous Progeny"*; and Judith Barbour, "Mary Shelley: Writing / Other Women in Godwin's 'Life,'" in Helen M. Buss, D. L. Macdonald, and Anne McWhir, eds., *Mary Wollstonecraft and Mary Shelley: Writing Lives* (Waterloo, Ont., 2001), 139–157.

26. MWS to Gisborne, Oct. 30–Nov. 17, [1834], in Bennett, ed., *Letters of Mary Wollstonecraft*

Claire complained that her stepsister was too generous because she declined to give an "immense drubbing" to men who mistreated women. But Mary was hardly naive. She knew from her own experience that romantic love was "imperious, intense and pervading." The challenge for "women, whose being is formed for tenderness and sympathy" was to decipher "among whom in the harder, harsher sex this feeling [of love] exists in its greatest purity and force." Not surprisingly, she identified a poet as a man who understood love as sympathy, as an expression of attention to his lover. And yet even a poet allowed that wanton, the imagination, to conjure a woman as he wanted her to be, unaware that "the beauty of the object resides in his eyes instead of in her mind or form." In fact, few women would find men willing to engage with them as friends rather than objects of their fancy.[27]

Successful marriages were uncommon because persuadable men were uncommon. But marriages, Mary came to believe, were necessary as a relatively secure space in which women could reasonably expect men to behave well. Obvious differences between the sexes required women to accept some level of dependence on men. "Human beings in every stage of life need companions," she wrote. But "women [need] protectors," although she was skeptical about whether there were "worthy companions and protectors" for any but "the highminded and delicate." Mary warned that a woman who found a "man on whom she may bestow without sorrow her tenderness" was unlikely to "find a second." That was tragic, for men and women were necessary to each other. A "solitary woman [was] the world's victim," and a man "not allied to a female" would never change. There was "something rugged, harsh, and unnatural in the very idea" of individuals living alone, or so Mary's experience suggested.[28]

Mary Shelley preferred to engage this cultural conundrum in fiction rather than biographies or essays. Because "reality and fiction" were "brother and sister," they "may not therefore too closely unite, marry, and produce an offspring which is neither true nor false." In novels, writers and characters could do work virtually impossible to accomplish in reality—that is, they could live out the imagined possibilities and perils of mixed-gender

Shelley, II, 214; [MWS], review of *The Loves of the Poets,* by [Anna Jameson], *Westminster Review,* XI (October 1829), 472, 473.

27. Claire Clairmont to MWS, Mar. 15, 1836, in Stocking, ed., *Clairmont Correspondence,* I, 342; [MWS], review of *Loves of the Poets,* by [Jameson], *Westminster Review,* XI (October 1829), 473, 475, 476.

28. [MWS], review of *Loves of the Poets,* by [Jameson], *Westminster Review,* XI (October 1829), 475, 476.

sociability. History was tied to examinations of the world as it was; fiction discussed the world as it might be. A novelist worked through "a converse with the world" as a whole rather than a study of the limited evidence that "'cribbed and cabined in'" a historian. As important, novels permitted immersion in the mysteries of human motivation. The wide latitude of "fictitious history" revealed more of "the science of man, than whatever can be exhibited by the historian." A good novelist, such as her father, deployed "a comprehensive and bold imagination" to examine the ambiguities of motivation. Godwin's genius lay in his ability to enter into "the very souls of his personages; he dives into their secret hearts, and lays bare, even to their anatomy, their workings" in order to blend all "into one whole, which forms the pervading impulse of the individual he brings before us." He was a master of empathy. His readers went with him "into the very form and frame of his creatures: our hearts swell responsive to every emotion he delineates." And they learned "'that the true key of the universe is love.'"[29]

After Godwin's death, Mary Shelley indulged her recurrent sense of her life as a gauntlet of grief. Suffering the deaths of three children and her husband, she endured "blow after blow" until "my heart dies within me." All she could do was "weep." Well, no, there was something else she could do. Like her mother and father, she could write. She could create characters living her dilemmas. She could talk with readers as friends "in peace of heart—the imagination at work alone—some warmth imparted to them by the strong conjuring up of fictitious woes—but tranquil in their own bosoms." Writing fiction was not a diversion for women with too much time on their hands. More than a source of income, novels were a means of social engagement. Like marriages, they were bounded by conventions. But honoring literary borders, like honoring legal borders, did not preclude experimentation or challenges to authority. To the contrary, novels often encouraged them.[30]

"The Soul of Woman" and "The Character of Men"

Published first in London and then in New York, Mary Shelley's last two novels, *Lodore* (1835) and *Falkner* (1837), offered nuanced explorations of the power of love to encourage mutuality between men and women. Continuing a conversation begun by her mother and her friends in the 1790s

29. [MWS], review of *Loves of the Poets*, by [Jameson], *Westminster Review*, XI (October 1829), 474; [MWS], review of *Cloudesley: A Tale*, by William Godwin, *Blackwood's Edinburgh Magazine*, XXVII (May 1830), 711, 712, 716.

30. June 7, 1836, in Feldman and Scott-Kilvert, eds., *Journals of Mary Shelley*, II, 548.

and developed by her father and other novelists around the Atlantic in the early 1800s, she was particularly interested in the consequences of a general male failure to substitute intimate friendship for egocentric self-love. Too often, men lived in isolation from women, whether they were by themselves or dependent on relationships with other men. Older men identified primarily as fathers suffered most acutely from this problem, usually with profound consequences for themselves and their daughters or surrogate daughters. Lodore and Falkner are middle-aged figures tortured by the unmediated choices of their youth. Their only companions are motherless daughters shaped by their behavior. The behavior of the fathers or surrogate fathers shapes the lives of everyone around them. Young women trying to make lives for themselves with confused young men cannot escape the legacy of their fathers.[31]

Contemporary critics, commending Mary Shelley's success in *Lodore* and *Falkner* in creating real people in real situations, were especially taken with

31. See Anne K. Mellor, *Mary Shelley: Her Life, Her Fiction, Her Monsters* (New York, 1989); Hill-Miller, *"My Hideous Progeny"*; Lisa Vargo, "Introduction," in Shelley, *Lodore,* ed. Vargo, 9–40; and Vargo, "Further Thoughts on the Education of Daughters: *Lodore* as an Imagined Conversation with Mary Wollstonecraft," in Buss, Macdonald, and McWhir, eds., *Mary Wollstonecraft and Mary Shelley,* 177–187; Charlene E. Bunnell, "The Illusion of 'Great Expectations': Manners and Morals in Mary Shelley's *Lodore* and *Falkner,*" in Conger, Frank, and O'Dea, eds., *Iconoclastic Departures,* 275–293; Sharon L. Jowell, "Mary Shelley's Mothers: The Weak, the Absent, and the Silent in *Lodore* and *Falkner,*" *European Romantic Review,* VIII (1997), 298–322; David Vallins, "Mary Shelley and the Lake Poets: Negation and Transcendence in *Lodore,*" 164–180, Julia Saunders, "Rehabilitating the Family in Mary Shelley's *Falkner,*" 211–223, and Graham Allen, "Public and Private Fidelity: Mary Shelley's 'Life of William Godwin' and *Falkner,*" 224–242, all in Eberle-Sinatra and Crook, eds., *Mary Shelley's Fictions;* Betty T. Bennett, "'Not This Time, Victor': Mary Shelley's Reversioning of Elizabeth, from *Frankenstein* to *Falkner,*" in Bennett and Curran, eds., *Mary Shelley in Her Times,* 1–17; Lisa Hopkins, "'A Medea, in More Sense Than the More Glorious One': Motherhood in Mary Shelley's *Lodore* and *Falkner,*" *Eighteenth-Century Novel,* II (2002), 383–405; Kate Ferguson Ellis, "*Falkner* and Other Fictions," in Schor, ed., *Cambridge Companion to Mary Shelley,* 151–162; and Melissa Stites, "Utopian Domesticity as Social Reform in Mary Shelley's *Falkner,*" *Keats-Shelley Journal,* LIV (2005), 148–172. More generally, see Sandra M. Gilbert and Susan Gubar, *The Madwoman in the Attic: The Woman Writer and the Nineteenth-Century Literary Imagination,* 2d ed. (1979; rpt. New Haven, Conn., 2000), 213–247; Margaret Homans, "Bearing Demons: *Frankenstein's* Circumvention of the Maternal," *Bearing the Word: Language and the Female Experience in Nineteenth-Century Women's Writing* (Chicago, 1986), 100–119; Paul A. Cantor, "Mary Shelley and the Taming of the Byronic Hero: 'Transformation' and *The Deformed Transformed,*" in Audrey A. Fisch, Anne K. Mellor, and Esther H. Schor, eds., *The Other Mary Shelley* (New York, 1993), 89–106; and Annette R. Federico, ed., *Gilbert and Gubar's "The Madwoman in the Attic" after Thirty Years* (Columbia, Mo., 2009), esp. Katey Castellano, "Feminism to Ecofeminism: The Legacy of Gilbert and Gubar's Readings of Mary Shelley's *Frankenstein* and *The Last Man,*" 76–93.

her male characters. One reviewer thought her "a remarkable exception" to the rule that female writers were "incapable of creating a strongly-marked masculine character." She was particularly adept at studying "the anatomy of feelings and of thoughts" that "work below the surface." Another writer commented that she was able to "unveil the soul of woman to its very uttermost" and "divine, appreciate, and depict the character of men." Her work was serious in ways that many "modern novels," with their "faded anthology of *effeté* jests, of shrivelled gallantries, and impassible sentimentalities," were not. Her meandering plots only slightly detracted from her investigation of the impact of well-intentioned human beings on one another. Time and again, she developed the theme of love, treating "the hopes and fears, the joys and sorrows, the delights and dangers, the blessings and the evils, of the fierce and tender passion" and warning that social commerce between men and women had unanticipated as well as beneficial consequences.[32]

The behavior of Henry, Lord Lodore, and his wife, Cornelia, affirms the social critique laid out in Wollstonecraft's *Vindication of the Rights of Woman.* Lodore exemplifies the danger of male self-love. Squashing "the smallest resistance to his desires," he fails to consider the "feelings" of others beyond their presumed joy "in serving him." Like most men, he confuses independence with "freedom from all trammels, except those of which he was wholly unconscious, imposed on him by his passions and pride." More a slave of his sensibility than most women, he "appeared to live rather in a dream than in the actual world." Cherishing "an ideal of what he thought a woman ought to be," Lodore cannot respect any woman as an independent human being. But he has the same problem with men, indeed, with everyone. Educated to command and to obsess about his honor, or reputation, Lodore has no idea of how to persuade or even of the need to persuade. He is insensible to the truth that those who exercise power "must in some degree follow, if they would lead, and it is by adapting themselves to the humour of those they would command, that they establish the law of their own will." Lodore "was imperious: opposition startled and disconcerted him." His choice of wife is therefore predictable. Smart, confident, older women make good mistresses. Wives should be pliable, subservient girls notable for their sexual allure. A female version of Lodore in her self-love, Cornelia is obsessed with fashion, parties, and love as sensation. Preoccupied with satisfying her own desires, she has no time for either her husband or their daughter, Ethel. Underneath the surface, of course, both

32. Bentley, review of *Lodore,* by MWS, *Examiner,* no. 1425 (May 24, 1835), 323, 324; *Fraser's Magazine for Town and Country,* XI, no. 65 (May 1835), 600–601.

Lodore and Cornelia are miserably unhappy. Men educated to be tyrants and women trained to be dolls cannot sustain useful lives or build happy families. They do not understand friendship, let alone love, as social processes. The chief victim of her parents' self-love is Ethel.[33]

Mary Shelley insists, as always, that the love of a parent for a child is the only worthy rival of the affection shared by lovers. But they are not mutually exclusive. Parental love, in fact, enhances romantic love. In the novels, men tend to awaken through engagement with daughters rather than wives. Humiliated by his wife's flirtations and his related loss of honor, Lodore leaves London for Illinois, taking Ethel with him. Cornelia chooses not to accompany them. Under her father's tutelage in an isolated setting, Ethel grows into a sympathetic, weak young woman. The antithesis of an ambitious male, she is every bit as enslaved to her imagination. "Nothing with her centred in self; she was always ready to give her soul away: to please her father was the unsleeping law of all her actions." Ethel grows up believing she ought to devote herself to pleasing a lover as she does her father. On their journey back to England, Lodore is killed in New York in a duel precipitated by gossip about his past. Ethel arrives in London where she falls in love with a young man struggling to make the transition from an aristocratic to a commercial world. The young lovers are too naive to confront reality. If they are more sincerely attached than the Lodores, they still live in a world as they imagine it should be.[34]

The alternative to Ethel is her new friend, Fanny Derham, the daughter of an old companion of Lodore. Fanny is intellectual and assertive. She loves her "darling books." Men are uncomfortable with Fanny because she will not allow them to construct her. Fanny, indeed, "was more made to be loved by her own sex than by the opposite one." "Superiority of intellect, joined to acquisitions beyond those usual even to men; and both announced with frankness, though without pretension, forms a kind of anomaly little in accord with masculine taste." Fanny and Ethel are different because of different educations supervised by different fathers. "Each had been the favourite daughter of men of superior qualities of mind" who wanted to do well by daughters they loved. But Ethel had received a sexual education. Lord Lodore had formed his ideal of what a woman ought to be, of what he had wished to find in his wife, and sought to mold his daughter accordingly. Mr. Derham contemplated the duties and objects befitting an

33. MWS, *Lodore,* ed. Vargo, 81, 82, 86, 101, 102.
34. Ibid., 63.

immortal soul and had educated his child for the performance of them. "The one fashioned his offspring to be the wife of a frail human being, instructed her to be yielding, and to make it her duty to devote herself to his happiness, and to obey his will. The other sought to guard his from all weakness, to make her complete in herself, and to render her independent and self-sufficing." Their education shaped their choices. Ethel gave "herself away with unreserved prodigality" to an equally profligate (emotionally as well as financially) lover, whereas Fanny "zealously guarded her individuality." Ethel "was guided by the tenderness of her heart, while [Fanny] consulted her understanding." Where Ethel was too deferential, Fanny was too "Quixotic." In the end, however, Fanny is more successful at blending judgment and empathy, although at the cost of never experiencing romantic love herself. Her life may "be presented as a useful lesson . . . to teach what goodness and genius can achieve in palliating the woes of life, and to encourage" women to imitate her example of "undeviating observance of those moral laws on which all human excellence is founded—a love of truth in ourselves, and a sincere sympathy with our fellow-creatures." Ethel and Fanny improve each other. Like the love of a parent for a child, the love of two friends does not detract from the possibilities of heterosexual romance. To the contrary, the love shared by the two women, like any form of love experienced as a cultivation of mutuality, complements heterosexual relationships.[35]

The happy ending of *Lodore*—Cornelia, realizing the folly of her selfish life, finds true love and provides her daughter and her lover with an income—is not convincing. Like Charles Brockden Brown in *Clara Howard* and *Jane Talbot,* Mary Shelley was too good at dramatizing the tenacity of self-love and the rarity of love practiced as engagement between two individuals who respect each other. The revolution called for in *Vindication* is incomplete at best. Cornelia's late awakening is too convenient. Lodore dies not really understanding what he has wrought. The future of Ethel's husband hardly seems promising. Most ominous is the sense that young women who reject the model of Cornelia must choose between the extremes of Ethel and Fanny.

Published two years after *Lodore* and written during the death of William Godwin, *Falkner* offers a qualified affirmation of the power of love to transform men as well as a social role for strong women. Falkner is another un-

---

35. Ibid., 316, 317, 321–322, 323, 448. See Sharon Marcus, *Between Women: Friendship, Desire, and Marriage in Victorian England* (Princeton, N.J., 2007).

happy middle-aged man who finds the possibility of redemption for his sins in his love for a young orphan he makes his surrogate daughter. Staying away from England as much as possible, Falkner raises Elizabeth (with the occasional help of a female governess) while traveling incessantly on the European continent. Mary Shelley does not commend this exile any more than she does Lodore's isolation of Ethel on the Illinois prairie. Although Elizabeth meets many people, she has no real friends, especially women who could function as mothers or mentors. The narrator warns that their sojourn on the Continent is "a fearful experiment" by an impetuous man who has taken Elizabeth "away from all the ties of blood—the manners and customs of her country—from the discipline of regular education, and the society of others of her sex." The upside is that Elizabeth has come to accept that powerful men dominate her life. For better or worse, she "early learn[ed] the woman's first and hardest lesson, to bear in silence the advance of an evil which might be avoided, but for the unconquerable will of another." Elizabeth grows into an independent woman, a mixture of Ethel's empathy and Fanny's assertiveness. When Falkner finally returns to London, Elizabeth takes charge of his household. Blessed with a "true feminine love of home," she possesses initiative and impatience with the "frivolous and indifferent." Elizabeth becomes friends with Gerard Neville, a young man whose mother disappeared when he was a child. Like Elizabeth, Gerard has learned to manage his passions. The "boy driven to wildness by a sense of injury . . . had subdued the selfish portion of his feeling—grown kind as a woman—active, friendly, and sympathizing, as few men are." The two friends share an affinity that slowly grows into love.[36]

Just as Elizabeth is more complex than Ethel, Falkner is more complex than Lodore. He wants to shape Elizabeth so that she will be "centred in him." But he also strives to love her, not as he had loved a woman in his youth, "only in imagination, but in every thought and sensation, to the end of time." Eventually, compelled to explain his odd behavior, Falkner tells Elizabeth the story of his life. It is an orgy of remorse intensified by his surrogate daughter's growing love for Gerard, a man Falkner knows is the son of a woman who died thwarting his desire for her. Revealing his real name is Rupert, he confesses that, if he is not a "monster," he is a criminal. Orphaned at an early age and indifferently educated, he never experienced love or friendship and became a slave to his sensibility. Strongly attracted to a beautiful woman named Alithea, he cannot have her because he sees her only as a projection of his desire. Not even a decade of self-imposed exile

---

36. MWS, *Falkner: A Novel* (New York, 1837), 35, 63, 83–84, 88, 93.

in India cures him of lust he mistakes as love. He does not esteem her; he simply wants her.[37]

Back in England, Falkner will not accept Alithea's choice to stay in a marriage she consented to while he was in India. Alithea admits her marriage is a disaster. Confessing her unhappiness to her would-be lover, she explains that she will not leave her monstrous husband because she will not abandon her child. "Let us be friends, Rupert," she pleads, "brother and sister." Miserable as she is, she "will not repine at the circumstances that lead me rather to devote my existence to my children, than to be that most blessed creature, a happy wife—I do not ask for that happiness." When Rupert reminds her of her husband's "base jealousy, his selfishness, his narrow soul, and brutish violence," she reminds him that *mother* is "a more sacred name than wife." Late one night, Alithea brings Gerard to a clandestine meeting where Falkner hopes to "induce her to assert her freedom, and follow me voluntarily" to America. When she refuses, he and his assistant kidnap her and take her to a hut on the beach where "she should be free." But Alithea is free only in her eager lover's mind. A slave to his fancy, Falkner cannot accommodate himself to "the real world." Too late, he realizes his problem is that he "never could force myself to do the thing I hated; I never could persuade myself to relinquish the thing I desired." In the middle of a powerful storm, replete with lightning, wind, and a roiled sea, Falkner finally accepts Alithea's choice and decides to take her home, seek her pardon, and confess to her husband. But, when he leaves her briefly, Alithea drowns attempting to escape.[38]

Falkner's behavior is far more heinous than Lodore's. But Elizabeth accepts his expiation as well as his transformation from ambitious egotist into a sympathetic man. The narrator worries that Elizabeth is too generous. "So engrossed by sympathy for others," she sometimes "forget[s] herself wholly." But her behavior is rational from her perspective. Falkner needs Elizabeth "to forgive and console" him. "He must feel that the hour of remorse was past; that of repentance and forgiveness come. He must be rewarded for all his goodness to her." Unlike the monster in *Frankenstein,* Falkner has found a loving companion in his surrogate daughter through whom he has enjoyed true love. But Mary Shelley makes it difficult for readers to empathize with a man responsible for the death of an innocent mother and the near ruin of her son. After all, as Elizabeth muses, we can find excuses for any crime. But loyal Elizabeth will *not* abandon Falkner, a man she loves

37. Ibid., 34, 150, 164, 166.
38. Ibid., 194, 195, 196, 197, 198, 199.

as a father, a man who has done well by her, a man who needs her. An honest woman who respects her conscience, she "had been brought up to regard feelings, rather than conventional observances; duties, not proprieties." Defiant Elizabeth will give up everything, including "every claim on my family," to be Falkner's friend.[39]

Men as well as women have to decide whether to forgive Falkner, a decision contingent on whether they believe his conversion is real. Gerard, more deeply injured than Elizabeth, is more profoundly conflicted. Reading Falkner's narrative, he feels pity and compassion because he understands the events from his perspective. Falkner had terrorized his mother and facilitated her death, but he is not a murderer. Gerard's love and respect for Elizabeth encourages him to forgive Falkner. She "had opened in his soul an unknown spring of sympathy, to relieve the melancholy which had hitherto overwhelmed him. With her he gave way freely to the impulses of a heart which longed to mingle its hitherto checked stream of feeling with other and sweeter waters. In every way he excited her admiration as well as kindness." He recites poetry; they listen to music. When Falkner is acquitted by a jury, all seems to have ended well. Love has triumphed. Or so Gerard ambiguously explains to his dying father: "Who would rule by power, when so much more absolute a tyranny is established through love!" The end, even for a sympathetic man, it would seem, is always tyranny.[40]

Because he is talking to another man about the exchange of his daughter, Gerard is more assertive with Falkner. He does not ask for Elizabeth; he proclaims his right to her. Their "mutual attachment" demands "extraordinary conduct." He will accept his "mother's destroyer" as his friend. But his actual declaration echoes the young Falkner's longing for his mother. Gerard and Elizabeth "love each other—no earthly power shall deprive me of her—sooner or later she must, she shall be mine; and meanwhile this continued separation is painful beyond my fortitude to bear." Falkner, in turn, is happy to hand over his surrogate daughter as if she is a beloved object. "I shall give my Elizabeth to you with confidence and pleasure. You deserve her." This exchange between two well-meaning men suggests that male self-love is never entirely extinguished. The novel concludes in peace, however. Falkner lives near Elizabeth, Gerard, and their children. The younger man, the narrator assures us, has never "repented the irresistible impulse that led him to become the friend of him whose act had rendered his childhood miserable, but who completed the happiness of his maturer years." Love

39. Ibid., 210, 248, 249.
40. Ibid., 236, 293.

had produced a revolution, however incomplete and fraught with peril. A man with every reason to surrender to hatred had managed his passion in conversation with a woman he loved and respected.[41]

In *Lodore* and *Falkner,* Mary Shelley continued to investigate the issues that had preoccupied her parents. In the 1790s, they had lived in a time of revolution when anything seemed possible, or at least worth discussing. Four decades later, their daughter wrote books for an urban middle class in Great Britain and the United States committed to the sanctity of an affectionate nuclear family as the foundation of human progress. Many imagined themselves besieged by working-class, aristocratic, and diverse peoples around the world whom they fancied incapable of governing themselves, disqualified by race, religion, and inadequate education. The radical aspect of the Wollstonecraft-Godwin circle, their insistence that love could transform malleable human beings, acquired an imperial dimension, one that reflected the values of relatively fortunate and powerful people whose goal was to remake people all over the world in their image. Novelists in Britain and America were lucky that they had the time and income to support their commitment to thinking through the complexities of human relationships. Most people in the nineteenth century were preoccupied with more pressing problems, like having enough food to eat.

Still, if the writings of Mary Wollstonecraft, William Godwin, and Mary Shelley reflect the concerns of a cohort of middling English-speaking people steeped in the language of an eighteenth-century sensibility, they endure because we continue to recognize the questions they asked and the dilemmas they confronted. Their appeal lies not in their answers or solutions so much as in their expectation of our empathy, their demand that we engage with them, their revelation of their struggles to deal with grief, melancholy, disappointment, missed opportunities, and unexpected consequences. Human beings, they knew all too well, hurt and destroy one another, not just through conquest and enslavement but also through well-intentioned efforts to possess one another personally. Discarding institutions and ideas that had subjugated the mass of mankind for centuries, revolution in the name of liberty offered no obvious remedy for that particular problem. It merely underscored the challenge of imagining a way forward that honored the desires and ambitions of all people, women as well as men, children as well as parents.

Love, in their view, was a means to an end, an affirmation of the social

41. Ibid., 315, 317, 321.

value of mutuality. It was hard work that all too often ended in failure, a source of misery as well as joy, an erratic and, at best, incremental awakening by men and women to an understanding of how necessary they are to each other. The ultimate unanswered question posed by the time of revolution was whether a democratic culture of self-expression would produce anything more substantial than a cacophony of noise, the anarchy Edmund Burke and religious critics anticipated. Wollstonecraft, Godwin, and Mary Shelley did not envision a world of perfect people living in a society of complete freedom. In their world, nothing was free. But rather than manage human passions and conflict through coercion and repression, they argued for an open society that encouraged honest conversation among human beings who respected one another.

Even in the depths of personal misery and serious doubts about the impact of men and women on each other, Mary Shelley would not surrender this faith in the possibilities of romantic love. Her husband had written in the painful year of 1819 that people ought to strive

> To suffer woes which Hope thinks infinite;
> To forgive wrongs darker than Death or Night;
> To defy Power, which seems Omnipotent;
> To love, and bear; to hope till Hope creates
> From its own wreck the thing it contemplates."

Mary Wollstonecraft had put it less grandly when she told Gilbert Imlay that she wished to be as necessary to him as he was to her. Ultimately, what she wanted was not what he wanted. That wanton, the imagination, had brought her pain and despair. But the hope it offered was worth the price she paid. In the end, the daughter to whom she gave birth just days before she died, the daughter who survived the deaths of her own lover and their children, the daughter who lived surrounded by men who so often behaved like monsters, agreed. If it was too late for Imlay, it was not too late for everyone.[42]

---

42. Percy Bysshe Shelley, "Prometheus Unbound," in Donald H. Reiman and Neil Fraistat, eds., *Shelley's Poetry and Prose: Authoritative Texts, Criticism,* 2d ed. (New York, 2002), 285–286.

"The subject was of Love"

In 1825, forty-seven-year-old William Hazlitt published a collection of character sketches intended to reveal *The Spirit of the Age.* The names of several of his subjects—Jeremy Bentham, Samuel Taylor Coleridge, Walter Scott, Lord Byron, William Wordsworth, and Thomas Malthus—remain familiar to us. Most, however, have grown dim in memory, or vanished altogether. Some were disappearing while they still breathed. Preeminent in this regard was William Godwin. In the 1790s, Hazlitt claimed, "No one was more talked of, more looked up to, more sought after" than Godwin. His works *Political Justice* and *Caleb Williams* provoked discussion all over the North Atlantic world; his wife was the author of several controversial books, including, most famously, *A Vindication of the Rights of Woman;* and his "New Philosophy" had inspired admiration and outrage in equal measure. Now Godwin was "to all ordinary intents and purposes dead and buried." Hazlitt did not mention that Godwin's daughter and his recently deceased son-in-law were eclipsing him in reputation. In any case, the diffident radical had become "as easy as an old glove," a sentimental old man whose apparent preference for romancing the past over engaging the present had made him complicit in his own obscurity. Having "survived most of the celebrated persons with whom he [had] lived in habits of intimacy," Godwin dwelt "with peculiar delight on a day passed at John Kemble's in company with Mr Sheridan, Mr Curran, Mrs Wolstonecraft and Mrs Inchbald, when the conversation took a most animated turn and the subject was of Love." The world Godwin remembered was a world lost forever.[1]

1. William Hazlitt, "William Godwin," in Hazlitt, *The Spirit of the Age; or, Contemporary Portraits* (1825), in Duncan Wu, ed., *The Selected Writings of William Hazlitt,* 9 vols. (London, 1998),

Figure 14. William Godwin. *By Henry William Pickersgill. Oil on canvas, feigned oval, 1830.* © *National Portrait Gallery, London*

What had happened to Godwin and, by extension, to the radical cause he represented? In part, Hazlitt blamed an unreasonable idealism. Godwin had

> conceived too nobly of his fellows (the most unpardonable crime against them, for there is nothing that annoys our self-love so much as being complimented on imaginary achievements, to which we are

VII, 87, 97. See, among others, Kevin Gilmartin, "Hazlitt's Visionary London," in Heather Glen and Paul Hamilton, eds., *Repossessing the Romantic Past* (Cambridge, 2006), 40–62. See Duncan Wu, *William Hazlitt: The First Modern Man* (Oxford, 2008).

wholly unequal)—he raised the standard of morality above the reach of humanity, and by directing virtue to the most airy and romantic heights, made her path dangerous, solitary, and impracticable.

Human nature, it seemed, had defeated Godwin and company's dreams, just as it had undone the romance of Wollstonecraft and Imlay. The outcome was predictable because the enterprise was doomed from the start. Yet, Hazlitt insisted, Godwin's eclipse also reflected a major cultural transformation that accompanied a reaction against the French Revolution and the impact of two decades of global war. The British no longer recognized, let alone honored, the radical dimension of Godwin's philosophy. The habits of intimacy, the animated conversations, and the subject of love that had constituted a revolutionary agenda in the 1790s were becoming the markers of domesticity in the 1820s. A growing middle class ensconced in private homes, energized by evangelical Christianity, and bound together by affection normalized radical concepts of friendship between women and men and domesticated romantic love.[2]

Hazlitt's interest in "the subject of love" was profoundly personal. Born in Maidstone, Kent, in 1788 to a Unitarian minister and his wife, he had dabbled in religion, art, poetry, and philosophy before he found his vocation as an essayist in the 1810s. He had known many of the radical figures of the late eighteenth century and had traveled widely in Europe. He had also found dealing with women difficult, preferring the company of prostitutes and working women. In 1808, he married a middle-class woman with whom he had three sons, two of whom died in childbirth; but the couple was never really in love, and they drifted apart. While living alone in London in 1820, Hazlitt became obsessed with Sarah Walker, the nineteen-year-old daughter of his landlord. It was an all-encompassing passion, the most intense relationship of his life; it was also an exercise in self-deception and self-destruction. Hazlitt romanticized Sarah and their love beyond all recognition. So strong was his affection that he divorced his wife to make a life with Sarah. Alas, the woman he loved so fervently did not reciprocate his feelings. Taking up with another lodger behind Hazlitt's back, she eventually moved in with her new lover and bore his child. For months, a devastated Hazlitt could not stop talking about Sarah. His obsession reached a climax in the anonymous publication in 1823 of *Liber Amoris; or, The New Pygmalion*, a stream-of-consciousness, mixed-form tribute to a grand passion

2. Hazlitt, "William Godwin," in Hazlitt, *Spirit of the Age,* in Wu, ed., *Selected Writings of Hazlitt,* VII, 89.

that existed largely in his imagination. Marriage to Isabella Shaw Bridg-water, the widow of a West Indies planter, helped Hazlitt find some measure of peace. So did writing.[3]

Hazlitt's favorite trope was paradox. He did not try to reconcile contradictions; he sought to exploit them. Life was a constructed narrative of personal details unfolding in a relentless struggle between opposites. There was no middle ground, no resolution, and no answer; there was only contemplation, conversation, and change. Rejected by Sarah and ignored by his peers, a bitter Hazlitt composed "On the Pleasure of Hating" around the same time he wrote *The Spirit of the Age.* The essay was a brilliant and bilious argument for the social utility of the antithesis of love: hate. If nature was "made up of antipathies," it followed that hate and love were joined together in perpetuity. The existence of hate necessitated the existence of love. But hate was more than a foil. It had its own strange power. "Love turns, with a little indulgence, to indifference and disgust: hatred alone is immortal," observed a man who, like Mary Wollstonecraft, had experienced the pain of love denied. No matter "the spirit of the age (that is, the progress of intellectual refinement, warring with our natural infirmities)," we nurture "the phantoms of our terror and our hate, in imagination" while "love and friendship melt in their own fires."[4]

More than love was ephemeral, wrote Hazlitt, warming to his subject. The circles of friends he had known and enjoyed had disintegrated. Times changed; people changed; circumstances changed; behavior that once entranced, annoyed; and friendships "are scattered, like last year's snow." "We grow tired of every thing but turning others into ridicule, and congratulating ourselves on their defects." Disabused of his youthful notions "that genius was not a bawd—that virtue was not a mask—that liberty was not a name—that love had its seat in the human heart," he knew those words as "a mockery and a dream." In such a world, what "chance is there of the success of real passion," especially for a man who had long been "the dupe of friendship, and the fool of love"? Hazlitt was a man old before his time, disappointed by lovers and friends. But his self-pity should not obscure his central point: virtually all human connections eventually cooled and concluded.[5]

Hazlitt's perspective was not idiosyncratic; neither was it undisputed. The late-eighteenth-century culture of social commerce had been predi-

---

3. William Hazlitt, *Liber Amoris; or, The New Pygmalion* (1825), ibid., 1–74.

4. William Hazlitt, "Essay XIII: On the Pleasure of Hating," in Hazlitt, *The Plain Speaker: Opinions on Books, Men, and Things,* I (London, 1826), ibid., VIII, 118–119, 120.

5. Ibid., 121, 123, 125, 126.

cated upon the idea that people were always—or *ought* always to be—discovering themselves through interaction with others. Social commerce, because it centered on the exchange of ideas and feelings, inevitably engendered continual revision and reinvention, any conclusion furnishing a starting point for further conversation. It was inherently and necessarily unstable. Mary Wollstonecraft and Gilbert Imlay had known that in 1793. But rather than rail at the contingency and confusion of life, they sought to make sense of their experience through acts of imagination that unfolded in conversation with friends, readers, and characters. In so doing, they participated in the origins of a culture of engagement rooted in books, dramas, lectures, and private and public conversations that would flourish in the nineteenth and twentieth centuries. Love, Percy Shelley had explained, was "that powerful attraction towards all we conceive, or fear, or hope beyond ourselves, when we find within our own thoughts the chasms of an insufficient void, and seek to awaken in all things that are, a community with what we experience within ourselves." Love "is the bond and the sanction which connects not only man with man, but with every thing which exists." Without love, "man becomes a living sepulcher of himself."[6]

"The world we dwell in," observed Godwin in 1809, "is a curious object." "It is an ever-shifting scene, and by some moralists has been compared to a *camera obscura,* that affords us the prospect of a frequented road." Nothing, he realized, was more certain than that everything would change. Aware of his own mortality, conscious of the passing of others as well as the ebbing of his reputation, Godwin argued for the value of communing with "the Illustrious Dead" literally on their graves. The dead are "still with us," he insisted, "in their stories, in their words, in their writings, in the consequences that do not cease to flow fresh from what they did." As long as we engage with them, the dead are not really dead. They live, if only in our imaginations, because we wish them to be necessary to us.[7]

6. Christopher C. Nagle, *Sexuality and the Culture of Sensibility in the British Romantic Era* (New York, 2007), 7; Percy Bysshe Shelley, "On Love," in Zachary Leader and Michael O'Neill, eds., *Percy Bysshe Shelley: The Major Works* (New York, 2003), 631, 632.

7. William Godwin, *Essay on Sepulchres* (1809), in Mark Philp et al., eds., *Political and Philosophical Writings of William Godwin,* 7 vols. (London, 1993), VI, 22–23.

acknowledgments

I wish I could acknowledge adequately the influence of scholars I have never met. Without the work of G. J. Barker-Benfield, Pamela Clemit, Mark Philp, Barbara Taylor, Janet Todd, and Wil Verhoeven, among many others, I could never have imagined *Love in the Time of Revolution,* let alone written it. Luckily, I can thank the many people who helped shape this book in conversation as well as in print. In the late 1990s, while driving Mary Kelley to the airport after a lecture at Miami University, I mentioned the reaction of my teenage daughter Elizabeth to her presentation about women and writing in the early American Republic. After listening to Mary, Elizabeth had decided to start a journal, a practice she sustained for many years. I hope *Love in the Time of Revolution* persuades Mary that Elizabeth was not the only one paying attention.

For opportunities to present early versions of various parts of this book, I am grateful to the colloquium series of the Omohundro Institute of Early American History and Culture in Williamsburg, Virginia; Dan Richter and the McNeil Center for Early American Studies at the University of Pennsylvania; the Clark Library and the History Department at University of California, Los Angeles; the 2009 annual conference of the Omohundro Institute of Early American History and Culture at the University of Utah in Salt Lake City; the Early Modern Collective at Miami University; and my fellow panelists at a session at the 2011 meeting of the Organization of American Historians in Houston. The remarkably supportive staff of the National Humanities Center in Research Triangle Park, North Carolina, helped with last-minute queries, even though they clearly had nothing to do with the book Fred Anderson and I were supposed to be writing.

On these and other occasions, I have benefited from the questions and comments of such generous scholars as Virginia Anderson, Gail Biederman, Kon Dierks, Carolyn Eastman, Niki Eustace, François Furstenberg, Carolyn Goffman, Dan Goffman, Ed Gray, Susan Gray, David Hancock, Dan Howe, Bryan Waterman, Gordon Wood, and Rosie Zagarri. I especially want to mention the whip-smart advice of Michael Meranze and the enormously helpful readers' reports of Sarah Knott and Catherine O'Donnell. It's been a pleasure working with everyone at the Omohundro Institute of Early American History and Culture. I particularly thank Virginia Montijo Chew for her skillful and patient editing of a long manuscript.

Students rarely appreciate the impact they have on their teachers. Those in my classes at Ball State University in the 1980s and Miami University since 1990 gave me the confidence to take chances in and out of the classroom. Shevaun Watson and Beth Avila taught me how to think about the relationship between history and literature. Kalie Wetovick worked hard in the summer of 2011 checking notes and compiling the bibliography. The twenty-five undergraduates who joined me in the spring of 2011 in reading some late-eighteenth-century texts demonstrated the truth that teachers learn more from their students than the other way around. Rebecca Wanzo, an undergraduate at Miami in the late 1990s who is now on the faculty at Washington University in Saint Louis, encouraged me in ways she would probably dispute, most crucially by asking me why I didn't write in the same style in which I taught.

Colleagues pay more attention to one another than we think we do. I was fortunate to know Michael O'Brien early in my career at Miami University; he taught me pretty much all I know about writing history that I hadn't already learned from Jack Thomas as a graduate student at Brown University. My late colleague Jack Temple Kirby showed me it was possible to have eclectic scholarly interests and to age gracefully. I am lucky that Charlotte Newman Goldy, Steve Norris, Erik Jenson, and Amanda McVety share their love of fiction, theater, and film almost daily. I am even luckier that Amanda, a gifted stylist, enjoys talking about the craft of writing history. I have also learned much about reading literature from cris cheek, Fran Dolan, Sara First, Katharine Gillespie, Oana Godeanu-Kenworthy, Matthew Gordon, Irene Kleiman, Tim Melley, Susan Morgan, Marj Nadler, Tatiana Seijas, Allan Winkler, and Gretchen Ziolkowski. In addition to being wonderful friends, Carla Gardina Pestana and Wietse de Boer are model scholars who regularly exceed the professional standards to which I aspire.

Although they bear no responsibility for its final form, four people had a particularly decisive influence on *Love in the Time of Revolution*. My colleague in the Miami English Department, Mary Jean Corbett, generously agreed to an out-of-the-blue request from a wayward historian to audit one of her classes and then proceeded to encourage my waywardness. Mary Jean reminded me of how much I love what I do. Plus, she always makes me laugh. Fred Anderson and I have talked at length about history and even more important matters for more than three decades in no small part because we appreciate the ways in which our different interests and styles complement each other. Fred is an extraordinary collaborator and the best of friends, even when he is skeptical about my choices. Renée Baernstein and I have talked over weekly lunches for almost two decades without getting bored or irritated (for long). Every page of this book reflects her expertise, indignation, and compassion. *Love in the Time of Revolution* literally would not exist without Fredrika J. Teute. Since our initial conversations about the topic (some time toward the end of the twentieth century), she has waited, mainly patiently, while I worked on other things, and demanded, mainly politely, that I abandon my customary opaqueness and just say what I mean. I am grateful for the opportunity, finally, to thank Fredrika publicly for believing I could write *Love in the Time of Revolution* and for making sure I did.

When I met Mary Kupiec in Charlottesville, Virginia, in the fall of 1973, I quickly concluded that I had never known anyone smarter, more hardworking, and with a greater sense of integrity. I still think so. By her example she taught me how to think formally, how to appreciate subjects I once deemed esoteric, and always to wonder why anyone should care about what I thought. We only cursorily read each other's work. But Mary has made critical interventions that have substantially improved every major project I've undertaken. In this case, after skimming through a very early draft, she remarked that, although what I was saying might be true historically, it was not true psychologically. I thank her for offering that insight, which took me years to work through; for enduring my chronic ambivalence; and for sharing our wonderful daughters, Elizabeth Renanne (and her husband Victor Broccoli) and Hannah Kupiec Cayton.

The genesis of *Love in the Time of Revolution* occurred in a tiny house on Delmar Street in Covington, Kentucky, in the early 1960s. Generally ignoring my four younger sisters Nann, Amy, Ellen, and Daphne, my maternal grandfather and my father offered me competing notions of masculinity. Lee Pelley wanted me to be a baseball player, a teacher of history, and a benevolent patriarch; fonder of talking than of listening, he had no patience with fiction. Robert Cayton had no interest in sports and no aptitude for the practical. He loved the imagination and he loved the arts, especially novels, the theater, and music. My grandfather took me to any number of Cincinnati Reds games, delighting in detailing the achievements of Willie Mays, Stan Musial, and the other players we watched warm up from his preferred seats near first base. My father took me to musicals and operas, ensured that I watched Leonard Bernstein talk about music on television, and drove two hours across eastern England on a rainy Sunday afternoon in the summer of 1968 so we could hear Benjamin Britten conduct his own work. When, after weekly suppers at my grandparents' home, my grandfather started reading to me—at the age of three!—from the U.S. history textbook he used with his high school students, my father countered at home with *David Copperfield*.

I found refuge from these two very different men in my grandmother's kitchen. Irene Stephens Pelley was a self-sufficient woman who did not suffer fools, in which category she included both her husband (usually) and her son-in-law (always). Ignore them, she advised me. Say what you think, Drew, not what you think they want to hear. If *Love in the Time of Revolution*'s blend of history and literature, scholarship and passion embodies my overdeveloped desire to keep everybody happy, it also reflects my most sustained effort—at long last—to embrace the lessons I learned in conversations with my grandmother.

index